I0831791

Modernism and the Women's Popular Roma
in Britain, 1885–1925

MODERNISM AND THE WOMEN'S POPULAR ROMANCE IN BRITAIN, 1885–1925

Martin Hipsky

Ohio University Press ❖ Athens

Ohio University Press, Athens, Ohio 45701
ohioswallow.com

Printed in the United States of America
Ohio University Press books are printed on acid-free paper ∞ ™

20 19 18 17 16 15 14 13 12 11 5 4 3 2 1

Library of Congress Cataloging-in-Publication Data

Hipsky, Martin.
Modernism and the women's popular romance in Britain, 1885–1925 / Martin Hipsky.
p. cm.
Includes bibliographical references and index.
ISBN 978-0-8214-1970-0 (hc : acid-free paper) — ISBN 978-0-8214-4377-4 (electronic)
1. English fiction—Women authors—History and criticism. 2. Modernism (Literature)—Great Britain. 3. Women and literature—Great Britain—History—20th century. 4. Women and literature—Great Britain—History—19th century. 5. Popular literature—Great Britain. 6. Books and reading—Great Britain. I. Title.
PR116.H54 2011
823'.085099287—dc23

2011016430

To Jennifer Gretchen Wiest and Lily Catherine Wiest

CONTENTS

ACKNOWLEDGMENTS

This book is the product of years of multiday research trips to several excellent archives: the Special Collections archives at the Honnold Mudd Library of the Claremont Colleges; the Marie Corelli archive at the University of Detroit Mercy Library; the British Library archives in London; the Colindale Newspaper Archives in London; the Department of Special Collections at the McFarlin Library of the University of Tulsa; and the Beinecke Library at Yale University. The archival custodians at all of these libraries were unfailingly helpful.

A shorter version of chapter 2 was originally published in *Pierre Bourdieu: Fieldwork in Culture,* edited by Nicholas Brown and Imre Szeman (Lanham, MD: Rowman and Littlefield, 2000). A version of the second half of chapter 3 was originally published in "Marie Corelli," edited by Carol Margaret Davison and Elaine M. Hartnell, special issue, *Women's Writing* 13, no. 2 (June 2006).

The germ of this study came from discussions with my mentor at Duke University, Marianna Torgovnick. Having shepherded me through a dissertation on the London modernist avant-garde, she encouraged me to move in this new direction and was the generous reader of my very first drafted chapter, back in the 1990s. Professor Torgovnick's books, ideas, and professional example have been very important to me.

Duke comrades who have helped to shape my ideas here include Imre Szeman, Nicholas Brown, Charles Dan Blanton, Trent Hill, Martine DeVos, Joe McLaughlin, Glenn Willmott, and Bill Maxwell. James Ledbetter and Linda Marrow, from the world of New York publishing, offered useful advice in the early stages of my writing. Christopher Pavsek and Carolyn Lesjak were very dear intellectual supports throughout the early research. I also want to thank Deborah Lee Gross for her constant willingness to offer feedback in response to my most tenuous and ethereal of ideas.

I am indebted to my one-time colleagues at Ohio Wesleyan University, Jeffrey Peterson and Rebecca Steinitz, for the improvement of the Ward and Corelli chapters; I wish they had been around to offer their inimitably acute feedback on later-written sections. To those current colleagues in the English Department at OWU who critiqued the introductory chapters, I am also very grateful; this intense cadre includes Patricia DeMarco, David Caplan, Mark Allison, Zack Long, Nancy Comorau, Joe Musser, and Lynette Carpenter. (If it were not for Lynette, I would have tried to pass off Clara "Barton" as the "It Girl" of late '20s cinema.) Two colleagues at other universities, Jesse Matz and Elizabeth Outka, also gave me invaluable advice on parts of the manuscript. I am grateful to Jesse for inviting me to the Humanities Center at Harvard to try out some early material on Katherine Mansfield on a group of seminar students.

I must also mention my effervescent students in the upper-level seminar on realism, the romance, and modernism in the spring of 2009: Megan Abram, Bryant Dill, Christina Fesz, Lauren Gentene, Lauren Hall, Lauren Harvey, Jennifer Herron, Abbie Higgs, Christine Hurley, Brad Mann, Maryann Penzvalto, Lauren Reed, and Amanda Zechiel. Together, they provided stimulus, inspiration, and insight, and their presence suffuses this book.

When I wrote above that this book is a product of *years,* I should have said *summers.* I want to thank Jenny and Lily for keeping me healthy, both physically and mentally, through those summers of research and writing. We inhabit a household that lives for stories, stories, stories. This book is dedicated to them with great love.

Introduction

> All fiction contains two primary impulses: the impulse to imitate daily life, and the impulse to transcend it.
>
> Gillian Beer, *The Romance*

The "low modern" and the "popular modernist" are twin classifying categories, emerging in contemporary scholarship on the modernist era, that may help us to deepen our understanding of the most widely read British literature of the late nineteenth and early twentieth centuries. They offer a literary-historical register on which to record the social "pitch" or "range" of the era's distinctive genres of popular fiction, and they bring new tones into our concepts of high modernism. In recent years, scholarship on the New Woman novel, detective fiction, the adventure romance, and literary experiments of content (as distinct from form)[1] has restored such middlebrow and lowbrow genres to their proper centrality in the history of fiction, and narrative generally, through the decades straddling 1900. As recently as the early 1990s, a scholar of British fin-de-siècle-through-1920s fiction could decry the "rigid demarcation between highbrow (James,

Conrad, Lawrence, Joyce, Woolf), middlebrow (Wells, Bennett, Galsworthy, Forster) and lowbrow (names too numerous and repellent to mention)" and could observe that "[t]here are scrupulous and imaginative histories available which assess the first group critically, summarize the second sympathetically, and ignore the third."[2] Fifteen years later, the editors of the volume *Bad Modernisms* noted that some scholars had transformed the term *modernist* "from an evaluative and stylistic designation to a neutral and temporal one" to go "beyond such familiar figures as Eliot, Pound, Joyce and Woolf" and to embrace "less widely known women writers" and "authors of mass cultural fiction."[3] Our knowledge of the vast body of popular fiction from this era is, in this sense, being democratized.

Nonetheless, some of the most popular British fiction of a century ago—especially the work of women romance writers—has yet to be understood in relation to modernist literary history. With the exceptions of Marie Corelli, Elinor Glyn, and E. M. Hull, about whom new scholarship has been emerging in the past few years,[4] the most successful female romanciers of Britain's turn into the twentieth century have not yet received the kind of attention that their one-time cultural influence clearly merits. This would hardly have been surprising a few decades ago, but with the ascendance of gender studies and cultural studies, such an oversight might seem noteworthy. Rather than attributing the lack of attention to any putative neglect on the part of scholars of the period—and thereby implying terms of value regarding the aesthetic and cultural and political dimensions, real or presupposed, of these women's romances—I think it is probably safer to assume that we have not yet seen studies of many of these novelists and novels simply because there are so many of them to consider.

Indeed, where does one begin? My approach here is to examine a small group of romances, those that best exemplified the meteoric rise of the woman-authored love story in Britain. This study attempts to redress the "romance gap" in our literary-historical record; it analyzes the discursive woof and warp of once-best-selling texts and traces these threads outward, through the wider webs of social signification in which we situate high modernist narrative. Scrutinizing a set of best sellers by romancists from Mary Ward to E. M. Hull, I hope to respond to a challenge issued by and to twenty-first-century scholars of modernism: illumination of the cultural continuities and frictions that result when the traditional criteria of literary modernism are brought to bear upon texts that are usually thought neither to be art nor to be about art.

My original impetus to approach the popular romances examined in this study was the simple fact that all were among the best-selling novels of their era, both in Britain and in the rest of the anglophone world. All but one of the eleven British-authored romances closely examined here appear in extant catalogues of best sellers in Britain and the United States from 1885 to 1925.[5] A retrospective study published in London in 1934, Desmond Flower's pamphlet *A Century of Best Sellers,* offers an authoritative list; using as his criterion the sale of at least 100,000 copies, he catalogues one to four best-selling novels per year in Britain during the era straddling the turn of the century.[6] Seven of the romances scrutinized in this book appear on Flower's list for their respective years: Ward's *Robert Elsmere* (1888), Corelli's *The Sorrows of Satan* (1895), Cross's *Anna Lombard* (1901), Orczy's *The Scarlet Pimpernel* (1905), Glyn's *Three Weeks* (1907), Barclay's *The Rosary* (1909), and Dell's *The Way of an Eagle* (1912). I have also chosen to look closely at Ward's *Lady Rose's Daughter,* because it ranked among the top ten best sellers of 1903 and prompted the American *Literary News* to announce, "[I]t is estimated that Mrs. Ward will reap a tidy profit of over $150,000 [$3.75 million in 2010 dollars] on 'Lady Rose's Daughter.' No living author has ever received as much. . . . '[T]here is no doubt that Mrs. Humphry Ward is the best paid of living novelists.'"[7] Then there is Corelli's *The Treasure of Heaven* (1906), which was said to have sold 10,000 copies on the first day of its publication alone, largely because a rare photograph of its celebrity author appeared as the frontispiece.[8] Finally, Edith Maude Hull's *The Sheik* (1919) originally sold over a million copies (Waller, 644) and in its film version of 1921 launched the short but incandescent career of Rudolph Valentino. Some of these figures come from lists that register the sales, not of novels alone but of top-selling books tout court—fiction, nonfiction, poetry, drama, religion, and so forth—in the individual years indicated. And so we begin with a simple but sociologically meaningful fact: between 1885 and 1925, these women-authored romances loom as a series of pinnacles along the highest plateau of popular British reading.

The challenges here, for literary historian and cultural theorist alike, are to identify and to interpret continuities of form and content: what do these books share that is distinctive to their historical place and time? How should they be fitted into longer-term literary history, and how are they—as prime samples of "the low modern"—to be understood in relation to "high modernism"? If there exists such a phenomenon as "popular modernism," do these romances qualify for that term? The singularities of each of these romances are considerable and must be respected; the cultural conservatism of Ward's *Lady Rose's Daughter* or Barclay's *The Rosary* may seem, for example, to occupy an ideological pole opposite the sexual emancipation we may ascribe to Cross's *Anna Lombard* or Glyn's *Three Weeks.* Nevertheless, illuminating generalizations are suggested by the material and are necessary to any investigation that would, in the words of one leading scholar of fin-de-siècle popular culture, "go beyond empiricism and the mere notation of particulars to the construction of meaningful structures, connections, and arguments."[9]

What are the commonalities? Like the feathered dinosaur, these texts embody a phylogenetic chimera in the evolution of the romance mode. This study illustrates how these romances share a preoccupation with psychological transcendence, or affective transports, expressed in representations that both embedded the historical legacy (the "DNA") of the romance mode and constituted embryonic, historically new instances of the emergent cultural form that would come to be called the "romance novel" of the later twentieth century. Some of the popular romances under scrutiny here may be considered proto–women's romances, in the later acceptation of that mass-cultural, airport-rack term. (And some were indeed sold, in inexpensive editions, in the railway stalls of their own day.) Up to the twentieth century, the term *romance* had broadly denoted any narrative of love and adventure that entailed elements of the counter-real, such as magic, spells, enchantment, or the supernatural. By the 1920s, that now familiar subgenre of the romance that we call the mass-market "romance novel" had emerged as a flourishing genetic variation, complete with a suggestive cover illustration. This new species of romance narrative would come to be characterized by two criteria: it was a work of prose fiction telling the story of the courtship and betrothal of one or more heroines, and it was a product of the culture industry—specifically, of marketing to adult female demographies.[10] A fresh offshoot of the centuries-old tradition of romance narrative, it grew rapidly, developing into a product for which the publishing house or imprint—particularly Mills and Boon from the 1910s forward and Avon and Harlequin from the 1930s and '40s—was at least as significant as the individual author (with celebrated exceptions, such as Barbara Cartland and Georgette Heyer). At the same time, twentieth-century novels—say, the works of C. S. Lewis or J. R. R. Tolkien—that would have been called "romances" by the lay reader in any earlier era were eventually slotted into differently marketed categories, with different generic labels, such as "science fiction," "fantasy," "mystery," and so forth.

In addition, the best-selling romances of 1885–1925 offer representations of interiority paralleling the more self-conscious forms of psychic intensity explored in works of certain anglophone modernists: Mansfield, Woolf, Lawrence, the Rebecca West of *The Return of the Soldier*, and the Joyce of "The Dead" and *A Portrait of the Artist as a Young Man.* In their analogous representations of interior states, we may perceive a zone of convergence between these cultural expressions of "low" and "high" modernity.[11] Here my epigraph, an axiom from Gillian Beer's work on the romance mode,[12] is instructive and provides the widest conceptual horizon of this study as a whole. While these British women's romances assay to represent, especially in their climactic scenes, states of psychic transcendence, the modernist texts in question figure the quest for psychic transcendence that encodes the ultimate unattainability of that goal. The former narratives, though they often include episodic adventures, primarily offer interiorized, psychologized romances of the development of secular love or self-transformation; the latter narratives offer intermittent intensities of psychic questing that cumulatively constitute what I propose to call the romance of interiority. Both sets of narratives can be conceived as self-consciously resistant to or reactive against the representational modes of late nineteenth- and early twentieth-century high realism. If Beer is right and "all fiction contains two primary impulses: the impulse to imitate daily life, and the impulse to transcend it" (*Romance,* 10), then these women romancists and certain high modernists, I argue, together partook in the latter impulse—and for reasons specific to their shared historical moment in the development of capitalist society. My theoretical frame is informed by the recent discoveries and insights of feminist studies of modernism, and of gender-studies approaches more generally. That said, my readings of these texts draw on an eclectic array of literary and cultural critics, some of them theorists who might, I freely admit, appear contradictory in other contexts—from Gillian Beer to Pierre Bourdieu, from Rita Felski to Northrop Frye, from Jenny Sharpe to Harold Bloom, from Q. D. Leavis to Fredric Jameson. However, the various romance and modernist narratives at hand call for nuanced interarticulations and seem to me to legitimate such a bricolage of analytic resources; this discursive terrain resists the potentially foreclosing claims of any single theoretical master narrative.

The *low modern* and the *popular modernist* are recently emerging terms through which we may deepen our understanding of some of the most widely read literature of the late nineteenth and early twentieth centuries, even as we adjust our constructions of high modernism accordingly. In what follows, I rely more on the former notion, "low modern," than the latter, "popular modernist," because I do not want to be misunderstood as attempting to reinvent such figures as Marie Corelli and Elinor Glyn as modernist writers. They are, I argue, distinctly modern; but I am not claiming that these writers belong to a (conceptually expanded) literary modern*ism* from which they have allegedly been excluded in previous literary histories. Instead, this book is intended to contribute to the ongoing project of a more respectful, responsive understanding of a phenomenon in popular fiction whereby English-language romances of the period 1885 to 1925, especially those by certain women authors, were sold to and were read by more people than ever before in history. In investigating this series of representative writers and narratives, I hope to demonstrate a generic evolution—to show how both the traditional romance mode and sublimations of high Romanticism blossomed into unprecedented forms. Herein lies the general link to high modernism, a broad connection that is more a matter of heretofore-unnoticed homologies than of a putative continuum or spectrum between popular and high modernisms. I reconsider both well-known and less-familiar writing by Mansfield, Lawrence, Joyce, West, and Woolf to explore how these modernist writers incorporated elements of the romance mode and a related neo-Romanticism into their innovative fiction and (in the cases of West and Woolf) literary criticism.

In the chapters that follow, I begin with the complex definitions and institutional contexts of the entity designated by the term *romance,* as it was understood during its efflorescence over this forty-year period in British cultural history. Chapter 1, "Contexts of Popular Romance, 1885–1925," offers an overview of the romance mode through its seven centuries of tradition in British literary practice, with attention to its symbolic gendering and relation to the later modes of realism, melodrama, and the "sentimental" novel. I examine the institutional structures of the literary field emerging by 1885, and through a short look at the representative career of Elinor Glyn, I suggest how the evolving interrelations among a dominant realism, a renovating romance mode, and an emergent modernism force us to scrutinize our received notions of "high" and "low" forms through the period. Prior to the Great War, as literary historian Clive Bloom records, almost all popular novels were "designated with the vague title of 'romance,' which had not itself become a term used exclusively for women's fiction."[13] Nonetheless, amid these shifts in the literary field, what we today refer to as the "women's romance" started to take shape. Although the nineteenth century certainly witnessed its share of sensation fiction, adventure romances, domestic romances, sentimental novels, and (in George Eliot's notorious designation) "silly novels by lady novelists," not until the first decades of the twentieth did the vast category of novels by women writers begin to precipitate, in a calculatedly marketable form, this new and tremendously successful genre of fiction.

This evolution in the categories of popular fiction by women is the subject of the book's second chapter, "Mary Ward's Romances and the Literary Field." Here I bring Pierre Bourdieu's theories of literary production and reception to bear on the spectacular early success and later decline of the romance-writing career of Matthew Arnold's niece, Mary Ward. Her transatlantic phenomenon, the best-selling *Robert Elsmere,* offers the single most famous exhibit of the late-Victorian religious romance. The pained agnosticism of its eponymous hero provoked sober public commentary from none other than the former prime minister William Gladstone. Ward's trajectory on the literary field tells a representative story about the receding of religious and moral didacticism in novels written by and aimed primarily at women, even as it illustrates the complex interplay of economic, ideological, and aesthetic factors in the immediate precursors of the commercially conceived paperback romance of the twentieth century.

By the later years of Mary Ward's career, in the period of the Great War, developing romance genres had acquired market designations. Some of these—such as "the country novel," "the city novel," and "the society novel"—have since fallen out of general use, while others—such as detective fiction, mystery novels, and family sagas—marked categories destined to survive into the boom of so-called genre fiction in the later twentieth century. From a deeper historical perspective, there also persists, amid this early twentieth-century proliferation of subgenres, a mutating line of continuity between "old-world" significations of the term *romance*—those that originated with the medieval Arthurian legends, Malory, and Renaissance figures such as Sidney and Spenser—and the meaning understood to subtend the contemporaneous romance subgenres. This is the subject of chapter 3, "Marie Corelli and the Discourse of Romance," in which I offer readings of three of Corelli's novels published between 1895 and 1914. Corelli's fictions critique aspects of cultural modernity perceived to be dehumanizing, as well as defend the role of the romance form as a timeless purveyor of eternal human truths. Through both the voice of her omniscient narrators and the voices of her heroines and heroes, Corelli devises romances *about* the romance mode. Insisting on the mode's continuity with English Romanticism, she proposes the resurrection of allegedly traditional values in what is perceived to be an increasingly hostile and hypersecularized twentieth-century modernity. In relation to other representational modes, these novels (along with the rest of Corelli's oeuvre) may be said to represent the revenge of the romance on high realism—a deeply spiritualized counterblast to, in particular, the cultural consecration of naturalist fiction in the late Victorian and Edward eras. Paradoxically, too, these tendentious romances anticipate and refract certain of high modernism's emergent attitudes toward cultural modernity.

By the first decade of the 1900s, fellow women romance writers had become less concerned than Corelli with the alleged antagonism between realism and the romance; some of the most successful were grafting realist features to the romance frame. My fourth chapter, "The Women's Romance and the Ideology of Form," explores three Edwardian romances via that modal synthesis. Three best-selling novels—the Baroness Orczy's *The Scarlet Pimpernel,* Florence Barclay's *The Rosary,* and Elinor Glyn's *Three Weeks*—demonstrate how the Edwardian romance carries the vestiges or residues of religious and socially hierarchical themes from previous eras: the binary of good versus evil, the near-mythical characters, the idealized and inspirited environments, and the quest for transcendence. In varying ways, these texts illustrate that those residues continued to color the mutating romance form, even as that form soaked up the freshly secularizing and psychologizing tinctures of twentieth-century modernity. Close readings of these texts by Orczy, Barclay, and Glyn illustrate how they embody twentieth-century tendencies in the historical romance, the religious romance, and the erotic romance. I also elaborate further in this chapter on the affinity between the newly secularized women's romance and an emerging modernism. In ambivalent response to the dispiriting verisimilitude of such realist texts as those of Bennett and Galsworthy, the most popular romances of the Edwardian decade often attempted both to counter a naturalistic pessimism with romantic idealism and to represent male-female intimacy more honestly and "realistically" than in previous romance literature. In so doing, many early twentieth-century romances share with an emergent modernist fiction the quest for the readerly experience of transcendence through representations of characters' psychic interiority, especially via secular conceptions of the forces of the unconscious.

The forces of the unconscious are also on prominent display in British imperial romances, though often in ways that are unintended by their authors, as discussed in chapter 5, "The Imperial Erotic Romance." The masculine adventure romances of the British fin de siècle through the 1920s, such as the popular works of Rider Haggard and Rudyard Kipling, have long been noted to feature orientalist or primitivist versions of the non-European Other. But how do these cultural projections appear in the most popular imperial romances by women—in Victoria Cross's *Anna Lombard,* Ethel Dell's

The Way of an Eagle, and E. M. Hull's *The Sheik*? Like their masculinist counterparts, these romances do not schematize the forces of good and evil simplistically along racial lines, yet they do deploy the associated tropes of the "dark races" to conjure representations of uncivilized brutality. At the same time, these texts' anxious cathexes on racial identities elaborate new discourses of desire. The narratorial anxiety that the female protagonist may be raped by the "native" male is balanced, as on a knife-edge, with the libidinality of the encounter with a romanticized, "primitive" masculinity. Generating the story line is a complex of tensions between a self-willed British woman and an exoticized man; as in the traditional romance form, resolution arrives with the lovers' achievement of transcendence through one another, but here that consummation features the safe dissolution of the threatening, nonprotective side of masculine violence—which has been troped as racially Other. In light of postcolonial theory (I rely most on the work of Jenny Sharpe and Robert J. C. Young), we discern in these texts an ambivalent fascination with the "ungovernable" Indian or Arab male. The economies of desire circulating through these novels' "exotic" locales anticipate the metaphorics of erotic *agon* and romantic transport in the Harlequin- and Mills-and-Boon-style romances of the mid to late twentieth century. At the same time, as I show at the end of the chapter, Cross, Dell, and Hull share continuities with the modernist primitivism of Woolf's *The Voyage Out,* two of Lawrence's novels, and the journals and stories of Mansfield.

The argument of chapter 6, "Modernism and the Romance of Interiority," is that high modernism and popular romance fiction may have actually served similar psychic functions for their early twentieth-century readers, and that just as significant as the formal differences between these literary modes may have been their shared differences from the "high realism" inherited from the nineteenth century. This section takes as its opening exhibit an early short story by Katherine Mansfield, "The Tiredness of Rosabel." Written on the eve of modernist experimentation in British fiction, Mansfield's narrative offers a rich vignette of a day in the life of a shopgirl in a London millinery. The text combines elements of three literary modes—realist mise-en-scène, romance fantasy, modernist interiority—as it poignantly and self-referentially depicts the consolations of romance narrative amid the boredom and unfulfillment of everyday life in urban modernity. Mansfield's story anticipates how both the early twentieth-century romance and modernist fiction rely on the pleasures and mysteries of the quest for transcendence to enchant their subject matter and their reading audiences and in so doing offer a powerful contrast to the sober demystifications of realist and naturalist literary practice. In contrast to the social diagnoses of literary realism—intended to awaken, educate, even galvanize readers into action—the metaphors and symbols of both modernist and popular-romance narratives may have acted therapeutically upon the anxieties and longings that readers' quotidian social experience either actively engendered or did little to allay or satisfy.

I conclude the chapter by positing that popular romance fiction offered its substitute fulfillments unself-consciously, whereas some of the modernist narratives of Mansfield, Joyce, Lawrence, West, and Woolf treat the very problem of a social realm in which the mass-cultural compensations for and diversions from readers' social alienation should have to exist at all. Yet these modernists may be said to offer parallel compensations of their own, which, if considerably more intellectual in their complex symbolic systems, also succeed because of their psycho-emotional appeal, their affective—as opposed to abstract or "cerebral"—consolations, avowals, even affirmations. Lest we think that such an association flatters popular romance, we might consider its converse, the fact that modernism has itself been accused of an escapism not dissimilar from that of the romance, through a "perfected poetic apparatus" that "must be realistic in order in another moment to recontain that realism which it has awakened."[14] For all its utility and rationalism, for all its acuity and candor, literary realism alone was not—is not—enough for many readers. Through their venerable but renewed, humble but idealist means, the romance writers considered here followed the same directive as the high modernists: the imperative to loft us, however fleetingly or intermittently, into a refashioned symbolic order that would bridge us across the pain of the historical Real.

CHAPTER ONE

Contexts of Popular Romance, 1885–1925

For an initial consideration of the relation of the popular romance to an emergent modernism, feminist criticism and gender studies may offer the best framework, especially as regards theories of genre and mode. Suzanne Clark's work, for example, reveals the influence of the so-called (at the time) sentimental mode on important female modernists. In *Sentimental Modernism: Women Writers and the Revolution of the Word,* Clark restores this category to modernist literary history and vindicates the works of American (or New York–based) writers Emma Goldman, Edna St. Vincent Millay, Louise Bogan, and Kay Boyle.[1] Clark's critical investigation, published in 1991, anticipated by a few years the current revisionist impulse to reconfigure the "low modern," the "popular modernist," and the middlebrow within our regnant historiographies of modernist literature. In the present study, in parallel with Clark's revisionist work, I trace the evolution of an older tradition of narrative representation—in this case, the romance mode—through narrative specimens of the modernist era. However, I want neither to claim that women romance writers from Marie Corelli to Edith Maude Hull deserve to be elevated to high modernist status, nor to champion Virginia Woolf, Katherine Mansfield, or the Rebecca West of *The Return of the Soldier* as neglected women modernists (obviously, with the possible exception of West, this would be carrying coals to Newcastle). Though I am motivated by our need to take more seriously, as a chapter of cultural history, the turn-of-the-century women romance writers and to theorize the oft-overlooked Romantic and romance-mode dimensions of some high modernist texts, I am not presuming to offer a bid for the canonization of the neglected women writers or to describe the historical reading experience of the female audience.

In fact, the popular romances under scrutiny here had not yet taken on the ideological stigma of the "feminized 'other' discourse" (which Clark properly associates with the sentimental mode from the early nineteenth century on)—or, more accurately, they did not do so until the end of this period, with the appearance in the 1910s of Dell's *Way of an Eagle* and Hull's *Sheik*. As is discussed in later chapters, men of the period professed to reading and valuing the early works of Ward, Corelli, Orczy, and other writers discussed here.[2] Although the best-selling narratives covered here were at times tagged as "sentimental" (sometimes by fellow women writers, as discussed at the end of chapter 2), it was not generally by virtue of their romance mode per se that they were pejoratively gendered by cultural arbiters of the era. As Mary Hammond points out in her study of English literary taste in this period, it has become "a critical commonplace" in twenty-first-century criticism that "the romance . . . had very ill-defined and somewhat permeable boundaries, and that consequently the art/market opposition was less a divide than a negotiating table."[3] The women's romance novel, as a mass-market subcategory of the romance mode, began to acquire its pejorative (and, of course, deeply ideological) associations with exclusively female writers and readers only in the third decade of the twentieth century, in the years following E. M. Hull's publication of *The Sheik* in 1919. Even as late as 1932, the year in which Q. D. Leavis published *Fiction and the Reading Public*, the critic did not differentiate the sex of either author or reading public in her analysis of best-selling romances: Marie Corelli, Florence Barclay, Ethel M. Dell, Edgar Rice Burroughs, Gene Stratton Porter, and Horace de Vere Stacpoole—male authors as well as female ones (and American as well as British ones)—provided her prime instances of "fantasy-spinning . . . the kind of fiction classed as day-dreaming."[4] Prior to the 1920s, of course, "the romance" had had its detractors of various stripes for a long time; nonetheless, the ever-mutating forms, both poetic and fictional, ranged under this broad rubric were understood to be rooted in a native, organic, deeply British literary tradition going back six or more centuries, without a consistent gendering. Long past the medieval era of its importation from the Continent, "the romance" of whatever varietal was the gender-neutral fruit of homegrown vines. If the romance, as a narrative mode generally, has ever been a "discourse of the Other"—partitioned off, in the reading public's collective imagination, as a feminine genre—this did not occur until later in the twentieth century.

In the more-distant past, the lack of a gender-based stigma to the literary category of the romance narrative had to do, paradoxically, with the sex of its author—nearly always male, for centuries, and therefore ideologically "invisible." This began to change when the education of women allowed for the emergence of such gothic romance writers as Clara Reeve, Anne Radcliffe, and Regina Maria Roche in the later eighteenth century and Mary Wollstonecraft Shelley in the early nineteenth. Authorial gender became a conscious factor in the discursive constitution of the signifier *romance literature;* some literary historians, following the lead of Harold Bloom, have even suggested that the romance mode became "internalized" as the spiritual quests of the (primarily) male poets of English Romanticism and in this development took on a symbolic masculinity.[5] It can then be shown that the "domestic romance" narratives of Jane Austen and her nineteenth-century successors, while they partook in greater measure than their romance predecessors of the formal features of "masculine" realism, nonetheless "feminized" the romance mode and that the "adventure romances" of Rider Haggard, Robert Louis Stevenson, Arthur Conan Doyle, and H. G. Wells, while straying from disciplined realism into implausible dreamworlds, nonetheless displaced the serial incidents of the Arthurian quest-romance into a modernized masculinity. Then, too, it has been demonstrated that a renovated realism was the mode of the "New Woman" novels of the late 1880s through 1890s, and so romance's modal antonym became associated with woman novelists at the moment when Marie Corelli was the reigning "queen" of romance.

The history of the gendering of the romance mode, in short, is somewhat dizzying. The "romance" form inherited by the women romanciers of 1885–1925 cannot be identified as a distinct, ideologically "feminized rhetoric" in the way that Clark's discourse of the sentimental can be. When it comes to gender and genre, then, we may start with two stable facts: first, the romance writers considered in this study did not believe their novels to be a priori gendered forms; and second, they were (for the most part) quite deliberate in referring to their works as "romances" of varying genres, aimed no less than the romances of previous eras at both male and female readers. Ward labeled *Robert Elsmere* "a religious romance"; Corelli weighed in vehemently on the side of capital-R Romance in the late-Victorian realism-versus-romance debates; Elinor Glyn entitled her autobiography *Romantic Adventure.*

The Popular Sublime and Melodrama

Bracketing the question of gender for a moment, there is another difficulty here: in the culture of late nineteenth- and early twentieth-century Britain, "romance" can come to seem a rather thin and etiolated sign. For my understanding of the discursive strands woven into the term in its British usage during the period, I rely in part on Gillian Beer's diachronic account of the mode. Beer acknowledges that the romance is too broad to be considered a single genre, yet she traces lines of continuity that stretch from *Sir Gawain and the Green Knight* and Thomas Malory to the later twentieth century. She catalogues what she calls a "cluster of properties" that distinguish the romance from other literary kinds, the most significant of which are the following: content based in love and adventure; the hero's and/or heroine's partial withdrawal from society; broadly limned characters; the interfusing of the quotidian and the marvellous; a sustained series of actions or incidents; "a strongly enforced code of conduct to which all the characters must comply"; and a happy ending.[6] What I have found most pertinent here is twofold.

First, keeping in view the sheer length of time during which the romance form has been central to English-language traditions—well over six hundred years—helps us to avoid a reductive view of the romance as realism's determinate negation (a reductivism that, to be fair, is partly attributable to the late Victorians' own framings of "the realism versus romance debates"). There was the era of the Arthurian cycles, in the fourteenth and fifteenth centuries; the rush of new romance-writing energies in the Elizabethan period, when writers such as John Lyly and Philip Sidney were inspired by translations of ancient Greek romances; the gradual schematization of the romance narrative contra "the novel" (or what came retroactively to be labeled realist fiction) in the eighteenth century; the new offshoots of gothic romance and the English Romantic movement soon thereafter; and, in the nineteenth century, the energetic development of romance genres as a challenge to the deterministic realism coming over from France (G. Beer, *Romance*, 6). The "archaeological layering" of romance specimens over this span of literary history reminds us that the romance writer in the period 1885–1925 had at hand various narrative and rhetorical resources—stratified down through literary-institutional memory like so many energy sources, many of them long antedating both contemporary romance models and the realism-romance debate—through which to model her formal nostalgia. And this is to say nothing of the semi- or unconscious osmosis of romance models, from all eras of British cultural history, through the young middle-class woman's formal and informal education in the late nineteenth century (as Kate Flint has demonstrated).[7] Second, Beer's catalogue of enduring romance features intermingles specifications of content and form. She demonstrates that over the centuries, through various displacements and metaphorizations of content, the formal functions of the romance mode are increasingly what identify it. The romance is attributed a synchronic, enduring feature, whether literal or metaphorized: its heroines and heroes encode social class, and that class is often royal or aristocratic. That content-based characteristic is then effectively subsumed by a formal function: another of the synchronic features of the romance is proposed to be its use as a literature of wish fulfillment. Beer's invocation of dreams is one key to her claims for the mode's continuity across the centuries, as the simple assertion of dream-as-form carries with it the attendant structures of latent and manifest, of condensation and displacement, of dream work and dream interpretation, et cetera.

My argument regarding the "deep history" of this study's romances—and of the modernist metaphorizations of the romance—may be anticipated through Beer's formulation of the romance mode's tendency toward greater abstraction across the centuries of its transformations through British literary history.

> Whereas in the earlier part of its history, when it was the dominant form for fiction, the romance can be quite reliably recognized by its subject-matter, the distinction

> between [realist] novel and romance later becomes a matter of the balance of attention. The [realist] novel is more preoccupied with representing and interpreting a known world, the romance with making apparent the hidden dreams of that world. Romance is always concerned with the fulfillment of desires—and for that reason it takes many forms: the heroic, the pastoral, the exotic, the mysterious, the dream, childhood, and total passionate love. (*Romance,* 12)

With the roster of popular romanciers under consideration here, we may add to this catalogue various forms native to their era: the religious romance, the mystical romance, the historical romance, the erotic romance, the imperial erotic romance, and the romance of interiority. But the key feature of this formulation, subtending all of these later genres, is the persistence of encoded desires. Beer concludes her history of the English-language romance with this diachronic feature: the romance "remakes the world in the image of desire" (22). Here the dimension of gender returns to our investigation of the selected romances of Ward, Corelli, Orczy, Glyn, Barclay, Cross, Dell, and Hull. It returns, not as a question of discursive othering or as an essentializing claim to the expression of monolithically conceived "female desire" but rather as a matter of perceiving these texts as historically specific opportunities for plurally female and androgynous desires to be encoded in popular narrative.

We may begin to characterize the representation of desire in the texts at hand by noting what it is not: desire is not primarily configured through a female character's subjectivity, focused on the meeting-courtship-marriage arc. Only four of the eleven best sellers (Corelli's *Treasure of Heaven,* Barclay's *The Rosary,* Dell's *The Way of an Eagle,* and Hull's *The Sheik*) considered here may be seen to structure a stereotypically conceived, heterosexual female desire along the central narrative sequence that would later come to be identified with "the romance novel"—that is, through the exposition of a corrupt society, the meeting of heroine and hero, the obstacles to their mutual attraction, and their eventual declaration of love and betrothal.[8] Among that group of four, only two (Barclay and Hull) offer a narrative exclusively from the point of view of the female protagonist. Prior to their commodification via mass-market formulas, such narrative elements had not yet hardened into place. This is not to deny that the consummation of romantic heterosexual love is represented as the locus of transcendence in many of these romances, but it suggests that we need to avoid a reductive interpretation of that desire for transcendence through the lens of later critical stereotypes about the romance novel, in which that desire is minimized as purely "emotional" and as channeled into "safe," institutionally sanctioned desublimations. One crucial point to make here, variously elaborated in critical work by Melisa Brittain, Nickianne Moody, Ann Ardis, and Laura Frost (all of whom I draw on in later chapters),[9] is that the romances of Cross, Glyn, and Hull sympathetically portray female desires in extramarital libidinality, in transgressions that are neither exclusively emotional nor institutionally sanctioned.

However, this sympathy is not consciously shared by all eight of the romance novelists under scrutiny here. Instead, a common denominator is to be found in the phenomenon of "the popular sublime," which comprises broad continuities among the various encodings of desire in these romances. In Rita Felski's formulation, "the popular sublime" is a late nineteenth- through early twentieth-century cultural phenomenon that expresses "a romantic yearning for the ineffable."[10] Many popular romances of the period, Felski indicates, exhibit "utopian and quasi-transcendental aspirations, as exemplified in a gesturing toward an ineffable domain beyond the constraints of a mundane material reality" (117). As in other literary and artistic contexts, the sublime is "an index of the unrepresentable"; in the case of the popular romances in question, the sublime facets of the romance discourse are those discursive zones that would strain and stretch to express "that which exists beyond prevailing discourses, conventions, and systems of meaning" (119). It is not hard to see how women's sexual desires, in the period under study here, would reside along the edges of prevailing discourses and would thereby present a challenging complex of near-inexpressible energies to work into the romance narrative. But the virtue of "the popular sublime" as an interpretive category is that it does not delimit desires to narrowly defined libidinal intensities; it includes those desires that were considered spiritual but were felt to burst through the vocabulary of institutional religiosity. In all of the woman-authored romances explored here, libidinal and spiritual yearning are portrayed as on a continuum—even, and probably against the conscious will of their writers, in the cases of the putatively "conservative" texts.

Felski's primary examples of the popular sublime are the romances of Marie Corelli, but she demonstrates that these narratives represent a larger feature of emergent mass culture and, indeed, the culture of turn-of-the-century modernity more generally: the popular romance of this era, Felski suggests, is "a form often considered to be regressive and anachronistic but whose nostalgic yearning for an indeterminate 'elsewhere' is . . . a foundational trope within the modern itself" (31). The popular sublime of the 1880s through the 1920s, she suggests, is both "a central aspect of mass culture's interpellation of femininity" and "a key element of the modern" (121). A virtue of Felski's formulation is that it both enables us to see what may be shared by the best sellers under examination here and opens the door to connections with tropes from certain texts of the high modernists. I do not have space here to delve further into definitions of "the popular sublime"—its various facets are explored later in discussions of particular romances and modernist texts—but I will note that the sense of rapture, transport, or self-transcendence that Felski discerns in the popular sublime may have its close analogues in such modernist loci classici as the death scene of Mansfield's "The Garden-Party" or the snowy tableau that closes Joyce's "The Dead."

Before moving on to institutional conditions in which the popular women romancists were writing, I wish to mention a final dimension of the generic situation of the British romance mode, 1885–1925. Several recent critics of the late-Victorian-to-modernist period have noted that melodrama is a constantly recurring mode, or stylistic through-line, in all such romance best sellers, from Ward's *Robert Elsmere* through Hull's *The Sheik.* In the case of Marie Corelli's narratives, for example, Felski suggests that the popular sublime "is achieved through the combination of a formal register of melodramatic intensity with a thematic focus on the transcendence of quotidian reality and the material world" (120). In *The Melodramatic Imagination,* Peter Brooks has posited that from the Romantic era on, the melodramatic mode represented a means by which to dramatize spiritual meanings, as the "force of sacred myth lost its power, and its political and social representations lost their legitimacy":

> [B]y the end of the Enlightenment, there was
> clearly a renewed thirst for the Sacred, a reaction to

> desacralization expressed in the vast movement we think of as Romanticism. . . . Mythmaking could now only be individual, personal; and the promulgation of ethical imperatives had to depend on an individual act of self-understanding that would then—by an imaginative or even a terroristic leap—be offered as a foundation of a general ethics. . . . Melodrama represents both the urge toward resacralization and the impossibility of conceiving sacralization other than in personal terms.[11]

There is an almost oxymoronic characteristic to most of the romances on display here, and that is the coexistence within the same pages of the protagonists' desublimated libidinal energies, in representations that were vilified as base and sinful by many established critics, with "a strongly enforced code of conduct to which all the characters must comply" (G. Beer, *Romance,* 10) and by means of which the reader can easily identify heroines, heroes, and villains. In this connection, we might refer to Gillian Beer's suggestion that "the finest romances are always much preoccupied with psychic responsibilities. Because romance shows us the ideal it is implicitly instructive as well as escapist" (9). I do not think it is facile to suggest that, even in the case of a relatively respected best seller such as Ward's "religious romance" *Robert Elsmere,* these women romance writers engaged in the fictional creation of "do-it-yourself ethical imperatives." Most of these romance writers averred (or protested) that their works were informed by Christianity, but in practice the ethics they embedded were personalized ideals that deviated from church doctrine and in some cases even strayed far from institutional or organized religion's conceptions of ethics.

The Popular Romance and Literary Institutions: The Case of Elinor Glyn

An anecdote about a romance writer's affront to conventional ethics provides the pivot into institutional affinities between the popular romance and high modernism. Nowadays, we point to "December 1910" to symbolize the passage between Victorian and modern sensibilities. As if to answer Virginia Woolf's periodizing wager with a bid of his own, D. H. Lawrence suggests, "It was in 1915 the old world ended."[12] I will blend these two chronograms into one—December 1915—and, without claiming epochal punctuality, cite a lawsuit that might at first seem to be about a kind of literature unrelated to Woolf's and Lawrence's modernist experimentalism but that may figure instead its dialectical verso. The lawsuit concerned Elinor Glyn's fifth novel, *Three Weeks,* a *succès de scandale* that featured a torrid affair between a young man and an older married woman. Glyn's romance had by that time inspired an anonymous doggerel in the Edwardian press:

> Would you like to sin
> With Elinor Glyn
> On a tiger skin?
> Or would you prefer
> To err
> With her
> On some other fur?[13]

On 21 December 1915, a judge in London's Royal Courts of Justice rendered a decision in a case of alleged copyright infringement of *Three Weeks,* which by then had sold close to two million copies.[14] The purported infringers of Glyn's literary copyright were the creators of a motion picture called *Pimple's Three Weeks, Without the Option.* In deciding the case of *Elinor Glyn (Married woman) v. The Western Feature Film Co. Ltd. & G. Black,* the presiding Justice Younger, as recorded by the court stenographer, pronounced that the novel *Three Weeks* was

> fortunate enough to be condemned almost unanimously by the critics, and to be banned in all the libraries. In consequence, I doubt not, of these attentions, it has enjoyed a vogue denied to less daring rivals, and it has reached a sale in this country and America in numerous additions [*sic*], expensive and cheap, of, I was told, far over a million copies. . . . In all its essentials the so-called episode is as hackneyed and common-place a story as could well be conceived. If it is to be distinguished at all from innumerable anticipations in erotic literature, the distinction is to be found in the accessories of the tale. Mystery surrounds the lady: of a loveliness unaffected by the passage of time, she is said to be polished, *blasée, soignée.* Even in a Swiss country hotel, but notably at Lucerne and Venice, she is persuaded by a luxury as

> sybaritic as it is incongruous: no wine can pass her lips which is not either of the deepest red or the richest gold. . . . The episode described in the Plaintiff's novel, and which she alleges has been pirated by the Defendants is, in my opinion, grossly immoral, both in its essence, in its treatment, and in its tendency. Stripped of its trappings which are mere accident, it is nothing more or less than a sensual adulterous intrigue.[15]

This excerpt is only a fraction of Justice Younger's legal opinion regarding *Three Weeks.* His response runs to several pages of excoriation, replete with not only ethical revulsion but also severe aesthetic judgments. He rejects Glyn's legal case on the grounds of the novel's moral depravity, but as this passage shows, he is also offended from the point of view of the amateur literary critic, deeming *Three Weeks* to be an especially "meretricious" example of a "hackneyed and common-place" strain of popular literature. He further opines that the film in question is clearly "a burlesque of the Plaintiff's novel, and that a genuine burlesque of a serious work constitutes no infringement of copyright."[16]

Viewed within the cultural paradigm shift of modernism, the opinions of Justice Younger offer us lively reading today, not least because we may, from our post-Freudian vantage, suspect that a secret pleasure energizes them. The document reveals the hostility between residual Victorian values and the emergent desublimations of twentieth-century mass culture. But to read it as such a cultural synecdoche is not simply to project our predictably generalizing categories over its historical singularity. Though Glyn may have used different terms to name the cultural pivot or fulcrum that her romance novel exemplified, she would come to recognize the cultural shifts anticipated by more "properly" modernist observers of the period. A few years later, Glyn would characterize the symbolism of Queen Victoria's passing in a manner worthy of Lytton Strachey:

> It was generally felt that changes must follow the death of the Queen, and the inauguration of a new century, and that new ideas, new standards and new hopes were in the air. But I think that no one then dreamed how rapid, how complete . . . would be the transformation. The pace of development of the whole world had, it seems, been slowed down for a decade by the failing strength of the little form in the black-draped coffin, and

> the leisureliness of the 'nineties was really that of a slow-motion picture. In deference to the views of the beloved Empress who symbolized England's nineteenth-century glory, inevitable economic and social changes had been unconsciously held back.[17]

Glyn positively heralds "new ideas, new standards and new hopes"; she calls witness to a "rapid," "complete" transformation of the culture; she diagnoses the collective unleashing of long-repressed energies. As a child—Glyn was born in 1864—she recalls, "[I] refused to accept the current doctrines of the Church of the Victorian Age, for they offended my childish sense of logic and truth; they seemed hypocritical, and I resented the prohibitions and repressions which they imposed" (*Romantic*, 24).

We see here a popular novelist's articulation of the same cultural revolution indexed by Woolf's and Lawrence's portentous dates. But there is a further parallel with high modernist attitudes, one that is evident in certain of the popular romance writers discussed in this study. Glyn's progressivism is mixed with an aristocratic hauteur that is self-consciously ideological and performative. "I conceived a hatred of Puritanism in all its forms," she avers, "partly based no doubt on my Cavalier and Stuart predilections, but partly too because I felt that such an attitude was almost a blasphemy against the beauty and joy of my romantic dream world" (24–25). Paradoxically, Glyn's moral libertarianism represented a reaction formation against certain aspects of modernity. Her writings are symptomatic both of a nostalgia for premodern romance and of a secularizing, antirepressive, "modern" structure of feeling. With differing emphases, the two sides of this ideological amalgam came to be expressed in many British popular romances of the late nineteenth and early twentieth centuries. In Glyn's case, the reactionary and antibourgeois attitudes would appear in the idealization of the anciens régimes of the European Continent and of pre-1688 Britain; in the cases of Corelli and Orczy, as we will see, nostalgic constructions of British culture of earlier centuries would serve as idealized countervisions to middle-class efficiency, rationalization, and self-disciplinary repression.

A key point here is the analogy between these writers' valorized constructions of the pre-Victorian past, and the antibourgeois and reactionary attitudes that would characterize certain figures of anglophone high modernism. It is certainly true that Elinor Glyn's hindsight regarding the symbolic turn of Victoria's death adds little to our received ideas about the modernist moment. But if the content of Glyn's description is fully predictable, the *source* of this description, a popular romance author, is worthy of note. By the time she published the words quoted above, in 1937, Glyn had long since established herself both as a celebrated romancist and as a Hollywood screenwriter with a high-profile public image—among other achievements, she was the cocreator of the first "It" girl of world cinema, Clara Bow. From one angle of view, then, her words are those of a literary lowbrow, a cultural figure from the demotic flank of Andreas Huyssen's "Great Divide" between mass and high culture. From another angle, these words—and, I later argue, such novels as her *Three Weeks*—offer a discourse of cultural change and a set of attitudes toward twentieth-century cultural energies that situate Glyn in the company of Woolf and Lawrence, marking her as a discursive and ideological, if not a formal and stylistic, purveyor of the cultural new.

In short, the cultural ideologies and career activities of Elinor Glyn serve as an institutional index of the "low modern," a category that can be put into illuminative relation with traditionally defined high modernism. Three further aspects of Glyn's courtroom experience in 1915 bear this out. The first is the fact that Glyn was a woman novelist whose legal case was supported by the Incorporated Society of Authors, Playwrights, and Composers, an organization created in 1883 to extend and enforce the copyright protection of literary authors.[18] In its role here as a kind of collective literary agent, the Society of Authors (as it was generally called) exemplified the increasing rationalization and professionalization of fiction publishing in the years around the turn of the century. Moreover, the society's willingness to espouse Glyn's cause represented a new phenomenon of the pre–World War I moment: the acceptance of successful female writers, no matter how "scandalous" or "frivolous" their works were labeled by the putative arbiters of literary and moral values, as the effective equals of male writers, in the eyes of an increasingly amoral publishing industry. Glyn was accepted for membership in the Society of Authors in April 1912; she followed such equally successful romance writers as Florence Barclay, Marie Corelli, Victoria Cross, Ethel Dell, and "The Baroness"

Emma Orczy, all of whom joined the society between 1908 and 1910.[19] In 1918, when the Society of Authors was presided over by Thomas Hardy, two women—Corelli and Mary Augusta Ward—numbered among the twelve members of the society's governing council, which also included J. M. Barrie, Arnold Bennett, Arthur Conan Doyle, H. Rider Haggard, H. G. Wells, and the former viceroy of India, Lord George Nathaniel Curzon. The list indicates that both literary respectability and popular stature were represented in the society's leadership and that female authors such as Corelli and Ward were seen to partake of such qualities. As a member of this literary guild, Glyn thus represents an important shift, incipient in the Edwardian period, in the relationship of women writers to the literary mass market: "respectability" in that marketplace was increasingly a matter, not of the moral content of one's fiction, but of the volume of one's sales.

The second aspect also concerns the developing logic of the fiction market but might on the face of it seem to contradict the first. Glyn's failed court case illustrates how, in the years before the Great War, the pervasive, all-penetrating commodification that we associate with later twentieth-century mass culture was a relatively crude and embryonic affair. By the time of her legal case against the Western Feature Film Company, in fact, Glyn had invoked the power of the Society of Authors to defend herself against three previous instances of copyright infringement. In 1912, newspaper notices had gone out to warn readers in New York against the claim that an anonymously authored novel called *One Day* was, as its title page announced, "A Sequel to Three Weeks."[20] In the same year, Cecil Spooner's theater stock company in New York City was warned to cease linking its dramatic production of *One Day,* advertised as "the greatest love story ever written" and "A Sequel to 'Three Weeks,'" to Glyn's creation.[21] And in 1913, Glyn had lost the cinema rights to her novel in the United States because of a loophole in American copyright law (she later regained her rights and wrote the screenplay for the 1924 Hollywood motion picture version of *Three Weeks*). These details of Glyn's experience offer a paradox: just as the newfound liberality and efficiency of the print industry enabled Glyn's tremendous authorial success, so too the enlarging capacities of the early twentieth-century mass media threatened an anarchic proliferation of copies and imitations. The same marketplace that was offering to more and more women writers a cultural prominence and social agency that had theretofore been available, almost exclusively, to a small number of male figures, was simultaneously threatening to strip them of their newfound autonomy and identity. Nonetheless, this early culture industry was as yet a far cry from the condition of literary mass culture that Fredric Jameson associates with a later moment, when "in mass culture, repetition effectively volatilizes the original object—the 'text,' the 'work of art'—so that the student of mass culture has no primary object of study."[22] Jameson here decries the only-too-familiar tendency of literary commodification, which, as another Marxist scholar has suggested, today "turns genre into a brand-name," so that "the brand-name supplants the genre itself, as Mills and Boon has done in the case of romance."[23] These latter economic tendencies in literary production did already exist—they had seen their lowbrow origins in the serial literature and penny dreadfuls of the nineteenth century—but they were not extensively developed in the mass-market literature of Britain until the last three decades of the twentieth century.[24] A century ago, by contrast, Elinor Glyn had every intention of ensuring that she be seen as an "original," of protecting what we would today call the "brand" of her individual literary name—not that of her publishing imprint, Gerald Duckworth—and during her lifetime she succeeded in doing just that. In another example of the female romance writer "carrying" her publisher, Methuen Publishers admitted in 1925 that "but for the novels of the late Miss Corelli," the company's "prosperity must have been far less notable."[25] Such singularity of authorial persona was maintained by the rest of those romance writers, from 1885 to 1925, who are the objects of study here: not for them the authorial interchangeability of the Mills and Boon romances or the ghostwriting behind a V. C. Andrews–style franchise. We may have since forgotten most of them, but during their lives they quite deliberately, and for the most part successfully, established and managed their authorial identities, or even celebrity status, without heeding the marketing directives that came from their relatively disempowered publishers.

A third significant facet of the Glyn incident is the fact that the genteel disapproval of her novel's "gross immorality" reflected the Edwardian media's categorization of her as a "sex novelist." That Justice Younger viewed *Three Weeks* in the context of "innumerable anticipations in" the "erotic literature" of his day is not surprising. In the wake of the progressive and experimental "New Woman" novelists of the 1890s, the decade 1905 to 1915 witnessed the rise of what literary journalists and moral reformers censoriously dubbed "the sex novel," a label that referred not to pornographic writing but to the preoccupation of certain early twentieth-century writers with questions of sexual psychology. As Peter Keating explains, "The crucial change lay in tone and attitude. Quite suddenly the time for defensive experimentation seemed to be over, and attention began to switch to a close analysis of the proven results of those experiments. It could now be assumed that there was no such thing as normal or orthodox sexuality."[26] A representative list of Glyn's contemporaries, the "sex-novelists," cuts across our standard groupings of "low," "middle," and "high" Edwardian fiction-writers: Arnold Bennett, Gilbert Cannan, Horace de Vere Stacpoole, Ford Madox Ford, E. M. Forster, John Galsworthy, Violet Hunt, D. H. Lawrence, Compton Mackenzie, John Masefield, Somerset Maugham, Elizabeth Robins, May Sinclair, and Hubert Wales (Keating, *Haunted,* 209). Some critics suggest that even H. G. Wells should be seen as having written at least one "sex novel": *Ann Veronica: A Modern Love Story* (1909). As produced by any of these novelists, says Keating, the sex novel "could be silly, serious, or sensational, but it always focused on the need to rid the self of sexual repression and honestly face the consequences" (209). Two things are noteworthy about the roster of "sex-novelists": first, for a strain of popular fiction that may be seen as the further development of the "New Woman" novel,[27] it was clearly the product of both male and female authors; second, cohabiting the same generic neighborhood are the modernists Ford and Lawrence, the Edwardian realist triumvirate of Bennett, Galsworthy, and Wells,[28] and the "lowbrow" Glyn and de Vere Stacpoole (author of the much-derided *Blue Lagoon* [1908]). Lawrence, for one, was not especially comfortable in this company. "Is the book so erotic?" he reportedly asked a friend, regarding his novel *The Trespasser.* "I don't want to be talked about in an *Ann Veronica* fashion."[29] Lawrence's uneasiness was well founded, as the scandalized reception of his works from *The Trespasser* through *Lady Chatterley's Lover* was to bear out.

To place a D. H. Lawrence novel in the same generic category as a romance such as *Three Weeks* is to invite well-deserved objections, not least because the formal and stylistic differences between the two are numerous. Yet the juxtaposition, which would have sounded more appropriate to the critics and readers of 1915, foregrounds their broad parallels of content, at once appealingly risqué and threateningly modern. As we have seen, Justice Younger said of *Three Weeks* that "[s]tripped of its trappings which are mere accident, it is nothing more or less than a sensual adulterous intrigue." It is tempting to imagine the words of Justice Younger's decision as applicable, however reductively, to another modernist magnum opus: Joyce's *Ulysses,* a tale of the all-too-human infidelities of Leopold and Molly Bloom. Such an imaginary substitution may be useful in its quick-flash defamiliarization of our critical categories—of low versus high, of "feminized" popular versus "masculinized" elite—but I make no claim to originality with this kind of thought experiment. Andreas Huyssen's paradigm of the "Great Divide," for all its critical purchase and well-deserved influence, has provoked many qualifications and emendations over the past two decades, in particular from feminist and cultural studies–oriented criticism. In her revisionist study of women modernists, *Sentimental Modernism,* Suzanne Clark demonstrates that "modernism is both caught in and stabilized by a system of gendered binaries: male/female, serious/sentimental, critical/popular. Upsetting the system—as women do—introduces an instability and reveals the contradictions. As we acknowledge the contributions of women, we see that modernism was both revolutionary and reactionary; the sentimental was both banal and transgressive" (8). By rediscovering what she calls "the necessary dialogue of modernism with the sentimental" (38), Clark unearths a critically neglected continuity between "high" and "low" literary strains, a continuity distinct from yet parallel to the one I have indicated, in the form of the "sex novel." Similarly, in *The Gender of Modernity,* Rita Felski rethinks the popular romance, "a form often considered to be regressive and anachronistic but whose nostalgic yearning for an indeterminate 'elsewhere' is . . . a foundational trope within the modern itself" (31). The "popular sublime," as embodied in the novels of Marie Corelli and other romancists of the period, strove after a "transcendence of quotidian reality and the material world" (120) in a variation on the same mythic and metaphoric quests for transcendence, specific to early twentieth-century forms of social alienation in the metropolitan sphere, that we associate with such modernist writers as Woolf, Lawrence, Mansfield, and others. The chapters that follow explore such continuities.

CHAPTER TWO

Mary Ward's Romances and the Literary Field

In this chapter, I examine the publishing history of a fin-de-siècle British novelist, Mary Arnold (Mrs. Humphry Ward), whose somewhat unenviable career vector—from Victorian totem of propriety to modernists' lightning rod of abuse—illuminates the various material, social, and ideological forces that shaped the woman-authored romance into its secularized, liberal individualist form. Her surprise best seller of 1888, *Robert Elsmere,* is the most philosophically ambitious of the popular novels interpreted in this study and hardly qualifies for the category of "romance" except that it offers the story of a spiritual questing and was referred to as a religious or a philosophical romance in its own time.[1] Only later in her career, by the middle of the Edwardian period, did Ward's evolving approach to fiction make her representative of the kind of popular romance writers covered in this study. That said, Ward's cultural impact as a best-selling author should also be seen as specific and irreducible—as a singularity of literary history, a unique trajectory that should no more be reduced to features of an abstract discourse of romance than it should be idealized as an expression of Ward's individuality. Ward's career arc is fascinating in and of itself, partly because of the wide-ranging effects of her decisions about what and how to write and publish; at the same time, that arc was also plotted by the conditions of the literary field in her time. In fact, I would argue that the story of how cultural institutions and social ideologies shaped Ward's career vector is more complex than that of any of the other romance writers under discussion in this study and that by virtue of her originally high prestige in the literary field, Ward indirectly affected the careers of all of the rest. As some other recent scholars of turn-of-the-century British literature have done, I refer to some useful Bourdieuan categories in elucidating the meanings of Ward's writing career, especially as pertaining to the evolving status of the woman-authored romance. This chapter, unlike those that follow, focuses less on close readings of the romances at hand—in this case, Ward's *Robert Elsmere* and her later *Lady Rose's Daughter* (1903)—than on their representative status in the history of the British literary field, with a view toward enlightening our understanding of the relationships between the texts and the sociocultural positions of the women romanciers, as well as those of (especially female) modernist writers such as Woolf and West.

The Literary Field in Late Victorian Britain

I start my discussion of Ward with the judgment of literary historian Peter Keating, who offers a commonly accepted account of the literary canonization of women fiction-writers in Britain after the passing of George Eliot: "[A]round the turn of the century, there were no women novelists of a literary stature remotely comparable to that of James, Hardy, Conrad, Meredith, Bennett, Wells, Gissing, or a dozen other men. This situation was itself a specifically late Victorian phenomenon[:] . . . from the death of George Eliot in 1880 until the publication of Virginia Woolf's novel *The Voyage Out* (1915), there was a break in the great tradition . . . even though there were more women publishing fiction and earning a living from it than ever before."[2] However we may feel about the mystical continuity of "the great tradition," the period in question does seem to offer a conspicuous hiatus in the "high" canon of fiction by women writing in Britain. Between the demise of Eliot and the appearance of Woolf's earliest novels, we witness the allegedly fallow period of what Raymond Williams, referring to fin-de-siècle British literature generally, calls "The Interregnum."[3] While the works of such New Woman novelists as Sarah Grand, Mona Caird, George Egerton, Ella D'Arcy, and Ella Hepworth Dixon were sometimes best sellers and are now properly understood to have been culturally transformative in the 1880s and 1890s, our era mirrors their own in denying them the literary stature of an Austen, a Brontë, or an Eliot. Elaine Showalter has shown that, among many ambitious female novelists of the 1880s and '90s, "Eliot's unquestioned dominance as a literary realist and moralist had long defined the unattainable boundaries of aspiration for other women writers. They had looked on her as 'somehow uncanny,' regarding her from afar with an admiration severely tempered by envy and with a depressing recognition of their artistic inferiority."[4] Showalter demonstrates that many women writers attempted to break from the fictional model provided by Eliot's high solemnity and quasi-"masculine role" as a literary forebear and "attempted to redefine the genre of the woman's novel through a fiction that was often sexually suggestive as well as formally experimental and innovative" (*Literature,* 63–64). The more daring among these writers succeeded in differentiating their fictions sharply from the models provided by Eliot, in ways that today's critics recognize as progressive. Jane Eldridge Miller has even suggested that some New Woman (and non–New Woman) fiction writers of the period, both female and male, effectively forged a modernism of social content, if not of literary form, in anticipation of the innovations to come.[5]

Such recognition, however, has mainly arrived with critical hindsight, and in their own time, the New Woman novelists, while sometimes commercially successful, were not generally praised in the male-dominated, "respectable" cultural institutions, whether journalistic or belles-lettrist. In fact, there is much evidence to suggest that by the mid-Victorian period, the popular image of women's literary production in Britain had bifurcated into two general categories: popular "sensation" fiction, meant for light entertainment; and the morally serious novel, devoted to exploring ethical questions stemming from the relationship between the individual and society. By 1880, the year of Eliot's death, evidence suggests that there existed in the world of English letters these two ready-made roles for any would-be fiction-writer who happened to be female: on the one hand, there was the "serious lady novelist," staking her claim to verisimilitude and the complex portrayal of moral problems and psychological truths and thereby taking on the mantle of Jane Austen, Charlotte Brontë, Elizabeth Gaskell, and George Eliot; on the other, there were the writers of melodramatic popular novels for the entertainment of a less-educated audience, in a tradition spanning from Ann Radcliffe to Mrs. Henry Wood and Mary Elizabeth Braddon. The former category was understood to be a very small club, yet its members were accepted as the peers of the greatest male novelists. Late-Victorian male critics in positions of cultural power regularly listed women writers as among the best in the English tradition, as attested by this catalogue from an 1877 article in *Nineteenth Century:* "our greatest English novelists—Miss Austen, Scott, Dickens, Thackeray," with "the greatest name of all, George Eliot, in the present."[6] One midcentury critic, François Guizot, went as far as to rhapsodize on how he delighted in reading "English novels, particularly those written by women. *C'est tout une école de morale.* Miss Austen, Miss Ferrier, Charlotte Brontë, George Eliot, Mrs. Gaskell, and many others almost as remarkable, form a school which . . . resembles the cloud of dramatic poets of the great Athenian age."[7] A recent survey of novel reviews in the influential journal *The Athenaeum* between 1860 and 1900 exhibits gender parity among those novelists to whom the words *artist, genius,* or *great* were applied: twelve men, thirteen women, two women under male pseudonyms (whose actual sex, unlike that of George Eliot and George Sand, was unknown to reviewers), and one anonymous author who was female.[8]

The women writers of the romance or the melodramatic novel, by contrast, had been belittled by none other than George Eliot, in her well-known derogation of "silly novels by lady novelists."[9] On the occasion of Eliot's death, a female critic approvingly cited the great author's dictum: "As an artist, [Eliot] wrote in 1852, Miss Austen surpasses all the male novelists that ever lived, and for eloquence and depth of feeling no man approaches George Sand. But in general the literature of women may be compared to that of Rome—a literature of imitation."[10] By critical consensus, female literary genius exhibited two special features: it expressed moral vision, and it was exceedingly rare. So too, of course, was male genius. What interests me here is the fact that by the closing decades of the nineteenth century, women authors of genius had begun to be perceived as a phenomenon of the past. Among those thirteen identifiably female novelists that the *Athenaeum* reviewers described as an "artist," a "genius," or "great," only five were British writers active in the closing decades of the century—Frances Ternan Trollope, Margaret L. Woods, Margaret Oliphant, Olive Schreiner, and John Oliver Hobbes (Pearl Richards Craigie)—and none was destined to achieve the cultural prestige of an Austen, a Gaskell, or a Brontë.

The categories of "woman novelist of genius" and "silly lady novelist"—the one enumerable on one hand, the other embracing an undifferentiated mass—might be said to correspond to two poles on the late-Victorian literary field, as hypothetically charted in the accompanying figure. Bourdieu defines the field generally as a competitive system of social relations, operating under the rules specific to its domain—be it the economic, the political, the educational, the cultural, or the social.[11] He describes the literary field, a subset of the field of cultural production, as "neither a vague social background nor even a *milieu artistique* like a universe of personal relations between artists and writers (perspectives adopted by those who 'study influences'). It is a veritable social universe where, in accordance with its particular laws, there accumulates a particular form of capital and where relations of force of a particular type are exerted. This universe is the place of entirely specific struggles, notably concerning the question of knowing who is part of the universe, who is a real writer and who is not."[12] According to this view, the literary field is best envisioned as a two-dimensional, metaphorical arena of cultural reception, in which are constellated the dominant works, authors, and genres of a given historical moment. The field's horizontal axis measures the relative popularity and profitability of a given work or writer or genre; relative positions of figures and texts are, in an obvious borrowing from Marx, calculable via their "economic capital," which in this specifically cultural context signifies their commercial success. The vertical axis measures the relative prestige of the work, writer, or genre in question; its measure of success is what Bourdieu calls "a particular form of capital"—*symbolic* capital, or relative cultural prestige (although the term is not strictly synonymous with the term *prestige* as traditionally understood). This second form of capital here is figurative; it conveys the risk of the original venture of seeking recognition on the literary field, as well as the propensity of cultural prestige, once established, to feed on itself or accumulate if it is carefully "managed." The metaphor connotes the investment, accumulation, and convertibility of such prestige within the social context of a given field.

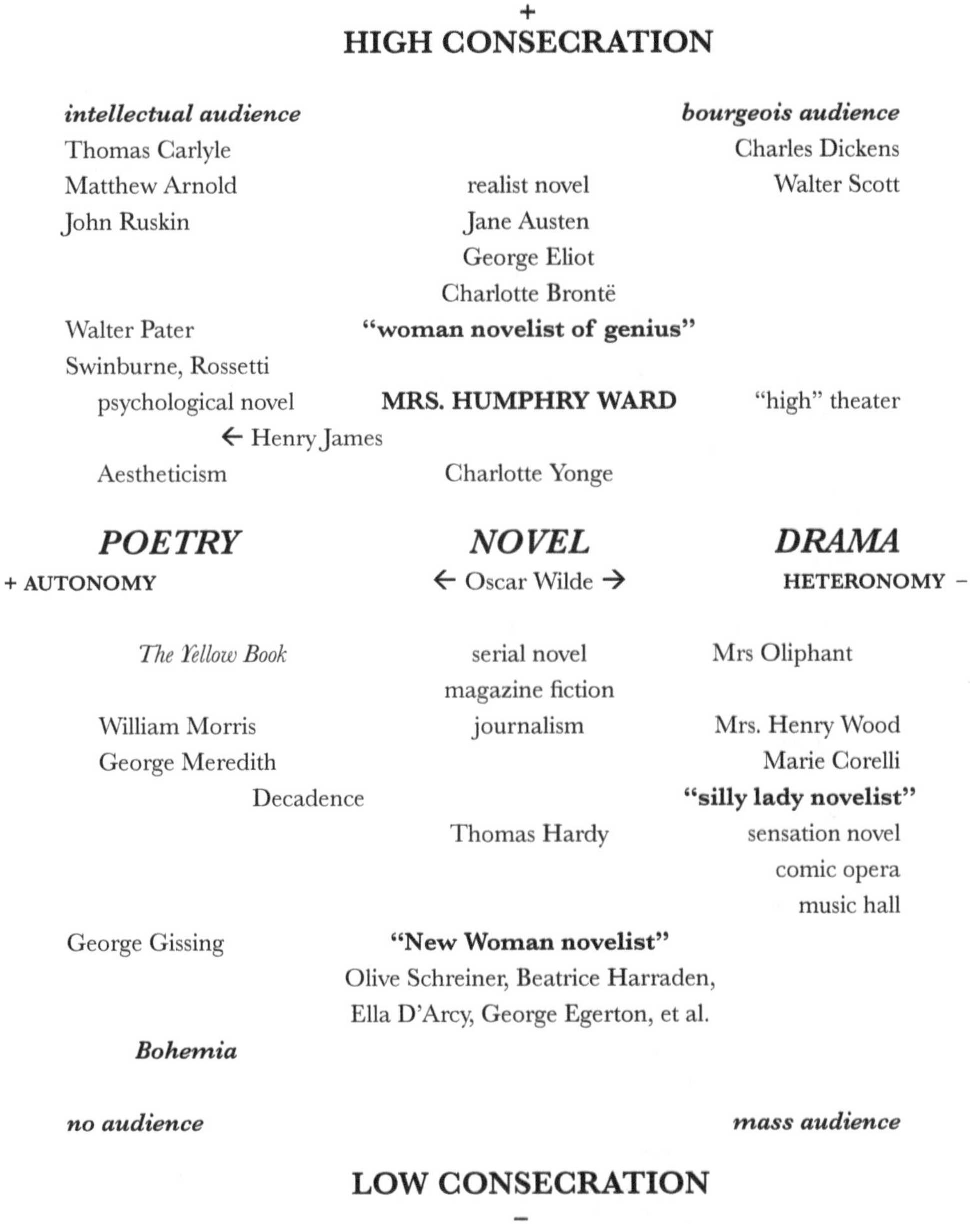

+

HIGH CONSECRATION

intellectual audience | ***bourgeois audience***

Thomas Carlyle
Charles Dickens
Matthew Arnold
realist novel
Walter Scott
John Ruskin
Jane Austen
George Eliot
Charlotte Brontë
Walter Pater
"woman novelist of genius"
Swinburne, Rossetti
psychological novel
MRS. HUMPHRY WARD
"high" theater
← Henry James
Aestheticism
Charlotte Yonge

POETRY | ***NOVEL*** | ***DRAMA***

+ AUTONOMY
← Oscar Wilde →
HETERONOMY –

The Yellow Book
serial novel
Mrs Oliphant
magazine fiction
William Morris
journalism
Mrs. Henry Wood
George Meredith
Marie Corelli
Decadence
"silly lady novelist"
Thomas Hardy
sensation novel
comic opera
music hall
George Gissing
"New Woman novelist"
Olive Schreiner, Beatrice Harraden,
Ella D'Arcy, George Egerton, et al.

Bohemia

no audience | ***mass audience***

LOW CONSECRATION

–

Hypothetical Configuration of the Literary Field in Britain, 1890s

"Literature no longer holds its former high prestige,—there are too many in **the field,**—too many newspaper-scribblers, all believing they are geniuses,—too many ill-educated lady-paragraphists and 'new' women, who think they are as gifted as George Sand . . ." [emphasis added]

—Marie Corelli, *The Sorrows of Satan*, 1895

Literary field is a sharper analytic term than *social background,* as it involves such factors as the writer's parentage, schooling, religious upbringing, regional identity, et cetera, specifically via their effects upon that writer's position on the field. At the same time, as Bourdieu indicates in this passage, the term is wider than *influences,* as it encompasses both the "gravitational pull" of significant fellow writers (whether living or historical) and a writer's relations with publishers, marketers, critics, and readers. The metaphor of "gravitational pull" (my own, not Bourdieu's) is meant to suggest that fellow writers' influences on a given author are at once *conscious,* in the sense of deliberate stylistic or generic emulation; *unconscious,* in the sense of stylistic and generic imitation that is not even perceived by the writer herself; and *structural,* in the sense of the "slotting" of the author (as, say, "Dickensian" or "Eliotic") by critics and readers, whose reception of the work is beyond the control of the individual writer and can sometimes be unpredictable.

Before considering the career of Ward, I offer one more extended passage from Bourdieu, in which he brings together his conceptions of structure and the forms of capital. He suggests that the study of any given literary field (that is, whether of 1890s Britain or 1990s France, and so forth) is

> a form of *analysis situs* which establishes that each position—e.g., the one which corresponds to a genre such as the novel or, within this, to a sub-category such as "the society novel" or the "popular" novel—is subjectively defined by the system of distinctive properties by which it can be situated relative to other positions; that every position, even the dominant one, depends for its very existence, and for the determinations it imposes on its occupants, on the other positions constituting the field; and that the structure of the field, i.e. the open space of positions, is nothing other than the structure of the distribution of capital of specific properties which governs success in the field and the winning of external or specific profits (such as literary prestige) which are at stake in the field. (*Field,* 30)

In this dense passage, Bourdieu reveals the structuralist underpinnings of his theory. He posits that the field is not ontologically grounded but is instead constituted of ever-changing relations—it is not a static thing but a dynamic process in which fluid relationality is the source of structure. He also refers to a universal aspect of all fields, cultural and otherwise: each involves specific forms of capital, which the agents aim to accumulate and increase through their varying "strategies."[13] The term *capital,* again, while used literally in the case of "economic capital," is in its other designations figurative and functions as incarnated through the "specific properties" (cultural, symbolic, political, educational, linguistic) that govern success in a given field.[14] Though it is a complex structure, then, the literary field does in large measure take its form through the identifiable exertions of individual and collective will and agency. Writers do not only compete, through their strategies, to improve their relative positions on the field; they have also historically "struggled" (Bourdieu's term is quite deliberate here) for the opportunity to claim a position on it in the first place, to be considered "real writers." For the field is also "the site of struggles in which what is at stake is the power to impose the dominant definition of the writer and therefore to delimit the population of those entitled to take part in the struggle to define the writer" (Bourdieu, *Field,* 44).

Needless to say, in the literary history of nineteenth-century Britain, such struggles were experienced differently by female and male writers. While all strove individually or in movements to stake their claim in what it meant to be a writer, only female aspirants had the added challenge of struggling to legitimate themselves as women writers—to overcome, that is, powerful gender prejudice against their cultural productions. This observation may seem self-evident, but the point here is that, in the case of late-Victorian and Edwardian women novelists, authorial gender is one crucial, symbolic "property" among others—economic capital, social capital, and cultural capital—that together and in complex fashion helped to determine an author's or a text's success on the literary field. As we see in the case of Mrs. Humphry Ward, advantages in certain of these forms of capital could occasionally overcome the social handicap of gender. As Toril Moi suggests, "In general, the impact of femaleness as negative capital may be assumed to decline in direct proportion to the amount of other forms of symbolic capital amassed. Or to put it the other way around: although a woman rich in symbolic capital may lose some legitimacy because of her gender, she still has more than enough capital left to make her impact on the field. In the case of exceptionally high amounts of capital, femaleness may play a very small part indeed."[15] While Moi is referring here primarily to female cultural figures of the twentieth century (for example, Simone de Beauvoir), the point holds—though to a somewhat lesser extent—for the late-Victorian literary field. By the late-Victorian period, the positions available to the woman writer consisted mainly in the two roles or constructs noted in the accompanying chart: at one end, the "great" woman writer or even "the woman novelist of genius," with her high symbolic capital (at that historical juncture, perhaps the highest ever accorded the female writer in Britain); at the other, the "scribbling," "silly lady novelist," with her low symbolic capital but ever-increasing potential for high financial capital—that is, large popular sales and the very real possibility of the author's economic independence. Thus, to use Bourdieu's precise terms, the entire literary field of positions made possible by "the distribution of specific properties"—in this case, the degree of institutional "consecration" and the degree of success in the marketplace—is in the case of the woman writer's works narrowed down by the possession of another "distinctive property," the author's gender. If the opportunity of institutional "consecration" (again, as realized by Austen, the Brontës, and Eliot) had come only gradually to the woman writer and almost exclusively through the genre of the novel, her artistic autonomy from market forces was, by reason of that genre's "heteronomous"[16] position in the field, essentially nonexistent. But if by 1880 women novelists' victories on the literary field were few and hard won, they were nonetheless incontestable. Any review of the "respectable" cultural periodicals of the period—the *Academy*, the *Athenaeum*, *Blackwoods*, the *Saturday Review*, and so forth—confirms that the standards of excellence by which new novelists were judged included equal numbers of references to Austen and Scott, Gaskell and Thackeray, Charlotte Brontë and Dickens. As my chart of the literary field between 1880 and 1900 conveys, the "great" woman novelist can be said to have occupied a position of middle-range economic capital and high symbolic capital. The "silly lady novelist," by contrast, could be said to occupy the lower right-hand corner of the field, given her high earnings potential and abysmally low status in the eyes of the masculine arbiters of culture.

A last element in this consideration of the literary field should be considered: the fact that literary genres themselves acquire, maintain, and lose both economic and symbolic capital. In the case of the late-Victorian novel, we see a rise in the genre's stock, inflected by gender. As Gaye Tuchman and Nina Fortin have argued, the novel's prestige and profitability both rose in the years between 1840 and 1900, but the gender distribution of low-culture versus high-culture novelists underwent a change: "Before 1840 the British cultural elite accorded little prestige to the writing of novels, and most English novelists were women. By the turn of the twentieth century[,] 'men of letters' acclaimed novels as a form of literature, and most critically successful novelists were men. These two transitions—in the prestige of novel-writing and the gender distribution of lauded novelists—were related processes, constituting complementary elements in a classic confrontation between men and women in the same white-collar occupation."[17] Through a detailed study of the publishing records of such houses as Macmillan and Company, Tuchman and Fortin have shown how once such women writers as Austen, Gaskell, and the Brontës helped to establish the prestige of the novel as a preeminent English literary form, the male publishers and critics began to redefine the serious novel as a male province and to bar new women writers from the "high end" of the field. At the end of the century, in this well-documented account, "women were not edged out of all fiction writing; they were edged out of writing high-culture novels."[18] On the literary field, in other words, the novel as a genre began in this period to bifurcate into "high" and "low" embodiments; women writers were generally (though not, as we have seen, categorically or absolutely)[19] assumed to be capable of producing only the latter. The male publishing and critical establishments made no attempt to belittle the achievements of earlier female "greats"; in a neat ideological contradiction, the widespread belief in female literary exceptionalism allowed them both to revere these precedents and to routinely dismiss ambitious new women novelists.

As Tuchman and Fortin's terms for this evolution in the literary field indicate—"a classic confrontation between men and women in the same white-collar occupation"—their account of the Victorian "lady novelist" is a sociological one and as such focuses on the institutional structures of the period. Certainly, women writers were collective victims of male-dominated institutions, to say nothing of ideologies, yet the very language of the description—women were "edged out of writing high-culture novels"—reveals through its passive construction how focusing on these levels *exclusively* may obscure the singular writers' own agency in this literary history. For this evolution is also the history of the interplay between, on the one hand, the patriarchal structures of the publishing industry and wider late-Victorian society, and on the other, the actions of certain (relatively) empowered women, as individual agents, in the evolving social constructions of "the lady novelist." Given the lopsided binary of "serious" versus "frivolous" novel-writing roles, any aspiring young woman writer of the time must have felt powerfully the limited possibilities of the literary field. (How many, for instance, felt encouraged to designate themselves, vocationally, as "poet" or "playwright"?) Yet in the years following George Eliot's death, the list of those who did try to match Eliot's level of achievement is a long one, including Eliza Lynn Linton, Olive Schreiner, "John Oliver Hobbes" (Pearl Craigie), and Vernon Lee (Violet Paget).[20] Patriarchal ideologies notwithstanding, the flourishing career of such a "consecrated" and belaurelled predecessor, well within living memory, served as a powerful encouragement to ambitious women romance writers coming of intellectual age in the 1880s and 1890s.

The Success of *Robert Elsmere*

Nowhere is the aspiration to become "the next George Eliot" more apparent than in the early career of Mrs. Humphry Ward, née Mary Arnold. As the granddaughter of Dr. Thomas Arnold, niece of Matthew Arnold, and friend to Walter Pater, Robert Browning, T. H. Huxley, and Henry James, Mary Ward was arguably as well provided with social, cultural, and educational advantages—with high-cultural capital—as any woman of the period in England possibly could have been. Her family and social connections, as much as the achievements of the nineteenth century's great women writers, were what first provided her with her conviction of her literary potential. In fact, her social advantages empowered her to believe, as a married woman in the mid-1880s, that her gender should be no impediment to her making a mark on the world of letters. Notwithstanding her class privilege, the story of her rise to literary prominence is, from one angle of view, a record of personal courage and resourceful persistence. From another perspective, it is the story of a historically unprecedented convergence of liberalizing social ideologies and free-market forces in the field of literature.

By age thirty, Ward had been an occasional journalist for the *Manchester Guardian* and had published her first book, the children's story *Milly and Olly* (1881), with the prominent London publisher Alexander Macmillan. As her biographer John Sutherland suggests, by 1883, the thirty-two-year-old Londoner had become "a successful hostess, a successful journalist, a successful mother and wife. Yet she seems never to have relinquished for a minute her ambition to write a great book. Every other success was secondary."[21] So great was her determination that she asked for a £250 advance from Macmillan for another work, which was to be a study of the French Romantic movement. She immediately received the advance, but the book was never written; the scope was perhaps forbiddingly broad, and projects that were more focused supplanted the original one. By the end of 1884, she had instead published with Macmillan both a translation of the Swiss philosopher Henri Frédéric Amiel and a novella entitled *Miss Bretherton.* It is interesting, and perhaps understandable, that Ward did not overtly claim to have been influenced by George Eliot in writing either of these works; to admit too readily to the groundbreaking inspiration of Eliot would have been both to raise expectations and to legitimize the assumption that a woman could only go where a previous woman had been. As if to deny any emulation of Eliot, who had early translated the work of the philosopher David Friedrich Strauss, Ward actually criticizes Eliot in the introduction to the Amiel translation, speaking of "the incommunicable magic which a George Eliot seeks in vain."[22] As an unpublished 1884 article by Ward indicates, the main influence on *Miss Bretherton*'s literary form is actually her friend Henry James, who appears in the thinly veiled guise of a prominent character in the novel.[23]

Neither the Amiel translation nor the Jamesian novella achieved popular or critical success. As capable and energetic as she was ambitious, Ward ignored the stinging comment of her uncle Matthew—"No Arnold can write a novel; if they could, I should have done it"[24]—and took her publisher's advice, which was to attempt a novel on a more "generally popular subject."[25] She also clearly hoped that the new work would identify her as a novelist of ideas—that the novel would, ipso facto, show her to be the successor to George Eliot. Nonetheless, she avoids direct reference to the Eliotic model in her personal correspondence of the years of *Robert Elsmere*'s composition, 1885 to 1888. As she explains in her autobiography, Ward wanted to write a novel simultaneously popular and intellectually challenging: "[W]hat one had to aim at was so to use suggestion as to touch the two zones of thought—that of the scholar, and that of what one may call the educated populace."[26] The circumlocution of that statement hints at her concealed ambitions: having failed to create a stir either with her philosophical translation or with her 1881 pamphlet, "Unbelief and Sin," circulated in bookstores in an effort to join the fray of Oxford religious controversy, Ward had recalibrated and tried a new bid at intellectual prominence: the narrativized, more easily digested form of a religious romance.

When it came to launching and sustaining her writing career, Sutherland suggests, "It was one of Mary Ward's principal strengths that she was able to think and act strategically" (85). And indeed, after what she considered to be her false starts, Ward found a controversial theme equal to the task of making her mark in the literary world. Her social experience among the male Oxford intelligentsia of the 1870s and 1880s provided her with a complex and controversial donnée for the novel—the loss of religious faith. Harnessed to the dual structure of the domestic romance and the spiritual-quest romance, the novel of ideas might bring her symbolic capital both in the general literary field and, within that, amid the exclusively male domain of the Oxford academic-intellectual milieu. *Robert Elsmere,* published in late February 1888, is at once a passionate love story, a compendium of allusions to many major British thinkers of the nineteenth century (in a zealous and excessive display of its author's cultural capital), and the tale of a man's rejection of Christianity in favor of an ethical theism. In her later *Writer's Recollections,* Ward would describe the impetus behind the novel as her desire to appeal to "the floating interest and passion surrounding the great controversy—the *second* religious battle [after, presumably, the Oxford Movement of the 1830s and '40s] of the nineteenth century—with which it had seemed to me both in London and in Oxford that the intellectual air was charged" (233). This "second religious battle" refers to the challenges to established religious thought at Oxford during the 1860s and '70s, the liberalizing Christian "heresies" being propounded by Benjamin Jowett, T. H. Green, Mark Pattison, and others.

We need not revisit here the substance of these religious controversies to recognize how brilliantly Ward appropriated them to effect her successful arrival as an intellectual figure. By publishing a religious romance, she deflected attention from her gender, even as she drew attention to and popularized the avant-garde theological ideas that were preoccupying the leading lights of academia. It was what Bourdieu calls an effective "position-taking" *(prise de position)* on the field. As Randal Johnson, in a gloss on Bourdieu, explains,

> The cultural field is . . . structured by the distribution of available positions (e.g., consecrated artist vs striving artist, novel vs poetry, art for art's sake vs social art) and by the objective characteristics of the agents occupying them. The dynamic of the field is based on the struggles between positions, a struggle often expressed in the conflict between the orthodoxy of established traditions and the heretical challenge of new modes of cultural practice, manifested as *prises de position* or position-takings. . . . The space of position-takings can only be defined as a system of differential stances in relation to other possible position-takings, past and present. This is where the notion of intertextuality comes into the analysis. Unlike intertextuality as conceived by Bakhtin or Kristeva, however, which tends to relate texts only to other texts, for Bourdieu texts must be analysed both in relation to other texts and in relation to the structure of the field and to the specific agents involved. (*Field,* 16–17)

In publishing *Robert Elsmere,* Ward joined this cultural struggle between literary orthodoxy and heterodoxy by championing a heretical movement in religious thought. She did so with a very shrewd grasp of precisely the phenomenon described by Johnson; as she wrote in her *Writer's Recollections,* her declared literary models were the religious controversialists of the mid-Victorian period: "There were great precedents—[James Anthony] Froude's 'Nemesis of Faith' [1849], [John Henry Cardinal] Newman's 'Loss and Gain'

[1848], [Charles] Kingsley's 'Alton Locke' [1850]—for the novel of religious or social propaganda" (229). Each of these éminences grises had indeed published novels that had hit the intellectual scene with the force of their (very different) theological stances, and so Ward was right to shield the "heretical challenge" of her title character's agnosticism under the established "position-takings" of these (by 1888) consecrated thinkers/novelists. Moreover, few literary historians today would deny that *Robert Elsmere*'s exploration of ethical theism—in particular, the hero's rationalist rejection of supernaturalism, of the doctrine of Christian miracles—earns Ward a place on this list of religious propagandists. The brilliance of her strategy, however, lies in the fact that, behind her overt and successful tactic of religio-philosophical provocation, Ward was effectively camouflaging the move into what Randal Johnson calls a "new mode of cultural practice": a woman "novelist of ideas" asking to be taken as seriously as the most controversial male thinkers—and not *only* male novelists—of the era. It was Eliot and Eliot alone who had recently made a successful bid to extend the female novelist's authority beyond exclusively moral questions and into a more philosophical purview. In her later appraisal of what she was up to, Ward explicitly (to return to Randal Johnson's terms) relates her "text only to other texts," while eliding the facts, at least as interesting, of "the structure of the field and . . . the specific agents involved." Both early and late in her career (*A Writer's Recollections* was published in 1918), she knew how to play the literary field.

Even the gender representations within *Robert Elsmere* appear calculated and tactical. The novel is undergirded by a thoroughgoing ideology of male intellectual superiority over women, even as its emotional register seems to reside within the heroine, Catherine, and her sister, Rose. If the theological soul-searching of the hero was daring and progressive for its time, the social universe depicted here was retrograde in its gender relations. Catherine is as passionate in her self-denying adulation of her husband, Robert, as she is (evidently) incapable of comprehending his radical ideas about the social imperatives of a Christian morality unmoored by the traditional church. Rose, who has artistic ambitions and an urge toward independence, is eventually punished by the narrative for placing these goals before her feminine self-subordination to the right kind of man. This divide between the male and female characters is an aspect of the novel that has been most striking to contemporary critics; for example, Clyde Ryals notes that "the men in *Robert Elsmere* sometimes seem to be personifications of ideas more than flesh-and-blood human beings," whereas the women are "vivid" and intuitive characters who "gain in moral awareness through love and suffering."[27] Patricia Meyer Spacks argues that the love story between Robert and Catherine, plagued by great obstacles over the course of their marriage but emotionally consummated at the moment of Robert's death, is likely to have been what offered the vital interest to much of the reading public of the time. In addition to this, as Spacks points out, Rose inhabits a conventional love-romance plot, but one "with a difference, as she insists against all obstacles on preparing herself to be a vocational musician." Rose is a New Woman courted by an attractive, rich, aristocratic man. Spacks opines that "the novel offers something for everyone."[28] That "everyone" may well have included those readers who were attracted by the character of Rose, perhaps even against the didactically punitive intentions of Ward toward the character. (This pattern of the attractively independent woman who falls in love somewhat ill-advisedly and illicitly, and who is emotionally punished for it, can be seen in Ward's later *Lady Rose's Daughter.*)

In fact, *Robert Elsmere*'s vastly different representations of male and female figures could be seen as the novel's structuring tension, a fault line at once thematic and formal, ideological and generic. As noted above, the novel embodies both philosophical religious treatise and romantic love story, and while the former dimension is achieved through a set of debating men, the latter is experienced primarily through the heroine's devotion to her lover and eventual husband. The romantic plotline is the simple and time-honored tale of the hero's wooing, winning, losing (in this case, spiritually), and rewinning of the heroine. Although Robert Elsmere dies from overwork in the last two pages of the novel, this martyrdom only emphasizes his transcendent relationship with Catherine, who will dedicate the rest of her life to his cause. As Judith Wilt suggests, the male protagonist "dies holding hard to both marriage and God against the bleak pull of Hardyesque modernity."[29] Here and in her subsequent novels, Ward makes her love stories a conversion experience as well—the conversion of intellectually and psychologically dependent women to the beliefs of their superior male lovers or husbands.[30] We see this thematic and ideological pattern at both the level of overt theme and the level of genre itself; Ward cross-pollinates the subgenres of the novel of ideas and the romance novel.[31] Just as the male characters serve as the vehicles of ideas to be learned by the female characters, so too does the "feminine" narrative backbone of the love story help sustain the reader's interest in the "masculine" narrative of unfolding ideas. Thus, in the same stroke, Ward covers her "unwomanly" literary ambition by representing a profoundly patriarchal vision and aims for wide popular appeal by delivering her intellectual "position taking" through the vehicle of the romantic quest for transcendent heterosexual union.

I do not offer this thumbnail reading of the novel in the spirit of the hermeneutic of suspicion; it is instead meant to illustrate the resourcefulness of an ambitious and intellectually sophisticated writer operating under the broad social constraints of British culture in the 1880s—just a historical half step, as it were, before the explicit arrival of the "New Woman novel" of the 1890s.[32] Ward's professional moves on the occasion of her novel's publication further illustrate this resourcefulness. In the weeks before the publication date of 24 February 1888, her letters to her publisher, George Smith of Smith Elder and Company, carried a stream of subtle pleas that his house should take her novel seriously. In a letter of late January, she exaggerated about how well she had done in the United States with *Miss Bretherton* and the Amiel translation, while maintaining a tone of modesty: "The editor of the Century [a popular American magazine] wrote me a little while ago asking for an article, & saying that so far as he could judge Amiel's journal has made a distinct mark on the American reading public. So I cannot help thinking that a new book of mine will have a chance there. Not that I expect to profit by it!—at any rate for the present."[33] She also pestered Smith about the yet-to-appear agreement of terms: "I should be perfectly content, if you wd. write me a letter embodying the conditions named in my various letters to you"—namely, a request for a £200 advance and £50 for the "extra expenses" of printing and advertising.[34] Two days before publication, in a further effort to impress her publisher and motivate him to promote her new book, Ward wrote a contradictory account of the opinion of Edmond Scherer (whose original French manuscript of Amiel's journals Ward had translated) regarding *Robert Elsmere.* She let on that Scherer had praised her new novel but then turned around and admitted that his views were also "critical": "His own position . . . has become purely negative and pessimistic. But then I venture to think, the English public, for all its unbelief, will be with me, rather than with him!"[35] The purpose of this letter was evidently to let her publisher know that a Continental intellectual respected her enough to read her novel manuscript (or at least deliver opinions on it) in advance of its publication.

In the three weeks following publication—an unnervingly long time—*Robert Elsmere* received no significant reviews in the English press. There was one positive review that arrived a week after the book's appearance, in the *Scotsman,* which compared *Elsmere* favorably to George Eliot's novels.[36] Ward kept up a hopeful front and informed her publisher of some privately received reviews: "Yesterday brought me specially characteristic notes from the Master of Balliol, M[r]. Burne-Jones, and M[r.] Pater. The Master had read it 'nearly through' in five days, and says most warm and cordial things, and M[r]. Burne-Jones 'never thought he should devour a book about parsons.'"[37] Ward was in frenetic action behind the scenes, shrewdly manipulating her social connections, calling in her various investments of social capital among the producers of cultural meaning and value. She asked for and received a favorable published review from Pater; she had a copy of the novel sent to J. T. Knowles, the editor of the highbrow journal *Nineteenth Century,* with the audacious request that he pass it on to his mentor, ex–prime minister William Gladstone. On 14 March 1888, three weeks after publication, she wrote yet again to her publisher: "Knowles seems to be enthusiastic and is handing on his copy to Mr. Gladstone. But I am afraid R.E.'s opinions will be hardly as congenial to the G.O.M.['Grand Old Man'] as John Inglesant's were!"[38] Ward was later to provide an account of what happened next:

> All through March [1888] the tide of success was rapidly rising. . . . [Gladstone] happened to be staying for an Easter visit with the Warden of Keble [College, Oxford], and Mrs. Talbot, who was his niece by marriage. I was with my mother about a mile away, and Mrs. Talbot, who came to ask for news of her, reported to me that Mr. Gladstone was deep into the book. He was

> reading it with pencil in hand, marking all the passages he disliked or quarreled with, with the Italian *"Ma!"*—and those he approved with mysterious signs. . . . Mr. Knowles, she reported, the busy editor of the *Nineteenth Century*, was trying to persuade the great man to review it. But "Mr. G." had not made up his mind.[39]

It was actually in early April that Gladstone made his short visit to his relatives' home in Oxford and, preoccupied with the book's expression of the loss of High Church faith, summoned its author for an interview. Ward had been standing vigil over her dying mother, who lived in Oxford, but she would not let her grief get in the way of a potentially career-making encounter. Within a day of her mother's passing, she appeared at Gladstone's door for the requested interview and proceeded to debate with him about Christian miracles at some length.[40] Seven days later, uncle Matthew Arnold—astonished perhaps by the news of this imperial summons of his niece—dropped dead of cardiac arrest in a Liverpool street. Nor were the newspapers unimpressed; their reported rumors of this encounter sparked the novel's sales dramatically. At this point, according to Ward's account, Gladstone wrote to her, "I try to write upon you, [and] wholly despair of satisfying myself, cannot quite tell whether to persevere or desist." She reports that Pater told her, "It is a *chef d'ouevre* after its kind, and justifies the care you have devoted to it."[41]

The novel was becoming a popular success, and the critical response had begun to feature copious references to the Eliotic model. The *Academy* trumpeted, "Mrs. Ward's literary method is that of George Eliot. Indeed, there is a curious affinity in *Robert Elsmere* to *Adam Bede*."[42] The *Pall Mall Gazette* offered a more skeptical response to such comparisons: "On the one hand it has had the misfortune to be greeted with a salvo of mechanical applause from the log-rolling fraternity, with whom Mrs. Ward is in high favour. 'Behold,' they cry, 'a greater than George Eliot is here,' thereby making themselves more than usually ridiculous."[43]

As the novel entered its fourth edition only two months after its original publication, Ward began to follow the example of "the log-rolling fraternity" and to invoke the inspiration of Eliot. Again, she was nudging her publisher, George Smith, to promote her work.

> I am v. glad to hear that the 4th edition is doing so well. But do you anticipate a speedy slackening in the sale that you are only printing 250 copies instead of 500 as a fifth edition? On looking back at the facts of George Eliot's circulation I see that her great success in the case of *Adam Bede* was made with a 2 vol. edition which came out apparently after about 2750 copies of the 3rd edition had been dispensed of some three months after the appearance of the book and sold enormously. I don't mean to compare myself to G. E., whatever foolish and "irresponsible reviewers" may do![44]

Both the practical concern with sales figures and the half-modest suggestion about her own literary stature quickly became characteristic of Ward's correspondence; her revealed ambition took cover under a "feminine" self-effacement, yet she was never henceforth afraid to reveal to her editors an assertive business sense. In the same letter, she requested that George Smith put out a cheaper two-volume edition, but her editor demurred, fearing to offend the circulating libraries (chiefly, that of the powerful Charles Edward Mudie): "It would not, in my opinion, be advisable to print a cheap edition of 'RE' until some time after the demand for the edition in three volumes has ceased. To print a cheap edition so soon would cause an outcry from the librarians, and it would . . . affect the sale of any future novel from your pen."[45] But Ward persisted: "I own to an unreasonable hankering after a 2 volume edition!" She counterbalanced such demands with self-deprecating proclamations: "This news about the book is really very wonderful. I confess—not being used yet to being a popular author!—I find it a little bewildering."[46] This correspondence illustrates, to a degree we might find surprising today, that Ward did have a great deal of say in the commercial fortunes of her novel—though she often hankered for more say. Indeed, from the publication of *Robert Elsmere* until her death in 1920, Ward kept up a voluminous correspondence with her publishers, micromanaging (or attempting to do so) all of the commercial facets of her career: royalties, serial rights, prospective markets, cheap editions, copyright complexities, translations, dramatizations, illustrations, author's right of veto, and so forth. As the cover notes to one of the largest collections of her correspondence suggest, "All of these negotiations were carried on with the utmost courtesy and dignified diplomacy."[47] This pattern of deep involvement with business decisions was to appear in the publishing relations of most of the successful woman romancists discussed in later chapters.

Later in the same month, May 1888, Ward achieved one of her main goals: Gladstone published a long review essay attacking her novel and the late-Victorian theological tendencies—theism, agnosticism—that it represented. Over the course of the next few months, the resulting notoriety set into motion a *Robert Elsmere* juggernaut. The circulating libraries were barely able to keep up with the demand, as another three-volume edition rolled out every two or three weeks. George Smith waited until late July, when he judged that the lending libraries had been saturated, to issue a "cheap," one-volume edition, which went into seventeen editions in a year. By the end of 1888, more than 100,000 pirated copies had been sold in the United States alone (Sutherland, *Ward*, 129). In late summer, Ward found herself receiving biweekly royalties in £125 installments. Philip Waller describes how the novel thereafter grew into "a *succès fou*, in eighteen months selling about 40,000 copies in England and 200,000 in America" (1030). By 1911, as Ward reports in her memoir, she estimated that *Robert Elsmere* had sold nearly a million copies in the English-speaking world—a number that does not account for sales of translations, which were also considerable.

Why, during its first eighteen months, did *Robert Elsmere* sell five times as well in the United States as in England? In part, this had to do with book-selling practices—the triple-decker sold to the lending libraries (followed, after a few months' delay, by single-volume sales), while cheaper single-volume editions, often pirated, sold immediately to individual consumers. But the less-mediated consumption of books cannot ipso facto explain the tremendous popularity of the novel among Americans. The critics and reviewers of 1888–89 focused on the heterodox theology of the hero as the source of the book's appeal. One thrust of their interpretation was the notion that Ward was successfully popularizing the crisis-of-faith narrative that had been the fodder of intellectual readers a generation earlier. After a long lag, it was held, the general public was catching up with the intellectual avant-garde. Moreover, critics and reviewers certainly realized the significance of the Gladstone imprimatur, which I have been at pains to describe here. However, neither of these reasons suffices to explain *Robert Elsmere*'s best-seller status on the other side of the Atlantic.

The reason may instead lie in the love story that unfolds between Catherine and Robert. Shortly after their first encounter, early in the novel, Ward supplies a description of the connection between heroine and hero that characterizes the typical meeting of lovers in the romance mode: "She had not yet said a direct word to him, and yet he was curiously convinced that here was one of the most interesting persons, and one of the persons most interesting to *him,* that he had ever met. What mingled delicacy and strength in the hand that had laid beside her on the dinner table—what potential depths of feeling in the full dark-fringed eye!" (35). Unpacking this passage, Spacks identifies a libidinal/spiritual continuum that is elaborated much more extensively in the later romances discussed in this study. "Catherine," Spacks suggests, "embodies both moral importance and emotional appeal" (155); but more specifically, this heroine functions as a vehicle for the inexpressible—Catherine serves as what Rita Felski identifies, in the popular sublime, as "an index of the unrepresentable" (119). Spacks detects a hint of libido in Ward's passage: "As for the 'potential depths of feeling' in her eye, that Victorian code for erotic appeal—Ward comprehends (although Robert does not) not only erotic potential but [also] its capacity for transmutation into other forms of energy" (155). Here, Spacks draws our attention to the muffling layers of discursive protection from the "forms of energy" represented by Catherine: Robert doesn't *know* what he intuits about Catherine's libido. Ward does know, but only in a diffused fashion, such that eroticism is just one "potential" of the "depths of feeling" in that "dark-fringed eye."

The scene of Robert's death, arriving in the last two pages of this long novel, illustrates another facet of the popular sublime—one that may reveal continuities with the sentimental mode but is not reducible to sentimentality. It is worth quoting at some length:

> One morning he had just dropped into a fevered sleep. Catherine was sitting by the window gazing out into a dawn-world of sun. . . . She looked the shadow of herself. *Spiritually,* too, she was the shadow of herself. Her life was no longer her own: she lived in him—in

> every look of those eyes—in every movement of that wasted frame.
>
> As she sat there, her Bible on her knee, her strained unseeing gaze resting on the garden and the sea, a sort of *hallucination* took *possession* of her. It seemed to her that she saw the Son of man passing over the *misty* slope in front of her, that the *dim majestic figure* turned and beckoned. In her *half-dream* she fell on her knees. "Master!" she cried in agony, "I cannot leave him! Call me not! My life is here. I have no heart—it beats in his."
>
> And the figure passed, and the beckoning hand dropped at its side. She followed it with a sort of anguish, but it seemed to her as though *both mind and body were incapable of moving*—that she would not if she could. Then suddenly a sound from behind startled her. She turned, her *trance* suddenly shaken off in an instant, and saw Robert sitting up in his bed.
>
> For a moment her lover, her husband, of the early days was before her—as she ran to him. But he did not see her.
>
> An ecstasy of joy was on his face; the whole man bent forward listening.
>
> *"The child's cry!—thank God! Oh! Meyrick—Catherine—thank God!"*
>
> And she knew that he stood again on the stairs at Murewell in that September night which gave them their first-born, and that he thanked God because her pain was over.
>
> An instant's strained looking, and, sinking back into her arms, he gave two or three gasping breaths, and died. (603–4; my emphases)

Citing this passage and an earlier scene of Robert's tubercular decline, Spacks maintains that "[a]t these critical junctures, the domestic, in its specificity and emotional energy, takes precedence over the conventionally religious. Indeed, it defines a new realm of spirituality" (159). The supersession of "the conventionally religious," the definition of "a new realm of spirituality"—these are elements that foretell the shared characteristics of the best-selling

British romances that emerged during the thirty years subsequent to 1888. The divergence from Spack's appraisal that I would offer is a difference of emphasis. Reading against the grain of contemporaneous reviews of *Robert Elsmere,* Spacks connects it to nineteenth-century domestic romance; I would instead draw attention to the italicized words from the passage: *spiritually, hallucination, possession, misty, dim majestic figure, half-dream, trance, mind and body incapable of moving.* Here, at the climax of this turbulent love story, we are in the presence of an elevated mysticism. At the moment of her lover's death, the heroine experiences a psychological transcendence, or affective transport into sublime presence. We do not know which turn-of-the century romanciers read *Robert Elsmere,* but we can point to this scene as exemplifying the discursive intensities that also characterize the romances of Marie Corelli, Elinor Glyn, and others.

Lady Rose's Daughter: Ward's Turn to Melodrama

By the end of 1888, Mary Ward had come to be much in demand as a public persona, and she was enjoying her newfound independence as a novelist—she had her publisher at her command. At summer's end he wrote to her, "I very much hope you are going to allow us to have the honor of being the Publishers of your new novel. I am of course quite at your service and shall be delighted to be of every assistance to you in making arrangements so as to extract as much value as possible out of this new novel."[48] Smith knew what Ward wanted to hear. For if by then she had acquired a shrewd "sense of the game" in the literary field—a well-developed *habitus*—she had gained an attendant knack for converting her sudden literary status into the more concrete form of money. What is more, she had parlayed both her own and others' cultural, social, and even political capital into a firm reserve of symbolic capital on which to launch a successful career as late-Victorian Britain's most respected woman novelist.

In so suddenly establishing her cultural presence, Ward's canniest move had been the successful provocation of Gladstone. The tactic was to have broader repercussions. By taking serious but respectful issue with Ward's (as he called it) "propaganda romance," this dominant figure from the nation's ruling class—one of the country's most powerful individuals—not only legitimated her as a significant literary persona but also, on another level, helped to consolidate and sustain the high symbolic capital that could, after forebears such as the Brontës, potentially infuse the female-authored romance novel. Thereafter, until the early Edwardian period, "Mrs. Humphry Ward" managed to maintain both her vast popularity and her role as the standard-bearer of the "respectable lady novelist." During these years, 1888 to (roughly) 1905, the fate of the female "novelist of genius" arguably lay in her hands as in no one else's. She published a series of critically acclaimed novels—*The History of David Grieve* (1892), *Marcella* (1894), *Sir George Tressady* (1896), and *Helbeck of Bannisdale* (1898)—most of which, to our eyes today, appear as intellectually sophisticated as *Elsmere,* while de-emphasizing its romance mode and moving closer to social realism. Through the 1890s, Ward struck a middle course between provocative social themes and the perceived radicalism of the New Woman novelists. Recent critics have debated her relation to feminism in this period. Some see the novels as effectively antifeminist in their depiction of the female protagonist (especially in *Marcella* and *Tressady*), who is brought up short in her forays into the public sphere of progressive social reform;[49] at least one critic, Beth Sutton-Ramspeck, sees Ward espousing a "social feminist concept . . . based not on *rights* (as liberal feminists argued) but on *duties* and responsibilities" to the world beyond the domestic sphere.[50] We can safely say that her contemporaries did not put Ward into the camp of the New Woman novelists; one reason for this, no doubt, is that unlike some of her more radical contemporaries, she balanced her heroines' struggles of self-definition amid altering gender ideologies with a vision of marriage as sacrosanct. In these novels of the 1890s, as Valerie Sanders suggests, "Ward is confident that however challenging and complex the new situation for women, the old attraction between a strong, protecting man and a 'childish' and beautiful woman will make all come out right between them, and quietly diminish the woman's interest in political campaigning" (123). This ideological moderation evidently appealed to many of the critics and to nearly all of Ward's legions of avid readers. As evidence of her cultural status, she could boast in the first decade of the twentieth century of having received personal letters from such political personages as Queen Victoria, Arthur James Balfour, and Herbert Henry Asquith; literary correspondents included Rudyard Kipling, Sarah

Orne Jewett, Alfred Lord Tennyson, John Ruskin, Sir Leslie Stephen, George Meredith, and Rider Haggard, among others.[51]

And yet, despite Ward's successful self-cultivation among many of the key "players" on the turn-of-the-century literary field, she soon went on to help delegitimate and deconsecrate the same prestigious image of the high-end "lady novelist" that she had inherited and carried on; among the avant-garde of the intelligentsia, both female and male, she turned the corner from inspiration to opponent within the space of fifteen years. In part, as we might well imagine, her unfaltering opposition to women's suffrage would soon meet with distaste among younger and socially progressive readers, especially those influenced by the New Woman novels. At the same time, however, Ward's accretion of symbolic capital *outside* the literary field continued to swell well after the high-water mark of her critical reception in the mid-1890s. Her increasingly prominent role as an opponent of liberal feminism only reinforced her prestige among the moderate to conservative establishment through the Edwardian era, especially in the United States. She was invited to dinner with Teddy Roosevelt at the White House in 1908; in 1909–10, she corresponded with J. P. Morgan and Andrew Carnegie. The subtitle of John Sutherland's biography tells the story of her institutionalization in four words: *Eminent Victorian, Pre-eminent Edwardian.* Yet it was precisely through the Edwardian years that first her reviews, and then her reading public, steadily deflated.

Soon after her blockbuster religious romance and its successors had lifted Ward and her family out of shabby gentility and into the realm of the nouveau riche, she had assumed a new life of country houses, philanthropic projects, and elite education for her children. To sustain this upward mobility, Ward had transformed herself, in Sutherland's words, into a "money-generating fiction machine" (*Ward,* 133). After her reputation's apogee in the mid-1890s, her fiction became less ambitious. Any tincture of intellectual autonomy, any resistance to marketing and generic codification, was by the early 1900s draining out of her work. In novels she published between 1902 and 1914—*Lady Rose's Daughter* (1903), *Fenwick's Career* (1906), *The Testing of Diana Mallory* (1908), *The Case of Richard Meynell* (1911), *The Mating of Lydia* (1913), and *Delia Blanchflower* (1914)—she shifted her emphasis from subtle characterization and challenging ideas to heightened plotting and didacticism. To maintain her popular appeal, especially in the United States, she made her fallen antiheroines' subplots racier and more scandalous, even as she moralistically decried both the feminist explorations of the New Woman novelists and the women's suffrage movement.

Lady Rose's Daughter, a novel that exemplifies the romances of Ward's later career, was published at the start of her turn toward a more melodramatic fictional style.[52] Here, under self- and publisher-imposed commercial pressures, Ward began to feel artistically ambivalent. Elements of fine-tuned realism alternate with a heated discourse of romance; the narrative shifts from the sharply observed dialogue and behaviors of London's power élite to the inner turmoil of a passionate love triangle. The action is set "a good many years ago,"[53] just far enough back (by inference, the early to mid-1880s)[54] to allow for the idealization of the Victorian past. The title character is twenty-nine-year-old Julie Le Breton, who presides over an aging aristocrat's Mayfair salon, the weekly destination of the most influential members of London's high society. A web of mystery and intrigue envelops the heroine's origins. Few realize that Julie is the illegitimate child of an adulterous couple who fled to France thirty years earlier. One of the salon's regulars, Lord Lackington, is unaware that he is Julie's maternal grandfather, having long been estranged from his daughter—the rebellious, intellectual, atheist Lady Rose of the romance's title. The latter provides an example of Ward's typical antiheroine in this subplot regarding Julie's parentage—Ward's characters denigrate her as a flagrant adulterer. Likewise, Julie's father, described as "a Radical, a Socialist of the most extreme views" (Ward, *Lady*, 254), is by virtue of such politics understood to be just the kind of artist who would run off with a married woman. By way of realistic details illustrating romance-mode villainy, we are told how Julie's parents decorated their French abode with "photographs or newspaper portraits of modern men and women representing all possible revolt against authority, political, religious, even scientific, the Everlasting No of an untiring and ubiquitous dissent" (25). Both parents died when Julie was a child, and at the advice of a lawyer, she was then given the surname of her French *gouvernante*. Having reached her majority, possessed of high social graces and "the most extraordinary gift of conversation" (34), she was taken on by the high-society power broker of Mayfair, Lady Henry Seathwaite, to serve as factotum and social arranger.

So runs the narrative's exposition; we are meant to understand the kinds of errors to which the title character may be prone, if she does not learn to avoid the sins of the parents. But in the first third of the novel, before the love-narrative takes over, Julie's error threatens instead to be the product of reaction against her parents' (allegedly) venal bohemianism: a keen social ambition, as the "illegitimate" child of the title's aristocrat. Her benefactor, Lady Henry, has come to suspect her of being a backstabbing social climber and tells a confidant, "[T]hat woman has stripped me of all my friends! She has intrigued with them all in turn against me. . . . As for my salon . . . it has become hers. I am a mere courtesy-figurehead—her chaperon, in fact. I provide the house, the footmen, the champagne; the guests are hers. And she has done this by constant intrigue and deception—by flattery—by lying!" (37). This diatribe, appearing early in the novel, would appear to establish an antiheroine. Ward's narrative voice, however, displays a remarkable forgiveness for Julie's social schemes. Lady Henry is eventually shown to be an unreliable, paranoid source; sympathy then accrues to Julie when she holds the salon one evening in the absence of her mistress, who becomes outraged and unjustly dismisses her protégée. These early scenes support Sutherland's reading of the novel's implicit gender politics: "Ideologically, it articulates [Ward's] belief that women's political power is best exercised indirectly by the creation of quasi-domestic environments (here the salon) through which men may be influenced" (*Ward*, 241). The narrator suggests that Julie is largely blameless in her efforts to exploit her position in Lady Henry's establishment as a means of social climbing; she is pursuing economic security and social status via the exercise of her talents, in one of the rare milieux available to unmarried women, and is not (directly or primarily) husband seeking. At the same time, Ward's conservative attitudes regarding social class are here encoded: "illegitimate" or not, Julie Le Breton is the daughter of *Lady* Rose Delaney, and Julie's social ambition may also be construed as the reclaiming, by her strenuous efforts, of a class birthright.

Aside from the lapsarian exile of Julie's parents, there is little thus far to suggest the good-evil binaries of melodrama or the affective intensities of the romance mode. As I suggest above, Ward's scenes of drawing-room dialogue and high-society behaviors evince a careful realism. On the novel's publication, the *Times Saturday*

Review of London opined that "chapter after chapter reveals a curious and significant phase of what, if not English high life, is a most convincing semblance of it. These are living people to whom we are introduced, and we come to know and understand them much better than our next door neighbors and daily associates."[55] Many decades later, Sutherland contended that the "main attraction of *Lady Rose's Daughter* is its rendering of the conversation and gossip of the English power élite as they congregate under Lady Henry's and later Julie Le Breton's roof" (*Ward,* 240). Sutherland then complained of a "glaring fault": by transplanting into a British milieu the institution of the French salon (Ward's story adapts an account from Parisian high society of the eighteenth century, from what she called "that treasure house of human psychology, the world of the French memoirist"),[56] Ward violated credibility. Sutherland perceived another "glaring fault" in the fact that Ward's narrative ultimately strays from the account of the historical source: "[W]hereas the historical Julie eventually came to a suicidal end, Mary's fictional Julie is rewarded with the romantic novel's conventionally happy marriage to Jacob" (*Ward,* 240).

Both of these critical judgments hinge on the fact that Ward's narrative offers a realist-romance hybrid, in which the romance elements come by the end to predominate. Sutherland has found fault in the romance function of transporting a familiar society into a parallel universe of heightened meanings and has effectively dismissed the significance of two-thirds of the novel: those passages that record the doubled love story of Julie's relationships with Captain Harry Warkworth and Sir Jacob Delafield. Before I go on to discuss these romance elements of plot and style, it is worth recording the closing observation from the 1903 review of *Lady Rose's Daughter* in London's *Times Saturday Review:* "Mrs. Ward has outgrown her first public, and its members will be as slow to forgive the desertion of them as will those of the new public from which she seeks recognition to pardon her failure to seek them out in the beginning of her career."[57] This circumlocution goes unexplained, but we should interpret it to mean that, in the opinion of the reviewer, Ward was trying to appeal primarily to the mass of readers of popular romance and was neglecting her more intellectually sophisticated readers. In connection with this critical judgment from Ward's moment, it is interesting to note that Julie Le Breton bids fair, in the first third of the narrative, to become (to our twenty-first-century eyes) perhaps the most complex heroine in all of Ward's fiction. However, Ward adjusted the register of novelistic representation somewhere around the story's midpoint, and her heroine will effectively be saved by the same force, romantic love, that threatens to destroy her.

Ward's *Saturday Review* critic, then, may be on to something important. In *Lady Rose's Daughter*, Ward surreptitiously began to delink conventional ethics from the progress of the romantic relationship. In this way, the text strongly contrasts with Ward's earlier novels and foreshadows an approach to the romance mode that later became pronounced in such popular writers as Glyn and Dell. This approach goes beyond what I would call the fictional creation of "do-it-yourself ethical imperatives" seen in *Robert Elsmere*, where, after the hero wins his heroine, his romantic quest becomes the search for an ethical theism beyond that of any organized religion. *Lady Rose's Daughter* represents instead the kind of "do-it-yourself ethics" in which romantic love offers an avenue to the popular sublime and whereby "the moral fantasy of the romance is that of love triumphant and permanent, overcoming all obstacles and difficulties."[58] In the latter two-thirds of the novel, these aspects of the romance mode are to be observed, specifically, in an abrupt turn to melodramatic plot and characters and in the Romantic figurations of Alpine and colonial spaces. But there is a significant distinction here from historical melodrama, with its overt didacticism, implausible plots, stock characters, and enhanced emotionalism and expressivism. Given the well-elaborated interiority of both heroine (Julie) and hero (Jacob), labeling either as a stock character would be inaccurate. This holds true for most of the heroines and heroes of the romances discussed in this study; a great deal of discursive energy is expended on the depiction of changing psychic states (with the aim, in turn, of cathecting a great deal of readerly investment). Moreover, the function of the melodramatic narrative as a moral fable here lessens in relation to its efficacy as a vehicle of affective intensities that are not directly related to questions of right or wrong. These intensities often derive from eros but are not limited to scenes or feelings of romantic love alone; there are other, related but distinct avenues of sublime transcendence.

On her expulsion from Lady Henry's premises, Julie establishes her own modest household, plans to earn a living by journalism, and realizes that both the soldier Harry Warkworth and the aristocrat Jacob Delafield have been falling in love with her. At first she is helplessly drawn to the dashing young captain: "And now, here she sat in the dark, tortured by a passion of which she was ashamed, before which she was beginning to stand helpless in a kind of terror. The situation was developing, and she found herself wondering how much longer she would be able to control herself or it" (124). We see here the mode of interiority that comes to characterize Ward's later passages in the novel, whether displayed in the consciousness of Julie or in that of Jacob Delafield; both struggle with the force of romantic love as an instance of the insuperable sublime, by turns terrifying and ecstatic. Neither will be able to achieve the kind of "mastery of nature" that some critics have associated with a "masculine," capital-R Romantic sublime, but both will have moments of access to the "ineffable horizon of meaning" that, as Felski shows, characterizes the popular sublime. The irony of this passage is that (until the end of the narrative) Julie feels this intensity in the presence of Warkworth, who seems incapable of such inner vision, whereas Delafield feels it in the presence of Julie. The asymmetry of this arrangement, in turn, indicates what Sutherland identifies as this romance's "high melodrama" (*Ward,* 240). Julie's two suitors are schematically opposed, not as good against evil but as good against the worldly. Warkworth, we are told, "had desired only very simple, earthy things—money, position, success" (9), when he fell in love with Julie. By contrast, Delafield's epithets, "ascetic" and "mystical," are constantly echoing through Julie's thoughts. The tension of the romance plot is generated by her position as the third point in the love triangle: "[A] sort of ascetic and mystical note made itself heard in all [Jacob Delafield] said of the future, a note that before now had fascinated and controlled a woman whose ambition [associated with Harry Warkworth] was always strangely tempered with high, poetical imagination" (407). Though evil does not inhere in Warkworth's character, he tempts Julie to a sin that would reprise the villainous adultery of her parents. Although he has pledged his hand to another woman, Warkworth arranges a two-day assignation with a willing Julie in France, but the tryst is narrowly averted just as she arrives at the Gare du Nord: Delafield coincidentally appears in the station and informs her that her grandfather is on his deathbed, so that Julie has no choice but to rush back to London.

Delafield guesses at Julie's purpose in France but gallantly accedes to her pretense of telegraphing her "Parisian friends" to cancel her visit. By an improbably fated encounter, then, Delafield's virtue vanquishes Warkworth's vice. (Delafield will be assisted in this victory by Warkworth's death of fever, a few weeks later, on his "special mission" in central Africa—about which more below.)

These are conventional ethical binaries, but Delafield's passion for Julie transcends any potential aversion to her intended sin:

> The more clearly he saw the specks in her glory, the more vividly did she appear to him a princess in distress, bound by physical or moral fetters not of her own making. None of the well-born, well-trained damsels who had been freely thrown across his path had so far beguiled him in the least. Only this woman of doubtful birth and antecedents, lonely, sad, and enslaved amid what people called her social triumphs, stole into his heart—beautified by what he chose to consider her misfortunes, and made none the less attractive by the fact that as he pursued, she retreated; as he pressed, she grew cold. (222)

In Jacob Delafield, Ward has offered a hero in whose virtue no "specks" are to be seen; he is a paragon of Christian forgiveness. Here we also see an archaism that antedates melodrama, in a residual figuration of social class that recurs, diachronic and enduring, in the romance mode. Romance's heroines and heroes encode royal or aristocratic class, as we see here in the terms that bridge the literal (Delafield, Julie, and others around them are titled or come from titled families) and the metaphoric: "princess in distress," "well-born," "damsels," "of doubtful birth and antecedents." The chivalric code underlying this passage casts Delafield in the role of prince or knight. He strains realism with his devotion to the yet unresponsive Julie, as he muses, "If she would but put her hand in mine, I would so serve and worship her, she would have no need for these strange things she does—the doublings and ruses of the persecuted" (222). This pastiche of a medieval discourse of courtly love, as re-created by Ward (and, of course, many earlier Victorians, such as the Tennyson of *Idylls of the King*), would convey the absoluteness of the hero's love for his heroine, an affective intensity that disregards "the specks in her glory," the mix of her nobler and less noble motivations. In this passage, then, the melodramatic register is continuous with a reconstructed discourse of the Old World romance mode. We may theorize what is going on here by returning to Felski, who posits that in "refusing to accept that the world is drained of transcendence, melodrama relocates the spiritual at the level of the personal, endowing individual characters with auratic significance as representatives of moral absolutes" (125). If Delafield, the "mystical ascetic," is intended to present the reader with absolute good, the character himself, at the same time, is allowing moral absolutes to be subsumed by the intensity of his romantic love for Julie.

Another of Ward's discursive layerings here—and another residuum that characterizes romances discussed in later chapters—is that of the Romantic poets' representations of nature. The mountains of Tuscany bring out the noumenal glow of Delafield's goodness, as Julie observes after their wedding: "But it was at La Verna, the mountain height overshadowed by the memories of St Francis, that she seemed to have come nearest to the ascetic and mystical tendency in Delafield. He went about the mountain-paths a transformed being, like one long spiritually athirst who has found the springs and sources of life. Her impression was . . . as of 'something wearing through' to the light of day" (420). Here, the subtextual presence of William Wordsworth in Jacob's Apennine experience is suggested by reference to Ward's family history. Her grandfather, Dr. Thomas Arnold of Rugby, had been neighbors with William Wordsworth at Rydal in the Lake District for ten years, from 1832 to 1842. The *New York Times* obituary of Mary's father, Thomas Arnold the younger, refers to the Wordsworthian family tradition of his "long mountain walks" with his children, from "the Westmoreland property Wordsworth had assisted Dr. Arnold in securing."[59] Wordsworth is prominent in Ward's 1918 memoir, as she proudly recalls family letters in which the poet complained that "he could not see enough of his neighbor, the Doctor [Thomas Arnold of Rugby], on a mountain walk, because Arnold was always so surrounded with children and pupils" (*Writer's Recollections,* 102). In the memoir, Ward also compares her theories of exaltation in the presence of natural beauty with those of the Romantic poet: "[T]he delight in natural things—colors, forms, scents—when there was nothing to restrain or hamper it, has often been a kind of intoxication, in which thought and consciousness seemed suspended—'as though of hemlock one had drunk.' Wordsworth has of course expressed it constantly, though increasingly, as life went on, in combination with his pantheistic philosophy" (121–22). Mary Ward had internalized a conception of spectacular, wild landscapes as those rare spaces on earth where one had a greater chance than elsewhere to witness the face of divinity. She had also adopted a Romantic variation on that late eighteenth-century theme of the sublime, the notion that the supernatural lying just below the surface of such a landscape would be met by the supernatural rising up, from one's deepest interiority, into the consciousness of the beholding self.

For the character of Julie Le Breton, such Romantic encounters with the sublime in spaces of nature—Alpine meadow, coniferous crag, mountain lake—bring forth her moments of unbounded romantic passion, in forms both ecstatic and terror-stricken. The itinerary of their postwedding holiday (it is pointedly not a "honeymoon," as Delafield has agreed to Julie's terms that this be a wedded life of chaste companionship) takes Julie and Delafield from northern Italy to the banks of Lake Geneva, where, on learning of the death of her former lover, Warkworth, "her fancy, preternaturally alive, heard" a cry of grief "thrown back from the mountains outside—returned to her in wailing from the infinite depths of the lake. She was conscious of the vast forms and abysses of nature" (435). A few days later, as she begins to realize her love for her new husband, "Julie looked out upon a vast freedom of space, and by a natural connection she seemed to be also surveying her own world of life and feeling, her past and her future. . . . And the august Alpine beauty entered in, so that Julie, in this sad and thrilling act of self-probing, felt herself in the presence of powers and dominations divine" (464–65). These borrowings from early nineteenth-century Romantic topoi are emphasized by the geographic locale in which Ward has chosen to grant her heroine these epiphanies. The newlyweds' journey has taken them to the Swiss village of Chernex, just up the hillside from Montreux, ruffled by "the cool wind that blew . . . from the gates of Italy, down the winding recesses of that superb valley which has been a thoroughfare of nations from the beginning of time" (440–41). The valley in question is that of the upper

Rhône, and it was indeed the route of the ancient Roman road and of Wordsworth's 1790 walking tour. Ward likely had in mind that famous sojourn in Book VI of *The Prelude* (1850), in which the poet records his youthful encounter at the upper end of "that superb valley," near Simplon Pass, with a glimpse of the apocalyptic sublime in "the stationary blasts / Of waterfalls."

These pristine highlands offer readers a strong counterpoint to the gossipy whirl of the London parlors. There is, however, a third kind of space that contributes to the spiritual patterning of *Lady Rose's Daughter*—the imperial periphery. In part, this is a simple, unremarkable matter of the ideological "naturalization" of empire that Edward Said attributed to many nineteenth-century texts of the British canons of fiction, from Jane Austen to Dickens and Conrad. So it is that Sir Wilfrid Bury, the elderly gentleman who observes the social climbing of Julie Le Breton, has just returned from three years of colonial business in Persia and "was talking of Central Asian politics and the latest Simla gossip to his two companions" (14) in an early scene in Lady Henry's salon. So too, Sir Wilfrid first knew Julie's father in Damascus, when "he was beginning the series of Eastern journeys which had made him famous" (55), and "Lord Henry and Captain Warkworth's father went through the Indian Mutiny together" (66). Ward accepted that the maintenance and expansion of the British Empire afforded her male characters an arena in which to serve their country and prove their manhood. As John Sutherland has shown, by the end of the 1890s, Ward's support for the British Empire had become vocal, as she believed that English rule was "the natural discipline appointed to them by Providence" (*Ward,* 197). In 1898, in the context of the British Army's successes in the Sudan, the Anglo-Ashanti Wars, and the Northwest Frontier (present-day Afghanistan and Pakistan), she "crowed" that the "pride of the English name" had "never [been] greater—Kipling will have to write a new Recessional"; these were to be taken as "signs that at present we are fit to rule, and are meant to rule" (quoted in Sutherland, *Ward,* 197). At the time of her writing of *Lady Rose's Daughter,* circa 1902–3, her biographer Janet P. Trevelyan claimed, "[T]he end of the Boer War found her more staunch an imperialist, more definite a Conservative."[60]

It should therefore come as no surprise that *Lady Rose's Daughter* portrays the brash young Warkworth, in Sir Wilfrid's words, as "the man who distinguished himself in the Mahsud expedition [of 1881]" (11) or that Julie's efforts to help Warkworth take charge of an African "mission" prompt Wilfrid to ask, "What is the meaning, Jacob, of a young woman taking so keen an interest in the fortunes of a dashing soldier—for, between you and me, I hear she is moving heaven and earth to get him this post—and then concealing it?" (79). In Ward's hands, the peripheral spaces of empire are more than the distant cross-hatching behind the illuminated foreground of metropolitan and European spaces; they are the spaces of English masculine achievement, as we see in Sir Wilfrid's mental summation of his imperial work in the Middle East: "Fight on! It was only the long drudgery behind, under alien suns, together with the iron certainty of fresh drudgery ahead, that gave value, after all, to this rainy, this enchanting Piccadilly—that kept the string of feeling taut and all its notes clear" (74). Ward is not presenting this self-sacrificing view of imperial conquest with even the slightest degree of irony. She promoted the sanctity of "the White Man's Burden" no less than she would later proclaim the absolute rightness of the British cause in the Great War.

Given this ideological position, the spiritual utility of empire to *Lady Rose's Daughter* is to offer a single redemptive note to the character of the otherwise unprincipled and self-seeking Captain Harry Warkworth. Ward would justify Julie's passion for this soldier by virtue of his service to nation and empire. In a mystical passage, a moment before Warkworth's fiancée happens upon Julie on an Alpine byway (another extraordinary coincidence), the heroine witnesses Warkworth fulfilling the duty of his "special mission to Mokembe":

> Far, far in the African desert she followed the march of Warkworth's little troop. Ah, the blinding light—the African scrub and sand—the long, single line—the native porters with their loads—the handful of English officers with that slender figure at their head—the endless, waterless path with its palms and mangoes and mimosas—the scene rushed upon the inward eye and held it. She felt the heat, the thirst, the weariness of bone and brain—the spell and mystery of the unmapped, unconquered land.
>
> Did he think of her sometimes, at night, under the stars, or in the blaze and mirage of noon? Yes, yes; he

> thought of her. Each to the other their thoughts must travel while they lived. (421–22)

Throughout the novel, the nature of Captain Warkworth's "special mission" is left unexplained and ambiguous, connoting both the Protestant missionary work of David Livingstone and his successors of the 1880s, and the military work of British subjugation of the tribes of the African interior in the 1890s. Warkworth's march is elsewhere described as starting from the Angolan settlement of Denga, with a military escort of British officers, porters, and supplies (318). They are to march into the hinterland, to the outpost of "Mokembe"—but for what purpose is never mentioned. Present-day Mokembe is more than a thousand miles northeast of Denga, located in the swamp forests of the Congo basin. Julie's reverie of a "waterless path" amid "African scrub and sand" may therefore seem a bit geographically inaccurate. Its fictive purpose is symbolic: the exoticism of this most distant place imaginable, on the contested periphery of empire and beyond the border of "civilization," is used to enhance the heroine's belief in the transcendence of the passion she shares with her star-crossed lover. Colonial space—"the spell and mystery of the unmapped, unconquered land"—is being summoned here as a resource for conjuring the popular sublime.

Elsewhere, this spiritual ecstasy, or "standing outside oneself," is counterposed with the sublime's terrors, as Julie has a premonitory vision of Warkworth's fever-induced death in the African hinterland. There is even a gothic dimension introduced to the novel here: "Julie's eyes strained into the darkness. . . . Upon the darkness outside there rose a face, so sharply drawn, so life-like, that it printed itself forever upon the quivering tissues of the brain. It was Warkworth's face, not as she had seen it last, but in some strange extremity of physical ill—drawn, haggard, in a cold sweat. . . . Her whole sense was absorbed by the phantom; her being hung upon it" (295). Later, in the midst of her spiritual Alpine transports, Julie receives word of Warkworth's passing and has the vision again:

> Julie's mind . . . had passed for the second time into the grasp of an illusion which possessed itself of the whole being and all its perceptive powers. Before her wide, terror-stricken gaze there rose once more the same piteous vision which had tortured her in the crisis

> of her love for Warkworth. Against the eternal snows which close in the lake the phantom hovered in a ghastly relief—emaciated, with matted hair, and purpled cheeks, and eyes—not to be borne!—expressing the dumb anger of a man, still young, who parts unwillingly from life in a last lonely spasm of uncomforted pain. (432–33)

Warkworth's agonized spirit here seems to fill the vast Romantic space of the Alpine valley with its almost inexpressible intensity; spirit and landscape have intermingled in a darker version of the popular sublime.[61] As Gillian Beer reminds us, "The grip of a romance can be that of a dream or of a nightmare" (*Romance,* 9). Here, the nightmare takes its energy from the conjuring of a nonexistent space beyond the borders of "civilization," in the "unmapped, unconquered land" of the central African interior—a Congo Basin inaccurately imagined as "scrub and sand." In a passage that recalls the death by dysentery of the missionary David Livingstone in Zambia in 1873, Julie imagines herself at Warkworth's tropical deathbed: "She was in a low bell-tent. The sun burned through its sides; the air was stifling. . . . [S]he heard the clicking of the fan in the doctor's hands, she saw the flies in the poor damp brow" (435). Warkworth's "special mission" hereby loses its military significance and would rhyme with the putative martyrdom of the famed Scots clergyman. Contemplating this scene in her mind's eye, Julie intuits that "existence seemed to have ended in a gulf of horror, where youth and courage, repentance and high resolve, love and pleasure were all buried and annihilated together" (435). As if in counterpoint to the ecstasies induced by the spaces of the Swiss Alps, the imaginary African wilderness generates the fearful side of the sublime, an utter powerlessness in the face of the abyss. Ward illustrates the symbolic uses to which the imagined imperial periphery would later be put in romances by Cross, Dell and Hull (as discussed in chapter 5).

Woman Romancists and the Literary Field under Ward's Dominance

Henceforth, Mary Ward would strive to flatter her audience's chauvinisms and unexamined prejudices, to adjust her novels' ideological messages to appeal to the broadest book-buying public.

She would leave behind the spiritual and intellectual risks of *Elsmere* and her novels of the 1890s. The protagonist of *Fenwick's Career* inveighs against the newfangled corruption of French impressionist painting; the heroine of *The Testing of Diana Mallory* is vindicated in her faith in British imperialism; the villain of *Delia Blanchflower* is a militant suffragette (loosely based on Christabel Pankhurst). Increasingly, as her cultural politics moved rightward, Ward pitted herself against the ideological heterodoxies of the burgeoning avant-gardes of the pre–World War I years.

Her struggle to establish a high position in the literary field long since won, Mary Ward made the gradual transition into writing solely for the field of "large-scale production"—that is, for the broadest possible audience, with the aim of (as her publisher George Smith had put it) "extracting as much value as possible out of" her novels—rather than for the maintenance of her symbolic status as a prestigious writer. As a result, all talk of her putative stature as the "next George Eliot" rapidly faded into silence in the Edwardian years. Ward's 1908 invitation to the Roosevelt White House and her flattering correspondence thereafter with such power brokers as J. P. Morgan and Andrew Carnegie merely serve to illustrate the delay, common to a time before the electronic media, between the peak of one's literary achievement and the apogee of one's broader cultural celebrity. She morphed into, not George Eliot redux, but the twentieth-century phenomenon of the best-selling woman novelist, moving at least a hundred thousand copies of each of her most successful novels, quantities theretofore almost unheard of for women writers in Britain.[62] Ultimately, this was the new space that she carved for the younger "lady novelists" of her day—that of the professional writer for the mass market, the novelist who (in contrast to the less popular New Woman novelists) eschewed heterodox ideas and refined new romantic formulae for reaching hundreds of thousands of readers. Her only female rival in the years of her peak sales was Marie Corelli, who by the 1890s was outselling Ward—but Corelli was never accorded the early respect that Ward had enjoyed.

Meanwhile, Ward's most significant influence on the symbolic and economic status of women novelists in toto—of which vast group she was reductively, but inevitably, taken as a modern figurehead—had as much to do with the rapidly changing economy of the publishing industry as with her novel's implicit social ideologies. Ward's biggest impact on the future of the woman-authored romance may well have been her decision in 1894 to take on the monopoly of the circulating libraries. Since 1888, she had been arranging with her publisher to bring out the cheaper, faster-selling single-volume editions of her novels slightly earlier than the customary six-month lag after the original triple-decker publication. (In fact, Mudie was by the early 1890s requesting a year-long interval but was willing in practice to settle for six months.)[63] This lag enabled the major circulating libraries to earn substantial profits, and in return, the libraries' imprimatur of "respectability" was highly valued by the publishing houses. Thus, the gentlemen's understanding between fiction publishers and circulating libraries had traditionally been upheld. By the early 1890s, however, several publishers who wished to avoid the effective censorship of the circulating libraries—the requirement of a certain moral tone in the fiction they were willing to purchase for loan circulation—had begun to depart from the usual three-decker format and to sell their novels directly to the public in a cheap (usually around six shillings) single-volume format. But this practice was risky, balancing expressive autonomy against loss of respectability, and so it was not yet widely enough followed to usurp the libraries' hegemony.

As the highest-paid woman in 1890s Britain, Ward recognized that she had the power to dare what no male novelist or publisher had yet dared: direct defiance of the circulating libraries. Her third novel, *Marcella,* had come out in the three-volume format in early April 1894, but she was displeased with the modest number of copies that the libraries had been purchasing. She confidently—and, as it turned out, accurately—wagered that the big libraries, those of Edward Mudie and W. H. Smith, were underfeeding the public demand for her work and were effectively imposing a bottleneck on her publication numbers. She urged George Smith to cross these patriarchal arbiters: "What are you thinking about *Marcella?* I see the 5th edition is not out yet. Shall we fix the cheap edition for July? And is it worth printing the three volumes again?"[64] With this letter, she was calling for the single-volume edition to come out a full three months before the conventional interval had passed. Not only that, but she suggested dispensing altogether with the circulating libraries: "I have quite made up my mind if you will support me to try the English market next time as well as the American with a

2 volume book at 8/6. I am quite prepared to risk the money loss, which however I believe to be very small. If I can possibly avoid it, that is to say, if I can keep the ear of the public I never want to be dependent on the libraries again."[65] Such talk made her publisher nervous, and Smith stalled a bit on the one-volume edition of *Marcella.* Nonetheless, the inexpensive version did come out just three months after the initial publication of the three-volume edition.

This seemingly inconsequential event of early July 1894 was the proximate cause of a phenomenon that would partly enable the twentieth-century mass marketing of fiction in Britain: the extinction of that Victorian institution, the triple-decker novel. This moment had, of course, been coming for a while, given recent advances in publishing technologies, along with a book-buying public that had been swelling since the 1870 Education Act and its spread of literacy among the working classes. Some have even suggested that Mudie's and Smith's libraries had secretly been wanting the shift to a one-volume format and used the demands of Ward and others as a pretext for the change.[66] Nonetheless, Ward's pressure appears to have tipped the balance, and in the months that followed, the big publishers were proclaiming that their novels for the 1894–95 season would all be coming out in the single-volume format at six-shillings per—about one-fifth the cost of the three-deckers. The statistics illustrate the old format's rapid demise: in 1894, 184 new three-volume novels were published; in 1895, the number was 52; in 1897, it was 4.[67] Sutherland is not exaggerating when he claims, "The reprint of *Marcella* was the torpedo that sunk the three-decker" (*Ward,* 148).

Ward also understood that bypassing the lending libraries brought on the necessity of more direct advertisement, if she was to realize her full sales potential. Ever eager to micromanage her career, she insisted on an aggressive ad campaign for the one-volume *Marcella* as soon as it appeared. Again, she wrote her publisher:

> I am a little depressed about the coming out of the cheap edition of *Marcella.* There is no notice in the *Daily Chronicle* or *Standard,* and the notice in the *Times* is at the tail-end of the column where nobody will see it. And I have seen no announcement anywhere else so far. Has the subscription for it been so good that you feel there is not much need

> for advertisement? . . . I shd. be quite happy to meet you in the matter of expenses, if you thought any more advertisement wd. answer—I dislike columns of press-notices as you know, but on the other hand I like a good deal of plain and conspicuous announcement. I am afraid it pays! . . . I feel that one can only compete nowadays by a free use of *legitimate* advertisement.[68]

Ward is both candid and savvy here, counterbalancing her forceful self-interest with the generosity of offering to pay for her book's advertisements. These words reveal the frank, hard-nosed, but principled ("*legitimate* advertisement") businesswoman—well aware of the practicalities of a competitive marketplace—that she had learned to be. At the same time, the letter emblematizes what I have already suggested was a historically unprecedented convergence of liberalizing social ideology and free-market forces: the former, in the increasing legitimacy of women's professionalism and business orientation, and the latter in the conception of literary publishing as a field of competition, irrespective of the values conveyed by the literature.

Ward's publishing coup of 1894 had emancipatory effects, curtailing the circulating libraries' censorious and socially normative control of women's production and consumption of fiction. Indeed, after the mid-1890s, there would be virtually no mediating institutions between popular women writers and market forces; together with material gains in publishers' efficiency and huge leaps in literacy among the lower classes, the demise of the triple-decker changed the structure of the literary field as a whole. But of course, more direct exposure to market forces also brought with it those negative effects with which we, at the start of the twenty-first century, have become all too familiar. With unfiltered access to the ever-growing reading market, editors increasingly expected female writers to produce—as Ward soon did—the more immediately sensational and less morally complex romantic fiction that provided publishers their best profit margins. With less of the exploration of gender politics that had characterized the New Woman fiction at its peak, and more adherence to idealized love stories, the most successful female fiction writers in Edwardian England abandoned the model of George Eliot altogether. To a higher degree than ever before, they realized the writing profession for women, even as they weakened its intellectual autonomy and lowered its cultural status in the literary field. For example, between 1900 and the outbreak of the First World War there arrived the so-called sex novel, the embryo of the contemporary mass-market romance. Its most successful women practitioners, Victoria Cross and Elinor Glyn, came to represent women writers' most extreme strain of novelistic reaction against the residual Victorianism of Ward. In 1908, as if to consolidate this rebellion, the Mills and Boon publishing house was founded and began to feature "society romances" and "exotic romances," narratives that could matter-of-factly represent the taboo topics of the New Woman novels—such as divorce and premarital erotic encounters—without the agonized ethical explorations of that slightly earlier subgenre. These novels, the British equivalent of the later-arriving Harlequin Romance lines of the United States, began the codification and institutionalization of a previously familiar storyline—the tale of a heroine who changes a man through her redeeming love—into a specific genre of fiction, one that has come to represent the popularly understood meaning of the term *romance novel*.

Thus, from 1908 on, women's writing of popular romance was on the path to becoming a vocation of what Bourdieu labels "industrial art"—efficient, market-savvy cultural production with the primary purpose of moneymaking. The irony here—the ruse of literary history—may be that Ward, by marginalizing the library censor, enabled the widespread distribution of woman-authored "sex-novels," "society romances," and "exotic romances," whose implicit ideologies of women's right to erotic pleasure and secular self-definition Ward abhorred. It was at precisely the moment of these more "licentious" new novels' appearance within the field of large-scale literary production—the second half of Edward's reign—that Ward's popularity declined. Almost overnight, it seemed, the mass readership on both sides of the Atlantic began to find her novels too stuffy and sanctimonious in their treatments of women's public, psychological, and especially romantic lives.

Women novelists were by then capable of wider popular success and greater financial independence than ever before in British history. At the same time, their collective symbolic capital had sunk since the middle years of the previous century, when François Guizot had rhapsodized of their "great Athenian age." It would take the highbrow modernism of such writers as Virginia Woolf,

Rebecca West, Katherine Mansfield, Dorothy Richardson, and others to redeem the symbolic capital of the female literary writer as a social construct. But they did so at a familiar price: the increased polarization of the literary field. By 1920, these more intellectually ambitious writers were doing their utmost to distance themselves from the romance writers of large-scale literary production. Virginia Woolf wrote contemptuously of Mary Ward both in her personal letters and in her diary. On finishing Ward's memoir in 1919, she recorded her distaste for the kind of writing career this eminent Edwardian had allegedly represented: "The enormous sales, the American editions, the rumble & reverberation—Piccadilly placarded with posters 'Marcella out!'—seem like the drum & cymbals of a county fair."[69] Woolf would even go so far, upon reading Ward's novel *Eltham House* (1915), as to write, "It's a vile book, and after gulping it down I feel morally debased."[70] For her part, Rebecca West was decrying the best-selling novels of Ethel Dell, Florence Barclay, and Marie Corelli (all of whom are examined in this book) as "tosh," or nonsense, and proclaiming that Mary Ward's career had been "one long specialization in the *mot injuste*."[71] Had Ward been afforded the chance to read these words, she would have been offended in more ways than one. Not only had she been lumped in with her ideological foes, the newer kind of popular romancist, but she had even become the anti-Flaubert, triply scorned by the bohemian avant-garde for her bourgeois institutionalization, her formal and thematic conservatism, and her (one-time) mass appeal.

Whether explicitly or implicitly, the female renegades of modernism could define themselves as Ward's determinate negation, her converse image on the literary field. In her study of Ward's novels, Judith Wilt goes so far as to suggest that "Woolf steadily read Ward for a kind of enraged inspiration" (*Behind Her Times,* 211). There is evidence to support this view, in light of the darkly sarcastic observations of a young Woolf: "I have decided to write all the novels of Mrs. Humphry Ward and all the diaries of Mrs. Sidney Webb. It will be my life work."[72] In a review of Ward's penultimate novel, *Harvest* (1920),[73] Katherine Mansfield wrote that "the inaudible and noiseless foot of Time passed and repassed, and the problems which had seemed to her so worth the solving seemed to dissolve, and with them her intense intellectual activities. With the disappearance of the rich difficulties came the unbaring of the plot.

She seemed to see how weak it was, how scarcely it held, and her later books rely upon the story. They are failures for this reason."[74] The primary token of decline here is alleged to be the novel's reliance on plotting. Elsewhere in the review, Mansfield accuses Ward of being unable to capture in her fiction that highest and most secular of desiderata (in her own and Virginia Woolf's view), "Life."

By 1920, the year of her death, Ward had offered the model of female predominance in both symbolic and economic capital on the literary field, with a power that was only just then waning; yet her institutionalization was such that it precluded much sense of gender solidarity with her on the part of the women members of the literary avant-garde. She and those like her were the ones who had helped to structure the orthodox positions in a greatly changed field, upon which these modern writers were taking their unorthodox, even heretical positions. It was, as I suggest at the beginning of this chapter, the endpoint of a most unenviable career vector. Ward had become a stalking horse for the new highbrow writers, even as she was underappreciated by the new writers and readers of the popular woman-authored romance, for whom she had helped to clear a path.

CHAPTER THREE

Marie Corelli and the Discourse of Romance

—Have you found those six brave medicals, John Eglinton asked with elder's gall, to write *Paradise Lost* at your dictation? *The Sorrows of Satan* he calls it.

James Joyce, *Ulysses*

Joyce arrived late [at a Paris dinner party, 1922] and apologized for not having dressed; at this time he had no formal clothes. He was drinking heavily to cover his embarrassment when the door opened and Marcel Proust in a fur coat appeared, as Joyce said afterwards, "like the hero of *The Sorrows of Satan.*"

Richard Ellmann, *James Joyce*

That was my great ambition: to have my place on the shelves of the British Museum, rubbing shoulders with the other Cs, the great ones: Carlyle and Chaucer and Coleridge and Conrad. The joke is that my closest literary neighbor turned out to be Marie Corelli.

J. M. Coetzee, *Elizabeth Costello*

As these epigraphs show, Marie Corelli, author of the fin-de-siècle romance *The Sorrows of Satan,* has been a target of literary derision from her own time through the early twenty-first century. James Joyce used Corelli's most famous novel as both a parodic inversion of Milton's epic and a means to belittle a fellow modernist, Marcel Proust. More recently, Nobel Prize winner J. M. Coetzee set Corelli up as a noncanonical "joke," the antithesis of the male heavies of the British literary tradition.[1] Indeed, the cultural prestige of Joyce and Coetzee offers a symbolic counterpoint to the knowing contempt in which their target was generally held by the cultural elite of the late-Victorian and Edwardian eras. Even among her romance-writing peers, most of whom were periodically ridiculed by the cultural cognoscenti, Corelli stands out as especially derided in her own time. She sharply contrasts with Mary Ward, who, as we have seen, arguably achieved the highest prestige on the British literary field among the female writers of romance from 1885 to 1925. Ward was the oldest of the women romanciers under consideration in this study, born in that symbolic mid-Victorian year of 1851, the moment of the Great Exhibition in London, the historic juncture at which the British Empire would begin to assume unprecedented global power. Her nearest contemporary in age among the most popular turn-of-the-century women authors is Mary Mills McKay (b. 1855), who brought out her first novel, *A Romance of Two Worlds* (1886), two years after Ward had published her own first effort. Though McKay, who adopted the pen name Marie Corelli, was destined to surpass Ward in sales—the more than one hundred thousand copies of *Robert Elsmere* were topped by the hundreds of thousands of *The Sorrows of Satan* and other Corellian works—the younger writer never enjoyed any panoramic heights of esteem from which gradually to descend.[2] Rita Felski has described Corelli's appeal in sociological terms: "Affiliation with an increasingly educated and professionalized literary intelligentsia, rather than socioeconomic status alone, seemed to have been the crucial factor in determining whether one abhorred Corelli rather than adored her" (144). Readers' responses to her novels were startlingly polarized throughout her career, which spanned from the mid-1880s to the mid-1920s.

Having been born four years after Ward, Corelli died four years after her, in 1924. These nearly coterminous lifespans may encourage us to see Corelli as a foil to the more respected writer in other ways, too. From the perspective of the early twenty-first century, Ward seems to face rearward in history and to play the role of rearguard Victorian through the first two decades of the twentieth. Corelli, a more volatile writer, faces forward to the mass marketing of the popular sublime in ways that she may not always have realized or approved. Like Ward, Corelli benefited hugely from the sudden decline of the circulating libraries in 1894–95; during the years that followed, enjoying more direct access to her hundreds of thousands of buying readers, she became remarkably prolific, publishing nine novels in the first decade of the twentieth century alone.[3] For a good part of that time, she enjoyed the status of Britain's best-selling novelist.[4] Her career peaked slightly later than Ward's: by the mid-Edwardian moment, when Ward, reappearing with a new novel every three to four years, had begun to decline in popularity among the respectable classes of readers, there may not have been a single novel reader in Edwardian Britain unaware of the prolific output of Marie Corelli. She became a flamboyant *litteratrice* and celebrated controversialist, turning out both fantastic narratives and, through the thinly veiled mouthpieces who were her protagonists, streams of opinion on the urgent social issues of the moment. Most of her novels were romances, categorized by her contemporaries as "mystical" or "fantastic" variants of the genre; she offered tales that mingled romantic love with Christian spirituality, featured all manner of celestial voyaging, and hummed with affective intensities.

Corelli used her celebrity as the platform from which to declaim her evaluation of the turn-of-the-century literary field in Britain. Embedded within many of her novels we find a vividly narrativized cultural theory. Corelli's antielitist views regarding the literary practices of her time highlight her single biggest difference from Ward—her deficit, at any point in her career, of symbolic capital approaching the older writer's. Her extraordinary mass-market appeal is what has sparked contemporary interest in Corelli; after a long period of critical neglect, her literary and social significance have been reappraised in the decades since the 1970s.[5] In this chapter, I discuss three representative romances that appeared at decade intervals through her career: *The Sorrows of Satan* (1895), *The Treasure of Heaven* (1906), and *Innocent: Her Fancy and His Fact* (1914). My treatment of Corelli shifts from the previous chapter's focus on the evolving literary field to the sociocultural ideologies found in such romances. As Rita Felski, R. B. Kershner, and Annette Federico have shown, the social discourses layered through most of Corelli's novels are too contradictory to be tagged as either conservative or resistive; her literary phenomenon validates neither Frankfurt school pessimism nor cultural studies–inspired optimism regarding the sociopolitical valences of mass culture.[6] Corelli's contradictions are especially noteworthy with regard to representations of gender and literary activity, as they reflect the turmoil of a period of rising feminism, a great rise in literacy, and a rapidly advancing commercialization of popular culture in general, and romantic literature in particular. Just as Ward's fatal blow to the triple-decker novel led to unexpected ironies, so too did Corelli's exploitation of the new opportunity of bypassing the circulating libraries. The sudden fact of what we might call a "morally deregulated" market for novels gave greater play to the commodifying tendencies of culture that Corelli's works—free to enjoy their popular success precisely because of the newly liberated market—take it upon themselves to critique and attack. Amid the modernization of the British literary market, Corelli's romances are often morally unorthodox and, in contrast to the most widely read romances of the mid- to late-twentieth century, generically anarchic.[7]

Collective desires and anxieties fueled the consumption of these idiosyncratic romances. At the same time, we cannot deny the role of Corelli's individuality, her distinct personality. An obsessive "micro-manager" of the business aspects of her career, she refused to employ any literary agent until 1904, and thus for years she dealt directly with her publishers, the houses of Bentley and Son and Methuen. Nickianne Moody describes these authorial circumstances: "Early success and exclusion from literary social circles meant that Corelli could avoid being edited and was protected from peer criticism at a formative stage. Her novels are, consequently, unwieldy and lack restraint. They address numerous popular concerns, anxieties, and the hope of social change while expressing her own personal feelings."[8] Corelli's manuscripts were virtually untouched by house editors, so her singular novelistic discourse was generally unaffected by any conscious marketing considerations. Her narratives appear diversely motivated, zigzagging among moral didacticism, sensual melodrama, and cultural jeremiad; to read Corelli today is to be astounded by her sheer, ebullient digressiveness. Her narrative style is frothy and haphazard, yet it undoubtedly conveys, as R. B. Kershner suggests, "an especially extreme embodiment of many of the ideological contradictions of the late Victorian period."[9] Though aleatory in story line, her romances drilled straight into the mother lodes of mass opinion.

Indeed, the success of Corelli's writing was as much a function of social discourses as of her formidable agency. Viewed in the cool light of historical analysis, the novels may be said to represent modernized myths and to bear out Claude Lévi-Strauss's claim, from "The Structural Study of Myth," that "the purpose of myth is to provide a logical model capable of overcoming a contradiction."[10] Refashioning the resources of the romance genre, the three novels under scrutiny here can be shown to narrativize troubling symptoms of late-Victorian and Edwardian social experience: *The Sorrows of Satan* addresses collective anxieties over class antagonisms and the hypocrisies of Victorian liberalism; *The Treasure of Heaven* tries to resolve fears of technological advance and hyperurbanization; *Innocent* deals with the perceived threats of cultural modernization and of an aestheticizing, secular humanism.[11] Moreover, these three novels are informed by Britain's quickly evolving conditions of literary production, in the sense in which Pierre Macherey uses that latter term.[12] Arising in the historical interval between the opening of the literary field to large-scale production and the tight slotting of the mass-market genres of fiction, they refract the class antagonisms thereby given voice. In part, the neutral, value-free axioms of capitalism itself, with their tendential leveling of ethical, cultural, and social hierarchies, may be precisely what generated the Corellian anxieties—the anxieties of the author herself but also, and more important, of her thousands of readers—that led in turn to the Corelli phenomenon.

The Sorrows of Satan: Social Contradictions, Romantic Resolution

Please allow me to introduce myself,
I'm a man of wealth and taste.

Jagger and Richards, "Sympathy for the Devil"

Of all Corelli's novels, *The Sorrows of Satan* has received the most scholarly attention in recent years. In part, the interest derives from its tremendous popularity: the book's sales in the months following its initial publication, in August 1895, were the highest yet seen at that time in the history of the English novel.[13] Contemporary scholars do not have exact figures regarding the novel's original sales, but we do know that prepublication sales of the first two editions amounted to at least 20,000.[14] In his 1895 discussion of the book in the *Review of Reviews*, W. T. Stead recorded that it sold "some seventy thousand copies" within its first ten weeks of publication.[15] Moreover, as Julia Kuehn reports, *The National Union Catalogue* established that more than fifty-five British editions of the novel had been printed by 1909; she uses advertisements of the time to determine that 202,000 copies were sold by 1920.[16]

The Sorrows of Satan was Corelli's first novel to be issued directly to the buying public, appearing exclusively in the one-volume format—selling for about six shillings (in 2010 dollars, roughly $36.00). In connection with this new practice, Corelli for the first time refused to send any free copies of the novel to reviewers in the press and went so far as to include a notice in the book's opening pages: "No copies of this book are sent out for review. Members of the press will therefore obtain it (should they wish to do so) in the usual way with the rest of the public, i.e., through the booksellers and the libraries."[17] These establishment-defying moves imply an unmediated bond between author and reading public, and indeed the novel's heroine, fiction-writer Mavis Clare, champions an antielitist cultural politics. In his introduction to the 1996 Oxford Popular Fiction edition of *The Sorrows of Satan*, Peter Keating posits that Corelli's antielitist gestures in connection with this novel contribute to our contemporary critical interest in this particular specimen among her many works. Keating offers a historical reading of this romance that takes its place beside illuminating contemporary readings by Felski, Annette Federico, Teresa Ransom, Julia Kuehn, and others;[18] thanks to all of this recent scholarship, we now possess strong feminist readings of the book's discursive terrain and historical significance. Here I propose an ideological interpretation, one that grafts these feminist insights onto a broadly historicist approach.

As its title suggests, *The Sorrows of Satan* conjures an imaginary life-world in which evil is personified by the most famous fallen angel in the Western tradition. Corelli's devil is perhaps more Mephistophelean, after Goethe, than Satanic in the Miltonic sense: a suave personage consorting with the urban, upper-class society of 1890s England, a culture whose vulnerabilities to the devil's lures cause him both to exult and to sorrow. The tale's romance template also draws upon the native British tradition of melodrama, with its typically allegorical depiction of a Manichean human experience that is fused with immediate social circumstances and concerns.[19] In this text (as in *Innocent,* as I argue later), we see illustrated Rita Felski's assertion that "in the context of Corelli's fiction," the popular sublime "is achieved through the combination of a formal register of melodramatic intensity with a thematic focus on the transcendence of quotidian reality and the material world" (120). In *The Sorrows of Satan,* as in many of Corelli's early romances (those of the 1880s and 1890s), this transcendence of the everyday appears in her fictional attempts to reconcile Christianity with reincarnation, karma, astral projection, and other Buddhist, Hindu, and mystical topoi.[20] Here, as Felski indicates, melodrama, gender politics, and a hybrid religious conception commingle in a distinctly Corellian romance. Contra Felski, however, I will not argue that melodrama per se, as a literary mode, was a gendered discourse in the 1890s;[21] instead, I believe the evidence suggests that it is by means of melodrama that Corelli conveys her ideological messages regarding not only gender but also class inequality and capitalist excess. Some of this ideological "messaging" was quite intentional on the author's part—but some was not and constitutes a series of emanations from the text's political unconscious.

Stage melodrama had been central to British popular culture since the turn of the nineteenth century. Soon after its emergence in 1770s France, this stage genre became deeply intertwined with the British tradition of romance narrative. The gothic romances of Horace Walpole, Anne Radcliffe, Matthew G. Lewis, and others informed the French dramas of the 1790s, which were then adapted, in native English incarnations, to London stages starting around 1800.[22] Frank Rahill offers a historical definition of melodrama as a literary mode:

> Melodrama is a form of dramatic composition in prose partaking of the nature of tragedy, comedy, pantomime,

> and spectacle, and intended for a popular audience. Primarily concerned with situation and plot, it calls upon mimed action extensively and employs a more or less fixed complement of stock characters, the most important of which are a suffering hero or heroine, a persecuting villain, and a benevolent comic. It is conventionally moral and humanitarian in point of view and sentimental and optimistic in temper, concluding its fable happily with virtue rewarded after many trials and vice punished.[23]

Recent scholarship has demonstrated that elements of the melodramatic mode had been integrated in Victorian novels through the decades leading up to the appearance of Corelli's first romances, in writers as diverse as Charles Dickens, Elizabeth Gaskell, George Eliot, Edward Bulwer-Lytton, Thomas Hardy, Mona Caird, and George Gissing.[24] Although Corelli did not state that she drew upon the melodramatic mode—her fictional mode was instead, by her own account, "poetic" and "romantic"—scholars have seen in Corelli's romances the transposition of stage melodrama into fiction. This is especially true of *The Sorrows of Satan,* which was her only novel to be adapted to the stage and the Corelli work most often the subject of (attempted or realized) silent film treatments, in 1911, 1916, 1919, and 1926.[25] Only the last, directed by D. W. Griffith in Hollywood, tends to be mentioned in film histories.[26]

An overview of the plot of *The Sorrows of Satan* suggests its melodramatic conventions—an emphasis on situation, on a suffering hero/heroine and persecuting villains, a conventional morality, and a portrayal of virtue rewarded—at the same time that it suggests Corelli's tweakings of such conventions. The romance is narrated in the first-person voice of one Geoffrey Tempest, a frustrated London writer who chronicles his rags-to-riches-to-rags experience of 1890s England. Early in the novel, he inherits the fortune of a distant colonial kinsman in South America. No sooner does he receive word of this windfall than at his garret door arrives an aristocrat, Prince Lucio Rimânez, who introduces him to the various pleasures and vices of London "Society"—gormandizing, gambling, evenings at the club and theater, and flirtation with beautiful women seeking rich husbands. Tempest uses his money to publish his novel, which achieves a limited success, but he is envious of the popular adulation of his literary peer, the woman novelist Mavis Clare, and uses his newfound influence to pillory her romances anonymously in the press. Accompanied by his new friend Rimânez (who seems to have a supernatural comprehension of the manners and motives of Society), Tempest finds that he succeeds at anything that involves money—he bribes the literary reviewers, he dresses to perfection, he is seen at all the right social functions, his horse wins the Ascot Derby, and Londoners of power and influence seek his company. Yet the satisfactions of all of these conquests are hollow. Soon he meets and falls in love with a "modern woman" of aristocratic lineage, Sybil Elton, who is looking for a rich husband. Tempest purchases an elegant country house in Warwickshire and manages to convince Sibyl to marry him, in what soon proves to be a poor match, as she cannot feel any emotion for him. Increasingly unhappy, Tempest realizes that neither his great wealth nor its attendant fame has brought him the spiritual plenitude he seeks. What he really wants is literary glory—to be renowned as a writer of noble works—after the model of Mavis Clare, whom he spitefully envies but soon finds too virtuous to despise. The beautiful, nihilistic Sibyl kills herself; on reading her journal, Tempest learns that she was overcome with despair after discovering the demonic identity of the man she secretly loved, Rimânez. Tempest lays all the blame for his wife's death on Sibyl herself and will not acknowledge the much-hinted-at supernaturalism of his best friend, even when Mavis Clare subsequently urges him to dissociate from this "fiend in a beautiful human shape" (346). He sails with Rimânez up the Nile River, where, among the Egyptian ruins, he realizes that Sibyl was the metempsychosed spirit of a mummified Egyptian sybarite. On a storm-tossed yacht in the Atlantic Ocean, Rimânez at last reveals his true identity as Satan, and Tempest rejects him—much to Satan's relief, as the individual's renunciation of evil prompts God to allow the fallen angel to experience a single hour in Heaven. Clinging to a spar of the destroyed vessel, Tempest is discovered by a passing ship and returns to London, where he learns, to his relief, that he has lost his entire fortune to his unscrupulous attorneys. At novel's end, a humbled Tempest spies his erstwhile friend Rimânez walking arm-in-arm with a prominent government minister into the Houses of Parliament.

One of the earliest published defenses of Corelli's romances, Thomas F. G. Coates and R. S. Warren Bell's *Marie Corelli* (1903), admonished the scornful critics for "missing the point" that *The Sorrows of Satan* was intended as allegory.[27] While this charge of ignorance leveled at the other critics is dubious, Corelli plainly meant her characters to be metonymic embodiments of late-Victorian social types, especially those of London Society. Corelli cues her readers to view this romance as an allegorical melodrama through nomenclature: Geoffrey Tempest suffers a stormy unhappiness, Sibyl Elton represents a prophecy of "godless" modern women, Mavis Clare has the clarity of a song thrush, and Lucio Rimânez incarnates an up-to-date Lucifer.

Another cue to allegory is a self-referential dinner party scene, arriving at the narrative's midpoint, during which the characters witness a series of *tableaux vivants.* In generic terms, we might call this the melodrama-within-the-melodrama, conveying in concentrated images the leitmotifs of the romance as a whole. Tempest notes the curiosity of the high-society audience as they await the evening's entertainment; it will prove to be all about themselves, as a class. "Soon we were all studying our programmes with considerable interest, for the titles of the *tableaux* were somewhat original and mystifying. They were eight in number, and were respectively headed—'Society'—'Bravery: Ancient and Modern'—'A Lost Angel'—'The Autocrat'—'A Corner of Hell'—'Seeds of Corruption'—'His Latest Purchase'—and 'Faith and Materialism'" (220). Each tableau has a didactic point. Women play prominent roles, such as the "exquisite female figure" in "Society" who wears diamonds and sips champagne as "behind her, catching convulsively at the folds of her train, crouched another woman in rags, pinched and wretched, with starvation depicted in her face" (221). "Lost Angel" presents a white-clad female angel amid an oblivious set of "brilliantly attired people" who are "completely absorbed in their own concerns" and cause the ignored figure to seem to ask, "Will the world ever know that I am here?" (221).

The question is portentous, and Corelli's Manichean symmetries, so prominent throughout the novel, are here signaled by the ignored angel, contrasted with the much-fêted Lucio (who, paradoxically, has arranged the tableaux). Like the "Lost Angel," Corelli's Satan walks abroad in fin-de-siècle London unrecognized for who he really is; he is instead celebrated for his wealth and charisma. It is also significant to Corelli's schema that the angel is female, and the devil male. That said, Corelli's feminine icon does not denote Coventry Patmore's "Angel of the House"; instead, Tempest is struck by the angel's resemblance to Mavis Clare—self-sufficient, unmarried, the career woman of "genius" (compare this with the earlier discussion of Mary Ward on the literary field), and the darling of romance readers throughout Britain. This symbolic equivalence of the "Lost Angel" to a woman who is neither wife nor mother represents far more than any putative megalomania on the part of "M.C." the writer; in fact, it can be read as an aporia in the text's elaboration of late-Victorian gender ideology—a paradox that will generate a symbolic resolution to real contradictions.

Tempest also witnesses a tableau, correlative to the "Lost Angel," of the late-Victorian marriage market. In "His Latest Purchase," a group of men "in fashionable evening dress" rise from the gambling table to gaze upon the winner's spoils: "a beautiful woman. She was clad in glistening white like a bride, but she was bound, as prisoners are bound, to an upright column, on which the grinning head of marble Silenus leered" (223). Tempest overhears a dinner guest's cynical response, "A capital type of the most fashionable marriages!" (223). But Tempest recognizes the social criticism intended by the tableau: "Her head was flung back defiantly with an assumption of pride and scorn—her eyes alone expressed shame, self-contempt, and despair at her bondage. The man who owned this white slave was represented, by his attitude, as cataloguing and appraising her 'points' for the approval and applause of his comrades, whose faces variously and powerfully expressed the differing emotions of lust, cruelty, envy, callousness, derision, and selfishness, more admirably than the most gifted painter could imagine" (223). Here, the men's attitudes (or, in Corelli's term, "emotions") of "lust, cruelty, envy, callousness, derision, and selfishness" together generate the marriage market, an institution of "white slavery." The implicit critique, however, targets not the system of patriarchy but personally indulged vices, which are understood to lead to a collective sin. (Also prominent are the stylistic features of Corelli's writing catalogued in Julia Kuehn's study—repetition, pleonasm, and a rhetoric of excess—all of which contribute to the mode of melodrama [119–23]). To the list of standard vices Tempest sees embodied in the men here, another tableau, "A Corner of Hell," adds greed: a man counts out gold pieces that "change to fire" and constitute his demonic torture, in a Dantean conception of a tormented afterlife brought on by one's characteristic sins in life. Taken together, Tempest's interpretations of these tableaux conflate two registers: readings of timeless, individualized vices and sins are interfused with a critique of the collective phenomena of class inequities, capitalist hyperaccumulation, and the objectification of women. These mute scenes provide *The Sorrows of Satan* with its abstract, or "dumb show," in the *Hamlet* sense: an index of the didactic leitmotifs that we as readers are intended to trace through the romance as a whole.

I return to the romance's figurations of social ills below; before doing so, however, I wish to explore the religious content vis-à-vis Anglican and Catholic orthodoxies of the late Victorian period. Corelli was vague about her denomination and tended to describe herself simply as an adherent of "the Christian Church";[28] regarding her Anglicanism, it is probably most accurate to describe her as Latitudinarian in her sympathies.[29] The symbols of the white angel and the torments of hell were, of course, entirely conventional, intended as a religious rebuttal to the secularization and materialism of bourgeois and upper-class life under modernity, but the kind of spiritualist idiosyncrasies on display throughout this and her other romances brought Corelli under fire for heterodoxy. Corelli's representations of religion and spirituality engendered controversy among many of the leading clerics of her day: some saw her as recklessly reinventing Christian iconography, through her quirky, individual fictionalizations, into noninstitutional visions that approached paganism. Church leaders responded variously to Corelli's religious syncretism. One Father Ignatius, a monk at Llanthony Abbey, claimed in 1896, "*The Sorrows of Satan* is flung down into the midst of English society, as it is constituted at present, as an heroic challenge to that society and to the Church."[30] By contrast, the Reverend Father Joseph H. McMahon announced in 1903, "I have heard yards of Corelli's so-called philosophy spoken of favorably by the pulpits of my own Church, and it is too bad. These books stand for egoism, agnosticism, and paganism. The influence of the pulpit is on the wane, and what is going to happen?"[31] Phillip Waller is correct, then, in claiming that Corelli's popularity in such novels as *The*

Sorrows of Satan is "inexplicable unless historians recognize the religious fervour of her work" (*Writers*, 782); but he also acknowledges the extra-institutional vagueness of Corelli's fictionalized doctrines, whereby she "regarded all religions as variants of Christianity and, like the spiritualists, was professedly non-sectarian" (783).

As in most of Corelli's romances, pagan and paranormal conceptions abound in *The Sorrows.* Corelli depicts a world in which reincarnation is common. Satan proclaims, "My worshippers live on through a [*sic*] myriad worlds, a [*sic*] myriad phases, till they learn to shape their destinies for Heaven!" (372); Tempest realizes too late that Sibyl was the reincarnation of an ancient Egyptian sybarite. A life-world in which metempsychosis, karmic states, and the three Fates of ancient Greek mythology cohabit with biblical conceptions of Heaven and Hell was straying from the orthodoxies of any Christian denomination of the period.[32] As one critic says of Corelli's early romances, "Corelli's hybrid Christianity, like other hybrid religions of the late-Victorian decades, stakes out its own brand of spirituality by strategically incorporating elements drawn from the very sources that it demonizes: fundamentalist Christianity, market capitalism, science, spiritualism, and Buddhism."[33] Elaine M. Hartnell has taken this view even further, suggesting that several of Corelli's novels, *The Sorrows of Satan* foremost among them, "discard or redefine the verities of virtually all mainstream Christian traditions and posit an ontology embracing reincarnation."[34] Another literary historian has recently summarized Corelli's spiritual philosophy as "based on opportunistic interpretations of selected teachings of Christ" and as dismissing "traditional religious authority and observance, and the notion of a jealous and punitive God." Instead, Corelli substitutes the concept that "God is Love" and limns a "system of personal spirituality wherein love and sincerity are rewarded, and where every individual has unlimited opportunities to win these rewards."[35] It is not too much of a stretch to suggest, as do the Corelli archivists at the National Library of New Zealand, that her type of spiritual philosophy "became an important part of the foundation of today's New Age religion."[36]

The point here is not to claim for Corelli the status of a "New Ager" *avant la lettre;* it is instead to note that some of her contemporaries charged her with the putative egoism and paranormalism of the "do-it-yourself" religionist, even as she herself attacked the presumed irreligiosity of her writing peers. Despite his antihero role, Geoffrey Tempest serves in this respect as her literary-critical messenger-boy, levelling charges of egoism and godlessness against contemporary fiction writers. Singled out for special scorn are Émile Zola and the "New Woman" novelists, the favorite reading material of Sibyl Vane. Tempest signals this leitmotif—the destruction of young women's morality by a "decadent" literature—in another of the tableaux: "'Seeds of Corruption' was the next picture, and showed us a young and beautiful girl in her early teens, lying on a luxurious couch *en déshabillé*, with a novel in her hand, of which the title was plainly seen by all—a novel well known to everyone present, and the work of a much praised living author. Round her, on the floor, and cast carelessly on a chair at her side, were other novels of the same 'sexual' type—all their titles turned toward us, and the names of their authors equally made manifest" (222–23). Confronted by this image, Sibyl whispers, "Geoffrey, it is painfully true!" Tempest soon apprehends her in the act of reading a New Woman novel; disgusted, he snatches it from her hands and hurls it into a lake (245). Elsewhere, Lucio informs Tempest that "in these new days of Sodom and Gomorrah," his book would succeed if it offered "a judicious mixture of Zola, Huysmans, and Baudelaire" (50). Sibyl confesses, in her suicide note, that "Swinburne, among others, had helped me live mentally, if not physically, through such a phase of vice as had poisoned my thoughts for ever" (327). Corelli's war on realist fiction, amply documented in earlier romances such as *Ardath* (1889), has in *The Sorrows of Satan* moved on to decadence, aestheticism, naturalism, and feminist fiction. It is interesting, then, that the *New York Times* article recording Father Joseph H. McMahon's attacks on her works bears the subtitle "Zola, Hall Caine, and Marie Corelli in Their Works Would Substitute a Moral Mirage for True Religion." If the young reader *en déshabillé* announces a major moral theme of this romance as a whole—the pernicious effects of late-Victorian literary movements—then Corelli stood accused by some of the same species of offense, the corruption of religion and morality.

As we have seen, Corelli's Weltanschauung is highly "personal" in two senses: it represents an idiosyncratic synthesis of different religious and spiritual traditions through the crucible of the romance writer's imagination, and it posits "good and evil" in allegorized characters. Given that, through *The Sorrows of Satan*, Corelli's "philosophy" (to use Father McMahon's term) is conveyed through the melodramatic mode,[37] the historicizing account of melodrama in Peter Brooks's work helps us to situate her Christian/spiritualist syncretism within a larger ideological context. Central to this account is the emergence of "the personal" within literary representations of ethical conflict. Charting the rise of melodrama in the wake of the French Revolution of 1789, Brooks posits the personalization of the Sacred in Western European culture: "[B]y the end of the Enlightenment, there was clearly a renewed thirst for the Sacred, a reaction to desacralization expressed in the vast movement we think of as Romanticism. . . . Mythmaking could now only be individual, personal."[38] With the execution of royals and aristocrats (a cataclysmic event anticipated by the beheading of Charles I in England in 1649), the force of sacred mythologies, participated in communally and best represented by the tragic mode in literature, began by Brooks's account to be lost. The promulgation of ethical imperatives began to shake loose of the Old World institutions and to be resituated into the imaginations of individual artists.

Together with high Romantic poetry and the gothic novel, by Brooks's reckoning, the literary-dramatic mode of melodrama emerged in Western European culture as a response to the supersession of unifying religious mythologies. As Brooks suggests, "Melodrama represents both the urge toward resacralization and the impossibility of conceiving sacralization other than in personal terms. Melodramatic good and evil are highly personalized: they are assigned to, they inhabit persons who indeed have no psychological complexity but who are strongly characterized" (*Melodramatic*, 16). Readers of *The Sorrows of Satan* might expect to find the personal "sacralization" of those characters who resist the devil, and the personal demonization of not only the original demon but also those who succumb to his temptations. Brooks shows that in traditional melodrama, "good and evil can be named as persons are named—and melodramas tend to move toward a clear nomination of the moral universe" (17). This is the structural patterning in Corelli's romance, such that Satan either attracts or repels the primary characters, to the extent that they possess the virtues or vices that slot them into a Manichean order.

But only to a certain extent; such Manichean assignments depend on whether those characters are male or female—and to this feature of Corelli's romance, with its ideological consequences, I devote the remainder of my discussion of *The Sorrows of Satan.* The irruption of Corelli's gender ideology bends and distorts her intended social criticism; there is an odd asymmetry to her assignment of praise or blame to individual characters representing social types. Neither Tempest, who (prior to the novel's climactic scene) often succumbs to the devil's temptations, nor even Satan himself is "evil," in the melodramatic convention of a personalized menace that executes its declarations of malevolent intent and reduces innocence, temporarily, to powerlessness (Brooks, *Melodramatic,* 34). For all his apparent gaiety, this Satan is melancholy and self-divided; he is fated to tempt humankind but is ever lamenting his successes in doing so; his devil-may-care veneer hides a devil who in fact *does,* at some level, care, if only because he wishes to get back to Heaven. We are intended to pity Satan: to perceive his fallen nobility and his clarity of vision and to feel sorry for him.

This is not so for Sibyl Vane, who is unambiguously bad. The romance's two central females, not its more nuanced males, are the ones who represent moral antitheses. As Corelli's earliest biographers elucidate, "Now the idea of Lady Sibyl was an allegorical one. She represented, to Marie Corelli's mind, the brilliant, indifferent, selfish, vicious impersonation of *Society offering itself body and soul to the devil.* . . . Marie Corelli considers that the evils of society are wrought by women; hence the impersonation of Lady Sibyl as a woman, courting the devil. Secondly she considers that the reformation of society must be wrought by women; hence the impersonation of Mavis Clare, as a woman *repelling* the devil."[39] If Coates and Bell were correct in thus representing Corelli's authorial intention—and there is strong evidence to suggest that this 1903 explanation of her romance had the writer's blessing[40]—then we are seeing an allegory that mediates its social content in three distinct ways. First, there are various personifications of personal and individual sins, such as "lust, cruelty, envy, callousness, derision, and selfishness," encountered not only in some of the *tableaux vivants* but also in such secondary characters as Tempest's lawyers, his publisher, the gourmandizing nouveaux riches ("the Liver Brigade" [36–37]), and so forth. Second, there are embodiments of the social pathologies of class inequity (such as the starved wretch of the tableau "Society"), capitalist hyperaccumulation (such as the plutocrat of "A Corner of Hell"), and the objectification of women (such as the woman of "His Latest Purchase"). Third, there are these catch-all opposite numbers, Sybil Vane and Mavis Clare, who represent respectively "swagger society" (54) and the potential "reformation" of that society.

Thus far, I have been explicating *The Sorrows of Satan* on the level of Corelli's conscious intentions. But of course any fictional narrative may also be possessed of a political unconscious, which can be detected in certain gaps, omissions, and aporias. In the case of Corelli's romance, these features of the text can be elucidated by pushing deeper into the asymmetry of the gender representations (Sybil Vane and Mavis Clare representing "pure" vice and "pure" virtue, Geoffrey Tempest and Lucio Rimânez representing "mixed" characters), which, I would argue, hints at how this romance concocts, from the ingredients of contemporary social contradictions, a paradoxical mix of resentments—modern and reactionary, feminist and antifeminist, anticapitalist and pro–free market. The donnée of *The Sorrows of Satan,* as we have seen, is the sudden access to great riches and the irresistible temptations that accompany such an elevation. The story's most prominent aporia, or seemingly irresolvable contradiction, derives from Geoffrey Tempest's predicament: the mutual incompatibility, or seeming antinomy, between individual virtue and private wealth. Ideologically, Tempest represents a fictional symptom of what historian Eric Hobsbawm identifies as "an era of profound identity crisis and transformation for a bourgeoisie whose traditional moral foundation crumbled under the very pressure of its own accumulations of wealth and comfort."[41] The causes of this perceived or felt disjunction between individual wealth and the social good may be seen as systemic or structural, embodying the following contradictions: peacetime conditions that led to the unprecedented, cold efficiency of modern wars; social stability in the metropolis that was maintained by violence and exploitation at the imperial periphery; and (perhaps most to the point here) a liberal ideology of self-reliant individuals on a "level field" that engendered oligarchy, plutocracy, and corporate tyranny.[42]

In light of this last paradox, it should come as no surprise that at the midpoint of the forty-year period described by Hobsbawm in *The Age of Empire, 1875–1914,* the top-selling British novel that had yet been seen by 1895 offers a sustained attack on the era's plutolatry. From the perspective of a "muscular" Anglican Protestantism, the notion of the mutual exclusivity of virtue and great wealth might seem to be, at the same time, both proven across history (such as in the founding story of the Anglican Church, with the Catholic abbeys' hoards of wealth and Henry the Eighth's greedy depredations thereof) and contradicted by Victorian ideologies of free trade and economic opportunism. On the one hand, the humbling experience of Geoffrey Tempest, who deservedly loses his unearned millions, is meant to provide readers with a moral object lesson limited to no historical setting. On the other, Corelli published the novel at a moment when plutocrats from Cecil Rhodes to John D. Rockefeller were widely considered to represent object lessons in how earthly riches could be a divine dispensation, a sign of virtue rewarded—and indeed, Rockefelleresque nouveaux riches figure prominently in *The Sorrows of Satan*, in the characters of Diana Chesney and her father Nicodemus, "one of the great railway-kings." The fictional Tempest does not labor for his riches, whereas the real-life plutocrats were widely believed to have done so. Nonetheless, we may point to this locus between individual labor and vast wealth as the site of a *felt* contradiction. In reference to the most conspicuously wealthy individuals and families of the 1890s, the phrase *earned wealth* may well have functioned as an oxymoron, conjoining incommensurable social phenomena, as the economic but morally charged concept of one's "earning" remuneration was being dwarfed by the impersonality of deterritorialized capital accumulations whose magnitude had been hitherto unwitnessed on earth.[43] Certainly, aristocrats had enjoyed the fruits of unearned, inherited wealth for centuries, but there were by the 1890s two important differences from the past: the unprecedented magnitude of the personal fortunes that global capital was making possible, and the fact that these fortunes increasingly attached to nonaristocrats of unprivileged class origins and thereby threw into question the belief that personal "virtues" could merit such disproportionate rewards. Indeed, in this social context, the phrases *to earn* and *to create wealth* may be felt to operate on different semantic planes, the one verbal applying to living persons, the other to an increasingly complex abstraction of value.

Here, then, is a "logical scandal or double bind," "unthinkable and conceptually paradoxical," that comprehensively worries the text of *The Sorrows of Satan*—that, like a combustible psychic fuel, seems to power Corelli's narrative. The ideological resolution to these real-life contradictions is embodied in the one unambiguously "good" character, the romance-writing Mavis Clare. Tempest dreams of Mavis Clare as an angel, and indeed she will come to incarnate the qualities that lead to Tempest's spiritual survival and ultimate wisdom; she is the repository of those divine truths that Satan once renounced. As we have seen, she so unambiguously represents goodness and virtue in the novel as to embody (together with her opposite number, Sibyl Elton) its melodramatic register. Her example figures the redemption of nearly all the social pathologies depicted in the novel.

The character of Mavis Clare thus serves an ideological function, embodying the fantasy that individual will can, if pure enough, vanquish the systemic ills of patriarchy and the free market. When Tempest first meets Mavis Clare, he is consumed by envy, for her spiritually uplifting romances—unlike his newly published novel—seem to defy the corrupt workings of the London literary field. She is savaged by the critics but adored by the reading public, and she makes a handsome living by her pen. With the benefit of hindsight, Tempest comes to understand that "[t]here was some quality in the subtle glory which could not be won by either purchase or influence. The praise of the press could not give it. Mavis Clare, working for her bread, had it—I, with millions of money, had not. Like a fool I had thought to buy it; I had yet to learn that all the best, greatest, purest, and worthiest things in life are beyond all market-value and that the gifts of the gods are not for sale" (151). Tempest acknowledges that her writerly and moral genius were what caused him to agonize in a resentment that has finally been dissolved away.

If one of the climactic lessons that Mavis Clare teaches Tempest is art's transcendence of corrupting "market-value," the other concerns the value of work. The phantasmagoric climax of the novel, the midocean scene in which Tempest renounces a finally revealed Satan, is followed by the protagonist's shipwreck, rescue, and return to London, where he discovers that his lawyers have cheated him out of five million pounds. But Tempest has learned the true value of the work ethic; by this late moment in his experience, when he realizes that he has fallen in love with the unattainable "lady author," Tempest's great epiphany is that one's economic well-being must always be earned, and, though enough to provide material comfort, it should never be disproportionate or immodest. He will no longer complain about unremunerated effort: "Clear before me rose the vision of that most divine and beautiful necessity of happiness—Work!—the grand and too often misprized Angel of Labour, which moulds the mind of man, steadies his hands, controls his brain, purifies his passions, and strengthens his whole mental and physical being. . . . Gratitude there should be in every human soul for every gift of heaven—but nothing merits more thankfulness and praise to the Creator than the call to work, and the ability to respond to it" (385). Declining to pursue a case against his scoundrel solicitors, Tempest tells the "utterly confounded chief of the detective force" that "[a] man who has too much money *creates* forgers and thieves about him—he cannot expect to meet with honesty. Let the bank prosecute if it likes—I shall not. I am free!—free to work for my living. What I earn I shall enjoy—what I inherited, I have learnt to loathe!" (386). Of course, these are the words of the same character who earlier railed against a situation in which his most arduous efforts met with little to no reward. But now he has learned, and has taught the reader, as he promised to do at the outset, that it is the individual, and not the social structure, that is always to blame. Mavis Clare's example vindicates that bedrock belief of Victorian liberalism, that just rewards can indeed be earned through the efforts of the individual economic actor—all the more so, as she is a woman and miraculously overcomes masculine power and prejudice in her achievement of autonomy. Mavis Clare is not a representation of Coventry Patmore's "Angel of the House" but instead represents that most emancipated of late-Victorian women, the unmarried writer who earns her living in a fiercely competitive marketplace. In this fashion, Corelli champions a progressive feminism and reinforces the myths of liberal individualism in the same stroke.

In this paragon of virtue and artistic genius, Corelli brings together the resources of both her idiosyncratic Christianity and free-market liberalism to "square the circle" of the mutual incompatibility between wealth and virtue. We should recall that the first sentence of the novel is Tempest's address to the reader: "Do you know what it is to be poor?" (3). This sentence and the diatribe concerning poverty that follows it establish the chasm between wealth and poverty as a central preoccupation of the narrative. The novel's early premise—that great wealth and goodness of character do not mesh within the same individual—represents an implicit provocation: how does one reconcile a "Protestant work ethic" that creates globe-straddling millionaires with the gospel of Matthew, and its warning about the rich man, the camel, and the needle's eye? But the text would implicitly heal this scandal and would provide an imaginary resolution to the real problem. In a sense, the text has generated the character of Mavis Clare as the means to reconcile the terms of the antinomy.

Formally speaking, then, this narrative mechanism poses Mavis Clare as, on one level, the two-dimensionally virtuous character of traditional melodrama, but on another, a discursive vehicle of ideological resolution on the planes of gender, culture, and political economy. Following Jameson, I have invoked the notion of "squaring the circle" of an antinomy—of, that is, a conflict between two apparently valid ideas or principles that is insoluble in the light of available knowledge.[44] While this notion may sound abstract, it simply represents the overcoming of a logical circularity, the supersession of a conceptual problem wherein the mind has bounced back and forth without making progress in reconciling opposed principles that coexist, even as they seem to be mutually exclusive. If those opposed principles are social axioms, to find some way to reconcile them is to escape ideological closure, to overcome the oscillation of the double bind; and if that way takes the form of a narrative, we witness one of the means by which literature can be said to perform ideological work, as a story embodies the "thinking through," via its characters and events, of the problem caused by the antinomy. Another way to put this dynamic is to suggest that "squaring the circle" of an antinomy means breaking out of circularity by the introduction of two new concepts: the logical contradictories to the ideological contraries represented in the original two terms. What had been conceptually circular becomes, as it were, quadrangular, and the horizon of thought expands, giving the text greater latitude to worry through the original problem.

I have already suggested that in Corelli's novel, private wealth and personal virtue are not logically contradictory but are instead ethical contraries, conveyed through a particular transcription—and jarring juxtaposition—of popular Christian and capitalist discourses. Nonetheless, conceptually speaking, these terms also summon for readers the subtextual ghosts of their logical contradictories.[45] Using a Greimasian semiotic square, we can schematize the text's central issues in such a way that the contrary terms of the troubling antinomy also evoke their contradictories.

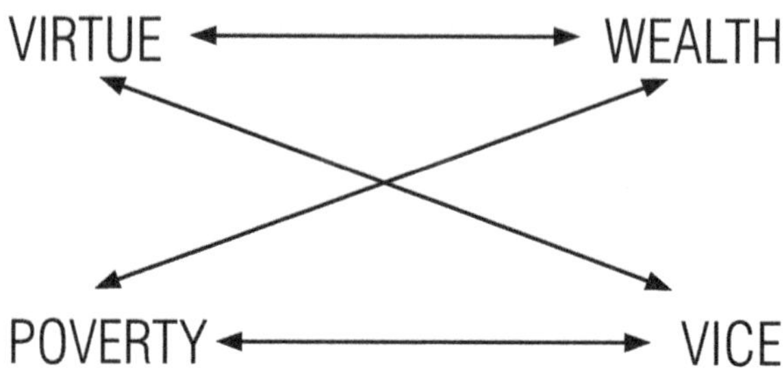

I would propose that all of these terms were central to the conscious social ideologies of Marie Corelli and her lower-middle- to middle-class readers. These concepts, in and of themselves, are, of course, abstractions, but to line each up directly, in static assignments to individual characters (after the fashion, say, of Bunyan's *Pilgrim's Progress*), would violate the conventions of the "romance" indicated in the book's title—conventions that Corelli does not intend, in her male leads, to be quite so obviously allegorical. Instead, the personae and events of the narrative effectively represent the terms' various combinations. The terms *wealth* and *vice* might seem most manifestly to cohabit in the figure of Satan, who professes to be limitlessly rich and appears at the moment when Tempest acquires his wealth. Likewise, as we have seen, the combination of poverty and sinful pride is embodied in Geoffrey Tempest at the start of his adventures, and the event of his inheritance projects him over onto the wealth-vice axis that comes with Lucio Rimânez's companionship. Likewise, another pair of events, Tempest's epiphanic shipwreck and the subsequent loss of all his money, later projects him across the semiotic square, as it were, to the position of virtuous poverty.

In the context of Corelli's Christian-spiritualist discourse, the concept of virtuous poverty could not help but connote, consciously or otherwise, the figure of Christ, and so it comes as no surprise to find that Mavis Clare, from whom Tempest has learned the value of Christian spirituality and the earning of one's daily bread, is compared explicitly to the Son of God. Earlier in the narrative,

Tempest's publisher has described a certain writer as "mocked and derided and opposed at every turn—and yet . . . winning a world-wide fame and power" (81). Tempest mockingly suggests the comparison of this author with Christ, to which his publisher solemnly responds, "But I was not thinking of the Great Example just then, Mr Tempest—I was thinking of a woman" (81). And so we come to the resolution offered by Mavis Clare, who as a Christ figure enables Tempest to take up this position as the unifier of virtue and poverty, at the same time that she alone unifies the system-originating poles of virtue and wealth. Mavis tells Lucio, "I would not be the possessor of wealth for all the world!" (277), and her relatively modest country home resembles neither a Mayfair townhouse nor an aristocratic estate. But how is it possible that an artist who has achieved "world-wide fame and power" does not also possess wealth? This gap is not explained; the romance text wishes away what common sense dictates must exist.

Mavis Clare, in other words, represents the dream-synthesis of the two major contraries of this semiotic system. Her virtue is so exemplary as to transcend the very problem of money—hers is a goodness that at last defies the seemingly ineradicable connection between riches and vice. How else would she be impervious to the devil, in the form of Lucio Rimânez? By emptying money of its power—by embodying the revealed truth that "the gifts of the gods are not for sale" (151)—Mavis Clare reconciles the antinomy between wealth and virtue. This apparent release from the ideological double bind can therefore be schematized with the characters thus ranged around the semiotic square.

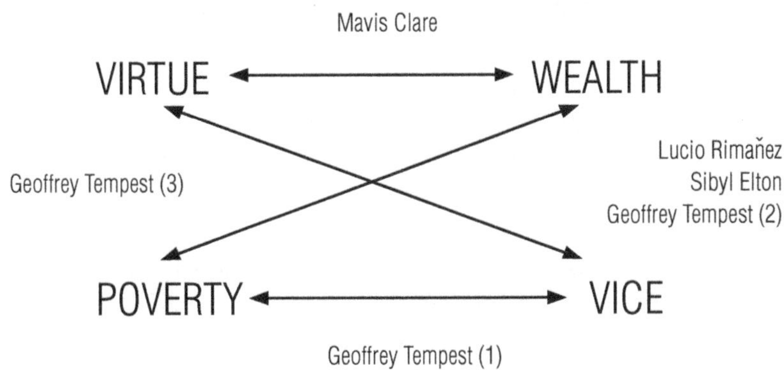

As the diagram suggests, Tempest may be seen as occupying three positions successively: the embodiment first of poverty and vice (an identification that emerges only retrospectively, after Tempest's class resentment of the opening pages is reframed as sinful), next of wealth and vice, and finally of poverty and virtue. Mavis Clare is the one character who at different moments in the novel serves as the opposite number to all of the other three major characters—as a writer, she is counterposed to Tempest; as a woman, she serves as Sibyl's foil; and as a spiritual figure, she opposes Satan. The character of Mavis Clare redeems woman, but just as important, she annuls the mystifying power of money. Satan has cynically portrayed the cash nexus as the Rosetta Stone to late-Victorian social meanings—or, to put it theoretically, to the capitalist recoding of formerly organic social value—but the grace of Mavis Clare restores meaning and spiritual order. In this manner, Corelli has generated an impossibly virtuous heroine and has offered a fantasy resolution to the novel's governing antinomy.

But that resolution has come at an ideological cost—the demonization, not of the male lead character or (ironically) the male devil but of the female lead, Sibyl Elton, who represents the principle of unearned wealth (via her roles as a decadent aristocrat and a "gold-digger") and is also, paradoxically, a victim of the patriarchal marriage market. The melodramatic vilification of Sibyl Elton put the feminist periodical *Shafts* into an uncomfortable double bind, as is evident in an 1895 review of Corelli's romance:

> Marie Corelli's pen of might has drawn for us a vivid description of her fancy's rich flight—the degradation through rebellious pride, and the descent into our sphere of an angel of light, and his transformation for the nonce into a cynical man upon town, who talks like a *roué*, worn out and disgusted with the life of society and all that it can yield. . . . This Self as Satan, or Satan as Self—as you will, for perchance we have not fully grasped the author's deepest meaning. . . . To say that a book of Marie Corelli's is well written is but a truism. This is in some respects especially good. . . . [Sibyl Elton's] story—her vindication, if it may be so called—written by herself, and the last, very last glimpses of her,

> are perhaps the cleverest parts of the book, which is . . . like a gleaming sword striking this way and that, never, save in the case of women, striking without good need, but there, like the world itself, somewhat merciless.[46]

Corelli clearly did not intend Sibyl Elton's suicide note to constitute her "vindication"—penned in a final moment of shame, it instead chronicles her slide into deception and degradation. *Shafts*'s general praise for Corelli's romance is handsome, but there is a veiled criticism here: the book, we are told, strikes at its women characters "without good need." Given the reviewer's effort to undo the demonization of Sibyl, the comment "perchance we have not fully grasped the author's deepest meaning" may be double-edged. And the reviewer's instinct may today seem fitting, given Sibyl's "merciless" overdetermination as both vice-ridden individual, fully responsible for her own downfall, and corrupt symbol of a feminized "high society."

In the end, it is another female character, herself a genius of the romance form, who represents the locus of transcendence, the avenue into an alternative reality—or in other words, the popular sublime. Original readers of *The Sorrows of Satan* were able to see themselves as participating in and promoting the spiritual phenomenon of M.C.'s romances and thereby participated in that transcendence, in the supersession of "decadent" and "vulgar" culture through the collective achievement of an ennobling, "holy" ideal. We twenty-first-century readers perceive that Corelli's heroine was intended to reconcile the dissonance between a Christian discourse of virtue and an emergent free-market fundamentalism. Sifting the evidence of letters and contemporary accounts, we see that many of her readers finished *The Sorrows of Satan* with a sense of reassurance.

It is interesting to juxtapose Corelli's inscription on her completed draft of *The Sorrows* with a comment by a novel reviewer in a respectable literary organ, the *Academy*. Corelli wrote, on the reverse of the manuscript's last blank page:

> Finished 15th August 1895
> Marie Corelli
> To Thee O God and my Saviour Christ
> I commend this work as all work I may do, or have done. Amen.
> *Ave Maria!*[47]

The Old World piety connoted by these words contrasts sharply with the modern sensibility that many of Corelli's readers perceived in such new romances as *The Sorrows of Satan.* One month later, in a review essay concerning several romance novels, James Stanley Little opened with this observation: "The modern novel, like the modern newspaper, must be accepted as the necessity of the hour. In any case there must be a great many persons who have come to regard it as a necessity, or there would be no market for the enormous number of new books that bear a general resemblance to romance."[48] The popular romance as a "necessity": this is a telling observation. What Jameson has written about Conrad's *Lord Jim,* a masculine adventure romance, may also be applied, with requisite modifications, here: romantically salving the tensions between "the energies of Western capitalism and the organic immanence of the religion of pre-capitalist societies," Corelli's romance may be said to have resolved the felt contradiction between wealth and virtue and to have "generated the impossible hero, who . . . now solicits that lowering of our reality principle necessary to accredit this final burst of legend."[49] Of course, in this case that hero is a heroine, and because of her status as a writer of mystical romances, she underscores precisely the self-aware suspension of the real*ism* principle, in favor of the glimpse of infinitude and boundlessness that the romance form can, however fleetingly or temporarily, achieve.[50]

The Corellian Romance contra Modernity: *The Treasure of Heaven* and *Innocent*

> For all her cleverness and culture, she was probably one of those soulless, atheistical women who have been so shown up by Miss Corelli.
>
> E. M. Forster, *Howards End*

> The people were dull and pretentious; old ladies with elderly maiden daughters; funny old bachelors with mincing ways; pale-faced, middle-aged clerks with wives, who talked of their married daughters and their sons who were in a very good position in the colonies. At table they discussed Miss Corelli's latest novel.
>
> W. Somerset Maugham, *Of Human Bondage*

In 1903, Corelli's first biographers wrote, "It may be asked—what is Marie Corelli's life-programme?" Their answer: "She would purify society."[51] Evidence suggests that thousands of her original readers believed that she succeeded in this pious "life-programme." Some wrote to her that her books had prevented them from committing suicide or drifting into agnosticism; others, that her work "had exercised a comforting and generally beneficent influence over them."[52] After encountering one of her romances, a correspondent wrote, "I felt a better woman for the reading of it twice; and I know others, too, who are higher and better women for such noble thoughts and teaching."[53] A male memoirist, the journalist Cecil Rolph Hewitt, recalled that during his Edwardian childhood in London, "Marie Corelli was more revered in our home than Thomas à Kempis himself."[54] Although no consistent demographic profile of Corelli's readers is recoverable, we can infer from scattered library and bookshop records[55] and literary references (such as those of Forster and Maugham in the epigraphs above) that her romances delighted middle- to lower-middle-class readers of both sexes. One reviewer asserted in 1909 that "many" of Corelli's "most enthusiastic admirers are men of the professional classes—doctors, barristers, lawyers, writers, men of education and intelligence."[56] The frequent translation of her novels into various European and South Asian languages attests that Corelli's dream-worlds also appealed to readers of non-anglophone and colonial cultures.

As we have seen in *The Sorrows of Satan,* one of the challenges of gauging Corelli's cultural impact is to connect her popular representations of spiritual transcendence to the contours of late nineteenth- and early twentieth-century social experience. If, as Felski has suggested, Corelli's "utopian gesturing toward an ineffable otherness can be seen as a critical response to irresolvable tensions within the social" (*Gender,* 143), then her novels' defiant planting of romance conventions within the contemporary ground of turn-of-the-century modernity must have spoken to the desires of both male and female readers. In part, Corelli's absolute figurations of good and evil seem to have salved the psyches of those bewildered by the ethical complexities of modernity. The recent feminist readings of Corelli's cultural significance to which I have referred may be supplemented with broadly historicist accounts of the development of the novel in the period in question. We may, without inconsistency or contradiction of method, consult a recent Marxist account of the role of the popular romance novel in the wake of nineteenth-century high realism and naturalism: "[R]omance once again comes to be felt as the place of narrative heterogeneity and of freedom from that reality principle to which a now oppressive realist representation is the hostage. Romance now again seems to offer the possibility of sensing other historical rhythms, and of the demonic or Utopian transformations of a real now unshakably set in place."[57] We have witnessed how *The Sorrows of Satan,* in the person of its title character, represented such a demonic transformation; I now turn to two Corelli romances that offer, in part, such utopian refashionings of reality.

In the reading that I wish to pursue here, we may take the "real now unshakably set in place," or the socially manifested "reality principle," to be embodied by those features of late nineteenth- and early twentieth-century modernity identified by sociologist Raymond Williams: the intensifying complexity of human communities in the industrialized world (especially in the context of imperialism); the unprecedented growth of the urban social space; the proliferating division of labor; and the altering relations between social classes (as exemplified in the explosion of lower-class literacy after England's 1870 Education Act) and within social classes (as instanced by the rise of women's rights).[58] All of these factors were causing ordinary people to become aware as never before of their connection with individuals and groups beyond their daily, face-to-face interactions; but this enlarging human network could hardly have been experienced as "community" in the traditional sense of the word, just as the ordinary person's awareness of that network could hardly have been comprehensive. If the realist novel reflected this "crisis of knowable community,"[59] the imaginary communities represented in the Corellian romance, with its moral certainties and fixed axis of good versus evil, may be supposed to have offered respite from such epistemological challenges and to have provided a kind of consolation, a "Utopian transformation" of bewildering social realities.

In the remainder of this chapter, I argue that both Corelli and many of her female and male readers experienced the turn-of-the-century romance through the historical self-consciousness articulated in Jameson's description—albeit in largely intuitive and commonsensical fashion. Through her updated use of romance traditions, Corelli presented her contemporary modernity as a reality quite "shakeable" by sheer force of moral will, in the spiritual regeneration provided by her premodern utopias. By way of examples, I look at two of Corelli's romances from the Edwardian period—*The Treasure of Heaven: A Romance of Riches* (1906) and *Innocent: Her Fancy and His Fact* (1914)—within the literary context of evolving relations among the fictional modes of the romance, realism, and a nascent modernism. Together, *The Treasure of Heaven* and *Innocent* thematize a key Corellian preoccupation, the fate of premodern romance ideologies and the romance mode of narrative under contemporary literary and social conditions in Britain. The two novels critique aspects of cultural modernity perceived to be dehumanizing, and they defend the role of the romance form as a timeless purveyor of "eternal" human truths. As do so many of Corelli's fictions, these narratives figure spirituality in ways that are at once Christian-salvationist and idiosyncratically modern: romantic battles between good and evil are interfused with a metaphysical feminism,[60] a defiant populism, and an idealistic rebellion against institutionalized masculine authority, whether it be that of the corrupt aristocracy, the calculating bourgeoisie, or the makers of cultural opinion. Through these thematic concerns, we can also discern a formal tendency that, with our benefit of hindsight, situates Corelli as representing a distinct stage within the history of literary modes. *The Treasure of Heaven* and *Innocent* may be said to represent the revenge of the traditional romance on turn-of-the-century realism, even as they prefigure certain of high modernism's emergent attitudes toward cultural modernity.

In the opening tableau of *The Treasure of Heaven*, Corelli depicts a high-society London so venal that the novel's main character, seventy-year-old millionaire David Helmsley, is undergoing a spiritual crisis. The protagonist feels beleaguered by twentieth-century metropolitan vices:

> London, with a million twinkling lights gleaming sharp upon its native blackness, and looking, to a dreamer's eye, like some gigantic Fortress, built line upon line and tower upon tower,—with huge ramparts raised about it frowningly as though in self-defence against

> Heaven. Around and above it the deep sky swept in a ring of sable blue, wherein a thousand stars were visible, encamped after the fashion of a mighty army, with sentinel planets taking their turns of duty in the watching of a rebellious world. A sulphureous wave of heat half asphyxiated the swarms of people who were hurrying to and fro. . . . [T]he swift whirr and warning hoot of coming and going motor vehicles, the hoarse cries of the newsboys, and the general insect-like drone and murmur of feverish human activity were as loud as at any busy time of the morning or the afternoon. . . . The public restaurants were crammed with luxury-loving men and women,—men and women to whom the mere suggestion of a quiet dinner in their own homes would have acted as a menace of infinite boredom. . . . No hint of pause or repose was offered in the ever-changing scene of uneasy and impetuous excitation of movement, save where, far up in the clear depths of space, the glittering star battalions of a wronged and forgotten God held their steadfast watch and kept their hourly chronicle.[61]

The city's nocturnal animation, hedonistic energy, mechanical conveyances, and "insect-like" inhabitants are together presented as nothing less than a hell on earth. The motor cars, newsboys, and "feverish human activity" foreshadow the main character's preoccupation throughout the novel with the ills of automobiles, the contemporary press, and corrupt modern business practices. The evils of modernity are established here at the outset as those of the urban metropolis (as implicitly opposed to the provinces, where there is still hope of utopia): this urban "Fortress" with "ramparts raised" defensively against the firmament is engaged in a war against heaven. God is preparing for martial conflict, recording the deeds of His ungrateful children, with His "sentinel planets" and "glittering star battalions" at the ready. In a manner opposed to the synecdochic social representations of realist or naturalist fiction, Corelli's romantic tableau depicts both secular and divine spheres. The life-world to be presented in this romance is immediately and unironically established as *total,* bridging earthly and heavenly realities. Not only, *pace* Raymond Williams, are we offered a knowable earthly community, but we are also privy to a celestial one.

Despite his despair at the decadence surrounding him, Helmsley will not surrender his instinctive need for the Christian faith: "Even I—old and frail and about to die—cannot rid myself of a belief in God, and in the ultimate happiness of each man's existence" (33). As he recalls the halcyon days of his rural childhood, he tells his only confidant, his lawyer Francis Vesey, "I had something then which I have never had since. . . . [I]t was merely—love!" (11). The pragmatic Vesey is dismayed: "I only wish you were not quite so—so romantic! . . . A man of your age doesn't want to be loved for himself alone unless he's very romantic indeed!" (15–16). This passage signals the theme that Corelli told her publisher she intended as the novel's moral: "The motive of the story is a very simple one—merely that happiness does not depend on money."[62] Indeed, the title of the romance telegraphs this theme, with its allusion to Jesus's words from Matthew 19:21, "go and sell that thou hast, and give to the poor, and thou shalt have treasure in heaven." If happiness in this novel does not derive from riches, what it does come to depend on, despite Helmsley's protestations, is *romance*, in at least three different senses of that multivalent term.

The first of these consists of the romantic search for an ineffable spirituality, as Helmsley determines to quit the city and roam rural Britain, disguised as a tramp, in an effort to rediscover the unfallen circumstances of his pastoral boyhood: "[H]e had started on a lonely quest,—a search for something vague and intangible, the very nature of which he himself could not tell" (58). The obstacles to this quest, as witnessed in the opening tableau, are twentieth-century materialism and its attendant unbelief, cynicism, and cold rationalism. Only a few days into his wanderings through southwestern England, Helmsley is exposed to a raging storm, loses consciousness, and awakens to find himself under the watchful care of a young woman. This Cordelia to his Lear is Mary Deane, a lace mender who nurses him through a two-month bout of rheumatic fever and, after inviting him to reside with her, eventually teaches Helmsley to weave baskets for his daily bread. Never divulging the facts of his high-society background, he secretly arranges for Mary to be his sole heir and encourages her courtship by a virtuous young writer, Angus Reay. Helmsley plays matchmaker out of the same altruism that Mary has shown to him, for he feels that at last "[h]e had attained what he never thought it would be possible to attain—a love which had been bestowed upon him for himself alone. He had found what he had judged would be impossible to find—two hearts which, so far as he personally was concerned, were utterly uninfluenced by considerations of self-interest" (311). Having achieved spiritual peace, Helmsley takes gentle leave of this world, whereupon Mary Deane finally learns of his riches, which she inherits as earthly reward for her goodness.

Her greater reward, though, is to be wooed and won by that paragon of nobility, Angus Reay. This love story, which finally takes center stage, demonstrates the two further senses in which the novel's subtitle, *A Romance of Riches,* is borne out. As Mary accepts Angus's proposal of marriage, they gaze upon a sunset of "burning rose," which prompts Angus to proclaim rapturously, "It is like the Holy Grail" (327). Corelli thus pays homage to the oldest traditions of the romance genre in English, with the grail here representing the achievement of oneness with divinity via earthly love. At the same time, she prefigures the emergent twentieth-century "women's romance," with its secular transcendence sited in the female protagonist's eventual emotional union with her male lover. In her work on popular fiction, Jean Radford shows how the spiritual transcendence that has long been characteristic of the mass-market romance would, in the decades after the Edwardian period, come to be bounded by human interiority: "[M]agic/supernatural/ Providential force is in today's romance represented as coming from *within:* as the magic and omnipotent power of sexual desire."[63] While the romantic experience portrayed in Corelli's passage may be intended as purely spiritual, this ecstatic moment is both psychologically realistic and believably earth-bound. This is the second sense in which happiness in *The Treasure of Heaven* comes to depend on romance: the romantic convention of the lovers' hard-earned union. The convention is so common in romantic literature across the centuries that it would hardly be worth mentioning but for the fact that Corelli's scene of romantic consummation is conveyed through an image of holiness: Christ's chalice. The scene thus offers an implicit riposte to what Corelli considered the profane depictions of heterosexual love in much of the fiction of her day.

But the third and most interesting sense in which "romance" brings happiness here, and in the novel as a whole, is generically self-referential. The passage just quoted continues with a self-conscious turn to Corelli's inspiration in the romantic literary tradition. Bathed in rosy light, Angus recites lines from "Idylls of the King," and muses,

> "That is Tennyson—the last great poet England can boast. . . . The poet who hated hate and loved love."
>
> "All poets are like that," she murmured.
>
> "Not all, Mary! Some of the modern ones hate love and love hate!"
>
> "Then they are not poets," she said. "They would not see any beauty in that lovely sky—and they would not understand—"
>
> "Us!" finished Angus. "And I assure you, Mary at the present moment, we are worth understanding!" (327–28)

For Mary Deane, the themes that "modern" poets would not understand are "the infinite joy of nature" (327)—as represented by the glorious sunset—and the spiritual consummation of romantic love. This scene of love between Mary and Angus illustrates something about Corelli's romance that we can discern only by keeping her many literary references in view. The long catalogue of allusions that pepper this novel includes Villon, Shakespeare, George Herbert, Bunyan, Coleridge, Byron, P. B. Shelley, Keats, the Brownings, and, repeatedly, Tennyson. Such literary wellsprings are in keeping with the education Corelli received as a girl, which featured readings in Shakespeare, Scott, Dickens, and the Romantic poets; we know that the adolescent Corelli hoped someday to emulate Byron and Keats.[64] As she described herself, she wrote out of a poetic, rather than a prose, tradition: "My education has been varied, almost desultory, half foreign, half English, the usual sort of thing bestowed on young ladies who are not expected to do aught in the world but dress fashionably and make themselves agreeable. For the rest I have educated myself. Always fond of literature, I have, by choice and free-will, studied Homer and the Classics, the best French, German and Italian authors, together with all the finest works in the

English language—particularly the poets, such as Byron, Keats, Shelley, and the king of them all, Shakespeare."[65] Corelli's construction of "literature," as it appears in this passage from 1890, had not discernably shifted by the time she published *The Treasure of Heaven.* The forms alluded to throughout the 1906 novel—Arthurian romance, Provençal lyric, English Romanticism, and the Victorian medieval revival—were clearly considered in and of themselves to convey spirituality. It is little wonder that Angus Reay is portrayed as vehemently rejecting writing journalism in favor of composing romances, as in the same autobiographical passage, Corelli pointedly contrasts such lofty forms with contemporary journalism: "I have systematically and persistently avoided reading the penny newspapers, detesting their morbidness, vulgarity, and triviality. The mere news, stated in the telegrams, has always sufficed for me; and I have fed my mind on books in lieu of reading articles."[66] This avowal reflects a polarity that she seemed to affirm through her entire career: the binary of "timeless" literature versus all other forms of writing (especially journalism), which were alleged to amount to mere ephemera.

Studding the narrative of *The Treasure of Heaven* from start to finish, the many references to English-language authors in the romance tradition, both poets and prose writers, constitute Corelli's secular scripture. In fact, for all of the opening scene's apocalypticism, the Bible is infrequently alluded to in this novel. Instead, Corelli's continuous braiding of the modes of premodern romance and English Romanticism serves the role of a para-religious canon. This romantic[67]—and itself romanticized—canon is opposed to both "modern" literary practices that allegedly "hate love and love hate," and "the sheer brutal selfishness of the modern social world" (156). David Helmsley, Mary Deane, and Angus Reay draw upon this romantic canon for their spiritual resources and as a defense against the depraved encroachments of "the modern." Just as these three characters embrace the seemingly timeless life of the pastoral community, so too are they well-read in seemingly timeless literature. In representing the continuity between the romance mode and social issues, they figure an imaginary resolution to what Williams identifies as "the crisis of knowable community." While the London of Corelli's opening tableau represents the demonic transformation of social reality into the community that is allegedly known to be evil, the rural Cornwall society that Helmsley discovers offers its utopian counterpoint—the "knowable community" that is virtuous.

It is telling to juxtapose *The Treasure of Heaven*'s representation of rural English society with a contemporary documentation of Edwardian village life. In his 1912 study, *Change in the Village,* wheelwright George Sturt compiled years' worth of observation of his home village of the Bourne, Surrey, and arrived at a pessimistic conclusion:

> We are shocked to think of the unenlightened peasants who broke up machines in the riots of the eighteen-twenties, but we are only now beginning to see fully what cruel havoc the victorious machines played with the defeated peasants. Living men were "scrapped"; and not only living men. What was really demolished in that struggle was the country skill, the country lore, the country outlook; so that now, though we have no smashed machinery, we have a people in whom the pride of life is broken down: a shattered section of the community; a living engine whose fly-wheel of tradition is in fragments and will not revolve again.[68]

It is precisely "the country skill" (in the form of basket weaving), "the country lore," and "the country outlook" that have come to heal David Helmsley; we may suspect that Corelli's romanticization of rural English life in the early twentieth century offers the diametrical opposite to Sturt's documentary realism. In contrast to the Corellian nostalgia for an organic community, Sturt offers a vision of rural dwellers who have lost their communitarian moorings: "In the new circumstances" of Free Trade, we are told, the village resident "lives in an environment never dreamed of by the peasant" (170). Horizons of social meaning have receded beyond the economic vanishing point, as "vast commercial and social movements, unfelt in the valley under the old system, are altering all its character; instead of being one of a group of villagers tolerably independent of the rest of the world, he is entangled in a network of economic forces as wide as the nation; and yet, to hold his own in this new environment, he has no new guidance" (Sturt, *Change,* 171).

Whether or not Corelli was acquainted with the contemporary rural existence chronicled by Sturt, her novel's implicit cure for the more general alienations of modernization is to be found in the secular scripture that is embedded throughout *The Treasure of Heaven.* In the end, this is a tale of individual alienation redeemed by a rediscovered collective ethos and communication with the cosmos, by the Corellian healing of what T. S. Eliot would famously call the "dissociated sensibility." As such, *The Treasure of Heaven* offers a modernization of the romance mode, as defined by Northrop Frye, who asserts that the genre traditionally "presents an idealized world: in romance heroes are brave, heroines beautiful, villains villainous, and the frustrations, ambiguities, and embarrassments of ordinary life are made little of. Hence its imagery presents a human counterpart of the apocalyptic world which we may call the *analogy of innocence.*"[69] This eschatological figure for the setting of all romance literature, which conflates a prelapsarian scene with the Bible's prophesied return of God's Kingdom to earth, well conveys the represented universe of Corelli's novel. We need only juxtapose the depiction of an Edenic Cornwall with the opening scene of an infernal London to discern the traditional Manicheanism of the romance mode. Within this represented life-world, the heroic "ambitions of man are identified with, adapted to, or projected on the gods"[70]—in this case, both the traditional Christian God and the "gods" of Corelli's selective canon of romantic literature, as assembled through the novel's series of allusions. Thus, Corelli adheres to such generic traditions of the romance form, even as she self-reflexively celebrates them. Ultimately, *The Treasure of Heaven* derives its narrative tension from the juxtaposition of this wellspring of romantic values with the allegedly soulless Edwardian metropolis—a fallen social reality, emblematized by the murderous motor car, and depraved precisely to the degree to which it partakes of modernity. To achieve this romance polarity, however, she must overlook the contemporary reality of the (in Sturt's eyewitness description) "shattered" and "fragmented" rural community.

As the plot of *The Treasure of Heaven* signified a pastoral wish fulfillment on behalf of the traditionally virtuous, so too did the novel's vast popularity—like that of many of her other best sellers—come to represent Corelli's revenge on the alleged cynicism of the high realist or naturalist modes, and the intelligentsia who favored them. Eight years later, she published *Innocent: Her Fancy and His Fact,* a romance that more directly indicts the cultural cognoscenti. Like the virtuous characters of *The Treasure of Heaven,* the eponymous protagonist of *Innocent* is a reader of romance literature. In this case, the values she learns from her reading bring her into tragic confrontation with the vanguard scene of the arts in London. The eighteen-year-old Innocent leaves the country for the city and eventually becomes a successful writer of romances, finding acclaim in the metropolis. In the end, she dies of a broken heart, metaphorically slain by the "modernist" attitudes toward life and love embodied in her would-be paramour, the bohemian artist Amadis de Jocelyn. The symbolic redemption of the romance mode, however, is figured in the glorious popular response to Innocent's books.

Historical ironies surround this work from the late period of Corelli's career.[71] Despite its depiction of Innocent's literary success, the novel was published just as Corelli's popularity had begun to decline.[72] Moreover, there is the matter of Corelli's portrayal of London's literary-artistic milieu. The eight years between *The Treasure of Heaven* and *Innocent,* 1906–14, were a time of ferment in the arts in London—witnessing the arrival of New Zealand writer Katherine Mansfield, the new literature of Ford Madox Ford's *English Review,* the advent of Ezra Pound and imagist poetry, the postimpressionist exhibit of Roger Fry, and the ascendance of painter Wyndham Lewis and his vorticist avant-garde, among other things. Together with the Bloomsbury Group of Fry, the intersecting coteries of Mansfield, Ford, Pound, and Lewis (referred to at the time as "les jeunes") are now, of course, recognized as the vanguard of high modernism in England, but the term *modernist,* while it had many and complex valences, did not yet refer to these artists or their movements. Before World War I, literature referred to as modernist corresponded generally to what is today classified as realism and naturalism. In the words of one Edwardian critic, in a 1908 study entitled *Modernism and Romance* (wherein modernism is denigrated and the romance is lauded), the "modernist" novelist "attempts to give to each note on a flute and each petal on a flower a significance which is measured only by its effect upon character. This is 'modernism' with a vengeance."[73] The critic is referring to popular novels—those of the New Woman writers, Arnold Bennett, G. K. Chesterton, John Galsworthy, and others—that we would today loosely group under the rubric of psychological realism. And so when *Innocent*'s narrator excoriates "modernist" attitudes, which serve here as a locus of evil as clearly as does high-society London in *Treasure of Heaven,* this semantic distinction must be recognized. What Corelli calls "modernism" in this novel refers to early twentieth-century discourses of sexuality, psychology, and materialism, as expressed both in contemporary literature and art and, more generally, in the talk and behaviors of metropolitan sophisticates. What we refer to currently as the cultural movements of high (or "classic") modernism are nowhere in evidence, as Corelli, resident of Stratford-on-Avon, appears to have been unaware of the literary-artistic innovators of London's prewar avant-garde. But by a paradox of literary history, Corelli's impassioned attack on "modernist" or materialist values resembles the idealist critique of modernity conveyed in much of the emergent art and literature now grouped under the rubric of high modernism.

In its use of the contrasting settings of country and city, *Innocent* inverts the plot trajectory of *The Treasure of Heaven.* In the earlier novel, as we have seen, the protagonist is spiritually poisoned by the city and thereafter redeemed by a rural community. In *Innocent,* the heroine is nurtured in the secluded, utopian world of the "yeoman" farmer and later victimized by the city. At the story's opening, we learn that Innocent has been lovingly reared by her adoptive father, Hugo Jocelyn, in a sixteenth-century farmhouse that retains the atmosphere of the 1500s. Briar Farm, we are told, was established during the reign of Queen Elizabeth by a French knight, Amadis de Jocelin, who left the intrigue-ridden court of the duke of Anjou to pursue a simpler, rural existence. We witness here, of course, a fictive-historical rhyme with Helmsley's flight from city to country in *The Treasure of Heaven.* Over the centuries, the original de Jocelin's farm has remained largely unchanged. With its artisanal fittings and furnishings, its gendered division of labor, and its freedom from the "morbid analysis of life" of "our present shiftless day," Briar Farm preserves as in a time capsule the social milieu of the premodern rural gentry.[74] Innocent derives her strong but humble character from the experience of this honest, rustic life and absorbs idealistic views of love through constant reading of the three-hundred-year-old "essays, sonnets, and rhymed pieces" of the farm's founder, in the form of manuscripts that she finds in a secret chamber.

The utopian microcosm of Briar Farm is portrayed as superior to urban modernity because Hugo Jocelyn embodies the values of the traditional yeoman farmer and eschews contemporary technologies.[75] In the second half of the novel, Corelli further protests modernity through her representation of London's cultural vanguard. Upon her arrival in the city, Innocent takes rooms with the kindly, aristocratic Lady Lavinia Leigh. Eighteen months later, when Innocent has published two romances to widespread acclaim, Lady Leigh has "guided and chaperoned" Innocent into "the mighty vortex of London" (254)—specifically, a metropolitan high society that celebrates its latest literary and artistic finds. In these later scenes of the novel, the allegorical force of Innocent's name becomes fully evident—she is diametrically opposed in spirit to the kind of artists and patrons who inhabit London's cultural coteries. A strain of populism informs Corelli's damning portrait of supercilious bohemianism, and, together with her implicit antielitism, Innocent also represents a spiritualized feminism. As one lord tells her, "You are famous and independent, but the world is not always kind to a clever woman even when she is visibly known to be earning her own living. There are always spiteful tongues wagging in the secret corners and byways, ready to assert that her work is not her own and that some man is in the background, helping to keep her!" (345). The humble Innocent, however, knows no bitterness. In succeeding against the odds in a masculine sphere of cultural accomplishment, this protagonist seems intended to inspire female readers by example rather than by explicit feminist philosophy. Moreover, unlike *The Sorrows of Satan,* this novel does not allegorize contemporary social ills through its female lead. Melodramatic evil will take masculine (but nonsupernatural) form, in a gendering that is doubly derived: both from Corelli's late-in-life experience of personal disappointment in heterosexual romance and from the social milieu of the new London art world of the 1910s.

The novel's prime incarnation of bohemian vice appears in the person of Amadis de Jocelyn, a London painter who bears the same name (with that telling vowel change) as Innocent's idolized French knight. Innocent falls in love with *this* de Jocelyn, who plays at passion but eventually abandons her. Innocent dies soon thereafter, the victim of de Jocelyn's ultramodern, antichivalric code of masculine self-regard. De Jocelyn indexes cultural tendencies antithetical to the small-r romance and capital-R Romantic canon arrayed through *The Treasure of Heaven,* which lacks any such villainous embodiments. In this way, Corelli returns to the mode of allegorical melodrama seen in *The Sorrows of Satan,* but there is a new generic touch here, as the character of de Jocelyn offers an element (rare in Corelli's romances) of the roman à clef. He is at least partly based on the non-avant-garde painter Arthur Severn, for whom Corelli was suffering an unrequited (if platonic) passion at the time of the novel's composition.[76] Severn (1842–1931), a protégé of John Ruskin's, was an occasional exhibitor at the Royal Academy and the New Watercolour Society; Corelli met him at Brantwood in the Lake District in 1906, and they sustained a friendship that had by 1914 become strained, as a result of Corelli's flirtatious pursuit of emotional intimacy with this married man. As her voluminous letters to him reveal, she felt spurned and was moving from frustration to rage at the time of *Innocent*'s writing.

Corelli believed that Severn was a great painter who had yet to garner the recognition he deserved; she considered him the reincarnation of J. M. W. Turner.[77] In reality, the seventy-year-old Severn had by 1912 achieved moderate success as a landscape artist in the Romantic tradition of Turner and John Constable. It is telling, then, that one of the villainous Amadis de Jocelyn's paintings, titled *Wild Weather,* is represented as Romantic: "It was what is called by dealers an 'important work,' and represented night closing in over a sea lashed into fury by the sweep of a stormy wind. So faithfully was the scene of terror and elemental confusion rendered that it was like nature itself, and the imaginative eye almost looked for the rising waves to tumble liquidly from the painted canvas." (267). Corelli's template here was likely one of Turner's turbulent seascapes, such as *The Junction of the Thames and the Medway* (1807) or *The Storm (Shipwreck)* (1823). This symbolic triangulation, then—J. M. W. Turner, Arthur Severn, and the fictional Amadis de Jocelyn—centrally informs the London art world depicted in *Innocent.* It also echoes, through the art world parallel, *The Treasure of Heaven*'s importation of Romanticism into an early twentieth-century social milieu. But here, in the hands of a bohemian, hypermasculine artist, that Romanticism is shown to be corrupted; the urban painter de Jocelyn presents the converse to the rural writer Angus Reay.

The real-life source of that imagined corruption of Romanticism is not hard to find. De Jocelyn's characterization represents the displacement of Corelli's personal symbols for Severn, as we find them preserved in her side of their many years' correspondence.[78] In the first year of their friendship, initiated in the summer of 1906, Corelli sent letters to husband and wife jointly, often addressing them as "Arthur Pendragon and Queen Joan." By June 1907, however, she had soured on Joan Severn and began to refer to her in letters addressed to Arthur alone as "Mrs. Cormorant McGlorious." There followed many long solo visits by Arthur to Corelli's home in Stratford-on-Avon—she would turn her music room into an artist's studio for his use at these times—and her correspondence became more frequent, sometimes near-daily, as is evidenced in the copious archives of the library at the University of Detroit Mercy. Her pet names for Severn varied from "Beloved Pendragon" to "Carissimo Benissimo Pendragonissimo" to the diminutive "Pen."

She did not merely couch her relationship with Severn in terms taken from medieval romance; she projected as its ideal form the bond between John Keats and Arthur's father, Joseph Severn. In 1820–21, the elder Severn had nursed the phthisic Keats during his last months in Rome; Severn's grave flanks Keats's in the Protestant cemetery of the Italian capital. Of these facts, of course, Corelli was abundantly aware. The fact that she had met Arthur in Wordsworth's Lake District, at the home of Ruskin, a key Victorian champion of Romanticism, only encouraged her quixotic urge to channel the spirit of the Romantic poets through her choice of a beloved. Commemorations of the poets are frequent topics of these letters, as in the case of Corelli's discussion of the Keats-Shelley Memorial Association and its purchase in 1907 of the house in which Keats and Joseph Severn had lived: "Oh, if I were a millionaire, £10,000 would be nothing to me in the cause of honouring the memory of great poets, the true apostles of a nation."[79] In subsequent letters, she refers to Arthur's attendance at Keats-Shelley Association meetings and writes of her own viewing of theatrical matinées for the benefit of the association.[80] She writes of motoring with her companion Bertha Vyver to see the monument to Shelley ("It depicts Mary Shelley supporting the drowned poet in her arms"), and she contemplates the genius of Byron, implicitly associating it with her own, in a play for Severn's sympathy: "[I]t is always unfortunate to have gifts like his so much above the average—genius always craves for beauty which it cannot find, and builds up ideals which are bound to be destroyed."[81] Reading *Fors Clavigera,* she muses on Ruskin's Romantic visions of an organic community, one that might join aesthetic idealism with the possibility of social regeneration: "I feel that the great Master was often very sorrowful—and must have been (in his heart) . . . disappointed in the people he sought to teach. What Utopian dreams!—and no one has yet realized Utopia!"[82] Corelli saw herself as having a profound emotional-intellectual connection with Severn; the Romantic inheritance she imagined his father had bequeathed to him would find its spiritual complement in her practice of romance writing.

Arthur Severn was willing to share Corelli's cultural enthusiasms and indulge her obsession with the male English Romantic poets; what he was unwilling to participate in, however, was the deeper emotional intimacy, verging on eroticism, that she was trying to achieve. She sometimes attempted advances through girlish flirtatiousness. By 1912, her letters had begun to be signed "studio-boy," in a playful and ironic reference to her imagined role as painter's assistant (in reality, she believed herself the established genius, and he the underappreciated artist who could profit by her influence and connections). In May of that year, she chided him for not taking care of his health, suggesting, "Play tennis in your birthday garment if Joan permits!—only don't tell *me* about it for I am teaching myself *not to care!* 'Caring' is only resented as a sort of stupid tyranny."[83] Three months later, on the occasion of flooding in England, she eroticized the swollen River Severn: "Oh, Severn!—what a relentless river you are to bear down on the gentle Avon in so ruthless and overwhelming a manner!"[84] The lightheartedness disguises the fact, evident elsewhere, that she yearned for Arthur to demonstrate the same devotion to her that his father had to the great poet. This is the emotional bond she sought from "the son of your father who had such sweet faith in Keats," from the scion of a man "immortalized as he is by tenderness in friendship."[85]

Corelli's fixation on homosociality between men from an earlier century presents interesting gender implications for her libidinal energies vis-à-vis Arthur Severn. Her casting herself as the servile "studio-boy" of the older artist, certainly, gives the archivist pause. Without psychoanalyzing, we might suppose that these male relationship paradigms offered a lighthearted cover of respectability to what might have become (on Corelli's side, at least) a potentially scandalous heterosexual intimacy between a married man and an unmarried woman. No matter how playfully she invoked these personal symbols, however, Corelli could not hide her pain when, in the spring of 1913, it finally sank in that Arthur could not be, and perhaps more important, did not wish to be, her tender *gallant.* A letter from this stage in the relationship contains the origins of the character of Amadis de Jocelyn:

> The "warm-hearted," "sensitive" temperament you have disparaged with such Schopenhauer-like scorn, shall be relegated to the forgotten "beginning of things"—say about 1909–10—when I knew a man named Arthur Severn, purporting to be the son of one Joseph Severn, whose *tenderness, patience, thoughtfulness,* and *sympathy* for the *too* sensitive "overwrought" Keats gave his name an imperishable glory. I rejoiced at my good fortune in being *allowed* a friendship with the son of such a man—this Arthur whom I named Pendragon—especially when *he* in turn seemed to like *me* so much as to make me his Studio-boy! . . . Anyhow, he *went,*—and *another* man came and *pretended* to be the real Arthur Pendragon . . . how *could* he be King Arthur? . . . who always remembered after all that the "boy" was a woman, not made of iron or steel, but soft flesh and blood, with impulses and emotions that could not be killed without killing *her* as well![86]

In *Innocent,* completed a year later and published (after delays brought on by the start of the Great War) in late October 1914, the antagonist is a would-be *gallant* who proves a heartless fiend and causes the heroine's death. Unusually among Corelli's romances—among any romances of the period—evil triumphs. In response to a sardonic comment on Severn's part, that reading *Innocent* had drawn from him "two big tears," Corelli replied that Innocent's "great mistake was the making of a *tender ideal* out of an ugly *'Real'!*"[87] Relatively late in her life (she was about to turn sixty), Corelli's sole experience of heterosexual love had led to this embittered comment on what was, after all, her own romance-writing career.

In the last letter quoted above, Corelli cites praise for her artistry by an acquaintance, the London playwright Charles Haddon Chambers: "[H]e could find 'thirteen of the dozen' even like 'Amadis de Jocelyn'—especially among artists!" De Jocelyn's depravity is inspired by Corelli's personal disappointment with the individual, but she is also depicting a contemporary social type, the cynical urban bohemian. As if to underscore the evils of de Jocelyn's fashionable secularism, Corelli's third-person narrator explains that

> he had joined one or two of the new schools of atheism and modernism started by certain self-opinionated young University men, and in the early stages of his career had in the cocksure impulse of youth designed schemes for the regeneration of the world, till the usual difficulties presented themselves as opposed to such vast business,—he had associated himself with men who followed what is called the "fleshly school" of poetry and art generally, and had evolved from his own mentality a comfortable faith of which the chief tenet was "Self for Self"—a religion which lifts the mind no higher than the purely animal plane;—and in its environment of physical consciousness and agreeable physical sensations, he was content to live. (363)

As in *The Treasure of Heaven,* so too here is one of the sources of corruption in modern attitudes labeled "atheism," but in this novel the term is paired with another: "modernism." Corelli's narrator goes on to associate these two "schools" of thought with the newer intellectual discourses of her Edwardian moment. "Schemes for the regeneration of the world" connote socialism; "the 'fleshly school' of poetry and art" hints at new explorations of sexuality in literature and the arts and the Decadence movement of the 1890s; the new "faith" of "Self for Self" and the "purely animal plane" smack of Darwinism; Jocelyn's focus on "physical consciousness and agreeable physical sensations" alludes to the emergent discourses of psychology and materialism. All of these tendencies are condemned as mean and cynical; indeed, our narrator elsewhere suggests that "to express sorrow, pity, tenderness, affection, or any sort of 'sentiment' whatever is to expose one's self to derision and contempt from the 'normal' modernist who cultivates cynicism as a fine art" (328). An example of the "normal modernist," then, Amadis de Jocelyn serves as an allegorical figure both for masculine sadism and for the intellectual and artistic tendencies of the secular vanguard.

It is important to keep in mind the dialectical turn in the semantics of "modernism" between Corelli's moment and our own. What she refers to here as "modernism" is the set of intellectual and artistic trends we now consider to have been subsumed and transformed by high modernism. As if to illuminate the distance between Corelli's and the current use of the term *modernist,* the artist Jocelyn is no postimpressionist, fauvist, or cubist but, rather, a figurative artist of landscapes and portraits.[88] But in character, if not in his neo-Romantic painting, the fictional Jocelyn today brings to mind the rebels of *les jeunes,* as in this description of his notoriety: "[H]e was a somewhat famous personage,—famous for his genius, his scorn of accepted rules . . . as well as for his *brusquerie* in society and carelessness of conventions" (265). We are also told that his paintings have been twice rejected by the stuffy Royal Academy but accepted by the French Salon and that he cuts a prickly figure on the London scene. Given this characterization, it may not be too fanciful to suggest that Jocelyn bears a certain resemblance to Percy Wyndham Lewis, leader of the vorticist avant-garde and chief editor in 1914 of its journal, *Blast.*

Although Corelli is unlikely to have even heard of Wyndham Lewis, much less the other members of the London avant-garde whom we now recognize as central figures in high modernism, the unintentional resemblance between the fictional character and the real artist may lead us to juxtapose *Innocent* and *Blast.* The avant-gardists, for their part, were aware of Corelli and used her name in the journal to help define the cultural tendencies that they wished to condemn. Lewis's manifestos in *Blast* ridicule both Corelli herself by name and "Corelli Lady Riders,"[89] the heroines of her romances. Such misogyny and stylized masculine aggression are to be found throughout the journal's pages, most notably in contributions from Ezra Pound, and notwithstanding the inclusion of one work by a woman, Rebecca West's short story "Indissoluble

Matrimony," which displays a stylistic bellicosity found nowhere else in her work.

In addition to misogyny, the jabs at Corelli likewise exemplify the antagonism that high modernist writers felt toward what they viewed as degraded popular culture. An unexpected irony arises in this juxtaposition: through the voice of her narrator in *Innocent*, Corelli offers as sharp an attack on the commercialization of the emergent mass-market fiction industry as may be found in *Blast*'s manifestos. Regarding Innocent's first, wildly successful romance, we learn that "she had produced a Book. Not an ephemeral piece of fiction,—not a 'Wells' effort of imagination under hydraulic pressure—not an hysterical outburst of sensual desire and disappointment such as moves the souls of *demimondaines* and dressmakers,—not even a 'detective' sensation—but just a Book—a real Book, likely to live as long as literature itself. It was something in the nature of a marvel, said those who knew what they were talking about, that such a book should have been written at all in these modern days" (243–44). Not only did Corelli here demonstrate her awareness of the embryonic categories of mass-market fiction—science fiction, the "sex novel," the detective story[90]—but also she clearly wanted to avoid any such market-based compartmentalizing of her own work, even as she recognized the near impossibility of doing so "in these modern days." As do her character Innocent's romances, so too would Corelli's novel redeem literature of the taint of commerce; almost despite herself she shared the high modernists' desire for an art that would transcend the incursions of market forces. And if the market-based fragmentation of the reading public is a symptom of what Raymond Williams calls "the crisis of knowable community," then both Innocent's fictional and Corelli's real reading publics, transcending the demographic categories of the incipient mass-culture industry, would fight that symptom with a de facto community of shared values.

For all their obvious differences from Corelli, then, if we step back and consider the subsequent history of Lewis, Pound, Eliot (a contributor to the second issue of *Blast*), and their fellow literary innovators, we can discern that both Corelli and this masculinist subset of the high modernists wrote works that represent reactions to the broadest social features of modernity. Corelli's stark moral polarity between the country and the city may imaginatively reflect the same nonsynchronous modernization that, by a broadly historicist account, catalyzed the modernists' intellectual formation. Jameson suggests that "what we now call artistic or aesthetic 'modernism' essentially corresponds to a situation of incomplete modernization."[91] At its material base, this uneven modernization consists of "a world that is still organized around two distinct temporalities: that of the new industrial big city and that of the peasant countryside" (Jameson, *Singular,* 141). Intellectuals and writers born in mid- to late nineteenth-century Europe, Jameson suggests, "live[d] in two distinct worlds simultaneously. This simultaneity can no doubt for the moment be cast in terms of some distinction between the metropolis and the provinces; but it might better be imagined in terms of a situation in which individuals originate in a *'pays,'* a local village or region to which they periodically return, while pursuing their life work in the very different world of the big city" (142). Despite the scorn directed toward her by other intellectuals of her time, Corelli deserves to be considered an intellectual of this description. Born in London, she grew up from age ten in the countryside of Surrey and thus experienced both the metropolitan and rural contexts. Given her romances' contrasting depictions of urban and agrarian settings, and the fact that she chose as an adult to settle in the little village of Stratford-on-Avon, it is not too hard to guess which of these contexts she preferred in her own life. In Corelli's writing, as we have seen, both the new technologies and the new worldviews of urban modernity are excoriated; and while in high modernist writers such as Pound and Eliot the evaluation of contemporary technologies and attitudes is two-sided—an amalgamation of Old World nostalgia and cosmopolitan iconoclasm—the powerful reactions likewise provide the intellectual grain of their literature. For both the romancier and these high modernists, in other words, the catalyst of modernity functions similarly: "[F]orm and content—the narrative concept of modernity, the implantation of . . . industrial machines—come together with a well-nigh gravitational impact" (Jameson, *Singular,* 145).

This argument may be broadened to apply to other, and slightly later, canonical modernist figures, beyond "the Men of 1914." Indeed, what such writers as Pound, Eliot, James Joyce, Virginia Woolf, and Katherine Mansfield published *after* 1914 presents the most important parallel with Corelli, because of their deepening reaction (through the 1910s, '20s and '30s) against a realist aesthetic.[92] The canonical works of modernism have been observed to be constituted in part by their writers' desire to resist easy consumption, by a kind of authenticity-through-difficulty, and this fact represents a resistance to the commercial categories of an emergent mass culture. As we have seen, Corelli works into her romances a way for her readers to understand how those romances are superior to other commercially successful fiction—they are special, set apart, the Platonic form of "the Book," rather than any degraded, modern facsimile thereof. Just as the heroic Angus Reay has turned from journalism to a romance writing charmed by his earthly love for Mary Deane, so too do Innocent's romances descend upon the jaded reading public like an enchantment. Corelli's romances of 1906 and 1914, like the canonical works of the high modernists, present allegories of their own production, inventing mythic claims for a unique formal status that has no current social recognition or acknowledgment. Corelli eschews the secular realist aesthetic, in the face of its prestige as the preeminent mode of serious fiction, in favor of a romance mode that she would endow with unique formal status (think of the romance tradition invoked throughout *The Treasure of Heaven*). The high modernists, to jolt their readers' expectations, subsume that secular realist aesthetic into something new and strange. But they share the self-consciousness of their defiance of conventional realism. The Corellian romances investigated here, through their thematization of romance writing against a hostile urban world, and the modernist poem or narrative, through its linguistic defamiliarization of everyday life in that world, both offer this kind of self-referentiality.

Like Corelli, too, the high modernists did not intend their works to be cordoned off from social reality in an aesthetic sanctum, with little bearing on everyday life. It is easy to lose sight of this fact, as the mid-twentieth-century institutionalizers of high modernism saw fit to put *Ulysses* and *Mrs Dalloway* on museum pedestals, granting them a timeless aura. But of course high modernism should not be characterized as art for art's sake, for this denies its original, radical force. So far from aesthetic autonomy, the high modernists understood that their call to the Absolute was highly political and availed itself of the category of the aesthetic as *semi*-autonomous—as an Archimedean point from which to gain a greater critical distance on social reality than realism was achieving—but emphatically *not* as sealed off from that reality. T. S. Eliot's famous notion of the dissociated sensibility suggests that he intended his poetry to offer "a vision of a total social transformation which includes a return of art to some putative earlier wholeness."[93] For modernists such as Pound, Eliot, and Joyce—just as for Corelli—modern, degraded, commercial life is not extrinsic to the work of art. Instead, it is critiqued within that work of art and is negated in that work of art's radical vision.

In the end, to situate Corelli's romances in the neighborhood of the rather exalted edifices of the high modernists may seem grandiose. After all, most critics agree that writers such as Joyce and Woolf attempted to supersede the conventional realism of their day by deepening the representation of quotidian experience into new revelations. Corelli, by contrast, has correctly been said to figure the ideal by "distanc[ing] authentic meaning from the realm of the quotidian in order to situate it in a remote and unattainable domain."[94] The former may seem to move deeper into reality, the latter to move away from it. But Woolf, for example, famously describes her literary goals in a fashion that hints at the absolute: "[L]ife is a luminous halo, a semi-transparent envelope surrounding us from the beginning of consciousness to the end. Is it not the task of the novelist to convey this varying, this unknown and uncircumscribed spirit, whatever aberration or complexity it may display, with as little mixture of the alien and external as possible?"[95] There is more than a hint here of a romantic quest on the part of the author herself—a seeking after the portrayal of noumenal realities in the work of art. However differently, and however less appealingly to our own sensibilities, Corelli also sought to capture spiritual absolutes in her writing, and many of Corelli's readers felt that she succeeded in this effort. I want therefore to conclude with a speculation about that readership. Not alone among the successful woman romanciers of Edwardian Britain—others include Victoria Cross, Emma Orczy, Elinor Glyn, Ethel Dell—Corelli apparently had powerful insights regarding her public. She seems to have understood that individuals' affective reality often lay elsewhere than in those exterior spaces and objects, institutions and ideologies, addressed in the heavily plotted realist fiction of her time. Both her class of romance writer and the emergent modernists sought to de-emphasize plot and exterior description and to focus instead on the interior worlds, either moral or aesthetic, of the human psyche. The former did so through the transplanting of the premodern romance mode into twentieth-century social conditions; the latter, through Joycean and Woolfian experiments with form, through the "revolution of the word." Despite their vast formal and intellectual differences, then, both modernist literature and the Corellian romance presupposed parallel understandings of the collective psychology of their readers and offered what we might call "romances of interiority" at a unique moment in the development of British society, a time when such forms of imagined community could offer resources of meaning in often routinized and stultified working lives.

CHAPTER FOUR

The Women's Romance and the Ideology of Form

As can be seen in the previous chapters, any simple model of high versus low in turn-of-the-century British fiction fails to account for certain beguiling complexities, such as the mobility of texts and authors on the evolving literary field, or the ideological striations of popular narrative. The relationships between fin-de-siècle through early twentieth-century popular romances and high modernist works, especially in the instances of authorship by women, are more complicated than the reverse mirroring that is implied in the views of contemporary writers from either side of the putative divide, such as Marie Corelli and Rebecca West,[1] or the signatories to *Blast*'s manifestos. Another dimension to these relationships that needs addressing is the ideology embedded within narrative form. In the Edwardian decade, the division between romance and realist modes of fiction, which had been hotly debated by prominent writers of the 1880s and '90s, was being complicated by the practices of some popular writers who were grafting realist features to the romance frame or vice versa. We have already witnessed an example of such a hybrid in Mary Ward's *Lady Rose's Daughter.*

In this chapter, I consider the generic constitution of popular romances by Emma Orczy, Florence Barclay, and Elinor Glyn, narratives that should be considered the immediate antecedents of the twentieth century's "women's romances"—of the (British) Mills and Boon love story, of the (North American) Harlequin romance, and of the (global) best seller by Barbara Cartland, Ida Cook, or Georgette Heyer. These forerunners of the mass-market women's romance should be seen as specimens of a genre that historically antedates the realist and modernist (and, of course, postmodern) literary modes yet is precipitated for critics categorically, as a literary phenomenon of the modernist era, through its formal relations with those historically subsequent modes. While the late nineteenth- through early twentieth-century romance form can be said to have subsisted, evolved, and subdivided apart from and alongside these historically younger modes, it can simultaneously be seen to have lived on in variously subsumed strains within each mode.[2] Conversely, certain "progressive" tendencies of realism and modernism—in particular, their discourses of secularization and psychic interiority—began to infect the popular or mass-market romance, which in its earlier Victorian forms had often seemed conventionally moralizing, but by this time had come to emit more overtly contradictory messages.

My viral or microbic figure of mutually infecting "strains" is not intended to portray this generic development as an autonomous, organic growth in an idealized petri dish of literary culture. Any discussion of literary mode and genre in the British contexts of the period must also account for how the literary field mediates the "external" forces of rapid social change, new publishing technologies, and perhaps most significantly, the commodification of culture. As I demonstrate in chapters 1 and 2, we should heed Pierre Bourdieu, who urges an intellectual framework "that transcends the opposition between internal analysis (text) and external analysis (context) by relating the literary . . . field in which producers evolve, and where they occupy dominant or dominated, central or marginal positions, on the one hand, and the field of works, defined relationally in their form, style, and manner, on the other."[3] My approach in the Ward chapter combines close readings of two of her best-selling romances with a consideration of the particular "players" in action on the literary field of the period. Having discussed in some depth two major "players" of the years 1885–1925—Ward and Corelli—I now will focus less on the career trajectories of the writers in question and instead foreground what Bourdieu calls "the field of works," defined as the cultural plane of evolving literary modes or genres. In this chapter, in other words, I bracket off those broader social phenomena that Bourdieu analyzes, and I focus on the generic relations of the romance to realism and to emergent modern discourses.

The novels discussed in this chapter—Orczy's *The Scarlet Pimpernel* (1905), Barclay's *The Rosary* (1909), and Glyn's *Three Weeks* (1907)—represent three key aspects of early twentieth-century transformations of the romance form. First, the quickly mutating popular romance of the 1900–1914 period became in many instances more "realistic." It adapted to its own ends the characteristic attempts of Edwardian realism to represent male-female intimacy and the psychic states brought on by romantic and erotic love. Second, the romance of this period shares with an emergent modernist fiction the quest for the readerly experience of transcendence through representations of characters' psychic interiority, especially via secular conceptions of the forces of the unconscious. With their parallel (though still quite distinct) metaphoric representations of psychic interiority, incipient modernism and the popular love-romance may be aligned together in contradistinction to the more metonymic or synecdochic representation of realist fiction. Third, I lay the groundwork here for chapters 5 and 6, with their readings of some canonical modernists, by suggesting through the cases of Orczy, Barclay, and Glyn that certain elements of the romance mode—its metaphysics, its affective intensities, and its popular sublime—are subsumed and renovated by modernizing discourses that we might have initially presumed to be antithetical to romance fiction.

Emma Orczy's *Scarlet Pimpernel:* Good and Evil in the Historical Romance

> Was I wrong? Were those business men right who kept their fingers on the pulse of the reading public and said to me with a shrug: "Yes, I rather like your book, but the public does not care for that sort of thing. . . . Give them something modern, true to the life of to-day, not the romantic imaginings of a past they care nothing about."
>
> Emmuska Orczy, recording her doubts about the rejected 1903 manuscript of *The Scarlet Pimpernel* (*Links in the Chain of Life*)

CHAPTER 4

> A second-rate talent, like that of the Baroness Orczy, is quite unfitted to deal with colossal movements such as the French Revolution. Her treatment of the events of 1793, in spite of its historical groundwork, is absolutely inadequate.
>
> Anonymous review of Orczy's second novel, *I Will Repay* (*Saturday Review of Politics, Literature, Science and Art,* 24 November 1906)

Among the romances discussed in this chapter, Emmuska Orczy's *The Scarlet Pimpernel* is the title most likely to be familiar to readers today. The novel has been adapted into numerous stage and screen productions over the decades since its original London publication in 1905. The most recent of these, a 1997 Broadway musical and a 1998–2001 BBC-produced television series, have sparked a revival of interest in the original novel and its sequels, as attested by the clutch of fan-oriented websites that discuss "Baroness" Orczy's romantic narratives.[4] An archetypal hero-in-disguise, the character of the Scarlet Pimpernel is now cited as a forerunner to such popular-culture figures as Zorro, Batman, and Superman; the popularity of Orczy's original story has dimmed considerably over the past century, but the character of the Pimpernel has managed to persist in the anglophone mass-cultural imaginary as a second- or third-tier icon. Unlike any of the other romances scrutinized in this study (with the possible exception of E. M. Hull's *The Sheik*), this book's title took on a life of its own as a media term for disguised leaders or rescuers. For example, in the 1940s, the Scots Reverend Donald Caskie was dubbed "the Tartan Pimpernel," and the journalist Varian Fry, "The American Pimpernel," for their success in smuggling refugees out of Nazi-occupied areas during the Second World War. In the early 1960s, *Time* magazine and others referred to antiapartheid leader Nelson Mandela, whose disguises often helped him elude capture by the South African government, as "The Black Pimpernel."

Another unique feature of this romance hero is the fact that he appeared as a character in a popular melodrama before emerging in fiction. Cowritten with Orczy's husband Montagu Barstow, the stage *Pimpernel* debuted in Nottingham in 1903 and was produced fifteen months later at London's New Theatre. According to Orczy's 1947 autobiography, *Links in the Chain of Life,* this London premiere of 5 January 1905 met with "hot and strong" popular success, and despite critical disdain, the play continued for more than two thousand performances in London.[5] She had written the novel alone in 1903, before coauthoring its play form with her husband, but her publishing house, Greening and Company, had agreed to publish only on condition of the play's success. Orczy parlayed her box-office hit into the rapid publication of the novel; it was issued in standard six-shilling form on 12 January 1905 (one week after the play's stage debut) and, after eleven impressions in eleven months,[6] reappeared at Christmas adorned with illustrations by H. M. Brock. Arthur Greening, who had founded Greening and Company in 1897, would later recall that *The Scarlet Pimpernel* and Guy Thorne's *When It Was Dark* (1903) were the two publications successful enough to "set the firm on its feet" and attract new authors.[7] Finding contemporaneous sales figures is difficult, but *The Scarlet Pimpernel* appears on Desmond Flower's list of those turn-of-the-century novels that sold over 100,000 copies.[8] Also telling is the fact that advertisements of the time for Orczy's *The Elusive Pimpernel* (1908) proclaim that that novel, a second sequel to the original romance (*I Will Repay* was the first), had by 1910 sold 111,000 copies.

Orczy's tale would seem to offer a classic example of the action- and adventure-oriented narrative—also known as the eventuary romance—popularized in Orczy's time by H. Rider Haggard, Robert Louis Stevenson, Anthony Hope, Bram Stoker, Arthur Conan Doyle, and others.[9] There is, however, a central difference from these male authors' romances: despite the swashbuckling exploits of its titular hero, *The Scarlet Pimpernel* is at its core a passionate love story, narrated primarily from the perspective of its female protagonist, the Lady Marguerite Blakeney. The novel opens in medias res, as we are transported to the revolutionary Paris of 1792 and the vengeful atmosphere of "Mademoiselle Guillotine." The intrepid and mysterious Scarlet Pimpernel has been rescuing aristocrats out from under the noses of the murderous Jacobins and depositing them in the safety of a sympathetic England. There we meet the novel's Gallic heroine, Marguerite, who fears for the life of her counterrevolutionary brother yet despairs of any help from her foppish English husband, Sir Percy Blakeney. Only after kidnappings, spying, and secret messages—amidst the taverns of seaside villages and the opulence of high-society London—does Marguerite come to find that the persona of the aristocratic buffoon has been but one of her husband's many disguises and that he is the elusive hero of the novel's title. The passionate love that once distinguished their courtship rekindles, and the Scarlet Pimpernel ultimately rescues both the abducted Marguerite and her noble brother from the clutches of the villainous revolutionaries.

If *The Scarlet Pimpernel* should be generically classed as an adventure romance in the contemporary popular vein of Haggard, it would also seem to participate in the same tradition of the historical novel that prevents us from categorizing such Walter Scott novels as *Ivanhoe* and *The Fair Maid of Perth* as "pure" romances. While, for instance, the Africa of Haggard's *She* and *King Solomon's Mines* is clearly an imaginary space, Orczy's novel would re-create the backdrop of factual European history, with pronounced specificity regarding dates and locales. It is thus useful to revisit the generic definition of historical realism, particularly as it is articulated through the example of Scott, whom many have considered the preeminent historical novelist in English. Georg Lukács is often cited regarding Scott's generic character; he asserts in *The Historical Novel* that "Scott's historical novel is the direct continuation of the great realistic social novels of the eighteenth century."[10] Lukács asserts that Scott takes the features of realism exhibited in the groundbreaking fiction of Defoe and Fielding—spatiotemporal specificity, the centrality of dialogue, careful depiction of cultural manners and social circumstances—and locates them in past eras, with a view toward mimetic fidelity to those contexts. By the Lukácsian account, unlike previous novelists whose settings were historical, Scott does not merely exploit those historical contexts as inert backdrops, by superimposing the language and concerns of his present moment onto his locales; instead, he offers the fine-textured verisimilitude that critics traditionally associate with novelistic realism.

To a limited extent, Orczy's *Scarlet Pimpernel* exhibits such historical realism; one need only dip into the first pages of the novel to see that she is attempting a Scott-like fealty to the social contexts of late eighteenth-century France and Britain. The first chapter, "Paris: September, 1792," locates us at the West Barricade of the city and offers a restless panorama of shopkeepers, military officers, peasants, and leading Jacobins, all vexed by the derring-do of the anonymous Pimpernel. The second chapter, "Dover: 'The Fisherman's Rest,'" transports us to a rustic and comparatively peaceful Britain, peopled by common English social types as we might imagine them to have existed in the late eighteenth century. Orczy would capture the flavor of the yeoman and peasant classes' talk, as we see in this opening colloquy among young kitchen-maids and their thirsty publicans:

> "What ho! Sally!" came in cheerful if none too melodious accents from the coffee-room close by.
>
> "Lud bless my soul!" exclaimed Sally, with a good-humoured laugh, "what be they all wanting now, I wonder?"
>
> "Beer, of course," grumbled Jemima, "you don't 'xpect Jimmy Pitkin to 'ave done with one tankard, do ye?"[11]

Lest readers feel that Orczy fails in re-creating historically specific dialogue, her third-person omniscient narrator makes a point of informing us that these characters are typical of their time and place, as we see in this description of the pub's owner: "Mr. Jellyband was indeed a typical rural John Bull of those days—the days when our prejudiced insularity was at its height, when to an Englishman, be he lord, yeoman, or peasant, the whole of the continent of Europe was a den of immorality, and the rest of the world an unexploited land of savages and cannibals" (11). With such Fieldingesque commentary, the narrator pokes affectionate fun at English chauvinism, but at the same time Orczy is seeking to achieve Scott's goal: "to portray the struggles and antagonisms of history by means of characters who, in their psychology and destiny, always represent social trends and historical forces."[12]

More precisely, Orczy intended the Scarlet Pimpernel to represent the quintessence, as a foreign-born writer saw it, of the male English aristocrat. So much she claims in her memoir; when her readers ask her how she came to have "such a wonderful understanding of the British character," she confesses that this "tribute to my Scarlet Pimpernel always pleases me more than any other. . . . For that was what I aimed at when I first conceived him: a perfect presentation of an English gentleman" (*Links,* 7). In comparing the epic to the historical novel, Lukács tells us that "[t]he principal figures in Scott's novels are also typical characters nationally, but in the sense of the decent and the average, rather than the eminent and all-embracing. The latter are the national heroes of a poetic view of life, the former of a prosaic one" (*Historical Novel,* 36). Generically, then, Orczy's novel approximates the historical vein of Walter Scott's works (and more obviously, of Dickens's *A Tale of Two Cities*), but as these passages suggest, the novel's depicted universe is populated by characters who would not be out of place as the supporting personae, affectionately satirized, of a Fielding novel (one thinks, for example, of the blustery Squire Western from *Tom Jones*).While, as Lukács asserts, "Scott's greatness lies in his capacity to give living human embodiment to historical-social types" (35), Orczy's intense narrative preoccupation with social class and British national character yields a heroine, a hero, and supporting characters who function as sociohistorical ciphers, at the expense of their representational individuation. Moreover, the novel chronicles a linear plot of encounters between villains and heroes/heroines, in which the side of the good does eventually prevail, in the escape of the Pimpernel's victorious band and the scores of aristocrats they have rescued from the guillotine.

To invoke "the side of the good" is to return us to the traditional romance's plot-driving binarism of good versus evil, and thus to tip the text away from realism on the generic fulcrum. Apropos here is a modal definition that Northrop Frye offers in *Anatomy of Criticism;* in all romances, we are told, "[c]haracters tend to be either for or against the quest. If they assist it they are idealized as gallant and pure; if they obstruct it they are caricatured as simply villainous or cowardly. Hence every typical character in romance tends to have his moral opposite confronting him, like black and white pieces in a chess game" (195). In *The Scarlet Pimpernel,* the two-dimensional character who qualifies as an archetypal melodramatic villain—representative, like the Pimpernel himself, of a social category—is the Jacobin leader Citoyen Chauvelin, tireless obstructer of Marguerite and the Pimpernel. With his "shrewd, foxlike face" and "snakelike, noiseless movements,"

> Chauvelin had a purpose at heart. He firmly believed that the French aristocrat was the most bitter enemy of France; he would have wished to see every one of them annihilated: he was one of those who, during this awful

> Reign of Terror, had been the first to utter the historic and ferocious desire "that aristocrats might have but one head between them, so that it might be cut off with a single stroke of the guillotine." . . .
>
> Small wonder, therefore, that the romantic and mysterious personality of the Scarlet Pimpernel was a source of bitter hatred to Chauvelin. (87)

The narrator depicts Chauvelin as a representative of the class bias behind the Reign of Terror (characteristic of a historical novel) and posits these social passions as originating in the timeless evil of human malice (characteristic of the romance mode). Although there is no prominent religious thematic in the novel—indeed, one of its striking characteristics for the romance of the period is the absence of references to heroic piety—here we find a metaphysical force working as what Frye would refer to as a romance "displacement": in this instance, the character who embodies the social-class Other as an ur-source of evil. We might even say that Orczy's narrative has found its substitutions for the premodern romance's raw materials of magic and Otherness in the Scarlet Pimpernel and the Jacobin Chauvelin. In his remarkable ability to don disguises—as a knitting "old hag" at the West Barricade of Paris, as a "stooped" and "elderly" Jew in dirty gabardine—the Pimpernel effects a romantic magic that makes its peace with the historical novel, insofar as it is rationally explicable. Chauvelin, meanwhile, represents one face of the Other, that of preternatural malice, not because he is French (the good Marguerite is also French) but because he opposes the aristocracy. In this tale, the villain's evil is both metaphysical and socially contingent, based as it is in the familiar reality of class resentment. Chauvelin's attitude toward the upper class, then, is what channels his evil energy, and that frames the novel within the ethical binary characteristic of the romance and melodramatic modes.

Chauvelin's romance function as a force for evil qualifies all the more as traditionally melodramatic when we consider his psychic provenance in the life of the novel's author. Born and reared on the rural estate of Tarna-Örs in north-central Hungary, she spent her later youth in Budapest, Brussels, and Paris, before her family settled in London in 1880, when she was fifteen. She devotes the first chapters of her autobiography to her earliest remembered trauma, an attack by Hungarian peasants on her aristocratic family's farm in "an appalling tragedy which has never faded from my mind from that day to this" (*Links,* 11). As an adult, Orczy would recall this personal experience as a late marker of the collapse of feudalism in central Europe, and by her own admission, this historical phenomenon came to occupy a central, highly conscious place in her life and art. The first page of her memoir announces that "the ancestry of the Orczy family is traced back to the entry of Arpád and his knights into Hungary nearly two hundred years before the Norman Conquest" (*Links,* 7). Orczy's date is accurate; the year A.D. 895 is generally accepted as the moment at which the Magyars, under the leader Arpád, first settled in Hungary. In establishing her lineage, Orczy suggests a thousand-year continuity of eastern European feudalism, a social stasis that was finally broken by the tardy Hungarian modernization of the late nineteenth and early twentieth centuries. She tells us of her celebrated grandfather, who had a "taste for that extravagant and large-hearted hospitality for which the Hungarian landowners will always remain famous even in these days of poverty and democratic government" (*Links,* 10). Orczy assumes that her English-speaking readers of 1947 (the year of her autobiography's publication, and of her death) will sympathize with her nostalgia for an eastern Europe of the ancien régime, no matter how exotic to most of them, and will share her longing to return to a time before the crises of the twentieth century.

Born in 1865, Orczy tells us, she was able as a child to experience her nation's "brilliant declining years":

> [T]here were no wars or rumours of war, none at any rate that reached the ears of those splendid feudal lords ensconced in their opulent châteaux, mediaeval still in their magnificence, their hospitality; their contemptuous disregard of every innovation that threatened the even tenor of their lives—new-fangled rubbish, or inventions of the devil did they dub that abominable railway which cut through *their* estate, *their* forests, *their* fields; bolshevism they would have called it had the word been coined then, or communism which was the catchword of politicians and had no meaning that any sensible man could discern. (*Links,* 8)

She intends a gentle irony in this depiction of Old World attitudes among the Hungarian upper classes, but her tone is affectionate. It is telling that she does not correct the feudal lords' misattribution of nineteenth-century eastern European modernization to "communists"—they would seem to elide capitalism as the mode of production emerging after feudalism. Or perhaps the labeling of railway infrastructure as "communist" is Orczy's invention, imported into the mouths of nineteenth-century aristocrats and thus revealing her own prejudices. As in *The Scarlet Pimpernel,* here her atavistic social imaginary does not include the entrepreneurial classes of capitalist modernization. Instead, there are only peasants and aristocrats, classes that came into conflict over the building of a steam mill and the importation of farm machinery into the Orczy estate. Threatened by these technological advances, we are told, the peasants responded, in the summer of 1869, by burning all of the estate's crops while the feudal masters were occupied with celebrating the fifth birthday of Orczy's older sister. "The tragedy of that memorable 22nd of July," we are told, "was so appalling that I don't wonder my parents turned their back on it and never wished to see it again" (*Links,* 12). Orczy recounts the terror of a four-year-old girl snatched from the gaiety of a birthday party, only to witness the despair and resulting emigration of her aristocratic family to a series of European capitals.

It may be that Orczy's identification here with a premodern aristocratic ideology is a performance—after all, fans of *The Scarlet Pimpernel* are the presumed readership of the autobiography, and Orczy probably felt she had to maintain her nostalgia for *l'ancien régime.* But the question of whether her explicit social ideology, in both novel and memoir, is sincere or performed may be less significant than the fact that Orczy experienced this trauma as a very young girl, and so suggests that we may read *The Scarlet Pimpernel* as the trauma's working-out or displacement. Evidence can be found in the novel's first sentence, a depiction of the Parisian proletariat milling about the West Barricade, reveling in bloody upheaval: "A surging, seething, murmuring crowd of beings that are human only in name, for to the eye and ear they seem naught but savage creatures, animated by vile passions and by the lust of vengeance and hate" (1). The tale's portrayal of evil is consistently vehement; it is more expressive and seemingly *motivated* than the casual, understated portrayal of good. Not only in Chauvelin, then, but also in this mob scene do we see, in Frye's classic definition of the romance mode, the "stylized figures which expand into psychological archetypes" (*Anatomy*, 304). Orczy's public text may represent a private dream: a vengeful wish fulfillment for its author's dislocating childhood experience, as mediated through a romance in which that trauma is symbolically resolved.[13]

It is important finally to scrutinize the other protagonist of Orczy's tale, Marguerite Blakeney, from whose perspective, after her appearance in the sixth chapter, the bulk of the novel's action is witnessed. Referring again to Frye's features of the romance mode, we may note that Sir Percy Blakeney (the Pimpernel) represents a traditional romance protagonist—"superior in degree to other men and his environment" (*Anatomy*, 33). Lady Blakeney, via whose point of view most of the third-person narrative unfolds, is no less active a protagonist, but of course she diverges from Frye's criteria by virtue of her sex. She is nonetheless portrayed as "superior in degree to other" *women*, and not merely for her great beauty: her epithet is "the cleverest woman in Europe," and we are told that, prior to her marriage to Sir Percy Blakeney, this "fascinating young actress . . . glided through republican, revolutionary, bloodthirsty Paris like a shining comet with a trail behind her of all that was most distinguished, most interesting, in intellectual Europe" (40). At the same time, Marguerite is humanized by her nonaristocratic birth and her moral error, as she is blackmailed by Chauvelin into revealing the whereabouts of the Pimpernel in exchange for the life of her beloved brother back in France ("she had not been strong enough to do right for right's sake, and to sacrifice her brother to the dictates of her conscience" [118]). Marguerite is just ordinary enough, in these respects, to encourage Orczy's original middle- to lower-middle-class readers to identify with her. What is more, the character's strong meritocratic beliefs ("the only inequality she admitted was that of talent" [39]) probably reinforced that sense of connection, helping to overcome the potential hurdle of readerly identification with rich French aristocrats over the egalitarian, albeit militant, Parisian commoners. So it is that one of the enduring features of the romance mode identified by Gillian Beer—that its heroines and heroes often encode royal and/or aristocratic class status—may be said to accommodate itself to the early twentieth-century reading audience.

As an active female protagonist with an egalitarian streak, Marguerite Blakeney may be classified as a romance heroine with a tincture of contemporary realism. But *The Scarlet Pimpernel*'s romantic quest concedes less to such touches of modernized realism, even as it offers a generic suturing of its own. This romance features two separate quests, very different in kind: the metaphorically displaced slaying of the dragon that is the defeat of Chauvelin by the Scarlet Pimpernel, and the consummation of the romantic relationship between Marguerite and Percy, in a union that is at once physical and metaphysical. Although they were married a year before the time of the narrated action, the lovers have never consummated their marriage, because of a sudden estrangement that occurred hours after their wedding. The final achievement of their love is portrayed as fulfilling a spiritual ideal, but one that is morally and philosophically unconnected to the foiling of the Jacobin purges. The public quest is pursued in a romantic universe of good and evil, such that, as in Frye's conception of the romance mode, the hero's motives are in the end perfectly expressed and uncontradicted by his actions and the villain's corrupt heart is visible for all to see.[14] The private quest, however, is expressed on a different plane, one "beyond good and evil": the zone of romantic-erotic transcendence. In a line that we might now consider typical of the mass-market women's romance, the narrator says of Marguerite, "[I]t seemed to her that the only happiness life could ever hold for her again would be in feeling that man's kiss once more upon her lips" (123).[15] We should not allow our familiarity with popular or "soap opera" romance narratives, however, to blur the significance of such a depiction of passion for its own sake, lacking in moral edification. The estrangement and ultimate reconciliation of Orczy's male and female protagonists leaves them with a greater passion than their original love and hence represents the fulfillment of a spiritual ideal, but, in a manner that both breaks with the sentimental romance of the nineteenth century[16] and anticipates the twentieth-century mass-market romance, this is an ideal through which ethical categories recede in significance. It is transcendence as earth-bound intensity of affect—as the popular sublime—rather than as communication with godhead, as realization of a spiritual absolute, or as the supreme self-mastery of moral development.

In this kind of romance narrative, lovers are subject to a boundlessness of passion that takes them outside of themselves. Here is a typical love scene from Orczy's novel:

> Had she but turned back then, and looked out once more on the rose-lit garden, she would have seen that which would have made her own sufferings seem but light and easy to bear—a strong man, overwhelmed with his own passion and his own despair. Pride had given way at last, obstinacy was gone: the will was powerless. He was but a man madly, blindly, passionately in love, and as soon as her light footsteps had died away within the house, he knelt down upon the terrace steps, and in the very madness of his love he kissed one by one the places where her small foot had trodden. (139)

As we have seen in the case of Ward's *Lady Rose's Daughter*, the melodramatic mode may be said to relocate spiritual absolutes in the material world, through rhetorical excess—the recording of overwhelming yearnings and oceanic passions.[17] Meanwhile, traditional definitions of the sublime, derived from such sources as Kant and Burke, will tend to emphasize a paradoxical combination of fear and beneficent awe in the presence of a vast natural object or phenomenon; here, in its "popular" instantiation, the sublime may be said to combine a sweetness or delight with pain, in the presence of the overwhelming force—not the loved one, but rather the love itself. In some definitions, the sublime involves a positive self-forgetfulness, such that quotidian anxieties are superseded by a paradoxical sense of well-being and security in the very recognition of one's powerlessness. Yet other accounts tell us that the experience of the sublime entails a beneficial suspension of human reason. There are traces of each of these affective phenomena represented in Orczy's passage, but they are present in a fashion that is far from philosophically abstract, and indeed quite accessible to readers.

The twentieth-century romance of erotic fulfillment emphasizes a setting in everyday reality and represents a transcendence that is, to a degree unprecedented within the English-language tradition, contained by that secular universe, without the channeling to an otherworldly absolute.[18] At the same time, this emergent type of romance retains its roots in the centuries-old generic form; as Frye suggests, "[T]he quest-romance is the search of the libido or desiring self for a fulfillment that will deliver it from the anxieties of reality but will still contain that reality" (*Anatomy*, 193).[19] Orczy thus presages the movement beyond the slightly older mode of the popular sublime evidenced by the sometimes otherworldly romances of Corelli, which, in the cases of *The Sorrows of Satan* and *The Treasure of Heaven,* invoked angels and the devil. Readers will instead be channeled imaginatively toward inward absolutes, toward new accesses of interiority; the emerging language of the romance will not disregard the divine, but it will stretch beyond institutional religious discourses to broaden the scope of a natural divinity within, the divinity of desire.

Florence Barclay's *The Rosary:* The Religious Romance Meets Psychologism

> Heaven knows how in the tepid pages of *The Rosary* its million readers detected the power that lived in Mrs. Florence Barclay, that made her physically radiant as a young girl when she was a woman of sixty and permitted her to enjoy complete confidence that she was directly inspired by the Holy Ghost; but it must have leaked through some channel.
>
> Rebecca West, *Strange Necessity*

> The modern "Christianised" morality tale (albeit bereft of an overtly religious message) was exemplified in the work of Florence L. Barclay, one of Britain's most successful writers. In her work, religion is replaced by religiosity.
>
> Clive Bloom, *Bestsellers*

In *The Scarlet Pimpernel,* we detect an evolving strain of the romance that looks, from the perspective of our own era, like the embryo of what is to come. Readers had by that time come to feel the "popular sublimity" of this romance subgenre through its central romantic-erotic relationship, and this feature, in the first two decades of the twentieth century, characterized the generic precursor to what would later be known as the "women's romance." Both the battle between good and evil and the engagement with a personified natural environment (central elements in Frye's definition of the romance mode) rapidly receded in importance, even as they often continued, in secularized and displaced ways, to take pride of place in the other modern subgenres of romance, such as the mystery, the fantasy, detective fiction, science fiction, and the adventure story.

Another feature of the modern love-oriented romance that precipitated this subgenre as distinct from the others is that, with a few notable exceptions, the narrative point of view became exclusively that of the female protagonist. Writing of the popular women's romance of the mid- to late twentieth century, Jean Radford identifies these features:

> (*a*) the centrality of the love relationship with adventure/incident as subsidiary elements (whereas in the thriller/adventure story, incident is central and love element subsidiary or illustrative); (*b*) . . . the major relationship is between heroine and hero, whereas in male-directed genres it is between hero and villain; (*c*) most contemporary romance has a female protagonist, whereas most adventure stories star a male protagonist; (*d*) romance depends on a special relationship of identification between reader and protagonist whether the narration is in the first or the third person.[20]

All four of these tendencies can be discerned in Orczy's 1905 best-seller, which predates by a few years the arrival of the Mills and Boon romances (and later, the Harlequin romances) to which this catalogue primarily refers. However, there are two important reasons to hold off labeling Orczy's novel and its kind as "women's romances," in the later sense that concerns Radford. The first is not generic but rather a matter of reception: the best-selling novels discussed in this chapter were demonstrably aimed at and read by both women and men. In her autobiography, Orczy makes a point of thanking the many thousands of "men and women" who "took [her] books to their hearts"; the biographies of her contemporaries, other female romance writers, offer similar evidence that many of their appreciative readers were men.[21]

The second reason, more to the point in light of the genre, is that some of these proto–"women's romances" continued, through the Edwardian era and beyond, to be overtly religious in theme. The still-publishing Mrs. Humphry Ward, having earlier lost her elite readership, was by 1910 also beginning to lose her mass audience. The religious romance was on the wane but was not yet a defunct subgenre, as Florence Barclay was to prove with her 1909 novel, *The Rosary*. Written in 1905–7, it was published simultaneously in London and New York in November 1909; by October of 1910, it had, according to an advertisement in *Publishers' Weekly*, sold 100,000 copies, thereby becoming the highest-selling novel in both Britain and the United States in that year. The ad reads as follows:

> Nearly a year ago, *The Rosary* was published. . . . [I]ntelligent booksellers began to read it and discovered that rare and peculiar quality that commends it to *all classes* of readers, men and women, young and old. . . . Today, after a period when the life of most so-called "best-sellers" would have ended, *The Rosary* is preeminently the most popular book in the United States. . . . It has become evident that *The Rosary* is going to take its place with those few unusual books, such as *Henry Esmond*, *Uncle Tom's Cabin*, and *Ben-Hur*, whose life is not for a season or two, but for all time. OVER 100,000 SOLD.[22]

In 1912, the *Newsbasket*, a trade publication of the book retailer W. H. Smith, announced that "Florence Barclay's books are now more popular than [those of] the well-known authoress Marie Corelli."[23] Within a decade, *The Rosary* had been translated into eight European languages.[24] Contemporary reviews, however, tended to be critical of its sanguine religiosity. A critic in the *Nation* declared that the novel had a "sprinkling of humor, with sugar, honey, glucose, and saccharine in amounts bordering on the indigestable."[25] *Bookman* proclaimed *The Rosary* to be full of "religiously sensuous stories which ought to be as unwholesome to a normal mentality as candied rose-leaves to a college athlete."[26] The perception that this romance was both religious and "sensuous," as we will see, was astute and suggests Barclay's subtle receptivity to the modernizing romance discourse of her Edwardian moment.

While in certain respects Barclay was both Mary Ward's and Marie Corelli's literary descendant (born in 1862, she was eleven years Ward's junior, and seven years Corelli's), *The Rosary* is considerably more straightforward than *Robert Elsmere* in its plot and is closer to realism than anything published by Corelli. The thirty-year-old protagonist, Jane Champion, is a leisured aristocrat who maintains friendships with several eligible bachelors but as a "plain" and unusually tall woman does not manage to excite the amorous feelings of any man whom she feels worthy of her attention. Early in the story, there arrives in her coterie a witty and promising young painter, Garth Dalmain, who converts simultaneously to Christian belief and to the love of Jane, upon hearing her sing the popular hymn of the title. Despite her feelings for him, she rebuffs his proposal of marriage, privately deciding that this artist requires a beautiful wife to keep him satisfied; she flees on a three-year voyage to see the sights of North America, Japan, and the Middle East. In Egypt, she overhears fellow English tourists discussing a newspaper account of the blinding of her former suitor by a poacher's rifle. Rushing back to England, she disguises herself as a nurse, takes on a position as Garth's caretaker, and gradually realizes that he has been tending the flame of his love for her over the years. Upon revealing her identity to him, she accepts his standing offer of marriage and leads him to discover a new avenue for his artistic talents through musical composition.

Recent critics have attempted to explain the immense popularity of Barclay's romance. Philip Waller emphasizes the modern, tolerant nonintellectuality of Barclay's mix of romantic ecstasy and spiritual goodness[27]—a feature that may be contrasted with the late-Victorian intensity of *Elsmere*'s theology and the religious phantasms of Corelli's earlier romances. Joseph MacAleer calls Barclay a transitional figure in the development of British mass-market fiction and sees a more sophisticated publicity machine than had existed for the slightly earlier romance writers; by this account, Barclay's public image as an "everywoman" presages the post–Great War ascendance of the publisher, the imprint, and more targeted marketing, as distinct from literary celebrity.[28] This claim of targeted marketing, however, is partially undercut by evidence that, like nearly all other pre-1914 romances by women, Barclay's book appealed to readers of different classes and to men as much as women. For instance, Field Marshall Evelyn Wood, a "hero" of the 1857 Indian rebellion, and Edward Lyttleton, a public-school headmaster, were public admirers of *The Rosary*.[29] The boasts of magazine advertisements must be treated skeptically, but it is worth returning to the G. P. Putnam's Sons' ad quoted above, which found in *The Rosary* "that rare and peculiar quality that commends it to *all classes* of readers, men and women, young and old."

The most compelling account of Barclay's phenomenal success is to be found in the work of Mary Hammond, who also sees

The Rosary as marking a literary-historical watershed, for paradoxical reasons. First, there is Barclay's diluted religiosity, which makes few demands upon the British readers of 1910; the characters' High Anglican faith is thin gruel—vague, indistinct, and so unexamined as to be effectively ecumenical. As Hammond says, "[I]f further proof were needed of the shift from organized religion to the spiritual in novels that occurred during this crucial period, then this [novel] is probably it" (163). The prayer beads of the title[30] were not generally associated with Anglicanism, being used instead by Roman Catholics (as well as, in different forms and with different names, by Muslims, Buddhists, Hindus, and Sikhs). Second, in contrast to Ward's and Corelli's heroines, the highly independent Jane Champion (as her name conveys) is so athletic, healthy, and physically active as to constitute a feminist statement; she represents a thoroughly modern woman. Third, Barclay's book offered a riposte to the Edwardian "sex-novel," the emergent genre that, as mentioned in my introduction, was effectively bridging the lowbrow and the highbrow in fiction (Hammond, 167, 173). In this regard, the best-selling phenomenon of *The Rosary*—a reaction-formation against the modernized sexual discourse of both an Elinor Glyn and an H. G. Wells—serves as another illustration of "the low modern." We witness a contradiction: just as Barclay "owes a lot to the reworked depictions of femininity for which the New Woman novelists were famous, embracing their hard-won freedom from weakness, incompetence, and restrictive clothing" (Hammond, 168), so too does she offer a novel-length retort to depictions of "impurity" in fictional women.

In certain passages, that retort participates in the very discourse of sexuality that it would presume to counter. While the spiritual didacticism of Barclay's religious romance does parallel, in a less elaborated fashion, that of *Robert Elsmere,* the central love relationship is here staged quite differently. Not only is romantic love the primary raison d'être of the narrative but also, no matter how proper and pious its external manifestations, this romantic love is a different matter on the inside, as it were—Jane experiences it as a font of irresistible, unconscious drives. Garth's first onrush of love for Jane, on her singing of "The Rosary," is figured in Christian imagery of humble subservience. He asks himself, "Must there be a cross to every true rosary? Then God give me the heavy end, and may the mutual bearing of it bind us together."[31] Yet in the moments after Garth's proposal, as Jane takes time to ponder it, she envisions his soul and her own as two animals preparing to mate:

> Garth, tonight, was like a royal tiger who had tasted blood. It seemed a queer simile, as she thought of him in his conventional evening clothes, correct in every line, well-groomed, smart almost to a fault. But out on the terrace she had realised, for the first time, the primal elements which go to the making of a man—a forceful, determined, ruling man—creation's king. They echo of primeval forests. The roar of the lion is in them, the fierceness of the tiger; the instinct of dominant possession, which says: "Mine to have and hold, to fight for and enjoy; and I slay all comers!" She had felt it, and her own brave soul had understood it and responded to it, unafraid; and been ready to mate with it, if only—ah! (109)

This inner life of love is the stuff of the sex-novel, against which *The Rosary* is a putative reaction. Such a passage would be unthinkable in any romance by Mrs. Humphry Ward. By earlier revealing Garth's noble intentions, Barclay's narrator has effectively erected moral barriers for her readers, in advance of this fantasy on the part of the heroine; but the fact remains that such representations of erotic passion were not found in the respectable anglophone romance before the turn of the century.

Jane imagines that her physical appearance will not keep such an appetitive man satisfied for long, and so she resolves not to appease his desire for her: "But things could never be again as they had been before. If she meant to starve her tiger, steel bars must be between them for evermore. None of those sentimental suggestions of attempts to be a sort of unsatisfactory cross between a sister and friend would do for the man whose head she had held unconsciously against her breast. Jane knew this" (109–10). There may be no Elinor Glyn–style tiger-skin rug in *The Rosary,* but a tiger there is. The eroticized "taste" of "blood," "the primal elements," "the instinct of dominant possession," the dismissal of "sentimental suggestions," the "unconsciously" clutched head: this is a discourse of human instinctualism heretofore unseen in the religious romance—unless applied, in negative terms, to fallen characters who will see their moral comeuppance.

Barclay's narrative would, of course, insist on reconciling such animal spirits with Christian virtue. Woven through Jane's romantic transport—"The loneliness of years slipped from her. Life became rich and purposeful" (111)—are reminders that the argot of the primeval forest is strictly metaphorical. But it would be only too easy for the reader of 1910 to reimagine the first sentence of the following passage without its opening qualifier, "in her soul": "In her soul she met her tiger and mated with him. He had not asked whether she loved him or not, and she did not need to ask herself. She surrendered her proud liberty, and tenderly, humbly, wistfully, yet with all the strength of her strong nature, promised to love, honour, and obey him. . . . She had locked her body out. She was alone with her soul; and her soul was all-beautiful—perfect for him" (111). Through Jane's interior state, readers are likely meant to enjoy the metaphysical vindication of such a "plain" woman possessing an "all-beautiful" soul. But there is a different kind of irony in the buildup of animalistic tropes to the climactic assertion of a wild mating, complete with the disclaimer, "She had locked her body out." Under the cover of overt piety—the passionate conversion of the man to Christian belief, the Christian wedding vows—Barclay's version of romantic attraction is instinctualized in a way that seems to have eluded the contemporary guardians of propriety, who would go no further than the *Bookman,* which characterized the romance as a "religiously sensual" tale. In *The Rosary,* Barclay got away with stealth eroticism.

Barclay also illuminated the discursive field of the religious romance with flashes of psychological realism. Just as Garth realizes his God-given male predominance in finding his soul mate ("the primal elements which go to the making of a man—a forceful, determined, ruling man—creation's king"), so too the plenitude that Jane feels in imagining her self-submission is described as an "unspeakable sweetness, an understanding of the secret of a woman's bliss" (111). While such phrasings may strike us today as sexist boilerplate, Barclay's narrator would seemingly counterbalance this inequality by offering insight into the psychic condition of the love-struck male as, in essence, an infantile "weakness":

"Thus she gave herself completely; gathering him into the shelter of her love; and her generous heart expanded to the greatness of the gift. Then the mother in her awoke and realised how much of the maternal flows into the love of a true woman when she understands how largely the child-nature predominates in the man in love, and how the very strength of his need of her, reduces to unaccustomed weakness the strong nature to which she has become essential" (111–12). The first English translation of Freud appeared in 1909, the same year in which Barclay was writing *The Rosary*, but given her immediate social environment—as a Christian philanthropist married to a conservative parson—it is rather unlikely that she would have read him. It is probably safer to assume instead that even as devout a writer of "the religious novel" as Barclay had absorbed the increasingly psychological discourse of the popular "sex-novel." And as the case of Elinor Glyn shows, Barclay is not alone in paralleling heterosexual love with the mother-child bond. Barclay's analogy for the intensity of the romantic emotions seems intended to evoke not Freudian paradigms but the Madonna and Child; thus, what might have been taken by a few readers as a psychoanalytic insight into the protagonists' love could at the same time be compatible with Christian typology. With or without its author's awareness, in such passages *The Rosary* effectively legitimizes a secular, Darwinian discourse of erotic attraction by smuggling it in under the "official" Christian rubric of the Ward-style religious romance. Ironically, in her muted way, Barclay may even have lent weight to the normativity of psychoanalytic discourse, given the fact that hers was the highest-selling novel of the year 1910 in England.

Barclay's passages of psychologized interiority return us to wider issues in the development of the romance mode. As we have seen, Gillian Beer defines the romance psychoanalytically as the mode of wish fulfillment. Jameson elaborates on that psychic effect, proposing that romance develops "under the sign of destiny and providence, and takes as its outer horizon the transformation of a whole world, ultimately sealed by those revelations of which the enigmatic Grail is itself the emblem. . . . [R]omance remains metaphysical . . . romance would seem to betray older, more archaic fantasy material [than does the comic genre] and to reenact the oral stage, its anxieties (the baleful spell of the intruding father-magician-villain) and its appeasement (the providential vision), reawakening the more passive and symbiotic relationship of infant to mother."[32] Following Jane's epiphanic analogy of Garth's love for her to the child-mother bond, her love reverie climaxes with a "providential vision" of transcendence: "The lonely years of the past, the perplexing moments of the present, the uncertain vistas of the future, all rolled away. She sailed with Garth upon a golden ocean far removed from the shores of time. For love is eternal; and the birth of love frees the spirit from all limitations of the flesh" (112). In these passages lies the metaphysical kernel of the novel, its central spiritual mystery of the instinctive union of two dissimilar individuals. Despite having glimpsed this vision of romantic transcendence, however, Jane allows her censorious conscience to obstruct its realization. Only when Garth has been crippled by blindness is the presumed power of his animalistic masculinity symbolically tamed, in a plot development meant to reassure Barclay's readers, we might suspect, as much as the heroine. Primitive anxieties are thus dispelled, even as the "archaic fantasy material" of the Oedipal/Electral moment is allowed its wish fulfillment.

My final point about *The Rosary* is that the mother-child trope for romantic love places Barclay's novel as a historically specific instance of the romance mode in two respects. The first is the layering of two seemingly contradictory discourses: the premodern typology of Barclay's Anglicanism; and the emergent and resolutely secular language of popular psychology, different from previous languages of psychology in that it foregrounds the forces of the unconscious. This discursive discontinuity may be described in literary terms as a *generic* discontinuity, marbled through *The Rosary,* between two subgenres of the romance—the religious romance, with its grail being the achievement of oneness with divinity via earthly love, and the emergent twentieth-century women's romance, with its secular transcendence sited in the female protagonist's eventual emotional union with her male lover. Despite the zoological turn in Jane's imagination, the narratorial surveillance of *The Rosary*'s scenes of passion would ensure their spiritual conservatism. The narrative telos of these scenes is, after all, the heroine's and hero's sacred marriage in Christ; such an end would justify the means of figuratively animalistic transports.

Even the chivalric, romance-mode paradigm of chaste love overcoming all external obstacles, however, is modernized and inverted. The only moral challenge that faces the heroine is her self-imposed renunciation of her love for the hero, on the grounds that she is not physically beautiful enough for him. She will come to render caretaking service to her champion only when he is symbolically emasculated by blindness. What Northrop Frye characterizes as the romance's baleful spell of the intruding father-magician-villain is displaced, not into a malevolent character like Orczy's Chauvelin, but into an interiorized entity, the demon of Jane's low self-esteem. *The Rosary* is also quite modern in this respect, inasmuch as it lacks (again, unlike the religious romances of Corelli and Ward) the ideologeme of good versus evil; every character in this novel is patently virtuous, in keeping with Barclay's stated aim "[n]ever to write a line which could introduce the taint of sin or the shadow of shame into any home."[33] But this policy does illustrate Frye's romantic criterion of an idealized world in which "heroes are brave, heroines beautiful." If in Frye's premodern romance "the frustrations, ambiguities, and embarrassments of ordinary life are made little of,"[34] Barclay turns the mundane frustration of Jane's plain appearance into an inner demon that serves as obstacle to the quest-object, her eventual emotional union with her man, and with it the realization of her own inner beauty.

The transcendence brought on by consummated romantic love, both in *The Rosary* and in the mass-market romances that it prefigures, may have its metaphysics rooted in a specific form of appeal to the unconscious. True, if we accept that the pleasures of the romance mode may correspond to the gratifications of the oral stage, we might be tempted into familiar habits of condescension to this form. However, to suggest this is not necessarily to trivialize the women's romance, any more than Frye or Beer intends to trivialize the romance mode generally by correlating it to psychic drives to wish fulfillment. Adult sexuality, as expressed in narrative representations, may be no more privileged a reenactment of that moment in the formation of the unconscious than any other kind. Jameson's account of the romance mode may be accused of Olympian sweep, but it is suggestive here: "[T]he archaic fantasy material that psychoanalytic criticism feels able to detect in such forms can never be imagined as emerging in any pure state, but must always pass through a determinate social and historical situation, in which it is both universalized and reappropriated by 'adult' ideology."[35] Barclay's depiction of passionate emotion can be seen as an embedding of such "archaic fantasy material" within the twin "adult" ideologies of Christian spirituality and the popular psychology of her day.

If the popular discourse of psychology seeps into Barclay's best-selling religious romance, it might be said to suffuse the most well-known romance by Elinor Glyn, *Three Weeks.* Before moving on to Glyn, however, I examine a view of the relationship between the popular romance and the psychologization of fiction, as it was perceived by critics contemporary with Barclay and Glyn. Here again, we should not allow our interpretive ideas about later women's romances to efface their historical differences from the earlier narratives under consideration here. Male critics of Barclay's moment anticipated later critical prejudices regarding the presumed quality of such popular texts, but they often attributed the presumed inferiority of the novels more to their "degraded" realism than to their romantic excesses. In his 1908 study *Modernism and Romance,* R. A. Scott-James describes "the typical modern novel" as follows:

> [T]here really is not a great fund of emotion in the typical modern novel. The one great emotional theme in five novels out of six is the sentiment of love presented under various disguises of plot and circumstance, complications and cross-issues. The great sex-question, the relations between men and women before or after marriage, the complex circumstances of society into which the love passion obtrudes itself—these alone afford the appeal to the heart in the bulk of modern novels. . . . [T]he abundance of love sentiment in the modern novel exists at the expense of the more various and deeper emotions portrayed by Scott, Dickens, Thackeray, George Eliot, Kingsley, Borrow, Stevenson, and Anthony Trollope. (93)

Scott-James here cites some of the famous romance and realist novelists of the Victorian era to contrast their works qualitatively with the Edwardian novel, as he and other critics perceived it. The inclusion of Walter Scott on the list suggests that Scott-James may be thinking of the alleged decline in the historical romance (embodied by such novels as *The Scarlet Pimpernel*), but the thrust of the comparison seems aimed at the Edwardian "sex-novel."

At the time of Scott-James's observations, fictions depicting sexual psychology had proliferated. Among the more notorious "sex-novels" were Somerset Maugham's *Mrs Craddock* (1902), Arnold Bennett's *Leonora* (1903) and *Sacred and Profane Love* (1905), H. G. Wells's *Kipps* (1905), E. M. Forster's *Where Angels Fear to Tread* (1905), and Elizabeth Robins's *A Dark Lantern* (1905). We should add to this list less-familiar authors whose romances were either censored by their publishers or suppressed by public-spirited "purity groups": Hubert Wales, author of *The Yoke* (1907); Robert Hichens, author of *Felix* (1903); and Maud Churton Braby, author of *Downward: A Slice of Life* (circa 1910).[36] By 1908, the year of Scott-James's study, the sex-novel had arrived at the forefront of popular consciousness in Britain. In 1909, the National Home-Reading Union issued a report that denounced such "worthless and demoralising publications" as "a grave national peril."[37] In this context, however, it is important to point out that the immediate precursors to the "sex-novel" of the first decade of the twentieth century were not romance writers at all, but instead late nineteenth-century realists: Hardy, Gissing, Meredith, and such New Woman novelists as Sarah Grand, George Egerton, Grant Allen, Emma Frances Brooke, Mona Caird, Ella Hepworth Dixon, and Ménie Muriel Dowie.[38] The prominence of socially progressive female writers on this list informs Scott-James's characterization of the Edwardian novel; his disparagement of "the abundance of love sentiment" is a coded reference to the perceived feminization of popular fiction.

As discussed in the introduction to this study, Suzanne Clark has demonstrated that the terms *sentiment* and *sentimental* connote well-documented prejudices against the supposed effusions of "effeminate" fiction. Yet the term *sex-novel* engendered a different set of anxieties—fears not of the alleged saccharine of idealization but of a greater realism in the popular novel, based specifically in its representations of the female libido. Peter Keating records that "the sex novel marked a distinctive phase in the growing interest of novelists in psychology. . . . [A]lways it focused on the need to rid the self of sexual repressions and honestly face the consequences."[39] The novelists in question tended to view their works as liberatory, as an opening up of heretofore closed mysteries and occluded energies. Elite critics such as Scott-James saw instead a constriction of fiction's thematic range. Addressing the popular novel's concern with "the great sex-question," Scott-James emphasizes its representation of what he calls "emotion," an umbrella term denoting in part both female and male erotic drives. Scott-James is alleging a superficiality in the popular novel's affective register, relative to the assumed profundity of his popular Victorian exemplars. The majority of Edwardian fiction, he euphemistically suggests, offers a close focus on "the mental and moral tissues of husband and wife. The novelist attempts to give to each note on a flute and each petal on a flower a significance which is measured only by its effect upon character. This is 'modernism' with a vengeance" (109).

This early use of the term *modernism* in connection with English literature is notable not only for its derogatory reference to a new focus on character's psychological states but also for its connection to popular fiction. Indeed, such use of the term *modernism* in 1908 offers a moment of critical self-reflection for us today (one my reasons for citing this passage): its context here is so unfamiliar to us as to have the salutary effect of reminding us of the dialectical history of any such generic or formal category, of forcing us to realize again the constant evolution of the fit between critical concept and literary object. While, as I have just argued, it is accurate to see Edwardian popular fiction focused on "the relations between men and women before or after marriage" as a precursor to mass-market "women's romance," Scott-James illustrates the terminology of his moment: such fiction should actually be labeled "modernist" wherever that fiction is informed by the discourse of an up-to-date "science" of romantic-erotic attraction. This "science," in the view of Scott-James and other conservative Edwardians, impoverishes the literary imagination with a demystifying realism. Near the conclusion of *Modernism and Romance,* Scott-James asserts, "I have tried to show how science, claiming to exhaust the whole field of human knowledge, has starved some of the instincts and faculties of men" (236). One of these instincts, he laments, is the capacity for wonder and "romance" that has allegedly been stripped out of most popular fiction of his day.

On the literary evidence that Scott-James provides, we may today perceive that the evolving popular "science" of male-female relations seemed not to starve but instead to nourish the "instincts and faculties" of many female—and many male—writers of romance. Scott-James was protesting the emergent popularity of novelistic representation that fused the traditional romance with the secular and psychologically refined perception of character. In Scott-James's discourse, the term *modernism* signifies, above all, the pivot of the romance mode from a conservative and patriarchal literary form to one that appears, to our twenty-first-century view, to embody a freer and riskier representation of erotic love.

Elinor Glyn's *Three Weeks:* "The Great Sex-Question"

> She set out to write a story of mere animal passion, but she succumbed to the atmosphere of the moral idea, which is still characteristic of literature in these islands, and she ended in a melodrama.
>
> Anonymous review of *Three Weeks* (*Saturday Review of Politics, Literature, Science and Art,* 15 June 1907)

Although Scott-James does not mention Elinor Glyn by name, her notorious *Three Weeks* provides a good example of the kind of popular "modernism" that he identifies. In keeping with the frank treatment of female sexuality pioneered by the New Woman novels, this 1907 romance tells of the gradual seduction of a respectable young man by a sensuous, liberated older woman. Paul Verdayne is an English country aristocrat in his early twenties, sent by his parents on the Grand European Tour as a means of delaying his intention to wed a parson's daughter, whom they believe to be below his station. At a pension in Switzerland, he meets and falls in love with the self-exiled queen of an unnamed Slavic kingdom. "The lady," Madame Zalenska, has long been estranged from her emotionally brutal husband. Through a series of intense encounters in Switzerland and Venice—the three-week affair of the title—Paul is educated in the ways of physical passion and romantic love. On his return to England, the lovesick youth keeps his promise not to attempt any communication with his lady until she contacts him.

Nine months later, she finally does—to tell him of their newborn son and of her husband's murderous rage. The villainous tyrant has discovered his unfaithful wife to be taking refuge on a Mediterranean island. Paul sets out from England on a yacht to rescue her but does not arrive in time to prevent the drunken royal from running a dagger through Mme. Zalenska's heart. Moments after the murder, the king is strangled by the lady's avenging groom. The novel's brief epilogue is set five years later, as Paul, finally over his grief, travels to Mme. Zalenska's eastern European kingdom at the invitation of its regent to witness the fifth birthday celebration of his royal son, who will eventually be crowned.

Upon its publication in June 1907, *Three Weeks* was attacked for immorality in the London press, and its instant scandal brought Glyn a celebrity that she successfully cultivated for the rest of her life, through her later years as Hollywood screenplay writer and beyond.[40] Previously she had made her presence known in the English world of letters through a series of moderately racy romances and society novels published by Duckworth Press: *The Visits of Elizabeth* (1900), *The Reflections of Ambrosine* (1902), *The Damsel and the Sage* (1903), *The Vicissitudes of Evangeline* (1905), and *Beyond the Rocks* (1906). Although the first of these had created something of a stir, because of its thinly veiled portraits of figures from high-society London, only *Three Weeks* qualified as a genuine best seller, the single book of 1907 that Desmond Flower records as having sold over 100,000 copies.[41] That King Edward was said to have insisted that the scandalous text must not be mentioned in his presence did not hurt the book's sales.[42] Nor did the fact that it was banned at Eton. In a 1955 biography, Anthony Glyn described his grandmother's experience: "The book sold sensationally fast, but even faster went its reputation for immorality. Lady Warwick had read the manuscript and sternly advised Elinor not to publish it, as, if she did, none of her friends would ever speak to her again. It was bad enough for a Society Lady to write books at all, without perpetrating books of that sort" (133). Anthony Glyn recorded that all the newspaper critics except those of the *London Times Literary Supplement* were hostile to his grandmother's most well-known novel. Calculating exact figures for the initial sales of *Three Weeks* was impossible, but he did note that in 1916, nine years after it appeared (and just prior to the production of the first "cheap" edition), its combined sales in the

United Kingdom, the United States, and the British Empire were just short of two million copies. By 1933, he added, world sales had reached five million copies (132).

The initial fuss over *Three Weeks* was caused by both the affirming depiction of an extramarital love affair, and the allegedly salacious language:

> A rage of passion was racing through Paul, his incoherent thoughts were that he did not want to talk—only to kiss her—to devour her—to strangle her with love if necessary.
>
> He bit the rose.
>
> "You see, Paul, love is a purely physical emotion," she continued. "We could speak an immense amount about souls, and sympathy, and understanding, and devotion. All beautiful things in their way, and possible to be enjoyed at a distance from one another. All the things which make passion noble—but without love—which *is* passion—these things dwindle and become duties presently, when the hysterical exaltation cools. Love is *tangible*—it means to be close—close—to be clasped—to be touching—to be One!"[43]

Glyn's narrator follows such declarations of passion by inserting elliptical interludes, in the form of asterisks or broad metaphors, by way of textually veiling the lovers' erotic consummation. Mme. Zalenska takes the lead in all such encounters, stoking Paul's sexual desire each time to the point that it cannot be denied and arranging for the affair to end at the peak of its intensity, in a final Venetian episode featuring a bed covered in rose petals. The sensuality of this novel remained striking enough in the late twentieth century that Barbara Cartland, in her Library of Love reprint series of classic romances of the past, passed over the novel that made Glyn's name in favor of nine of the same author's less well-known, and less racy, works.[44]

Glyn avowed that she had a serious purpose with such provocative material. As discussed in the introduction to this study, she was an outspoken critic of the perceived repressions of the Victorian age. She wrote of the 1901 funeral rites for the monarch that "the slow progress of that solemn procession marked the passing of that period of repose and security, and of all those things which leisure and security imply—peace, order, confidence, contentment, rest and material well-being on the one hand; self-satisfaction, blindness, prejudice and stagnation on the other."[45] It was in a spirit of emotional emancipation, and not soft-pornographic stimulation, that she claimed to offer such scenes as the one quoted above. In justification of her eroticism, she affirmed in her autobiography that "[t]he psychological emotion in itself—as distinct from lust—is far from base, and when it accompanies real love I believe it provides the most perfect expression of joy attainable on earth; which is why the real spirit of romance must soon return, even to our modern, matter-of-fact world—if indeed it has ever departed from it in reality" (*Romantic Adventure,* 2–3). This declaration strikes two of the keynotes of the emergent popular romance of the period: an amoral emphasis on human psychology ("the psychological emotion in itself"), and a secular telos ("joy attainable on earth"). The disavowal of lust is crucial, as Glyn wished to ennoble the experience of romantic transport or rapture. Her language approaches the conception of the popular sublime that we have been elaborating here, with its textual transcendence of quotidian reality.

Glyn's agenda here reveals that her romances are specimens of literary "modernism," as it was defined in 1908 by her contemporary, R. A. Scott-James. Surprisingly, however, the connection with the modern "sex-novel" is precisely what she would deny: "As I see it, the word 'romantic' represents the true opposite to the word 'sordid'; romance is a spiritual disguise, created by the imagination, with which to envelop material happenings and desires, and thus bring them into greater harmony with the soul" (*Romantic Adventure,* 2). In part, one suspects, this insistence on romantic spirituality is a self-defensive performance—the author's dramatization of her noble motives, intended to deflect charges of immoral sensualism. Glyn opens her memoir, in fact, with a dramatic pronouncement: "On looking back at my life, I see that the dominant interest, in fact the fundamental impulse behind every action, has been the desire for *romance*" (*Romantic Adventure,* 2; italics in original). Among the romance writers I have thus far discussed, Glyn may have the strongest affinity with Corelli, who was also emphatic about the spiritual, soulful *health* of "the romantic" as a category. It is true that

Corelli more aggressively advocated for the romance as the literary mode to combat realism, whereas Glyn was a bit more vague, seeing a "spirit of romance" gone semidormant amid contemporary "reality" more generally. But Glyn insisted, in accord with the older writer, that that spirit of romance "must soon return, even to our modern, matter-of-fact world."

As does Corelli, moreover, Glyn emphasizes the continuity of her narratives with the premodern romance tradition. In *Three Weeks,* the hero is an aristocrat, the heroine a royal; we see another modern love story reshaping a tradition, the narrative of upper-class adventure and eros, that dates back to the earliest English-language romances. By her own account, Glyn's spiritual attraction to the romance mode emerged in her childhood and was at odds from the start with traditional Christianity. When one of George MacDonald's romances for children was read to her, she recalled, it was "a turning point in my life, and influenced me more than any other which I have ever read. It aroused a sleeping interest in mystic things, and turned my religious ideas into these channels, and away from orthodox beliefs" (*Romantic Adventure,* 14). In this context, it is no accident that Paul Verdayne's lover is referred to as "his lady" and that his attitude is worshipful[46] or that the affair starts with the lady's teasing of her lover and the delaying of erotic consummation through her provocative poses and gestures. Glyn is consciously resituating the ideals of medieval courtly love in a modern context, as do Orczy in *Pimpernel* and Corelli (with tragic irony) in *Innocent.* But of course the sexuality is far more literalized here, and Glyn is diametrically opposed to the democratic Corelli in her attitude to high "Society," a social milieu that, unlike the fleshpots of *The Sorrows of Satan,* is always romanticized in her works. The omniscient narrator of *Three Weeks* functions as a playfully aristocratic voice in her own right and represents the elegant persona that Glyn would consistently offer to the magazines and newspapers. Capitalizing on the success of her romance, Glyn kicked off her 1907 American book tour with an interview announcing this persona: "I have often been asked . . . why it is that I only write about one class of people. I always reply that it is the only class I know. Why should I write stories about suburban London? I have never been there. I don't know what kind of doors the houses there have, and what colour the wallpaper is. In reading a book by Marie Corelli recently I was greatly amused by her description of a butler with a powdered wig."[47] The quotation is notable not only for her use of the middle-class Corelli as an ill-informed foil but also for its symbolic initiation of her longstanding social pose for the benefit of the Americans. Glyn was no British aristocrat by birth, but from the moment of the appearance of *Three Weeks* in the United States, she performed as one for the anglophiles of the country at large—and, later, of Hollywood in particular. (The screenplay-writing phase of Glyn's career is beyond the purview of this study, but recent scholarship is rediscovering the film-professional "player" that she embodied in 1920s Hollywood.)[48] As suggested in the introduction, Glyn's writings and public persona are symptomatic both of a nostalgia for the romance of the anciens régimes and of a secularizing, antirepressive, "modern" structure of feeling. The parallel with Orczy's *Scarlet Pimpernel* is obvious.

Glyn's romance even shares a commonality with Barclay's *The Rosary* (published two years later than *Three Weeks*): the discourse of popular psychology. Glyn's narrator, too, celebrates the lovers' subjection to their libidinal urges and instinctual drives—though in a tone that is, through the novel's opening passages, far more playful and hardly compatible with upstanding morals. Implying that there is no romantic chemistry between Paul Verdayne and his original betrothed, an English parson's daughter, the narrator informs that the two "were dressed alike, and at a little distance, but for the lady's scanty petticoat, it would have been difficult to establish her sex" (*Three Weeks,* 9–10). Paul, about to embark on his Continental tour, is chummy with his fiancée: "Good-bye, old chap. . . . We have been real pals, and I'll not forget you! . . . I shall never love any woman but you—never, never in my life" (10). In the next sentence, the winking narrator notes, "Cuckoo! Screamed the bird in the tree" (10). Later, in the presence of Mme. Zalenska, Paul is repeatedly overtaken by a passion that comes on "unconsciously" and "subconsciously," as the mere sound of her voice sends him into waking dreams.

This is indeed a psychologism well outside the lines of Barclayan Christianity: under his lady's sway, Glyn's hero becomes an amoral creature, subject to aggressive, even hostile undercurrents of erotic attraction. At Paul's first sight of the lady, as each is seated alone at a Swiss hotel restaurant, his immediate fascination morphs into a violent resentment of her allure:

> All this time the lady had never once looked at him. . . . [Her] white lids with their heavy lashes began to irritate him. What colour could they be? those eyes underneath. They were not very large, that was certain—probably black, too, like her hair. Little black eyes! That was ugly enough, surely! And he hated heavy black hair growing in those unusual great waves. Women's hair should be light and fluffy and fuzzy, and kept tidy in a net. . . . This looked so thick—enough to strangle one, if she twisted it round one's throat. (18)

Glyn depicts a common enough form of self-deceiving denial, as her character is unwillingly transfixed by the lady's beauty and experiences the powerful threat, indeed danger, of erotic attraction, in a psychic self-division our narrator calls a "disapproving irritated interest" (19). This arresting hint of sadomasochism, the image of strangulation-by-hair, anticipates the intertwining of Eros and Thanatos to be theorized by Freud a decade later in *Beyond the Pleasure Principle* (1920).

In the same vein of psychic ambivalence—again, reminiscent of *The Rosary*—the lady assumes a semimaternal voice as the lovers first converse: "You are beautiful, you know, Paul. . . . So tall and straight like you English, with curly hair of gold. Your mother must have loved you, as a baby" (41). Such motherly condescension from the object of his erotic attraction only goads Paul into an explicitly libidinal approach; when his lady again insists, "Yes, you are a baby! . . . A great, big, beautiful baby, Paul" (50–51), he resents this endearment ("If Paul had been a girl, he would have pouted") and refigures their budding relationship in animal terms that emphasize his initiative. "I raced about after you like a dog after a hare," he tells her of his pursuit, to which she laughingly concedes, "And so I was the true hare—I ran away!" (52). A consummate psychologist of passion, the lady knows how to alternate teasing with surrender, how to keep the balance of erotic power in constant tension. In keeping with R. A. Scott-James's characterization of the popular "modernist" novel, Glyn "attempts to give to each note on a flute and each petal on a flower a significance which is measured only by its effect upon character"—or, more accurately in this instance, upon the character's psyche and libido.

But if Glyn's carefully recorded "notes" and "petals" should undoubtedly qualify as the frank recording of romantic-erotic response, it bears repeating that the narrative's idealized love-relationship aims to represent the earthly transcendence of the traditional romance mode. To an even greater extent than the other romances, *Three Weeks* epitomizes a central paradox of the emergent women's romance. The frequently elevated diction and the underpinning ideologeme of good versus evil—good being the achievement of a transcendent love, and evil the obstructive behavior of the villainous king-husband—evoke premodern chivalry and do so in a highly self-conscious manner. At the same time, the defiant celebration of the feminine libido, that symbolic source of the novel's romantic transports, breaks popular British precedent with its ultramodern daring and joie de vivre. The fusion of these two elements leads to the phenomenon of "do-it-yourself" ethical imperatives that would increasingly characterize the secular romance.

The anonymous 1907 reviewer from the *Saturday Review* quoted in the epigraph to this section is commenting on such morality when s/he opines that this is a story of animal passion and melodrama. Not only does Paul fancy animal metaphors for his own amorousness, but also, we are reminded, the narrator compares Mme. Zalenska to a tiger and a snake: "Then a madness of tender caressing seized her. She purred as a tiger might have done, while she undulated around him like a snake" (113). Later, the reviewer laments, Mme. Zalenska—Paul's "Tiger Queen" (192)—"undulated about, creeping like a serpent over her lover, and kissing his eyelids and hair" (175). The reviewer concludes that when "Mrs. Glyn exalts this animal fascination into an affair of the soul, declares that there was in it 'an essence about which only angels could write,' and that 'with all the lady's intense seriousness, and absence of what the Europeans call morality,' the 'tendency of her influences was to exalt and elevate into broad views and logical reasonings,' she ceases to be edifying."[49] The *Saturday Review* hereby lodges a protest, characteristic of most reviews of the time, against *Three Weeks*'s alleged permissiveness and liberality regarding moral behavior. The reviewer also perceives (quite accurately) that the novel ends in melodrama—in a battle between good and evil—but objects to the final portrayal of Mme. Zalenska and Paul as on the side of the angels, "exalted" and "elevated." Glyn had gone further than any of the romance writers thus far surveyed here in inverting conventional morality; she had, by the common critical view of the time, turned Victorian propriety on its head.

The concluding actions of *Three Weeks*'s plot provide an example of prose melodrama that illustrates Peter Brooks's historical claim, "Mythmaking could now only be individual, personal; and the promulgation of ethical imperatives had to depend on an individual act of self-understanding that would then—by an imaginative or even a terroristic leap—be offered as a foundation of a general ethics. . . . Melodrama represents both the urge toward resacralization and the impossibility of conceiving sacralization other than in personal terms."[50] Glyn's romance elevates short-term adulterous passion over long-term married commitment as a higher good. Her donnée is "the paradox that marriage is supposed to be the goal and fulfillment of romance, but romance is identified with brief intense affairs."[51] In parallel with the New Woman novel's interrogation of social conventions, Glyn's heroine brazenly critiques the British institution of marriage. Mme. Zalenska, who is wedded not to Paul but to a "mad, drunken husband" in eastern Europe, urges her paramour never to make any permanent vows in the name of love, telling him that they will eventually become "chains as heavy as lead" and that fate "will force you to break them" (108). She takes a rebellious stance:

> "Paul," she said presently, "how small seem the puny conventions of the world, do they not, beloved? . . . Here are you and I, mated and wedded and perfectly happy—and yet by these foolish laws we are sinning, and you would be more nobly employed yawning with some bony English miss for your wife—and I by the side of a mad, drunken husband. All because the law made us swear a vow to keep for ever stationary an emotion! Emotion which we can no more control than the trees can which way the wind will blow their branches! To love! Oh! yes, they call it that at the altar—'joined together by God!' As likely as not two human creatures who hate each other, and are standing there swearing those impossibilities for some political purpose and advantage of their family. They desecrate the word love. Love is for us, Paul, who

came together because our beings cried, 'This is my mate!'" (106–7)

Glyn's justification for the cry "This is my mate!" is derived in part from the new discourse of popular psychology, which accepts our animal instincts as healthy and irrepressible. At the same time, as we have seen, that justification is also derived from the very old discourse of courtly romance. If such passages lodge a social protest, they do so, Glyn implies, safely within the generic parameters of the romance mode.

Like the New Woman novelists, then, Glyn challenges marital conventions,[52] yet she does so in the name of a nostalgic ideal of romantic love, not of gender equality or women's rights. As she later asserted in her memoir,

> The word Romance has been narrowed and cheapened in modern times until it has been thought of little account, and for many it no longer represents the beautiful and inspiring ideal that it has always meant, and still means for me. . . . [R]omance is a spiritual disguise, created by the imagination, with which to envelop material happenings and desires, and thus bring them into greater harmony with the soul. It is the essence of chivalry, that is, of the fine actions inspired by delicate sentiments which are not aroused by thoughts of personal gain, but rather by the impulse to render homage to another. (*Romantic Adventure,* 2)

This is the same erotic atavism that inspires the erudite Mme. Zalenska to compare her relationship with Paul to a series of legendary loves of myth, literature, and history, including Cupid and Psyche, Pericles and Aspasia, Anthony and Cleopatra, Justinian and Theodora, Belisarius and Antonina, Lancelot and Elaine, Desdemona and Othello, Huldebrand and Undine, and Marguerite and Faust. Despite—or because of—the tragic fates of so many on this list, each pair is offered as an illustration of the short-lived, secular transcendence reexperienced by our twentieth-century hero and heroine.

In other words, though she does not offer a Corellian allegory of the production of romance (as seen in *The Treasure of Heaven* and

Innocent), Glyn shows a historical consciousness of her position as a revivalist of the venerable English tradition of the chivalric romance. At the same time, her brash modernity generates the paradoxes delineated here. What distinguishes her from the historical romancier of the Orczy variety—and from such Victorian revivalists of the Arthurian romance as Alfred Lord Tennyson[53]—is her intermingling of premodern chivalric ideals with an avant-garde liberality regarding sexuality, especially women's erotic desire. Invoking the myths of Galahad and Lancelot, Glyn insists in her memoir that "the essential element in romance is love, but it is love in the highest sense, in which it becomes selfless devotion to a spiritual ideal . . . and not the debased form which is associated with the mere psychological emotion of the mating season" (*Romantic Adventure,* 2). Moreover, on the question of gender relations, the lady seems to denigrate the modern practice of educating women, arguing that it interferes with their capacity for domestic excellence and the fulfillment of "a man's ideal," yet implies that she herself embodies the model of the sophisticated ancient Greek *hetaerae,* those unmarriageable but highly educated women who would represent an exciting counterideal to feminine domesticity.[54] And finally, although she wishes to distance her fiction from "debased" erotica, her narrator often employs the frank modern terms of secularized and materialist popular psychology—in acknowledgment of the newer discourses of the "psychological emotion of the mating season." *Three Weeks* thus offers another Edwardian anticipation of the popular women's romance of the mid- to late twentieth century, which completes the secularization of the romance mode even as it often refashions the old literary discourses, as idealized by Glyn, of premodern visions of transcendence.

In Glyn's hands—as, variously, in Orczy's and Barclay's hands—the ideology of the romance as a form is therefore Janus-faced. It is at once regressive and progressive; it is implicitly feminist throughout its renovation of an Old World Weltanschauung rooted in aristocracy and patriarchy. In *The Gender of Modernity,* Felski argues that the progressive elements outweigh the retrograde in this kind of early twentieth-century romance, in such vehicles of the popular sublime: "A romantic yearning for the ineffable, rather than exemplifying a conservative and anachronistic throwback to an earlier epoch, as writers on kitsch often imply, emerges as a key element of the modern and a central aspect of mass culture's interpellation of femininity" (120–21). Whether Felski is correct to see the progressive "modern" as weighing more heavily in the balance, I do not know; my interest has been to suggest that the "romantic yearning for the ineffable" is a key element, not simply in "the modern" as a cultural category but more specifically in a modernity of literary content, within differently inflected "high" *and* "low" forms. It is in this specific sense, as specimens of a new romance form, that *The Scarlet Pimpernel, The Rosary,* and *Three Weeks* may be considered "low modern" narratives.

CHAPTER FIVE

The Imperial Erotic Romance

If the romances of Orczy, Barclay, and Glyn secularize and psychologize the romance genre in the first years of the twentieth century, then what we might call the "imperial erotic romance"—the white woman's love story in a colonial setting—explicitly racializes the genre. Scholars have long noted that the masculine adventure romances of the period, such as H. Rider Haggard's *King Solomon's Mines* (1885) and Rudyard Kipling's *Kim* (1901), feature orientalist or primitivist versions of the non-European Other.[1] The term *imperial romance* has commonly been applied to "a complex group of fictions appearing in Britain between the 1880s and the 1920s, which were devoted to narrating adventure in colonial settings."[2] This is a familiar subgenre of the romance, one that emerged well before the turn of the century; alongside Haggard and Kipling, Robert Louis Stevenson, Joseph Conrad, John Buchan, and others were in this period extending and transforming the tradition of "boys' own adventure" that was developed earlier in the nineteenth century by G. A. Henty, Mayne Reid, Frederick Chamier, Frederick Marryat, and R. M. Ballantyne. This masculine strain of the romance has sparked recent scholarship on the ideological hybridity, the mesh of conservative and progressive discourses, that constitutes these subliminally anxious texts and on the continuities with modernist experimentalism, particularly in the cases of Conrad's primitivism and Forster's *A Passage to India*. Postcolonial criticism on the imperial romance has brought to our attention the protomodernist interrogations of the bourgeois subject, generated by narrative explorations of the non-Western Other, that began to appear in imperial romances from the 1880s and thereafter.[3]

But critical attention has only recently turned to those European constructions of colonized non-European peoples that appear in imperial romances by women writers. Here I look primarily at three such texts, published in the years bridging the decline of the moralizing Victorian romance and the rise of the mass-market woman's romance: Victoria Cross's *Anna Lombard* (1901), Ethel Dell's *The Way of an Eagle* (1912), and E. M. Hull's *The Sheik* (1919). To understand the popularity of these three romances, we have to reimagine the structure of feeling that came with being British subjects of a global empire—or, more generally, anglophone readers of European descent, subject to the ideologies of empire. I argue that libidinal investments in racial fantasies, on the part of author and reading audience, provided the narratives with much of their energy and suspense; ideologies of race fueled the combustible discourses of desire.[4] Informing each narrative is a complex of tensions between a willful British woman and an exotic or "Othered" man; resolution arrives with the "taming" or domestication of the white woman and with her disarming of the thrillingly dangerous element represented in an "exotic" male lover—whether through his death *(Anna Lombard)* or through the emergence of his "better" self, as nurtured by the heroine's love *(The Way of an Eagle, The Sheik)*. Bringing to bear some of the more recent articulations of postcolonial theory, we find in these romances both implicit critiques of discursive constructions of the feminine and an ambivalent fascination with the "ungovernable" Indian or Arab male. The elements of "uncivilized" or non-European masculinity, portrayed as at once threatening and attractive, may be seen to test the independence of the New Woman heroines and, in the case of Dell's and Hull's novels, to refract through the "barbaric" side of the white male heroes. In all three romances, the fear of rape by the "native" male is balanced, as on a knife-edge, with the libidinality of the encounter with a romanticized, "primitive" masculinity. Almost entirely missing from the triangulation of signifying nodes—"white woman," "dark man," "white man"—is the figure of the "dark," or non-European, woman. This absence is doubly symptomatic of new developments in the early twentieth-century romance mode. First, it suggests the discursive confluence of what Jenny Sharpe, in her groundbreaking study of the same name, calls "allegories of empire";[5] and second, it indexes these novels' economies of desire, which would come to characterize the mass-market women's romance.

The bulk of this chapter is devoted to exploring these interlinked phenomena, through readings of works by three of the preeminent authors of the imperial erotic romance. In the last section, I examine the correlative primitivist discourses of writings by Woolf, Lawrence, and Mansfield that explicitly thematize the European experience of "exotic" landscapes and peoples. In the end, we may see how modernist narratives serve, ambivalently, as parallel sites of both the perpetuation of racialist ideology and of discursive rupture and shift—not against but in tandem with the unprepossessing tales of love and intrigue found in the works of Cross, Dell, and Hull.

Victoria Cross's *Anna Lombard*: "Those Voluptuous Tropic Nights"

> She sat down next to a girl very much her own age who was reading *Anna Lombard* in a cheap, paper-covered edition. . . . She glanced at the book which the girl read so earnestly, mouthing the words in a way that Rosabel detested, licking her first finger and thumb each time that she turned the page. She could not see very clearly; it was something about a hot, voluptuous night, a band playing, and a girl with lovely, white shoulders. Oh Heavens!
>
> Katherine Mansfield, "The Tiredness of Rosabel"

Contemporary criticism of the fiction of Victoria Cross (pseudonym of Vivian Cory), especially of her best-selling novel *Anna Lombard* (1901), has considered her writing in light of the late nineteenth-century social phenomenon of the New Woman. Cross's career began with the publication in 1895 of the novel *The Woman Who Didn't,* which was widely taken to be a rejoinder to one of the most scandalous of the New Woman novels, Grant Allen's *The Woman Who Did* (1895). In the same year, there also appeared, between the covers of the notorious *Yellow Book,* Cross's erotically suggestive short story "Theodora: A Fragment." This is Cross's most frequently discussed work today; its violation of gender taboos, through the approving depiction of its female protagonist's frank sensuality and heterosexual desire, illustrates the New Woman writers' attempts to legitimate women's social and erotic energies.[6] What is less commonly remarked, however, is the fact that "Theodora" and *The Woman Who Didn't* derive their eroticism in part from symbolic connections between sexual desire and the exoticizing of colonized "Eastern" lands. In these narratives, the peoples and cultures of Egypt, Arabia, Mesopotamia, and India serve as the sources of ambient metaphors, primitivist tropes that would wreathe the romantic encounters of their English protagonists in erotic suggestion. Enfolded within the colonial discourses of turn-of-the-century Britain, Cross's fictions represented the libidinal charge that their white British readers may have felt on contemplating racial Others, imagined as the denizens of North Africa or the Middle East or South Asia.

Six years later, with the publication in 1901 of *Anna Lombard,* Victoria Cross literalized these cultural metaphors in a story of sexual obsession between an Anglo-Indian and a Pathan of India's Northwest Frontier. As Shoshana Milgram Knapp suggests, *Anna Lombard* "tested [Cross's] readers by breaking more taboos than in all of her earlier works put together."[7] Indeed, the amalgam of colonialist desires and anxieties seen in Cross's earlier works finds vivid expression in the heroine and plotline of *Anna Lombard,* a novel whose psychosexual iconoclasm, at once racially ambivalent and uncharacteristically daring for a writer of Cross's era, still astounds today. In Edward Said's discussion of Kipling's *Kim,* a novel published in the same year as *Anna Lombard,* the critic suggests that "[t]he division between white and non-white, in India and elsewhere, was absolute. . . . [A] Sahib is a Sahib, and no amount of friendship or camaraderie can change the rudiments of racial difference."[8] Yet Cross's 1901 novel represented a prohibited interracial relationship that went well beyond "friendship or camaraderie": the marriage of a white Englishwoman and her Indian servant. For all of its melodrama, this popular romance, which eventually sold more than six million copies,[9] offers a complex staging of what we might have supposed ideologically unthinkable to the common British reader of 1901.

A child of Anglo-Indian parents, Vivian Cory grew up immersed in the tensions and contradictions of Anglo-Indian life, the taboos and prohibitions of colonialist discourse. She spent much of her youth in Lahore, Karachi, and other locales of present-day Pakistan, observing her father's role as a major, and later colonel, of the Raj. Born in 1868 in Rawalpindi, sibling-city to present-day Islamabad, she would have heard stories of the East India Company's recent conquest of the Sikh kingdom of the Punjab (1849), as well as the sepoy rebellion of 1857, after which (in 1858) India was politically annexed to the British Empire. Vivian and her two sisters spent time in England to be schooled, and they returned to India to stay with their parents in the intervals. Their experiences among schoolmates back in England may have encouraged the sisters to embrace and to foster the belief that romantic risk and danger characterized their upbringing in India's Northwest Frontier. We are limited to speculating about such feelings,[10] as virtually the only archival material from Vivian Cory's lifetime consists of her adult, professional correspondence with publishers. But it is safe to say that the literary romanticization of India was a Cory family practice. Vivian's older sister Adela (1865–1904), who wrote under the pen name "Laurence Hope," enjoyed a brief fame in the first years of the twentieth century for the lyric volumes *The Garden of Kama and Other Love Lyrics from India* (1901), *Stars of the Desert* (1903), and the posthumous *Last Poems: Translations from the Book of Indian Love* (1905). One of Adela Cory's most popular poems, "Kashmiri Song," was destined to provide a crucial plot element in E. M. Hull's *The Sheik.*[11]

More prolific than her older sister, Vivian Cory indulged this mystical and romanticizing impulse in her literary representations of not only India but also other cultures under European rule. Within the context of British and imperial social relations of the fin de siècle, her fiction implicitly promotes a progressive social agenda, rife though it may appear today with epistemological gaps and puzzling contradictions, not least of which is her idiosyncratic Othering of her non-European characters. But to make ethically condescending claims regarding the "exotic" libidinal projections of Cross's fin-de-siècle fiction is to risk overwrought generalizations about the psychic energies of her readers. As I note elsewhere in this study, we do not have enough information about the buyers and readers of the period's popular fiction to verify, in any positivist fashion, our hypotheses regarding its specific psychological appeal to British and other anglophone readers. I survey some of the more compelling theories about readerly engagement with women's romances generally in chapter 6, where Katherine Mansfield's fictional depiction of a reader of Victoria Cross provides an opening into the question. For the time being, I am interested in the discourse of race in Cross's fiction—a discourse seemingly informed by an imperial-political unconscious that, as the novels' sales figures attest, must have "spoken to" the social psychology of the predominantly white readers of fin-de-siècle Britain.

In recent years, in fact, emerging scholarship has unearthed extraliterary discursive evidence to provide fairly firm support to certain generalizations regarding the British public's psychic investments in the racialized tropes of empire. We may turn by way of example to the work of Robert J. C. Young, whose book on the psychoanalytics of empire can be summarized in this tersely worded thesis: "Theories of race were . . . also covert theories of desire."[12] Surveying the works of eighteenth- through twentieth-century historians, social scientists, anatomists, zoologists, anthropologists, philosophers, and sociologists, Young finds continuities between these writers' tropes for racial difference and those of popular novelists and canonical literary figures of the Victorian and modernist periods. He draws special attention to British writers of the adventure romance: "The many colonial novels in English betray themselves as driven by desire for the cultural other, for forsaking their own culture: the novels of Burton [translator of *The Arabian Nights*], Haggard, Stevenson, Kipling, Allen [author of *The Woman Who Did*], or Buchan [author of *Sir Quixote of the Moors*] are all concerned with forms of cross-cultural contact, interaction, an active desire, frequently sexual, for the other" (*Colonial Desire,* 3). With few exceptions, in these writers' fictions the desire for the cultural Other is gendered masculine, and the desire's object is gendered feminine. Victoria Cross, whose most interesting writings are contemporaneous with most of these authors', is now a relatively obscure figure, yet I suggest that *Anna Lombard*—which is concerned precisely with the European *female*'s "active desire, frequently sexual, for the other"—offers as fascinating a configuration of the tensions and aporias of racialist discourse as do any of Kipling's or Stevenson's works. Like these better-known writers, Cross was an implicit elaborator of racial difference, and *Anna Lombard* is (together with her novel *Life of My Heart* [1905]) her racial ideology's preeminent site of expression.

Young's analysis of colonial discourse "traces the emergence of desire in history, its genealogy and its disavowal in the history of racialized thought" and thereby offers a set of conceptual tools with which to dismantle the discursive patterning of Cross's novel. Regarding the European (especially British) history of racialized thought, Young offers first a theatrical, then a procreative metaphor:

> The impresario that stages this patriarchal drama is called "culture," itself the production of an emergent European capitalist society; the conflictual structures generated by its imbalances of power are consistently articulated through points of tension and forms of difference that are then superimposed upon each other: class, gender and race are circulated promiscuously and crossed with each other, transformed into mutually defining metaphors that mutate within intricate webs surreptitious cultural values that are then internalized by those whom they define. . . . And so too racial theory, which ostensibly seeks to keep races forever apart, transmutes into expressions of the clandestine, furtive forms of what can be called "colonial desire": a covert but insistent obsession with transgressive, inter-racial sex, hybridity and miscegenation. (xi–xii)

One of Young's main ideas here is that racial theories and literary constructions of race, intertwined with those of gender and class, have often been mutually constitutive. But there is another crucial idea, one conveyed by a subtle metaphor in Young's passage—the figure of *wiring,* of an arrangement of electrical conduits. Gender and race may be "crossed with each other" in a procreative figure, but here the "intricate webs" may also appear to us as containing multitudes of crossed wires—precisely the sites where, to our eyes, the tangled conduits of desire that power the narrative's libidinal motor seem to short-circuit on their own gaps and contradictions. To posit such aporias, which we as contemporary readers might presume to identify through historically informed insight, is to risk an unwarranted assumption of our superior epistemological or ethical vantage, as compared with that of Cross and her original readers. Another of Young's observations—one that is intended self-reflexively to inform my readings of Cross, Dell, and Hull in this chapter—is that, in mediated ways, the same "covert but insistent obsession" found in European racial theory of the past may be a motivating force behind some postcolonial literary criticism of recent decades. Reminding us that contemporary "forms of racism remain so intimately bound up with sexuality and desire," Young warns us that "[t]he fantasy of postcolonial cultural theory . . . is that those in the Western academy at least have managed to free themselves from this hybrid commerce of colonialism, as from every other aspect of the colonial legacy" (182). A self-reflexive and dialectical awareness of this "fantasy" should guard against the inert and sterile binaries of a judgmental reading of the colonial discourse of these romances, whereby individual authors would either be championed for their implicit challenges to imperial ideologies or unmasked as perpetuating such ideologies.

With these caveats in mind, I want to show how Cross's novel is concerned precisely with Young's topoi of turn-of-the-century racial theory in Britain: interracial sex and that singularly nineteenth-century construct, miscegenation.[13] Before examining the novel, I would like to cite Melisa Brittain, the one critic (to my knowledge) who has offered an analysis of *Anna Lombard* that is informed by recent postcolonial theory. Brittain demonstrates that, because of the racial transgression on which the plot turns, critical reception of the novel was almost uniformly pejorative.[14] As she observes, "Negative reactions to the novel by the majority of reviewers suggest that *Anna Lombard* posed a significant challenge to gender and race categories that underwrote patriarchal colonial prestige" ("Erasing," 91). Nonetheless, Brittain suggests that the novel's "configuration of interracial sexuality simultaneously challenged and reinstated dominant ideologies of race, gender, and class hierarchies" (75). While I generally agree with Brittain about the probable discursive effects of this novel among its original readers, I believe that she understates its arresting strangeness and anomalous popularity—the book eventually sold more than six million copies, saw at least forty editions,[15] and served as a catalyst in an early literary experiment by Katherine Mansfield (see chapter 6). In what follows, I highlight the novel's psychosexual singularity, which, more than simply "challenging" its readers, was perhaps radically freethinking, even as Cross publically announced that her open-ended racial imaginary was intended to stage a lesson in old-fashioned Christian tolerance. The erotics of the novel, with their discursively "crossed wires," serve at once to legitimate British colonial power and to violate gender and racial taboos. The iconoclastic representation of the title character's erotic encounters might be seen as both a sublimate of hegemonic imperial discourse and a collective fantasy that we might otherwise have guessed to be inexpressible in 1901.

Not long after the first edition of *Anna Lombard* was published in 1901, Victoria Cross added a one-page preface to ensuing editions. It begins, "I have been challenged by certain papers to state my intentions in writing *Anna Lombard*."[16] Cross laments that an influential London newspaper, the *Daily Chronicle*, has seen fit to hold the "conduct" of the novel's first-person narrator, Gerald Ethridge, "up to ridicule and contempt" and to "stigmatise it as a 'horrid absurdity'" (1). An overview of the novel's plot helps us imagine why the Edwardian editors of the *Daily Chronicle* rendered such a harsh judgment. It is the 1890s; at a dance held by the Indian Civil Service in Kalatu, a village of northwestern India (present-day Pakistan), assistant commissioner Gerald Ethridge meets and falls in love with the twenty-one-year-old Anna Lombard. Anna, the daughter of an Anglo-Indian general, is a woman of artistic temperament who has just completed her education in England. Gerald is called away the next day to civil service in Burma and returns a year later to become engaged to Anna. However, she soon reveals that, unbeknownst to her father, she has in the interim married their household servant, Gaida Khan. When Anna vows to Gerald that she still loves her original fiancé, he decides to wait until her passion for the proud young Pathan has faded and the secret marriage can be quietly annulled. Cholera strikes Gaida, and despite Gerald's altruistic efforts to nurse him back to health, the Pathan dies. When Anna reveals that she is carrying Gaida's child, Gerald decides to preserve her reputation by immediately marrying her. But her maternal love for the baby boy incurs the jealousy of her long-suffering husband, and, guilt-stricken, she murders her child. After Anna has spent a cloistered year of self-imposed penance for this murder, she returns to Gerald, who again forgives her and welcomes her to a long-deferred life of conventional, socially sanctioned marriage with her Anglo-Indian husband.

In the preface, Cross defends herself against the allegation of this plot's "horrid absurdity" by invoking Christian doctrine: "I endeavored to draw in Gerald Ethridge a character whose actions should be in accordance with the principles laid down by Christ, one that would display, not in words but in his actual life, that gentleness, humility, patience, charity, and self-sacrifice that our Redeemer himself enjoined. . . . He forgives the sinner, raises the fallen, comforts the weak. He works and suffers to reclaim the Pagan and almost-lost soul of Anna Lombard" (1). Cross professes here that she wants her readers to believe that the novel's moral is "hate the sin, love the sinner," even when that love is tested by the "sins" of interracial sex and miscegenation. Without speculating on Cross's sincerity in claiming such didactic motives for publishing the novel, we observe that this apology codes the racial transgression as a religious one: Anna Lombard's soul is ultimately saved from "Paganism," as the heathen sin is implied to be (a barely averted) bigamy. In fact, this preface would divert us from the novel's central taboo of a sexual relationship between a white woman and a "black" man, for it focuses on the upright conduct of Gerald and thereby avoids mentioning directly the obvious scandal of Anna's sexual misconduct. Cross thus skirts the most likely reason for the novel's popularity: the mysterious character and forbidden experiences of the Anglo-Indian woman who is, after all, the title character.

Without engaging in a pointlessly self-congratulatory hermeneutic of suspicion—whereby we might convict the author of bad faith, participation in racist ideology, perpetuation of imperialist discourse, and so forth—we may perceive that Cross's *apologia pro novella sua* is precisely the kind of disavowal of racialized desire that Young has broadly theorized as informing many tracts and fictions of colonial discourse. Cross's evasive preface suggests the contradictory repression/indulgence of the prohibited desire that is the psychic motor propelling the novel's plot. In the novel itself, the narrating character of Gerald Ethridge professes to be shocked—shocked!—to find out what is going on, even as he becomes more obsessed by Anna Lombard with each new revelation of her deepening misconduct, as she progresses from interracial marriage to de facto bigamy to miscegenation to infanticide.

From the moment of Gerald's first encounter with Anna, she is established as a paragon of feminine virtues, so that her fall may be the more dramatic. Bored by the "frivolous" chatter of his first dance partner at the commissioner's ball, Gerald says, "[J]ust as we passed a corner my gaze fell suddenly on a figure in white sitting alone on a *fauteuil.* I don't know why, but something in the figure caught and held my eyes" (10). After asking his companion for the woman's name, he is told,

> "Why, you must know her, surely; she's the General's daughter, Anna Lombard."
>
> "Anna Lombard," I repeated. "It's a curious name; it sounds somehow to me mediaeval, a middle-age sort of name."
>
> "Oh Anna's not middle-aged," returned inconsequentially my rather flighty companion. (10)

Anna's name strikes our narrator as antique, which of course it is; the recorded history of the Lombards goes back at least as far as the Roman Empire in Germany, circa A.D. 50.[17] Moreover, Anna is the daughter of a high-ranking official, symbolically separated from the crowd of shallow Anglo-Indian women around her, and we are soon to learn that she has received an excellent education in the classics (13). She has about her an aura of aristocracy, a superiority of spirit and intellect that would justify Gerald's instant enamorment.

On closer inspection, the character of Anna Lombard has about her an air of semiotic overdetermination. Not only is she suggested to be an aristocrat and a model of feminine virtue—innocent of coquetry ("this was her first 'real ball'"), with "a sort of appealing timidity . . . united with such an obviously clever and gifted mind and such a sweet face and form" (14)—but also her racial characteristics are repeatedly emphasized: she is "that girl in white," with "fair" hair and a "soft, white forehead"; "Her eyes were blue, like pieces cut from a summer's sky, and her skin like the wild rose in the English hedgerow, first opening after a summer shower" (12). Given Anna's central transgression in the novel, this will inevitably be read as a deliberately racialized description, both intended to heighten the tragic irony of her later fall and unconsciously echoing Western racial theorists' catalogues of European features. (We might compare the passage just quoted with a notorious racial categorization from John Burke's *The Wild Man's Pedigree* [1758]: "European. Fair, sanguine . . . hair yellow, brown, flowing; eyes blue; gentle, acute, inventive.")[18] Noteworthy here is the one-to-one correspondence between Anna's features and the characteristics of the eighteenth-century theorist's ideal European. Moreover, Cross's romantic simile ("like the wild rose in the English hedgerow") serves to link Anna Lombard organically to the terrain of the British Isles, in a symbolic conflation of nation and race. Anna is racially desirable, as it were, "to the second power"—the quintessence of a Britishness that is itself the quintessence of Europeanness. Young's previously quoted observation regarding the history of racialized desire under European imperialism as creating "metaphors that mutate within intricate webs" is particularly germane here. The first few pages of Cross's novel thus function as a discursive matrix, generating a Victorian hologram of femininity along the vectors of upper-class status and racial superiority.

However, Cross projects this hologram to serve the ends of narrative irony. The first third of the novel chronicles Gerald's resistance to the temptations of interracial promiscuity for the sake of his "pure" white ideal, Anna Lombard.[19] Transferred to Burma, far from Anna, Gerald is encouraged by other British officers to take on a Burmese mate for the duration of his five-year posting. He refuses to do this, even when courted by a young Burmese snake-handler, who hangs herself in despair at his rejection. Distraught and desperate for advice, Gerald seeks out a fellow colonial, who has taken a Burmese wife. Gerald witnesses an exotic scene of domestic bliss:

> When I went round to see him in the evening, I used to find him generally smoking peacefully in his dining-room with his wife and family crawling about on the floor round his chair. He had three little round, fat, toddling bunches of babies, the youngest of whom was as white as its father.
>
> "But, Knight, what *will* you do with all these when your term is up, and you have to leave?" I asked

> him one evening when I came upon the scene of happy domesticity.
>
> "Oh, well, she," with an airy wave of his hand, "will go back to her people, you know, with the kids."
>
> "But what about the little one? It's a girl, isn't it? and as white as we are. You won't want her to go into the bazaar, surely, and lead a dog's life among these blacks—your own daughter with your blood in her veins? It's horrible!"
>
> "You're quite right, perfectly right, my dear fellow; it *is* a horrible thought, and that's why I never encourage it. I never think about disagreeable things. What's the use?"
>
> I gazed at him, fat, rubicund, cheerful and comfortable, as he leant back in his chair, then at the pretty, child-like being who sat on her heels under the table, weaving a garland of clematis and crooning to herself, and then at the three little creatures, tumbling round her, that he had seen fit, for his own amusement, to bring into the world and to such a miserable heritage. (68)

Gerald is unsettled by this mock-bourgeois proscenium of "miscegenation"—with its head of household presenting a counterimage of the Victorian paterfamilias in a drawing room back in middle-class England—but he has also made it clear that, after the tragedy of the love-struck snake handler, he has come to Knight to discuss the possibility of "taking a Burmese wife." He decides to remain true to Anna, but Cross will soon reveal that the idealized Anna is the one who is being untrue—and with a "native." Gerald's rejection of the possibility of a Burmese wife serves as an ironic foreshadowing, enhancing readers' presumed shock at the eventual revelation of Anna's interracial liaison.

At the same time, however, Cross conveys a very different ideological lesson: Gerald's sexual liaison, though unrealized, would have been socially acceptable on the margins of the empire; Anna's realized union with a "native," by contrast, was utterly taboo. Had Gerald chosen to take a temporary Burmese mate, he could, by the social codes of the subcontinental empire before 1900, have suffered no ill effects to his career and eventually have married Anna without social repercussion.[20] It so happens, however, that Anna, who never made any explicit promises to Gerald, has taken a Pathan husband, yet this must remain a deep secret. What can be shrugged off merely as Knight's "own amusement" is later portrayed to be Anna's unthinkable transgression. The novel's moral register and its sociopolitical critique work at cross-purposes here: are readers meant to be more scandalized by Anna's choice to take an Indian lover, or by the stark double standards of Anglo-Indian patriarchy? So far from merely condemning Knight's marriage and procreation on simple grounds of racial pollution, then, Cross draws attention to the hypocrisy of British colonial practice: the gender asymmetry of its ideology regarding interracial sex.[21]

If the tableau of Knight's domestic bliss suggests that Cross is critiquing a patriarchal structuring of race relations, the imbrication of the racial and sexual registers is less ideologically legible. Upon his return to India, Gerald admits to a perverse fantasy about Anna, which he expresses shortly after she has accepted his proposal of marriage:

> Amongst the other things I had studied, the history of the Middle Ages had always possessed a great fascination for me, and now I was suddenly drawn again towards it by the name of the girl I loved, and by the peculiar timbre of her nature that seemed familiar to me and came to me as an echo of the past. . . . One night I came suddenly upon the biography of Catherine Sforza, and read it through from beginning to end. At the end of the old quarto volume was a full-page portrait of this notorious and evil woman. . . . There was something curiously familiar in the expression, in the look about the luminous eyes of force—great mental force and power; and all at once, in a flash, it came to me whence arose that feeling of recognition. . . . "Anna could look like that, I am sure she could," I thought. (93)

Gerald begs his fiancée to masquerade as a "notorious and evil woman" in a tableau vivant performed for the Anglo-Indian colony at Kalatu. Anna balks at the idea but, after being confronted by her suitor's ardent desire to see her acting the part of a murderer, eventually consents to appear as Catherine Sforza, a late-medieval, Florentine personage, allusive to Macchiavelli's *The Prince.* Anna's impersonation of "the Sforza" prompts the audience to ask for five encores, which makes all the other Anglo-Indian women jealous and leads to an intimate exchange with Gerald:

> "You were splendid to-night—perfect!"
>
> "Was I?" she said very softly, nestling up close and putting her arms around me. "I am so glad you were pleased with me."
>
> When with me, all her arrogance, coldness and contemptuous indolence of manner, with which she often treated her enemies or faced the world, disappeared. With me, whatever pride she might possess, she put at my feet. To me, she was always yielding, submissive, clinging, loving and simple. This change, this distinction she made for me, had in it a subtle and intoxicating flattery.
>
> I crushed her up to me and kissed her again and again on her red hair and painted eyes and fresh mouth, and she yielded herself passionately to me.
>
> "I don't want to be the Sforza," she whispered in my ear, "nor anybody except just your own little girl." (109)

Gerald seems to relish the "arrogance, coldness and contemptuous indolence" of his love object, and thus, what he calls the "strange fancy" of seeing her in this murderous guise reflects a desire to exaggerate those qualities of character, to make his conquest of her heart all the more exciting and erotically charged. This passage signifies the wish fulfillment of a dominant male exerting mastery over a strong, independent female who becomes, at his touch, "yielding, submissive, clinging, loving and simple." Gerald admits to the irrationality of his whim; Anna says of Gerald's desire to see her in the garb of a violent criminal, "I really do think you might have found some more orthodox person for me," and he can only respond enigmatically, "I do not think that would have been nearly so suitable, you see" (98). He does not attempt to explain his erotic caprice, as he does not understand it himself, conceding that his fantasy is socially perverse.

But the performativity of Anna's masquerade limns the very qualities that Gerald will perceive—or, more accurately, project—in

Anna's lover, Gaida Khan: fierce beauty, haughtiness, indomitability, capacity for violence. The point of the Catherine Sforza scenes is thus to illustrate that Gerald is subject to the same ungovernable, libidinal impulses that will pull at Anna, who cannot repress her passion for an "Oriental." In his erotic fantasy, Gerald remakes Anna into the Other, inducing her to perform the role of a historical femme fatale. Here is his tortured rationalization of his desire: "[Sforza's] crimes were the crimes of her century. Her great mental force threw her into crime, because crime was the order of her time, and you have that same force which you would throw into great and heroic deeds if they were to be done" (98). This convoluted analogy, which might be initially perceived as gratuitous, prepares the reader to forgive the taboo violated through Anna's secret marriage to the racial Other. At the moment when a shocked Gerald is about to be introduced to Gaida Khan, whom Anna has revealed to be her secret husband, he considers,

> True, she was my Anna Lombard, that I had thought of when I had first heard her name, stepped out of the Middle Ages before me. And I looked at her sitting not far from me, pale, calm, composed as a statue, and my eyes seemed to see, only through a mist of pain, a shade from those times of blood and lust and passion and crime; times when swift poisons were made by white fingers, and when women loved as men, as strongly, and often as briefly. When they laughed at the idea of one lover, yet were ready to die with, for, or by the hand of, any one of the many; times when the very air they breathed seemed charged with treachery, cunning and danger—from these a shade had returned and confounded itself with the clear white soul of an English girl in a body beautiful and innocent to look upon as the sunlight of a summer day. (143–44)

The same metaphor with which Gerald had represented his love-object in the full glory of her irresistible beauty returns as a means for him to try to understand her appalling transgression. In Gerald's superheated imagination, Anna's Otherness derives of a savage race-memory, the collective barbarism of the European Middle

Ages. If Catherine Sforza's feminine sins were "the crimes of her century," they find their contemporary equivalent in the sexual and racial transgression of Anna Lombard.

And then we witness one of the most daring conjunctures of Cross's novel. Anna discloses to Gerald her forbidden erotic sanctum; the white woman summons her "black" lover into her chambers, for the inspection of the white man. In portraying Anna as an avatar of the phantasmatic medieval woman, as "a shade from those times of blood and lust and passion and crime," the hero would both damn and exculpate his heroine. In a remarkable assertion of moral relativism, Gerald decides that Anna is channeling a past era "when women loved as men, as strongly, and often as briefly"—an epoch when European women had allegedly acted on their libidinal impulses as English men did in the Indian empire, whether by marrying across race or engaging multiple lovers or doing both at once. All the while, too, the text reminds us of the fact that these racial/sexual constructions are the projected interpretations of the white male narrator and are not without their blind spots. In considering the "physical danger" of the "native's insensate jealousy, unreasoning rage, and childish yet fiendish revenge" (137), Gerald is pointedly unaware that he is attributing the same qualities to the atavistic "shade" that has "returned and confounded itself with the clear white soul of an English girl in a body beautiful and innocent to look upon." Lest such ironies undermine our presumptive identification with Cross's narrator, Gerald regains his philosophical reflexivity, reminding himself of the subjectivity of the European view of Indians. He reflects, "Could I desert her? Married to a native! One needs to have lived in India to fully understand the horror contained in those words." But he then goes on to assert that it is only "according to the British standpoint" that the native "has no moral sense" (137).

For all his exculpatory musings, Gerald seems to accept the word *crime* as appropriate for Anna's secret marriage to Gaida Khan. That such a coupling between a white woman and a "black" man was viewed as a crime among British authorities of the period is well documented. Historian Kumari Jayawardena reveals that in 1902 "a British official deplored the recent 'craze of white women for running after black men,' adding that 'it pervades all classes of society' from peeresses to working-class women. White women who married Indians were denounced as deviant; 'unless she is sexually perverted,' wrote an Englishman in the early 1900s, 'she has violated her own nature in marrying a man of coloured race.'"[22] In this discursive context, Cross is clearly interrogating the double standard applying to Anglo-Indian men and women, but there remains an ambivalence around the phenomenon of interracial passion.

The novel turns a sharp discursive corner when the child of Anna's furtive liaison arrives, and the narrative swiftly culminates. After the death of Gaida Khan from cholera, Gerald can barely look upon the issue of Anna's secret marriage, the "half-caste" infant: "It was hideous with that curious hideousness of aspect that belongs usually to the fruit of Eurasian marriages . . . horrible in its suggestion of mixed blood" (276–78). The agonized waves of empathy that Gerald had felt for his erring beloved—the stuff of many pages at the novel's core—are extinguished abruptly when she shows signs of love for her mixed-blood infant. Sensing this antipathy and fearing that Gerald will leave her, Anna smothers the baby. Then, after having spent one year in repentant seclusion in a "white bungalow" on the Indian plain, she resummons Gerald, and all guilt is dispelled in a scene of reconciliation:

> "Dearest Anna, you are beautiful, but it is not for these things that I love you, you know."
>
> "I know, I know," she murmured, throwing herself into my arms . . . "but you are human and you like to have them, and I am human and I like to give them, and we have both suffered so much no one would grudge us our happiness now, and oh, I have prayed for God to give me back my good looks to reward you with, and that He has done so is a sign of His forgiveness; don't you think so?"
>
> And I answered softly, "Yes, dear." (297)

And so the novel ends; henceforth, neither Gerald nor Anna will dwell on her experiences of interracial marriage, de facto bigamy, so-called miscegenation, and infanticide.

The contradictions of this hasty resolution are, to say the least, rather stark. Just as Anna was drawn to Gaida for his beauty, so too is it emphasized in the end that Gerald loves Anna for hers, and the compelling rhetorical agenda of the novel has been, until these last pages, to reveal precisely this equivalence or symmetry of passionate desire. But the force of social prohibitions converts this symmetry into an asymmetry: the unnatural crime of the white woman's active desire for the "black" man finds its reverse image in the domestic bliss, sanctioned by God, of the white man's desire for the white woman. Likewise, the Christian virtues that Cross ascribes to Gerald in her preface—"He forgives the sinner, raises the fallen, comforts the weak"—instantly evaporate when he witnesses Anna's adoration of her infant, feels a fury of jealousy, and decides to abandon her and the half-caste child, despite his promises to stay. If Cross has gone to great pains to portray the human dignity of Gaida Khan, she has not done so on behalf of the infant, whose casual murder, on account of Gerald's jealousy, is rewarded in the end.

Ultimately, there are two very different ways of reading the ideological import of *Anna Lombard*'s resolution. The first is offered by Brittain, who judges that this scene of closure effectively shuts down all of the subversive potential that has been opened up by the preceding narrative: the New Woman and her unruly desires have been domesticated, and the titillating transgressions of the interracial liaison have, from the standpoint of legitimizing social discourses, been "properly" disavowed and punished. The second is to see the "safe" recontainment at the narrative's closure as forced and aporetic, as too hurried and too cursorily "decided" to settle comfortably all the questions raised by Anna's choices and actions throughout the narrative or to lay to rest the narrator's agonized, complex ruminations over them. However we choose to interpret the novel's conclusion, what is clear is that this fictive heroine's transgressions appalled most reviewers of Cross's day and led them to ignore any redemptive moral lesson in the resolution. Taking the cue of those disapproving reviewers—though in a very different spirit from their own—I am tempted to suggest that this text is the one that, among the various popular romances discussed in this book, offers us today the most surprisingly radical interrogation of social ideologies, the most daring test of the discursive boundaries of its time.

Ethel M. Dell's *The Way of an Eagle:* "Omnia Vincit Amor"

> Dell! The lowness of it! The books these lower classes read! [thought Gordon Comstock.] . . .

> "I b'lieve I'll jest 'ave *The Way of an Eagle* over again," said Mrs. Weaver finally. "You don't never seem to get tired of *The Way of an Eagle,* do you now?"
>
> "It's certainly astonishingly popular," said Gordon, diplomatically, his eye on Mrs. Penn.
>
> George Orwell, *Keep the Aspidistra Flying*

Romance editor jay dixon has suggested that the most common formal feature of the mass-market women's romance is that it is told from the heroine's point of view and that its most common theme is "that women can change men through love."[23] The romance novel has also been described as, by definition, putting "the heroine at the center of the book, at least coequal with the hero, or occupying more of the spotlight than he does."[24] If these descriptors hold, then *Anna Lombard,* told from the perspective of the hero and chronicling his fidelity to a "sinning" heroine who repents by killing her own infant, is too quirky and singular to conform to this formula. Perhaps more to the point, the formula did not yet exist. Although we cannot precisely date the emergence of what we today categorize as the mass-market "women's romance," *Anna Lombard* antedates that emergence by at least a decade.

The two romances that remain to be discussed in this chapter, Ethel M. Dell's *The Way of an Eagle* and E. M. Hull's *The Sheik,* share with Cross's romance the implicitly conservative "taming" of the rebellious heroine. But they also portray the female protagonist's experience from her point of view, effecting positive change in her chosen man. Circumstantial evidence suggests that these two novels' primary readership consisted more disproportionately of women than did the readerships of any of the other romances that I have so far discussed in this study. Clive Bloom shows that Florence Barclay's *The Rosary* and Dell's *The Way of an Eagle* were among the first successful examples of the modern romance aimed explicitly at women readers.[25] For her part, Pamela Regis demonstrates that Hull's *The Sheik* "embodies the spirit and essence of the romance novel," in its twentieth-century, mass-market incarnation.[26] Ethel Dell's biographer makes the same claim on behalf of her subject: "At the time they were written, Ethel's books seemed shockingly lucid. No woman novelist had ever provided the woman's eye view of the approaching lustful man. She spares her readers no detail of what ensues, yet she is never pornographic, never vulgar, there is no shedding of clothes."[27] It has also been shown that the modern women's romance emerged with the creation of the Mills and Boon publishing line in 1908, as the first of this firm's novels to resemble the contemporary genre were published a couple of years later, with books such as Sophie Cole's *A Wardour Street Idyll* (1910) and Laura Troubridge's *Body and Soul* (1911).[28]

Putting these facts and judgments together, we may propose that the mass-market women's romance, as we today understand it, came into being in Britain in the decade between 1910 and 1920. That the novels that made Ethel Mary Dell and Edith Maude Hull famous, and associated them thenceforth with the origins of the women's erotic romance, should also have been prime examples of the imperial romance is perhaps no coincidence. As I suggest at the opening of this chapter, these two works most clearly embody the discursive confluence of this romance genre's economies of "exotic" desire and allegorizations of the British Empire. A lifelong editor with Mills and Boon, jay dixon, has recently traced the historical development of the changing representations of "exotic" desire in her firm's early women's romances. Dixon suggests that

> [a]lthough in their early years [1908 through the First World War] Mills and Boon recognized a division between categories of fiction in their catalogues, such as crime and their "Laughter Library," the only romance category they acknowledged was the society novel, set among the English upper classes. But it is possible to discern three more categories of romance from this early period that were not officially recognized—the country novel, the city novel and the exotic novel. The first two of these are set in England, in the countryside or in a large town (usually London) respectively; the latter is set abroad, generally in a country belonging to the British Empire. (*Romance,* 5)

Of those three unofficial categories, dixon notes, the exotic novel was the one that regularly featured characters engaging in premarital or extramarital sex. The "more sexual books" of the 1910s, dixon informs us, were those "belong[ing] more to the society and exotic lines. The city and country novels are, as a whole, distrusting of passion and less sexual than those set abroad" (49). "In all these books the hero is the object of desire, but it is only in the society and exotic novels that the story revolves around his sexuality" (51). Explicit male sexuality is represented in characters from the English aristocracy and after 1914 and the demise of the "society" novel, in a class of characters that dixon characterizes as "Mediterranean heroes,"[29] who are often found in imperial settings. However, the "dark" foreign qualities of these French, Italian, and Spanish heroes, given their Caucasian racial provenance, are always clearly distinguished from the full-fledged status of the Other that would be represented by a non-European, "black" male character. "A book with a Latin hero is always 'hotter' than one with a British hero," as one editor from Mills and Boon is reported to have said (dixon, 51). At the same time, these "exotic romances" published by Mills and Boon never depicted anything more than dalliance between European and Arab or Indian characters—never, that is, allowed the ideologically policed border of interracial sexuality to be crossed. Evidence thus suggests that the popularity of the Mills and Boon exotic romance in the 1910s and '20s had to do with the greater erotic license that British readers associated, in the collective imagination, with tropical locations and non-English—but still safely European—"dark" lovers. The contrast between the Mills and Boon "exotic" plot and the transgressions depicted in *Anna Lombard* is bold and serves to suggest, again, the singularity of Cross's novel.

With few such exceptions, romance representations that approached the taboo of interracial sexuality offered the affrighted projections of the turn-of-the-century imperial allegory, which, as Jenny Sharpe has argued, frequently entails the narrative configuration of the "dark rapist" as a threat to British colonial order.[30] Sharpe and Nancy L. Paxton have demonstrated that the sepoy rebellion of 1857 triggered a late-Victorian shift in English representations of the Indian or colonized male, such that the threat of sexual violence was henceforth prominent in the cultural imagination of Anglo-Indians and the supporters of empire back home in Britain. In her survey of British and Anglo-Indian novels of the period, Paxton says, "[I]t is no accident that the dominance . . . of the colonial rape narrative which makes Englishwomen and their innocent children into a precious national sacrifice coincides with the most martial phase of British imperialism, between 1870 and

1914."[31] Such fictional depictions of the sexual menace of the "dark man" were based less in any reality than in the discursive imperatives of a threatened colonial authority:

> The binarism of Western civilization and Eastern barbarism is difficult to maintain when the colonizer is an agent of torture and massacre. A discourse of rape—that is, the violent reproduction of gender roles that positions English women as innocent victims and English men as their avengers—permits strategies of counterinsurgency to be recorded as the restoration of moral order. I am not suggesting that this representation was a "willed" operation but rather that it was a "reasonable" explanation within the logic of a civilizing mission. Governed by benevolence, moral fortitude, and rationality, the civilizing mission cannot accommodate signs of violence except where they exhibit the native's barbaric practices. (Sharpe, 6)

Indeed, recent scholarship illuminates that much literary fiction from the late nineteenth through mid-twentieth centuries evinces this allegorical "discourse of rape," whereby the colonial system shifts its underlying rationale from assumptions of self-interest and moral superiority to those of self-sacrifice and racial superiority. Among Sharpe's primary examples are G. A. Henty's *Rujub the Juggler* (1893), Bithia Mary Croker's *Mr. Jervis* (1895), Flora Annie Steel's *On the Face of the Waters* (1896), E. M. Forster's *A Passage to India* (1924), and Paul Scott's *The Jewel in the Crown* (1966) (7). The figure of the English woman who is sexually threatened or violated in a colonial setting, by Sharpe's reading, becomes a metonym for the violation of the "noble" aims of the British imperialists—even when, as in the cases of Forster and Scott, those aims are being damningly interrogated.

The Way of an Eagle and *The Sheik* are romances aimed to please and entertain the general public and thus are not texts in which we should expect to find strong indictments of colonialist beliefs and practices, any more than we would expect the English women who are presented as their female protagonists to be consciously intended as allegorical figures. Instead, bracketing the issue of authorial intentionality, we may perceive that these romance heroines constitute the textual sites of the refractory collision of, on the one hand, the fear of sexual violence and, on the other, the libidinal desire for the "exotic." The protagonists' emotional and erotic ambivalence toward their male antagonists-turned-lovers, a pattern common in the later evolution of the mass-market women's romance, is in these earlier instances heavily freighted with the ballast of an imperial history that cannot be ignored if, as Sharpe suggests, "we are attentive to the geohistorical specificity of such figures and are keenly aware that they are received rather than invented" by the authors in question (140–41). In these two iconic texts, whatever mystery and danger are to be found in the hero are "borrowed" from the racial Other, whose "exotic" proximity is a feature of the colonial landscape. Ania Loomba has demonstrated that in imperial-era writings, "aggression, violence, greed, sexual promiscuity, bestiality, primitivism, innocence, and irrationality are attributed (often contradictorily and inconsistently) by the English, French, Dutch, Spanish, and Portuguese colonists to Turks, Africans, Native Americans, Jews, Indians, the Irish, and others."[32] Keeping in mind this typical list of presumptive racial attributes, we will see that Dell and Hull, by setting their narratives amid the colonized peoples (Indians and North African Arabs, respectively), symbolically extract these hypermasculine characteristics from the "dark races" and, resituating them in the British hero, sufficiently mitigate their danger so as to tip the balance over to romantic appeal. An unconscious transference or "borrowing" of character traits is enacted; through such displacement, the symbolic contents of terrifying "black" men are effectively "whitewashed"—lodged within a European male and so made safe for fantasy consumption. I argue that this displacement allowed these novels to enter that liminal arc between masculine sexual menace and thrilling mutual passion, a vector of libidinal tension that was at once daringly modern and more socially acceptable than the direct taboo-breaking of Victoria Cross's romance.

Like *Anna Lombard*, Ethel M. Dell's *The Way of an Eagle* is set, in large part, in the Northwest Frontier of India at the turn of the twentieth century. The opening scene features a British garrison led by a brigadier general whose adult daughter, Muriel Roscoe, is the sole European woman for many miles around. Together with a dwindling band of British soldiers, father and daughter are in mortal peril: "[S]he was with him among the Hills of the Frontier when, like a pent flood suddenly escaping, the storm of rebellion broke and seethed about them, threatening them with total annihilation."[33] The parallel with the 1857 uprising is clearly established, and the hero who delivers Muriel from the implied threat of violation by the Indian "tribesmen of the hills" is soldier Nick Ratcliffe, a master of disguise and of hand-to-hand combat. Nick spirits Muriel out of the mountain stronghold just as it succumbs to the tribesmen's siege. After squiring her through the frontier wilderness, he deposits her unharmed into the hands of her new British guardian at Simla. Nick has fallen in love with Muriel, but she is ambivalent, and, reneging on her initial assent to marry him, she flees to England. After losing an arm in battle with the Indian warriors, Nick also returns to the motherland, where a subplot involving the infirmities and infidelities of mutual friends—and the revelation of Nick's more tender side—leads Muriel to the brink of realizing that she loves Nick in return. But she shuns this self-knowledge, flees back to India, and is followed there by Nick, who disguises himself as an Indian beggar to keep secret watch over her. In this guise, Nick bravely prevents the assassination of a chief British administrator by the Indian rebels and in so doing proves his worth to Muriel, who suddenly accepts her true feelings about him. The novel closes with the newlyweds on their honeymoon in the foothills of the Himalayas, as Muriel informs her delighted husband that she is expecting a child.

In marked contrast to Cross's sympathetic portrayal of Gaida Khan, whose briefly heard voice is the vehicle of a "black" man's perspective, Dell deploys her Indian characters as stick figures, voiceless entities lurking about the perimeters of Anglo-Indian society. Their status as characters "received rather than invented" is unsurprising, in light of the fact that Dell, unlike Cross, never had occasion to experience India; she was intellectually formed under limitations shared by many middle-class women of late-Victorian England. Born 2 August 1881 in the fashionable Brixton suburb of Lambeth, she was raised in sheltered circumstances and only once in her life traveled outside of England. Her father, Vincent, worked as a clerk for the Old Equitable Insurance Company in the City of London; he was such a workaholic that, as Dell's biographer, her adoptive niece Penelope Dell, tells us, "Ethel's birth was engraved on his memory as a wasted work day" (*Nettie,* 2). Dell's religious background, which can be felt in the symbolism of her romances, was slightly unusual, inasmuch as her father's family were Roman Catholic, while her mother's (the Parotts) were Protestants.

The details surrounding the publication of *The Way of an Eagle,* Dell's first of several romances, seem to offer a vindication of the powerful work ethic she acquired through such an upbringing. Dell wrote the first versions of the novel when she was in her mid-twenties; the closest companion and best editor of the fledgling author was her older sister Ella Dell, who in 1907 encouraged her to submit the manuscript to the most famous literary agent of the day, James Brand (J. B.) Pinker. Four years and at least eight rejections later, Pinker, who was accustomed to the successes of such clients as Oscar Wilde, Arnold Bennett, Joseph Conrad, and H. G. Wells, had lost interest in promoting the work of such an unknown. In 1911, an undaunted Dell submitted the manuscript to the publishers T. Fisher Unwin, who were encouraging unknown writers to enter their "First Novel Library" contest. The thirty-one-year-old did not win the prize, but at Fisher Unwin's suggestion she reduced the novel by two-thirds, and they agreed to publish in early 1912. Immediately, as Penelope Dell tells us, "[t]he sales of *Way of an Eagle* outstripped the publishers' wildest dreams. Between 1912 and 1915 it went through no less than 27 printings, each larger than the one before. Ethel, though she was unaware of it at the time, was responsible for half [of] T. Fisher Unwin's hardly inconsiderable turnover" (34).

A probable cause of this novel's success was that it tapped into popular British conceptions of the "romance" of the Indian empire. Dell derived her representations of India from family oral history and from her reading of earlier popular novels set under the Raj. Penelope Dell boasts of her aunt that "in her many stories about India, not only were her descriptions of places reasonably correct, but she could seldom be faulted on dress or customs whether civil, military, Indian, or Anglo-Indian" (4). This is a notable claim to make about *The Way of an Eagle,* inasmuch as Dell seems to set her story both in real colonial locales, such as Simla and Bengal, and in evidently fictional sites, such as Sharapura and Gwawalkhand. The first of these latter two place-names is to be found in Hindu mythology but, as far as I can tell, on no contemporary map of the subcontinent; the second may be a reworking of Gwalior, a large town on the central Indian plain where in 1858, according to some historical records, the British turned back the tide of rebellion and regained control after the savage fighting of the uprising.[34] If "Gwawalkhand" is intended as a geographical analogue to Gwalior, then a veiled historical allusion to the quelling of the mutiny may also have been intended; certainly, such a reference would be in keeping with the novel's representation of native resistance being successfully "put down" by the valorous Nick Ratcliffe and the British army. Whether or not such a connection was meant—and at notable variance with Victoria Cross's fictions—this novel's representation of British colonists and Indian subjects runs unreservedly with the grain of post-1857 imperialist apologetics.

As for family lore about India, Ethel Dell's interest was spurred by talk with her younger cousins, who had been reared there, and by the possibly apocryphal tale of her great-great-uncle Edward de Worley, who was said to have fought and died in the early 1800s among the Pathans of the Northwest Frontier. Penelope Dell suggests, "Ethel's imagination must have been stimulated as she listened to this true story about a member of her family. Honour before dishonour, duty first, even unto death, were the keystones of many of her novels, and the inspiration for such idealism may well have been seeded by Edward de Worley" (11–12). The conservative ideals undergirding this romance likely derived as well from Dell's favorite reading about India: the popular turn-of-the-century novels of Flora Annie Steel, Maud Diver, Alice Perrin, and Fannie Farr Penny.[35] All of these texts, while not full-blown imperial romances like Dell's, probably reinforced the black-and-white patterns undergirding Dell's fictional representation of the putative sexuality and violence of subcontinental peoples.[36] We have no direct evidence that Dell read Victoria Cross; we may speculate that Cross's experience of being unmarried in India may have some bearing on her less conventional novelistic depiction of British-Indian relations. Penelope Dell characterizes Ethel Dell's immersion in the colonial novels that she read as follows: "A flood of information was pouring out of India from the wives of army officers, civil servants, tea planters, and engineers. Most of it was good, solid, mediocre stuff, such as one would expect from intelligent but not conspicuously talented women, turning the commonplace intrigues of isolated up-country stations into romantic stories" (21). In addition, we are told that "Ethel enjoyed searching through the writings of Rudyard Kipling, borrowing each book as it came out either from wealthier neighbours, or from Mudie's Library, from which she had a bundle of books each month" (21).

Together, these resources appear to have constituted Ethel Dell's research into colonial life in India at the time she wrote *The Way of an Eagle*. In his work on British fictional representations of colonial India, literary historian Peter Morey glosses the episteme in which European writers about India were immersed:

> We must examine the fictional strategies used to gain power over, depict and "speak for" India and, by extension, which narrative forms are chosen and what motifs and images circulate. Indeed, do the writers recognize that what they offer is a "re-presentation" of India and not the essence of the object itself, and are they conscious of themselves as belonging to a tradition of writing which purveys such "representations"? The answer to this question is particularly important for colonial novelists since Britain's knowledge of India was dependent on steadily accumulated texts of many kinds—geographical, anthropological, legislative, commercial, military and strategic and fictional. When these texts converge a corpus of knowledge is created and a sanctioned discourse about India is born which works to perpetuate the outlook and role of the colonizer.[37]

Morey extends the Foucaultian approach of Said's classic text of postcolonial theory, *Orientalism,* to the study of such male colonial novelists as the Forster of *A Passage to India,* John Masters, J. G. Farrell, and Paul Scott. The use of Morey's formulation here is to suggest that Dell, as a nonresident colonial writer of a mode of fiction distinguished by its appeal to popular idealities and fantasies, should (*a fortiori*) hardly be blamed personally if she turns out to be a perpetuator of sanctioned discourse about India. To a certain extent, and without discounting her authorial agency in engendering plot, characters, and themes, we might expect that that discourse will effectively "speak" through her.

Given this discursive provenance, and Dell's patent interest in colonial life, it is noteworthy that the novel's English characters evince little curiosity about the presumptively inferior Indian culture that surrounds them. At the novel's opening, Muriel's devotion to her brigadier-general father is portrayed as encompassing her life, and her lack of interest in Indian culture is put in a positive light: "[S]he had not been carried away by the gaieties of this new world. The fascinations of dance and gymkhana had not caught her. The joy of being with her father was too sacred and too precious to be foregone [*sic*] for these lesser pleasures. . . . He liked to have her with him, and soon it became a matter of course that she would accompany him on all his expeditions. She revelled in his tours of inspection. They were so many picnics to her, and she enjoyed them with the zest of a child" (12–13). This idyll of seeming innocence, the enjoyable lark of imperial administration, is shattered by the uprising of the hill tribesmen: "[T]he unexpected had come . . . like a thunderbolt" (13). No reason for the rebellion is divulged, beyond the unreasoning malevolence of the "tribesmen." The one Indian we see at close range during the siege, in the scene of Muriel's near-abduction, is linked to evil: "There, within a few yards of her and drawing nearer, ever nearer, with a beast-like stealth, was a tall, blackbearded tribesman. . . . His eyes, gleaming, devilish, were to her as the eyes of a devouring monster. . . . [S]he saw the narrow, sinewy hand and snakelike arm dart forward to seize her, felt every muscle in her body stiffen to rigidity in anticipation of its touch, and shrank" (35). The diction of the demonization—"beast-like," "blackbearded," "devilish," "devouring monster," "sinewy," "snakelike"—is juxtaposed with Muriel's physical revulsion. Suggestions abound that we are about to witness the rape of the white woman by a black "devil."

This is a scene of the impending violation of the female colonial by a composite projection of European anxieties, and it is deeply informed by post-1857 "allegories of empire." Jenny Sharpe suggests how such allegories may function: "The images of native men sexually assaulting white women is in keeping with the idea of the colonial encounter as a Manichean battle between civilization and barbarism. . . . When articulated through images of violence against women, a resistance to British rule does not look like the struggle for emancipation but rather an uncivilized eruption that must be contained. In turn, the brutalized bodies of defenseless English women serve as a metonym for a government that sees itself as the violated object of rebellion."[38] Ideologically, this analysis of imperial allegory seems to map neatly onto Dell's scene of peril. The Manicheanism and the sociopolitical displacements are also familiar features of the masculine imperial romance, especially in the works of Haggard.

There is, however, a second, different moment in Dell's demonization of the Other: the figure of the devil is transferred to the very man who saves Muriel from abduction. Nick Ratcliffe, reentering the scene at brink of disaster, is emphatically not portrayed as a vision of chivalry: "[S]he presently saw Nick's face bent above the black-bearded face of his enemy; and remembered suddenly and horribly a picture she had once seen of the devil in the wilderness" (36). After a fierce struggle, Nick slays the tribesman, but Muriel will thereafter recall this instant of her rescue as the very moment when Nick's visage seemed to her as "the face of the devil" (37) and will suffer an obsessive anxiety over this violent aspect to his character.

This mirroring between villain and hero conjoins the vocabulary of satanic possession with that of sexual assault, and indeed Nick has been depicted as symbolically raping Muriel only hours before. Here is the language used to describe Nick's drugging of Muriel to spirit her away from the barracks:

> Holding her with an arm that felt like iron, he forced the glass back between her teeth, and tilted the contents down her throat. She strove to resist him, strove wildly, frantically, not to swallow the draught. But he held her pitilessly. He compelled her, gripping her right hand with the glass, and pinning the other to her side.
>
> When it was over, when he had worked his will and the hateful draught was swallowed, he set her free and turned himself sharply from her.
>
> She sprang up trembling and hysterical. She could have slain him in that instant had she possessed the

> means to her hand. But her strength was more nearly exhausted than she knew. (22)

Dell here offers one of the first examples of a thematic motif that would become prominent in many mass-market women's romances of later decades: the hero's early act of brutality, either witnessed by or perpetrated upon the heroine, is eventually redeemed by the revelation of (or the development of) the tender, loving, and gentle side of his nature. But particularly interesting at this juncture is the imbrication of Nick's early acts of brutality—both the symbolic rape of Muriel and the killing of the tribesman with his bare hands—within the racial categories often associated in the European mind with the "barbarism" of "the darker races." Revisiting the list of racial attributes that the European colonists would often impute to the colonized races—aggression, violence, greed, sexual promiscuity, bestiality, primitivism, innocence, and irrationality—we observe that the white hero Nick Ratcliffe partakes of some (though not all) of them in his two early moments of brutality, especially in his struggle with the black-bearded tribesman. This "transracialization," as it were, of Nick's character even extends to his physical appearance: "It was a clean-shaven face that should have possessed a fair skin, but by reason of unfavourable circumstances it was burnt to a deep yellow-brown. The features were pinched and wrinkled—they might have belonged to a very old man; but the eyes that smiled down into the Brigadier's were shrewd, bright, monkey-like" (2). Certainly, the epithet *monkey-like* may here carry with it connotations of bestiality, though in this context its effect is probably intended to be humorous rather than threatening—to Muriel, Nick's eyes may be unattractive, but they are also keenly intelligent. Time after time, Muriel perceives anew Nick's "wrinkled" and "yellow-brown" skin at those moments when she doubts how to read his character. Through much of the narrative, the perceived color of the hero's skin clouds the heroine's recognition of his virtuous character. In fact, Dell was well known for creating outwardly "ugly" male protagonists, in order to set the ironic—and sometimes ideologically charged—contrast between their "unattractive" exteriors and their desirably sensitive interiors. (Conversely, in some of her romances, the male villains were depicted as dashingly good-looking.) In the following, characteristically ambivalent moment of Muriel's perception, Nick manifests putatively non-European elements, both internally and externally: "His patience—his almost womanly gentleness—notwithstanding, she could not forget the demon of violence and bloodshed she knew to be hidden away somewhere behind that smiling, yellow mask" (65). By the novel's end, in keeping with the conventions that would soon become prevalent in the genre, Muriel's influence brings Nick's "womanly gentleness" to the fore. His loss of a limb also serves as a plot device to soften his character, counterbalancing his forcefulness with an element of vulnerability.

Yet this male lead does not by the novel's end lose his capacity for decisive, defensive violence; the heroine has simply learned to change her metaphors for this aspect of his character to something more positive than "yellow-brown devil" or "demon of violence." This symbolic shift begins early in the novel, as Muriel watches Nick murder her Indian assailant: he is described as "bent to destroy like an eagle above his prey, merciless, full of strength, terrible" (37). The trope of the bird of prey will thereafter counterbalance her perception of Nick as a "demon" and eventually becomes her private explanation for the "darker" side of his character. The romantic transformation of the hero consists in the gradual supplanting of the one figure for the other. The symbolic displacement of the properties of the "beast-like tribesman" into Nick is gradually transmuted into an animalistic image that is positively charged. Muriel comes to fantasize a savage abduction, as Nick metamorphoses into an airborne raptor: "[S]he slept, and dreamed that an eagle had caught her and was bearing her swiftly, swiftly, through wide spaces to his eyrie in the mountains. It was a long, breathless flight fraught with excitement and a nameless exultation that pierced her like pain" (66). Where Dell's symbolic economy earlier demonized Nick, it now ennobles him, in a positive bestialization that again represents Dell's romantic Manicheanism. The recurrent avian metaphor, "The Way of an Eagle," exchanges Nick's primitive and aggressive facets for an extended, erotic dynamic of rapture and surrender. At the same time, too, it safely stands in (like Barclay's metaphor of the paired tigers) for any actual sexual contact between him and Muriel, until such is understood to have occurred with their marriage at novel's end.

There is another notable exchange in Dell's symbolic economy, the chain of displacements that moves us along her Manichean binary from evil to good. We are encouraged to interpret Nick's "ugly duckling" aquilinity as a sign of his grace, because the symbol of the eagle informs both the title of the romance and the book's epigraph, taken from the Old Testament:

> There are three things which are too wonderful for me,
> yea, four, which I know not—
> The way of an eagle in the air;
> the way of a serpent on a rock;
> the way of a ship in the midst of the sea;
> and the way of a man with a maid.
> (Proverbs 30:18–19)

By the romance's end, the hero's eagle-like nature has become something "too wonderful"; it represents his "way," as a man, with the "maid," or virgin, that Muriel has until recently been. We are left with the same glorification of love's mysteries that we saw in the work of Barclay, but the religious trappings are here much less significant to the novel than they were in the more overtly moralistic writer. In *Bestsellers,* Clive Bloom says of Barclay that "in her work, religion is replaced by religiosity," or a dilution of religious orthodoxy (88). *The Way of an Eagle,* published just two years after Barclay's *The Rosary,* indicates yet another increment of creeping secularization. Citing the scandal of Glyn's *Three Weeks,* Bloom observes that "[i]t was this reading with its 'less Christian,' more 'liberated' sense of women's role that finally put paid to the work of Ouida and Marie Corelli and opened the way for Ethel M. Dell and later Mills and Boon" (34–35). Regarding Dell's tendency to use biblical quotations as her thematic framing device, Penelope Dell suggests that "Ethel's heavenly 'pegs' made her acceptable, her passionate content irresistible. She had found a mixture that could be swallowed undiluted, enjoyed, and yet still perform its duty. It was strictly adult reading, though, and not even the moralising whitewashed the purple passages. They were too hot for the tender mind. That these tales were neither stuffy nor pious speaks for her lively talent as a storyteller" (*Nettie,* xiv). *The Way of an Eagle* concludes with another biblical quotation, Nick's final allusion to a line from II Kings 6:17: "[A]nd, behold, the mountain was full of horses and chariots of fire around Elisha." But such snippets of theological discourse do not provide any religious timbre to the novel; they act instead as camouflage, as a bit of ideological scaffolding to protect the novel's real business, which is to conjure an earthly, earthy passion. Penelope Dell suggests that alongside such lip service to religiosity, her aunt allows moralism to dissolve into insignificance: "Ethel holds up her finger and shakes it, indicating disapproval but at the same time behind her hand she seems to hide a smile of indulgent complicity. Herein lay her discernment of human frailty. Where other women novelists would indulge in downright moralizing in order to get published, Ethel merely shook her head and looked the other way" (*Nettie,* xiv).

With this observation, we return to the claim made at the opening of this section, that Dell may be called one of the originators of the mass-market women's romance. As Clive Bloom observes in *Bestsellers*, the genre has since "spread from Ethel Dell to Mills and Boon, Barbara Cartland and Joanna Trollope, but [they] still retain recognisable elements from their origins, providing continuity within creative traditions, based on a knowledge of possible variations" (13). If religion and traditional moralism are, by Dell's time, fading out of the romance, what becomes of the Manichean opposition of good and evil, that mainstay of the romance from time immemorial? The answer, I think, is connected to another claim I make at the start of this section—namely, that romances such as Dell's and Hull's bear the traces of both "exotic" desire and the allegorization of empire. But the answer is not the reductive notion that the white man and woman become the essential sites of good and the non-European male becomes the essential source, whether literal or figurative, of evil. Jenny Sharpe suggests that "[t]he images of native men sexually assaulting white women is in keeping with the idea of the colonial encounter as a Manichean battle between civilization and barbarism."[39] In other words, in Dell's romance—and in the colonial discourse of which this novel acts as a cipher—the fundamental evil consists in cultural behaviors, rather than in racial essences. Indeed, only in the "barbaric" rebellion against the "civilizing" rule of the British do the native Indians partake of evil in Dell's novel, and the manifestation of that evil comes in the attempted abduction of Muriel (in the scene already discussed). There is another eruption of evil in the assassination attempt against the British resident governor of Gwawalkhand, which is averted by the combined efforts of Nick and Muriel. So different from her earlier, more passive presence, the now-self-assured Muriel has become an active agent for good—she wrests the revolver from the native rebel, who is caught up in a tussle with the disguised Nick, and shoots the would-be assassin dead. For all that this scene suggests about the heroine's self-empowerment through love—the woman's revenge on the source of villainy, and the ultimate balancing of the woman's courage with her man's—it also represents the resolution of the imperial allegory, whereby the moral virtue of Muriel's and Nick's combined heroism stands in for the reassertion of European administrative control. For Nick's part, this reassertion of imperial control has been a function of his ability to "pass," like Rudyard Kipling's Kim, as a native beggar. As such, it provides the bridge into discussion of E. M. Hull's *The Sheik,* which centers on similar cross-racial disguise and offers another illustration of the transformed meanings of "good" versus "evil" in the women's imperial romance.

E. M. Hull's *The Sheik:* "The Mercy of an Arab Who Was Merciless"

In *Bestsellers,* Clive Bloom observes that "[a]lthough 'spiritual' and conservative, [Ethel M.] Dell's stories also contained the violent passions so enjoyed by women (especially young girls) before World War Two. Her influence on women's romance is still evident and can be clearly seen in the 'sexier' women's novels of a later age, but also in works like E. M. Hull's *The Sheik*" (134–35). The continuity between Dell and E. M. Hull (pseudonym of Edith Maude Winstanley) is aptly noted. At the opening of this chapter, I suggest that in the three romances under primary scrutiny here, the fear of rape by the "native" male is balanced, as on a knife-edge, with the libidinality of the encounter with a romanticized, "primitive" masculinity. If Cross causes the fear of rape by the native Other to be (uneasily) transfigured into interracial marriage and Dell converts that fear to erotic ends by means of symbolic transference of putative non-European behaviors, E. M. Hull combines both of these narrative arcs in her 1919 best seller, *The Sheik.*

Among the women's imperial romances of the early twentieth century, *The Sheik* is likely the best remembered today, as its

1921 Hollywood adaptation secured the story an enduring place in the history of popular culture. The movie triggered a series of least a hundred British editions of the novel by 1923, caused a spectacular run on the novel in the United States, and, most famously, launched the celebrity of Rudolph Valentino, who played the eponymous hero.[40] However, unlike Corelli, Orczy, and Glyn, three authors whose fiction was also adapted by the Hollywood movie industry of the 1920s, Hull never established her own media image as a larger-than-life romance author. Today, little is recorded of her life. The most frequently noted feature of Hull's home existence is that she was the spouse of "a dull pig-breeder called Percy."[41] One of the few media pieces on Hull published in her own time, a 1922 blurb in *Bookman,* suggests that she did not harbor the ambition to become a celebrity writer:

> One of the most popular of present-day novelists is Mrs E. M. Hull who is seldom to be met with in literary circles, for she spends a good deal of her time in traveling, and, when at home, prefers a country life in Derbyshire, and is keen on all manner of games and sports. She wrote her first novel "The Sheik" with no idea of publishing it, but as a means of personal distraction during the war, when she had to be very much alone. When it was finished she decided to let it try its fortune with a publisher, and its prompt and unexpected success encouraged her to write another book.[42]

Another reason that Hull did not cultivate a media personality after the fashion of Glyn was a lack of popular success with her subsequent romances. The second book, mentioned here—a romance set in modern Japan entitled *The Shadow of the East* (1921)—did not fare especially well in the fiction market; neither did her handful of sequels to and spin-offs of *The Sheik,* published through the 1920s and '30s.[43] Yet of all the romanciers discussed in this study, Hull enjoys a singular distinction: her first novel is generally seen as the initiator of a distinct subgenre of the women's romance—the "desert romance," or the "sheik romance."[44] Though finding a comprehensive catalogue of all the desert romances published in the United Kingdom and United States since 1919 is difficult, the following sample from the scores of sheik-themed romance titles of the previous three decades gives a sense of Hull's long-term influence: *Desert Hostage* (1982; Diane Dunaway), *Bedouin Bride* (1984; Barbara Faith), *Desert Princess* (1986; Hayton Monteith), *Fire and Sand* (1989; Sarah Edwards), *Sheik's Spell* (1991; Eboni Snoe), *Sands of Time* (1993; Terri Valentine), *Sheik* (1997; Connie Mason), *Sheikh Surrender* (2004; Jacqueline Diamond), *Possessed by the Sheikh* (2005; Penny Jordan), and *The Sheikh and the Bride Who Said No* (2005; Susan Mallery).[45]

Because of *The Sheik*'s initial popularity and lasting presence within this subgenre of the mass-market women's romance, Hull's narrative has sparked a good deal of critical discussion in recent years.[46] The novel's plot was indeed bold for its day. A young English aristocrat, Diana Mayo, sets off with a retinue of indigenous guides for a few weeks of wandering adventure in the remote regions of the Algerian Sahara, only to be abducted by a French-speaking Arab sheik, Ahmed Ben Hassan, who rapes her and imprisons her in his camp for several months. Against her better judgment, Diana finds herself falling in love with her haughty and powerful captor, who rescues her from the clutches of a second, even-more-brutal sheik and is critically wounded in the effort. As Ahmed teeters on the brink of death, a courteous Frenchman from his past, the Vicomte Raoul de Saint Hubert, reveals to an anguished Diana that Ahmed has all along been merely passing as an ethnic Arab; he is actually the son of a Spanish mother and an English aristocrat. In the novel's final pages, Ahmed recovers and declares his love for her, and an elated Diana accepts his proposal of marriage.

Unsurprisingly, the two elements of this romance to occasion recent critical comment are its eroticization of rape and its "racial bait-and-switch." Hull initially treats the fear of rape by the native Other very differently than do Cross and Dell, in whose romances this terror hovers as an unrealized possibility and so serves both as a means toward displaced eroticization and as a conduit of unconscious, imperial allegorization. In *The Sheik*, by contrast, the rape occurs early in the tale, when both heroine and reader believe that Sheik Ahmed is ethnically Arab. Yet the brutal act is doubly removed from realist representation. First, it is occluded by its absence from the narrative proper—it initially occurs in the white space between chapters and later only by implication, as Diana reflects on her day-to-day experiences in captivity. The scene of Diana's initial violation stops short of graphic description, closing as the just-kidnapped Diana resists the sheik's kisses and he laughs cruelly, asking, "Must I be valet as well as lover?"[47] The chapter ends, and the next picks up with Diana's morning-after reflections: "She had fought until the unequal struggle had left her exhausted and helpless in his arms, until her whole body was one agonised ache from the brutal hands that forced her to compliance" (60). Second, the rape is imaginatively distanced by the geographical setting of the story: the vast, sparsely populated deserts of French-held North Africa offer no identifiable locale (as compared to the Indian and Burmese settings of Cross and Dell) of the British experience of colonial rule. The sandy domain of the Bedouin tribes being largely unoccupied by English colonists or tourists, Hull safely distances her heroine's abduction and rape from the realm of real-life threats to women residing in the territories of the British Empire. If these nebulosities represent Diana's rape in veiled fashion, the late revelation of Sheik Ahmed's ethnic lineage further serves the purpose of fashioning the sexual violation into an acceptable topos of romance fantasy. When the kidnapper is revealed to have been a European all along, the specter of miscegenation is suddenly dispelled.

But just as central to the novel's racial imaginary is Diana's ethnic identity, which triggers the sheik's sexual sadism. Late in the novel, we learn that Ahmed detests his alcoholic, abusive father, who caused his pregnant mother to flee into the desert, where she died after giving birth. This original trauma has shaped Ahmed's entire character—has led him to eschew the English language and European culture (despite his European education) and to despise the English as the race of his violent father. A repentant Ahmed confesses as much to Diana, after she learns of his secret history: "I didn't love you when I took you, I only wanted you to satisfy the beast in me. And I was glad that you were English that I could make you suffer as an Englishman made my mother suffer, I so loathed the whole race. I have been mad all my life, I think—up till now" (288). The rape of Diana is not only the act of a man who has adopted (putatively) Arab ways and therefore (according to the discourse of the Other) is licensed to act upon his lust but also the symbolic reprisal of a man who loathes his English blood, and so takes a form of ethnic "revenge" on Diana for her Englishness. This confession represents a remarkable mutation of the type of imperial allegory we have seen theorized by Jenny Sharpe, in which the reprisal for the colonized males' sexual insubordination (itself an imaginary projection) is enacted by the white male protagonist. Here, by contrast, the sheik has sought his revenge against the European colonizers through sexual violence and then repented of the sentiment behind that revenge. Ahmed's confession, as he vanquishes the "madness" of his former brutality, is intended to redeem his character and to differentiate his rape of Diana from the rape, otherwise identical, that was *nearly* committed by Ahmed's evil alter ego, the ethnically Arab Sheik Ibraheim Omair.

That gulf of racial difference must, for the purposes of ideological closure, be hardened into essence. Once Ahmed's experience of "passing" as a non-European is behind him, he casts aside his Arab garb, and for the first time he appears before Diana in European clothes, using his native tongue: "[I]t was as a stranger that he had come back to her, divested of the flowing robes that had seemed *essentially* a part of him; an unfamiliar figure in silk shirt, riding breeches and high brown boots, still dust-covered from the long [horse] ride. A thin tweed coat lay in a heap on the carpet. . . . [W]ith a little start Diana realized he was speaking in English" (285–86; my italics). Despite Diana's feeling that the Arab robes had been an "essential" part of her captor, the narrative demonstrates that Ahmed's "essential" European characteristics (emblematized by his silk shirt, riding boots, riding jacket, and English language) emerge like the sun through the dissipating fogs of his "madness." Suddenly "civilized," Ahmed realizes the enormity of his crimes against the white woman: "You think you love me now, though God knows how you can after what I have done to you. . . . [M]arriage with me is unthinkable. You know what I am and what I have been. You know that I am not fit to live with, not fit to be near any decent woman. You know what sort of damnable life I have led; the memory of it would always come between us—you would never forget, and you would never trust me" (289). Having shed his archetypal status as the romance villain, Ahmed now embodies a different romance avatar: in a sudden access of chivalry, the mysterious equestrian has come to his senses, to acknowledge that only a "decent," or civilized, man is "fit to be near any decent," or civilized, woman. There are two levels to the hero's redemption. First, the heroine's moral rescue of the hero entails his return to his racial identity as a white Englishman. Second, in a narrative maneuver that would come to characterize many subsequent mass-market women's romances, the heroine's love has "saved" the character of the erstwhile remote, brutal, and unreadable hero, making him a better person by sensitizing his hypermasculinity. On both levels, generic form dovetails with ideological content.

It might seem that we could check these coded messages off a laundry list of items on *The Sheik*'s psycho-discursive agenda, the reaffirmed *doxa* of gender and race that we might well have expected to find in the imperial erotic romance of 1919. Through the tidy resolution of the plot, the imperial allegory dovetails with the development of a mass-market formula. Regarding the novel's racial dimensions, however, there is one more aspect to consider: the hero apparently cannot expunge all traces of his Otherness, lest he lose his erotic allure. Diana accepts the revelation that her sheik is racially European, but to accept Ahmed's cultural identity as a European would be to extinguish her desire for him:

> She did not blame him, she could only love him, no matter what his life had been. It was Ahmed as he was she loved, his faults, his vices were as much a part of him as his superb physique and the alternating moods that had been so hard to meet. She had never known him otherwise. . . . The proud, fierce nature and passionate temper that he had inherited, the position of despotic leadership in which he had been reared, the adulation of his followers and the savage life of the desert, free from all restraint, had combined to produce the haughty unconventionalism that would not submit to the ordinary rules of life. She could not think of him as an Englishman. The mere accident of his parentage was a factor that weighed nothing. He was and always would be an Arab of the wilderness. (258–59)

Here we see a gray area, a blurring of the black/white binaries structuring European culture in contrast to non-Western nature. Ahmed's "fierce nature and passionate temper" stem as much from his European parents as from his self-acculturation in the ways of the Arabs. Susan Blake has proposed that *The Sheik* can be read as saluting an assembly of reactionary constructions and retrograde essentialisms but arriving finally—through the concluding declaration of Diana's desire—at a culturalist construction of race: "As Raoul needs the Sheik to be English, Diana needs him to be Other, the antithesis of the English."[48] Blake's point here is that through the signifiers of race and culture that quilt Ahmed's identity, the text eventually deconstructs these particular binaries. Hardly an extraordinary fact in itself, this result nonetheless brings with it an interesting sociopolitical consequence: a novel that condones the rape of its heroine cannot so simply be decided as reactionary.[49]

In the end, then—to circle back to the claim made at the start of this chapter—we have again witnessed in Hull the feature found in the imperial erotic romances of Cross and Dell: this subgenre of romance balances the fear of rape by the "native" male with the libidinality of the encounter with a romanticized, "primitive" masculinity. There are other contexts in which Hull's ideologically overdetermined romance should be historically situated—in particular, vis-à-vis the First World War[50] and the New Woman[51]—but I will not here elaborate on those dimensions (the latter has been especially well defined by such recent critics as Laura Frost). Instead, I conclude my discussion of Hull's romance by looking at the subliminal continuities that this text shares with venerable strains of the adventure romance and, through striking discursive affinities, with the encoding of "primitive" zones and territories in contemporaneous modernist fiction by British writers.

In *The Sheik*, of course, emotional and spiritual transcendence takes the form of Diana's finding "true love." But deposits of affective intensity in the early stages of the text suggest a different form of romantic transcendence, illustrative of the popular sublime. As Diane sets out on her trek, the desert is presented as an enchanted and animistic space: "It was the desert at last, the desert that she felt she had been longing for all her life. She had never known until this moment how *intense the longing* had been. She felt strangely at home, as if the great, *silent emptiness* had been waiting for her as she had been waiting for it, and now that she had come it was welcoming her softly with the faint rustle of the whispering sand, the *mysterious*

charm of its billowy, shifting surface that seemed beckoning to her to penetrate further and further into its *unknown obscurities*" (24; my italics). In this uncanny and extraordinary passage, moments before Diana's abduction and the commencement of her erotic experience with the hero, she feels an "intense longing" for a geographical place that feels as if it exists before or beyond history. In what I will call the "desert-cathexis" of her desire—distinct from her later longing for her sheik-lover—we witness the vestige of a traditional romance practice: the setting of the hero's or heroine's experience within a counter-real world. On one level, Diana's yearning for the "silent emptiness" and "mysterious charm" of this place is revelatory of her independent character; on another, her character does not at this juncture matter at all, and she serves simply as a recorder of a space outside of history, as a subjective conduit of an exotic and enchanted locale. Diana's empty desert here functions both as a stopping place of the novel's plot progression, a fold in space imagined to be external to human culture (which, in reality, as a part of Bedouin territory and the French-administered colony of Algeria, it is not), and as the embedded node of a more archaic mode of romance, a "discontinuous pocket of homogeneous time and of heightened symbolic closure."[52] Through Diana's perception of the desert, we witness an example of how, as Phillip Wegner says in an analogous generic context (that of science fiction), "character functions in the romance form in a very different way than in the novel: as a formal 'registering apparatus' whose movements during the course of the narrative action produce a traveler's itinerary of both the 'local intensities' and 'horizons' of the space that the narrative itself calls into being."[53] This moment also offers continuities with high Romanticism, as the desert's invitation "to penetrate further and further into its unknown obscurities" is a call for the self to lose its customary bounds and to access the timeless noumena with which natural phenomena are infused.

As if to celebrate such spatiotemporal transcendence, Hull's narrator describes the heroine's feeling of union or connection with the natural landscape:

> The idea of danger brought a little laugh to her lips. How could anything in the desert hurt her? It had been calling to her always. There was nothing strange about

> the scene that lay all around her. Her surroundings seemed oddly familiar. The burning sun overhead in the cloudless sky, the shimmering haze rising from the hot, dry ground, the feathery outline of some clustering palm trees in a tiny distant oasis were like remembrances that she watched again with a feeling of gladness that was fuller and deeper than anything she had been conscious of before. She was radiantly happy. (33–34)

In this passage, we see the palimpsests of two romance topoi from Northrop Frye's catalogue in *Anatomy of Criticism:* the initiation of the journey into adventure, and a sentient natural environment, which may be seen to possess a will of its own toward the protagonist, be it wary and malevolent or (as here) welcoming and benevolent. The heroine's sense of being "strangely at home" in a desert she has never before experienced—the fact that "[t]here was nothing strange about the scene that lay all around her" and "[h]er surroundings seemed oddly familiar"—returns us to the "deep structure" of the romance mode. Diana's uncanny sense of the familiarity of a desert she has never before occupied and her emotional suffusion with inexplicable "remembrances" bring on the connection of internal and external worlds, in a Romantic bridging between the noumena of self and of natural environment. This representation of the protagonist in relation to a natural space at once defamiliarized and uncannily familiar ("strangely at home") is highly significant; I return to such correlations between the twentieth-century narrative at hand, and both the small-r romance mode and capital-R Romanticism, in the more "properly" modernist texts discussed below.

These two early passages of *The Sheik,* therefore, represent key apertures through which (as seen in Cross and Dell) readers are delivered nearly as much libidinal energy via the spaces of the imagined Other—the settings, places, and alternative worlds of the action—as via the mutual passions of heroine and hero. The passages suggest a different narrative trajectory that might have been followed through the rest of Hull's romance: they bring to mind the typical plot vector of the masculine imperial romance. In her discussion of the imperial tales of Buchan, Haggard, Kipling, and Stevenson, Susan Jones suggests, "Recurring generic features of imperial romance find their antecedents in older forms. Most of the novels under discussion illustrate the function of the journey as it appears in medieval romance quests. . . . As in earlier paradigms, the identity of the protagonist is at stake, he undergoes a 'test,' a number of trials and temptations in the encounter with the 'other' in exotic and hazardous locations, and ideally (but by no means exclusively) remains secure and attached to the mores of his society on the return."[54] In the present context, we can revisit a list of the traditional forms taken by these medieval romantic "tests": the goal of the hero of English chivalric romances was ever "opposing the ever-present enemy, the 'Saracen,' and various wicked kings, traitors, giants, and dragons."[55] "Saracen," of course, was the term employed by the medieval English and French to refer to the Arabs in particular, and by extension to Muslims generally. If the masculine imperial romances surveyed in Jones's study offer numerous up-to-date displacements of the Saracen and the other villains of the Middle Ages romance, it is a fitting coincidence that in Hull's feminine imperial romance, which by virtue of its female adventurer and modern context is at two removes from the medieval romance tradition, the presumptive villain is portrayed as a modern-day Saracen. As we have seen, this avatar of the medieval-romantic Saracen is effectively converted from evil to good under the influence of the heroine's love; the heroine might be said to succeed at this test. However, *The Sheik* inverts other aspects of the romance quest of Jones's description: the heroine's identity fundamentally changes as a result of her adventures; the temptations of her encounter with the Other are impossible to resist, as her individual agency is forcibly stripped away; and she does not remain secure and attached to the mores of her society on her return, in part because she does not return. As the conclusion of the novel shows us, her wish is never to be sent away from the desert; her desire is to remain in this enchanted space. She will be granted her desire, but the space, while yet enchanted, will be reterritorialized—that is, it will lose its intoxicating openness and be symbolically invested with an older form of patriarchal domination than that of capitalist Europe.

Just as *The Sheik* inverts the residual structures of the medieval romance, so too it anticipates the uses to which "enchanted" and "exotic" geographical spaces would be put in the popular women's romance of the decades that followed its publication. In *The Principle of Hope* (1959), Ernst Bloch theorizes the species of transcendence that we see Diana experience in her "desert moment." When the modern subject travels to "beautiful foreign lands," Bloch tells us, she is in a position "not to experience any of the deadening effects of everyday life and possibly see meanings in the objects which in everyday life only a competent painter would discover. Defamiliarization is here the exact opposite of alienation; within the bourgeois-private world, travel is the May which makes everything new."[56] Bloch goes on to link the positive defamiliarization of travel in beautiful foreign lands to the experience, both actual and textually represented, of the first flush of romantic love.

There is, then, a Janus-like quality to *The Sheik*, which at once conveys the "deep structures" of the older British romance form yet also, by remolding those structures around a female protagonist, faces forward into the future of the women's romance. The fantasized spaces of the North African desert provide the heroine with an imaginary, alternative society to that of the West; she has entered a new territory in which evaporate the discursive boundaries of the civilization that she has voluntarily left behind. In materialist-psychoanalytic terms, this romance has dissolved, through its desiring trajectories, certain values, beliefs, and practices regarding gender and sexuality—it has deterritorialized the heroine's body by opening it up to desire and by relocating it in a space external to the libidinal limitations of the society left behind. Diana's longing takes the unconventional form of cathexis on geographical territory, on a tract of nature, and this imaginary production of desire has (or is intended to have) an emancipatory effect on readers. The heroine has gone beyond the reach of any protection from kidnapping and rape, but she has also, at the same stroke, gone beyond the reach of any fetters on her now socially unconstrained libido; she has experienced a continuity between the territories of the body and terrene expanses that, however briefly, are felt to be outside of culture. Then, in a move of recontainment, the story's resolution reterritorializes the libidinal flows thus released, insofar as the heroine comes corporeally to belong to the now inhabited desert and to the converted hero. In an archaically patriarchal fantasy, she has chosen to belong to the now socialized place, as well as to him; this sense of belonging is what she most ardently wants. "'You won't send me away?' she whispered pleadingly, like a terrified child. . . . 'Never!' he said sternly. 'I will never let you go now'" (296). The space of the desert, which in its uninhabited form had made her feel "strangely at home" and "had been calling to her always," is ultimately realized as the place where she belongs, in a romantic consummation that represents true love both as a metaphysical and as a geographical form of homecoming. But that space is only so realized when it has been refigured as a "primitive," patriarchal community.

Modernist Primitivism, the Romance Mode, and Romanticism

This final instance from *The Sheik* leads to a larger speculation regarding a link between this form of the romance and certain examples of fiction more traditionally labeled modernist. Gilles Deleuze and Félix Guattari's trope of "territorialization," which I have been "unearthing" within romance representations, provides the correlation. In *A Thousand Plateaus,* this phenomenon is presented as a metaphor that is also a synecdoche—it is simultaneously corporeal, geographical, and the abstracting ground of an analogy.[57] Cross, Dell, and Hull figure libidinal flows of energy via representations of the spaces of the imagined Other—the exotic settings, the alternative worlds of the action—just as much as they do so via the depicted relations of the main characters. These romances enact what Deleuze and Guattari label decoding or deterritorializing flows—to wit, the dissolving, through their desiring trajectories, of older values, beliefs, and practices regarding race, gender, and sexuality—only to recode and reterritorialize, to produce new strictures and bounds, which may or may not be seen as socially progressive, depending on the instance in question and one's angle of view. In this respect, the mystifications of the imperial erotic romance may be said to offer "lowbrow" analogues of the "primitivist" imaginary seen in the works of such modernist writers as Woolf, Lawrence, and Mansfield.[58]

But this is not an argument about conscious influence between the popular romances and the modernist texts. The "primitivist" topoi of such modernist works rely on the same discursive resources, inherited within British culture at large, that are evident in the romances discussed here; in both low modern and modernist narratives, these tropes variously serve to subvert traditional representational codes to symbolically deterritorialize the represented life-material, that is, these primitivisms set adrift "schizophrenic fluxes of bits and scraps of things, people, words, customs, and beliefs,"[59] in ways that effectively scramble the Western discursive regimes of the time regarding "savage" or "uncivilized" peoples and cultures. As I begin to suggest here but explore more fully in the next chapter, these textual de- and reterritorializations (which, when we move beyond the specific context of primitivism and its literal geographies, will perhaps better be denoted by the more discursive terms *de-* and *recodings*) are enacted at the level of content in the popular romances under discussion here and at the levels of both content and form in certain modernist texts.

Woolf's first novel, *The Voyage Out* (1915), has commonly been considered a female bildungsroman that generically intertwines the love story and the quest narrative.[60] The novel stages the development of the young heroine, Rachel Vinrace, in the fictive South American colony of Santa Marina and, unusually for Woolf, offers representations of both "exotic" geography and the racialized Other. Critics have commented on the use of primitivist discourse in the symbolic structure of this protomodernist narrative, in which the heroine dies of illness at age twenty-four, before she has had the chance to consummate her love relationship or achieve her quest for self-definition. These critical responses address Woolf's ideological representations, conscious or unexamined, of the land, peoples, and culture of the South American expatriate colony and of the inland areas into which her English characters travel.

At the outset of the transatlantic voyage, Rachel's forty-something mentor, Helen Ambrose, offers a narrative emblem of their journey's destination: she is embroidering a piece of cloth with "a great design of a tropical river running through a tropical forest, where spotted deer would eventually browse upon masses of fruit, bananas, oranges, and giant pomegranates, while a troop of naked natives whirled darts into the air."[61] Does such a passage encode an ironic critique of Helen's imperialistic assumptions, or does it implicitly endorse this vision of the exotic "primitive"? The answer is uncertain in the early Woolf—by contrast with the later Woolf, who more radically interrogates the category of "civilization" on which such a question depends.[62] We might consider this question in light of a later moment in *The Voyage Out* when, on the boat journey upriver "into the heart of the night" in the tropical jungle (this novel's parallels to Conrad's *Heart of Darkness* have not gone unnoticed by commentators), the three women in the English party raise "the question of nakedness" and choose to sleep nude on mattresses laid out on the deck (the men follow their example, "at the other end of the boat") (259–60). Clearly, the white characters increasingly feel the lifting of civilization's codes of conduct as they steam up the Amazonian river ("As they moved on the country grew wilder and wilder" [261]), but does this indicate that Woolf is conjuring "enchanted" and "exotic" geographical space after the fashion of E. M. Hull's Saharan desert?

To this latter question, which has to do with the tropical territory, distinct from its indigenous people, I think the answer is yes. Strong evidence may be found in a scene in which dovetail the love story and the adventure quest—the romance material—of *The Voyage Out.* Perched atop a seaside cliff, a few days before the voyage upriver, Rachel and Terence Hewitt are thrilled by the panorama of continent and ocean:

> [H]ere the view was one of infinite sun-dried earth, earth pointed in pinnacles, heaped in vast barriers, earth widening and spreading away and away like the immense floor of the sea, earth chequered by day and night, and partitioned into different lands, where famous cities were founded, and the races of men changed from dark savages to white civilised men, and back to dark savages again. . . . [H]aving once turned their faces that way they next turned them to the sea. . . . It was this sea that flowed up to the mouth of the Thames, and the Thames washed the roots of the city of London. (200)

The view available to their eyes interiorizes; it elaborates itself on an inward screen and is recast as a cognitive map shared by the two characters. They project immensities of land, alternately bathed in daylight and shrouded in night; they "view" a chiaroscuro pattern by which those immensities are divided up among the "races" of "dark savages" and "white civilised men." So too the sight of South America's eastern seaboard conjures the image of a city-space three thousand miles across that water. As a counterpoint to the murk of the metropolitan river, the pristine waves at the base of the cliff offer an elating access to prehistory: "So it had been at the birth of the world, and so it had remained ever since. Probably no one had ever broken that water with boat or with body" (200–201). The lexical connection of this virgin sea with "body" libidinalizes the scene with a surge of romantic-erotic longing, as Terence, to whom these sights offer a "freshness and newness" that seem "wonderful," realizes that Rachel's "body" is "very attractive to him," and he is "overcome with the desire to hold her in his arms" (201). The territory—presenting him with imagined alternations between "savage" and "civilised," between "dark" and "white," and between a symbolic "night" and "day"—seems to trigger a sudden cathexis via which Rachel's body becomes, in the psychic experience of Terence, coextensive with the ground beneath their feet.

The trajectory of Woolf's heady passage moves from an exhilarating and shared cognitive mapping to the erotic impulse of the heterosexual man alone; this shift grants Woolf the possibility of some "wiggle room"—that is, the potential, by the end of the passage, for ironic, critical distance. Nonetheless, what we witness here might be seen to perpetuate the classic form of "territorialization" that is explored in Anne McClintock's *Imperial Leather,* in which the physical geography of the New World is both racially polarized and gendered as the sexualized feminine, through various tropes of colonization. Lest we worry about the naive entanglement of Woolf in such discursive webs, it should be repeated that her later works, especially *The Waves* and *Between the Acts,* suggest a much more self-conscious critique of the imperialist tropes that are spared narrative interrogation here; moreover, as is discussed below, the climactic passages of Rachel's voyage into the interior will unsettle this type of libidinal investment. But through much of *The Voyage Out,* Woolf seems to participate, however ambiguously, in the celebration of "the primitive" as a set of resources for recharging romantic-erotic energies and renovating Western cultural forms.

This participation is most evident in sequences describing the collective attitudes of the novel's British travellers. One early passage in particular merits a long quotation, as the narrator establishes the story's donnée:

> The reasons which had drawn the English across the sea to found a small colony within the last ten years

> are not so easily described, and will perhaps never be recorded in history books. Granted facility of travel, peace, good trade, and so on, there was besides a kind of dissatisfaction among the English with the older countries and the enormous accumulations of carved stone, stained glass, and rich brown painting which they offered to the tourist. The movement in search of something new was of course infinitely small, affecting only a handful of well-to-do people. It began by a few schoolmasters serving their passage out to South America as the pursers of tramp steamers. . . . The country itself taxed all their powers of description, for they said it was much bigger than Italy, and really nobler than Greece. Again, they declared that the natives were strangely beautiful, very big in stature, dark, passionate, and quick to seize the knife. The place seemed new and full of new forms of beauty, in proof of which they showed handkerchiefs which the women had worn round their heads, and primitive carvings coloured bright greens and blues. (85–86)

The comparison of South American indigenous culture with that of Italy and ancient Greece suggests the modernist turn to "the primitive"—itself a "movement in search of something new"—as an inspiration to the aesthetic sensibilities of Woolf's fellow Bloomsbury bohemians. The attraction of well-educated English tourists to Santa Marina, on account of the region's arts and crafts, likely refracts Woolf's own excitement about the non-Western elements of postimpressionist art and of the designs and products of the Omega Workshops, which her sister Vanessa and friend Roger Fry codirected.[63] The paintings of Matisse and Gauguin, the Congolese fabric patterns of the Omega artisans[64]—such were the "new forms of beauty," inspired by non-Western "primitive" cultures, that provided correlates to Woolf's fictional artifacts. The attraction of such newly discovered forms to "only a handful of well-to-do people" smacks of the avant-garde's selective appeal to a sophisticated elite; in contrast to the figurations of "the primitive" in Cross, Dell, and Hull, Woolf's exoticizing of the culture of the Other might seem, unsurprisingly, to be "caviare to the general." But the ideological parallel subsists.

Of course, it is true that Woolf's narrator attributes the description of the "natives"—"strangely beautiful, very big in stature, dark, passionate, and quick to seize the knife"—to the turn-of-the-century English "schoolmasters" who originated that modern "movement in search of something new." But we do not detect much daylight between the collective views of "the English" and Woolf's structure of feeling in this passage. This interpretation of Woolf's characteristic narratorial stance in *The Voyage Out* does not take for granted the ironic distancing that we attribute to the technique of free indirect discourse. While she may apply the technique in passages that concern the perspectives of individual characters, there is not much evidence that, in this first novel, it ironizes *collective* attitudes. On the contrary, we may discern here a high-modernist version of that eroticized projection of "native" physical energies that is to be found in the imperial erotic romance. Whether the schoolmasters' British usage of the term *native* here refers to Santa Marina's Spanish and Portuguese colonials, its mestizos, or its indigenous peoples is unclear. But Woolf's omniscient narrator leaves unironized the romantic exoticizing of a fiery, "dark," potentially violent populace. She also illustrates, without evident narratorial irony, the imperialistic attitude toward these people's lands in the dialogue of her British tourists. At the suggestion that he should "raise a troop and conquer some great territory and make it splendid," a male expeditionary asks, "They're all conquered already, aren't they?" His fellow-traveler's response is telling: "It's not any territory in particular. . . . It's the idea, don't you see? We lead such tame lives" (131). This latter sentiment seems to rearrange Marlowe's claim, in *Heart of Darkness,* about Western Europeans' "conquest of the earth," that "what redeems it is the idea only." Woolf may have been conscious of Conrad's novella as she penned such lines; regardless, what is noteworthy is the repetition of the term *territory* here and elsewhere in *The Voyage Out* and the difficulty of determining what attitude we as readers are intended to take toward that territory's "conquering."

The reconnection of such tropes of territory to romantic love arrives late in the text, when, at the culmination of the boat journey into the interior, Rachel and Terence become engaged. Immediately thereafter, their disembarked party laboriously pushes through the tall grasses of the rain forest; Rachel feels Helen's hand clap upon her shoulder, and Rachel falls, feeling herself "rolled this way and that, now seeing only forests of green, and now the high blue heaven" (276). Struck "speechless" and "almost without sense," Rachel sees the heads of Helen and Terence looming over her and hears them laughing: "She thought she heard them speak of love and then of marriage. Raising herself and sitting up, she too realised Helen's soft body, the strong and hospitable arms, and happiness swelling and breaking in one vast wave. When this fell away, and the grasses once more lay low, and the sky became horizontal, and the earth rolled out flat on each side, and the trees stood upright, she was the first to perceive a little row of human figures standing patiently in the distance" (276–77). Homoeroticism swells between Rachel and Helen; indeed, as Patricia Juliana Smith has shown, earlier drafts make the lesbian subtext explicit, as the erotic interplay between the two women is portrayed as mutually desiring, and Terence is absent.[65] I would complement Smith's reading by drawing attention to Rachel's next utterance: "Who are they?" (277). "They" are presumably the other members of the English band, but it is only seconds later that their leader walks them into the indigenous village that "was the goal of their journey" (277), and it is hard to miss the symbolic thrust of "she was the first to perceive a little row of human figures," as though Rachel is in the advance guard of an expeditionary force making first contact with native tribes of the New World. Rachel's "Who are they?" proleptically intertwines the European tourists and the members of the Amazonian tribe, the majority of whom are mothers and children, "soft instinctive people" who silently offer the visitors "sweetmeats" (277).

The English cohort has accomplished its quest, the journey-within-the-journey that is the upriver search for "a little row of human figures" that represent the Other to "civilized" Europeans. This achievement dovetails with the symbolic apex of the heroine's courtship narrative, the moment of supreme happiness when her betrothal is announced. But this "wild" space beyond the borders of Western civilization has enabled a self-forgetting on the part of the heroine in which she transgresses, at what would have been the conventional climax of the narrative, the heterosexual script that we have seen in the imperial erotic romances of Woolf's time. Soon after, Rachel's death from illness will interrupt the conventional *Bildung* of the heroine. As Smith notes, "[T]he village scene marks the beginning of Rachel's resistance to her own engagement, as the native women leave her with a sense of 'insignificance' and 'pain' in her being 'in love.'"[66] The tropes of the "primitive" are being put to ideological use here in the context of erotic love, but Woolf has inverted conventions that we have witnessed in the imperial erotic romance, by feminizing and, in effect, deheterosexualizing those tropes.

Like the popular romanciers, Woolf has indeed exoticized and enchanted the space of the "primitive." But in contrast to the three romances discussed in this chapter, Woolf does not reterritorialize the opened space of "the primitive" with patriarchal and/or imperial investments:

> Seeking each other, Terence and Rachel drew under a tree. Peaceful, and even beautiful at first, the sight of the women, who had given up looking at them, made them feel now very cold and melancholy.
>
> "Well," Terence sighed at length, "it makes us seem insignificant, doesn't it?"
>
> Rachel agreed. So it would go on forever and ever, she said, those women sitting under the trees, the trees and the river. (278)

This fold in space, this pocket of symbolically homogeneous time, is not enlisted in the ideological project of self-aggrandizement on the part of the British tourists. While Rachel has, perhaps inevitably, projected a symbolic meaning upon these women of foreign language and culture, she is also aware of their gaze and of her status as indifferent object to their subjectivity. Lacking any exoticizing qualifiers, the trees and the river represent an eddy in time that is not exclusive to such spaces at the margins of Western empire. At this climactic juncture of her novel, Woolf has disrupted the ideological patterns heretofore evident. She has effectively deterritorialized "the primitive"—has disinvested it as a geographical, corporeal, and metaphorical zone of cathexis. That this passage, much worried over and redrafted in her revisions, is from a formal perspective the novel's most elliptical, ambiguous, and disruptive of narrative convention is perhaps no accident.

D. H. Lawrence is another modernist fiction-writer on whose primitivist tropes the imperial erotic romance casts an illuminating light. Since the groundbreaking publication of Marianna Torgovnick's *Gone Primitive* (1990),[67] the most commented-on narratives encoding Lawrence's idiosyncratic primitivism, elaborated as in the work of no other canonical modernist fiction-writer except perhaps Conrad, have been *Women in Love* (1920) and *The Plumed Serpent* (1926). Torgovnick's detection of a symbolic "regendering" of the primitive—from feminine and degenerative in the former novel to masculine and regenerative in the latter—has spurred an ongoing exploration of the complexities and contradictions in this discursive matrix,[68] which was central to both Lawrence's literary corpus and the spiritual questing of his last decade of life, with his sojourns to Australia, Ceylon, Mexico, and New Mexico. Space forbids a re-elaboration of these readings of Lawrence; instead, we may briefly consider points of contact with the foregoing discussion of Cross, Dell, Hull, and Woolf.

First, *Women in Love* offers conceptions of "the primitive" parallel to those found among the characters in *The Voyage Out,* as a set of imaginative resources toward the putative liberation, romantic and libidinal, of English bourgeois-bohemians. Unlike Woolf, however, in this novel Lawrence does not represent exotic territories but instead portrays the emotions and interiorized visions spurred for his European characters by archaic or "savage"—Amazonian, Egyptian, Aztec, West African—artifacts and cultures. In the early chapter titled "Fetish," Gerald awakens from his sexual encounter with Pussum to discover that the men in Halliday's flat are padding about in a state of nudity; he is asked about his own experience "in hot countries where the people go about naked . . . South America—the Amazon.[69] Gerald is skeptical about his fellows' idealization of the tropics, which carries an implicit critique of the dissociated sensibility or limited sensorium of life lived in a cold climate. The "heavy, slack[,] . . . degenerate, perhaps slightly disintegrate" Halliday asserts, "Oh—one would *feel* things instead of merely looking at them. I should feel the air move against me, and feel the things I touched, instead of having only to look at them. I'm sure life is all wrong because it has become too visual—we can neither hear nor feel nor understand, we can only see. I'm sure that is entirely wrong" (77–78). Here as elsewhere in the novel, Gerald's resistance to such desiring projections is meant to be taken as obtuse, as the sign of a lack of cultural experimentalism that will eventually doom him. Birkin theorizes on Halliday's African fetish-object, asserting that, for the present company, this work of art "conveys a complete truth" about "culture in the physical consciousness, really *ultimate* physical consciousness, mindless, utterly sensual" (79). This is portrayed as a profound insight. Gerald resents the idea, the narrator asserts, "because he wanted to keep certain illusions" (79). For his own part, Birkin is unconcerned with the ritual or symbolic functions the carving might have held in its African setting;[70] he does not admit to the unknown—the lost symbolic coding that originally created the aura of this socially sanctioned fetish—but he recodes it, in the Deleuzian sense, as an index of the "primitive," as a relibidinalized fetish of his own people's putative lost psychic origins. The net effect of Birkin's reading of the "primitive" in *Women in Love* can be extrapolated from his rhetorical projection upon the carved figure of a woman in labor: just as he puts the artifact to his own idealizing uses as an organic, Romantic symbol (of the type Paul DeMan has identified in Coleridge's writing),[71] so too does he essentialize both race and gender via that symbol's putative timelessness.

When it comes to romantic love, *Women in Love*'s discourse of the racial Other is more abstract than that found in imperial erotic romances—there is no ambiguity, for instance, about the four central lovers' literal ethnicity as Anglo-Saxons. In concert with the passage just examined, Birkin, as Lawrence's mouthpiece, dreams up intense projections of "the primitive" as a means of comprehending his own experience of libidinal drives. Having had physical consummation with Ursula, he channels the energy he had earlier believed to emanate from the West African fetish and relocates it temporally as an ancient Egyptian "potency": "[H]e sat still like an Egyptian pharaoh. . . . He knew what it was to be awake and potent in that other basic mind, the deepest physical mind. And from this source he had a pure and magic control, magical, mystical" (318). If the contemporary West Africans have, according to Birkin, "gone beyond phallic knowledge" into a feminized sensuality outside linear Western time, this ancient North African source is alleged to align the feminine and masculine essences in balanced counterpoise, providing both Ursula and Birkin with the "star-equilibrium which is alone freedom" (253, 319). Lawrence's poetic formulation would seem to suggest an inverse use of the "primitive" to that found in Cross, Dell, and Hull. Their tales of heterosexual anxiety and desire worked through the complex of tensions between a willful British woman and an exotic or "Othered" man, and through the gendering of the "primitive" as masculine, to arrive at the libidinal balance of plot resolution. Here, the gender and sexual ideology is differently structured; Lawrence deploys his feminized "primitive" to the same end result, resolving Birkin's heterosexual anxieties and desires by means of this symbolic catalyst, rather than by a romantic relationship with the lover as "primitive" Other.

Perhaps it is no coincidence that this inverted gendering of the "primitive" occurs through the pen of a (notoriously, ever since Kate Millet's 1970 critique) sexist writer. Be that as it may, what remains constant between the women-authored imperial romances and this male-authored text is recurrent gesture, never quite total, toward essentialization of gender, as well as race. But we have seen that Lawrence would later regender the "primitive" as masculine and regenerative, both in *The Plumed Serpent* and, as Laura Frost has shown, in the 1924 short story "The Woman Who Rode Away."[72] In these two narratives, not only characters but also geographic territories represent uncivilized wildness, in parallel with the figurations we have observed in the imperial erotic romance. In Lawrence's work, Frost has demonstrated the exception to the general rule that there is little or no conscious influence of these popular romances on the modernist texts that also thematize the "primitive." Lawrence had not merely read *The Sheik* but had in these two narratives reimagined Hull's plot in portentous response to what he called, in his literary criticism, "the throb of *The Sheik*."[73] The erotic content of both "The Woman Who Rode Away" and *The Plumed Serpent* consists in encounters between the white woman and the racially Othered man, but these are by no means love stories; they instead offer abstract allegorizations of the romance arc. They pivot on the categories of race, nation, and exoticized land. But they are just as anxious about the prospect of the literal miscegenation of the races as are the texts of Cross, Dell, and Hull.

The white American protagonist of "The Woman Who Rode Away" ventures alone into the wilds of the Sierra Madre, on an obscure impulse similar to that impelling Hull's Diana Mayo. Gazing from the porch of her family home, she is beckoned by the vast expanse of empty Chihuahuan mountains: "To be sure, the great wooden doors were often open. And then she could stand outside, in the vast open world. And see great, void, tree-clad hills piling behind one another, from nowhere into nowhere. They were green in autumn time. For the rest, pinkish, stark dry, and abstract."[74] This depiction of a geographical space as before or beyond history—"void," "nowhere into nowhere," a "vast open world"—resembles the Sahara as perceived by Diana Mayo, and Lawrence's protagonist feels an intense longing to escape into it. As in Hull's romance, this initial deterritorialization leads to a symbolic reinvestment of the land with a plenitude of cultural meaning, but Lawrence turns the subsequent abduction, this time by Amerindians of the "savage" Chilchui tribe, into a story of impersonal race-retribution and Aztec-style human sacrifice. The threat of rape, so central to Dell's and Hull's romances, dissipates over the last stages of this narrative, as, after residing some days as a captive among the tribe—gently washed and anointed but never physically harmed or violated—the woman is drugged, stripped, and laid out upon a flat cave-stone. Moments before plunging a knife into her heart, the eldest tribal member gazes at the setting sun, and in his eyes "there was power, power intensely abstract and remote. . . . [T]he old man would strike, and strike home, accomplish the sacrifice and achieve the power. The mastery that man must hold, and that passes from race to race" (68). This quasi-rape will be nonsexual, an archaic religious rite that is justified by the didactic logic of the racial narrative. The communal bodies of the Amerindians would be coextensive with the wilds of the Sierra Madre; Lawrence reterritorializes both with significations that turn the erotics of this sacrifice into a metaphor for the power and mastery that his own race should learn from another.

So too, as Torgovnick has suggested, *The Plumed Serpent* transforms the marriage of European woman and Amerindian man into an allegory for masculinist primitivism as a source of renewal for Western civilization. Although the heroine, Kate, is mesmerized by the "primitive" sexuality of the indigenous people and is ritually anointed with the status of a fertility goddess, that fecundity is ultimately a metaphor, a matter of the insemination of one essentialized race with the putative energies of another. If, as we have seen, *The Sheik* finally arrives at an implicit blurring of the white/black binaries structuring European culture in opposition to non-Western nature, then the Lawrence of *The Plumed Serpent* blurs his categories in a way that is both more abstract and more explicitly ideological.

A third modernist case, that of Katherine Mansfield, presents a configuration of primitivism with its own distinctive emphases—and a shift, in parallel with Lawrence, from an earlier to a later literary attitude toward the material, both of which may be placed in illuminating relation to the imperial erotic romance. Mansfield shares with Victoria Cross and Ethel Dell the personal and/or familial experience of the British colonies—in her case, New Zealand, where she lived seventeen of the first twenty years of her short life. As do their romances, so too do some of Mansfield's writings transmute the "exotic" spaces and indigenous figures of the British imperial periphery, in this case "Maoriland,"[75] into the stuff of romance. Unlike the romancists, however, she does not stage heterosexual erotics within these Othered territories; nor does she follow the pattern of Lawrence and the early Woolf, in projecting a multifaceted critique of Western civilization through an idiosyncratic modernist primitivism. Instead, Mansfield mystifies and idealizes antipodal nature (and in her earlier phase, antipodal peoples) after the fashion of English Romantic poets, especially Wordsworth. Her youthful journals and some of her early vignettes feature what Nicholas Thomas identifies as a form of "settler primitivism," which can be distinguished from the modernist primitivism of radical formal innovation stimulated by tribal art (such as the primitivism of modernist art that we have glimpsed, indirectly, in art-oriented passages from *The Voyage Out* and *Women in Love*).[76] The adolescent Mansfield's settler primitivism represents instead a desire to establish an emotional and artistic connection, not with a generic "primitive" culture but with a particular local one—that of the Maori of New Zealand.

Mansfield's diaries record her interest in meeting Maori individuals, especially in the detailed account of a month-long camping trip, November to December 1907, into the interior of New Zealand's North Island, through the Urewera district: "Give me the Maori and the tourist and nothing between." She often idealized the individuals she encountered, as in her description of a Maori man in whose face she sees "passion might and strength" and another of a young Maori girl, silent and motionless, "all the lines" on whose face "are passionate, violent, crudely savage" but in whose "lifted eyes slumbers a tragic illimitable Peace. . . . She is the very incarnation of evening, and lo—the first star shines in her eyes."[77] While this latter passage may indeed reveal "a sense of the 'primitive' that curiously looks forward to D. H. Lawrence,"[78] one should recall that these are the observations of a nineteen-year-old, a white colonial youth who has not yet matured into artistic interrogation of the discourses of modernity, racialist or otherwise.

Likewise, Mansfield's only story featuring an erotic relationship between colonial and indigenous figures is a piece of juvenilia, the unpublished vignette "Summer Idylle" (1906). Mansfield sets "Summer Idylle" on the shore of "a gigantic amethyst" of a lake—the North Island's Lake Taupo, the site of the Maori legend of Hinemoa and Tutanekai.[79] The two main characters, one based on Mansfield and the other (probably) on her Maori school friend Maata Mahupuku, bear culturally transposed names, so that the white girl is called "Hinemoa," and the Maori girl, "Marina."[80] This languorous tale begins with the awakening of the white girl, who opens her blinds to the morning song of the New Zealand tui bird and enters Marina's bedroom, in which "the floor was strewn with blossoms" and "the scent of the Manuka [tree] was heavy and soothing." The language of Hinemoa's encounter with the sleeping Marina owes a stylistic debt to the adolescent Mansfield's literary idol, Oscar Wilde: "A faint thin colour like the petal of a dull rose leaf shone in the dusk of her skin. Hinemoa bent over her with a curious feeling of pleasure, intermingled with a sensation which she did not analyze. It came upon her if she had used too much perfume, if she had drunk wine that was too heavy & sweet, laid her hand on velvet that was too soft and smooth" (75). The pleasurable effect of the "dusk"-colored youth on the Mansfield surrogate is not only visual but also, by suggestion, olfactory, gustatory, and tactile; these sensory registers intermingle with a sensation that she does not analyze, perhaps because it hints at Lord Alfred Douglas's love that dare not speak its name. Marina opens her eyes, takes Hinemoa's face in her hands, and kisses her "just between her eyebrows" (75). The rest of this prose poem consists of the two girls' swimming and eating together, interspersed with gestures by the Maori girl that both frighten and beguile the white girl—Marina's baring of teeth, her teasing threat of cruelty, her recounted myth of trees that seize and kill warriors, and her consumption of blue yams (New Zealand kumara, of which the white girl says, "No, I don't like them. They're blue—they're too unnatural" [76]). If, as Nicholas Thomas posits, a "settler primitivism" (106) can be distinguished from a modernist primitivism, then the seventeen-year-old Mansfield (who had had three years of schooling in London) appears to have been influenced by both cultural attitudes.

Two features of the vignette are telling. First, with her fellow modernist, the Woolf of *The Voyage Out*, Mansfield shares the opportunity afforded by the setting of imperial periphery to take a risk (however brief and, in this case, unpublished) in representing homoeroticism. Second, unlike both the popular romanciers and her fellow modernist, the Lawrence of the three narratives discussed above, she does not gender her "primitive," despite—or because of—the lesbian subtext. The literal sex of Marina does not appear to be metaphorical or synecdochic with regard to her indigenous identity (and this impression is, I would argue, of a piece with the usual absence of gender essentialism in Mansfield's entire oeuvre). Like every other narrative, popular or experimental, scrutinized in this chapter, the vignette is shot through with the desire and anxiety that are constitutive of European primitivism. When the uneasy Hinemoa proclaims that she "lacks that congruity" that Marina enjoys with the land, her friend responds, "It is because you are so utterly the foreign element" (76). But the lambent counterworld of "Summer Idylle" is lyrical and Elysian, not edgy or dangerous; this youthful flight of fancy recontains the Mansfield figure's brief "terror" within an enchanted Romanticism.[81]

Mansfield's camping diary carries plentiful remarks upon the landscape and the indigenous inhabitants of the North Island, and her mature period also features stories—"The Garden-Party," "The Doll's House," and so forth—that are set in New Zealand. But "Summer Idylle" is the closest she ever came to a convergence of love story and primitivist tropes. Her lyrical reworking of the legend of the lovers Hinemoa and Tutanekai hints at the reason: it is as if the very proximity of the non-European native peoples caused her, through the discursive nimbus of "settler primitivism," to relocate her libidinal investment in constructs of the "noble savage" at a temporal remove, in the mythical past. In Mansfield's Urewera notebooks, the romance mode manifests itself both in a re-enchanted environment, inhabited by the ghosts of indigenous history, and in high Romanticism, through the revelation of Wordsworthian spots of time, catalyzed by antipodal nature. She projects Manichean animation out into her natural surroundings, as in her description of the Kaingaroa bush, its trees and logs "like strange fantastic beasts, a yawning crocodile, a headless horse, a gigantic gosling, a watchdog—to be smiled at and scorned in the daylight, but a veritable nightmare in the darkness" (Mansfield, *Notebooks,* 146). She goes on to people the landscape with indigenous revenants: "And now and again the silver tree trunks, a skeleton army, invade the hills. . . . Visions of long dead Maoris, of forgotten battles and vanished feuds stirred in me" (*Notebooks,* 136). The young Mansfield feels a melancholy sense of desertion emanating from the once-populated wilds: "And always through the bush this hushed sound of water running on brown pebbles. It seems to breathe the full deep bygone essence of it all—a fairy fountain of golden rings—then rounding a corner we pass several little whares [Maori dwellings], deserted & grey" (*Notebooks,* 140). Throughout the Urewera notebooks, we see again the palimpsests of two of the romance topoi catalogued by Northrop Frye: the journey into adventure, and a sentient natural environment, which may be portrayed as possessing a will of its own toward the protagonist.

Through the same diary pages, Mansfield records a series of Romantic epiphanic moments. One example is her description of an encounter with the Waikato River, which may recall Wordsworth's Simplon Pass in Book VI of *The Prelude:* "Then the climb, the rocks, the uncertain foot walk, higher & higher, clinging to the trees, the shrubs, . . . & then a tumultuous foaming torrent of water, leaping, crashing, snow white, like lions fighting, thundering. . . . It seems as if there is nothing in the world but this shattering sound of water—it casts into the air a shower of silver spray—it is one gigantic battle. I watch it and I am one with it" (Mansfield, *Notebooks,* 146). As the "sounding cataract" haunts the Wordsworth of "Tintern Abbey" "like a passion," so too does it elate the young Mansfield. She records moments of access to the traditionally conceived Sublime. A mountain scene summons the fierce and brutal music of a German Romantic composer, through the emotion she recollects in journal-writing tranquility. At sunset, her hiking party gazes upon "the lonely mountain outlined against a vivid orange sky," then sits "huddled up there alone—fiercely almost brutally thinking—like Wagner" (Mansfield, *Notebooks,* 145).

We have moved from primitivist tropes to the conjuring, via the New Zealand environment, of a conventional European Romanticism. But the two modes are interfused; here in the diaristic travel writing, Mansfield is unconsciously laying the early groundwork for their appearance in two of her most fully realized modernist ventures, "Prelude" (1917) and "At the Bay" (1922). These linked stories epitomize the narrative experimentalism that Mansfield pursued in the last seven years of her short life. "Prelude," its title a tribute to Wordsworth, fictionalizes the Beauchamp family's move in the 1890s from urban Wellington to a rural homestead; formally it de-emphasizes plot and occludes narratorial presence in a manner as groundbreaking as that of Woolf's novels of the 1920s (Woolf and her husband were the first to publish "Prelude," through their Hogarth Press). Its sequel, "At the Bay," which depicts a day in the same family's life at a seaside cottage, is one of Mansfield's final stories before she died of tuberculosis in January 1923; it may be seen to offer the most radical multiperspectivism that she was destined to achieve. The latter story, in particular, signals the formal direction that Virginia Woolf was to follow most vividly in her intersubjective novels *Mrs. Dalloway, To the Lighthouse, The Waves,* and *Between the Acts.* That the first of Woolf's experimental novels, *Jacob's Room,* appeared during her personal and professional association with Mansfield is no coincidence; of course, speculations abound about the profundity of their mutual influence, but clearly both writers were arriving simultaneously at narrative tactics of fragmented point of view and manifestation of the unconscious.

Here, the salient feature of the two Mansfield stories is the fusion of such a modernist form with the transmutation of the romance elements and the Romanticism of the juvenilia. Both dimensions, a small-r romance environment and a capital-R Romantic sublimity, are metaphorized through the two texts' highly self-conscious "New Zealand-ness," their use of the natural environment—in particular, its flora and fauna—as a symbolic wellspring of defamiliarizing effects. There is no longer any direct reference, after the manner of "Summer Idylle," to Maori culture or people as a symbolic matrix. Suffusing the narratives is a penumbra of exoticism that has in Mansfield's mature writing been expunged of primitivist racialism. Both the original title of "Prelude," "The Aloe," and the name of the central child-figure, Kezia (a variation on cassia),[82] allude to subtropical plants unfamiliar in anglophone lands of the northern hemisphere. The aloe plant looms over the narrative of "Prelude" like an otherworldly messenger from a mystical plane of existence. The great aloe growing in front of the Burnells' new home catches Kezia's attention as she explores the wild yard. Along the rural roadway to the house, there is an "island" of grass: "Nothing grew on the top except one huge plant with thick, grey-green, thorny leaves, and out of the middle there sprang up a tall stout stem."[83] She is frightened, feeling as if this plant "might have claws instead of roots. The curving leaves seemed to be hiding something; the blind stem cut into the air as if no wind could ever shake it" ("Prelude," 73). Upon asking her mother, Linda, about it, she is told that it is an aloe, a century plant that flowers "once every hundred years." Despite Kezia's fear of "the fat swelling plant with its cruel leaves and fleshy stem" (73), there is also a sense of wonder at the aloe's otherworldly quality, its inhabiting by a veiled spirit.

Here the child's perspective is what conveys the sense of a supernatural will manifested in the natural environment, but the aloe also beckons Kezia's mother with its promise to help her see into the life of things. When Linda's own mother, Mrs. Fairfield, later tells her, "I have been looking at the aloe," Linda becomes dreamy: "'Do you feel it, too,' said Linda, and she spoke to her mother with the special voice that women use at night to each other as though they spoke in their sleep or from some hollow cave—'Don't you feel that it is coming toward us?'" (90). Is this the "special voice" of an encaved sibyl, of a matriarchal oracle? We pivot into Linda's psychic interiority, as she daydreams of being pulled up out of cold water and onto a ship with a "budding mast." Exalted, she thinks "how much more real this dream was than that they should go back to the house where the sleeping children lay and where Stanley [her husband] and Beryl [her sister] played cribbage" (90). Although Linda has shared with her mother the hallucinatory sense of the aloe's motion, it comes to symbolize a psychic withdrawal, a place of refuge from contact with others, especially from the contacts necessitated by her roles as wife and mother.

Elsewhere, too, Linda and Kezia anthropomorphize and channel the vitality of the fauna around them. In one striking passage, animals and humans exchange voices: from the shelter of her bedroom, Kezia hears "tiny owls" calling "more pork, more pork," and the bush comes alive with a chatter of "Ha-ha-ha . . . ha-ha-ha"; simultaneously, "'Honk, honk,' came from the servant girl (she had adenoids)," and Kezia herself "gave a little squeak" (63). Later, in a striking instance of the manifestation of Linda's unconscious, she translates the laughing cries of mynahs and New Zealand tui-birds into her sunrise dream.

> She was walking with her father through a green paddock sprinkled with daisies. Suddenly he bent down and parted the grasses and showed her a tiny ball of fluff just at her feet. "Oh, Papa, the darling." She made a cup of her hands and caught the tiny bird and stroked its head with her finger. It was quite tame. But a funny thing happened. As she stroked it began to swell, it ruffled and pouched, it grew bigger and its round eyes seemed to smile knowingly at her. . . . It had become a baby with a big naked head and a gaping bird-mouth, opening and shutting. (64)

Other critics have subjected this uncanny passage to the Freudian reading for which it seems to beg;[84] more salient here, perhaps, is the subtle enchantment of reality, so prevalent throughout these stories, whereby the defamiliarized, exterior nature depicted by the narrative is continuous with characters' psychic interiority. As unstable as Linda's and Kezia's mental conditions may at times appear, they are also the wellsprings of the narratives' creativity, their dislocating freshness.

These encounters with aloe and birds suggest how, throughout both stories, Mansfield's technique of free indirect discourse depicts internalizations of the natural environment—perceptions on the border between realism and fantasy—and provides an ambivalent feeling-tone of fascination and disquiet. As a final example, we may consider a late scene from "At the Bay," in which Linda's sister, Beryl Fairfield, gazes out her bedroom window:

> The manuka tree, bent by the southerly winds, was like a bird on one leg stretching out a wing.
>
> But when Beryl looked at the bush, it seemed to her the bush was sad.
>
> "We are dumb trees, reaching up in the night, imploring we know not what," said the sorrowful bush.[85]

The New Zealand bush, that primeval zone of native flora and fauna, here speaks with the collectivized voice of a whole wild region. Mansfield records that she did indeed intend to fix the attention of British readers on such terrestrial exoticism. In her journal of early 1916, just before she returned to "The Aloe" to pare it down to the greater ellipticality of "Prelude," she planned that the revised narrative should "make our undiscovered country leap into the eyes of the Old World," should convey "a sense of mystery, a radiance, an afterglow."[86] The writer devised a project to make New Zealand strange, to invest the terrestrial Other with a mystery that would spark readers' desires. More specifically, in "Prelude" and "At the Bay," Mansfield may be said to have deterritorialized the representation of the "antipodes," Britain's geographical antonym, by her anthropomorphizing of the flora and fauna and by her gentle bestialization of the human characters. These defamiliarizations cross conceptual limits or frontiers and, I would venture, set deterritorialized flows of desire into textual circulation. Together with the anxieties that unsettle Linda and mesmerize her daughter Kezia (such as the imagined "hundreds of parrots . . . that persisted in flying past Kezia with her lamp" ["Prelude," 58]), those desires are enacted through the psyches of the characters; both psychic phenomena are also intended to affect Mansfield's readers. However, differently from every other narrative examined in this chapter (including Mansfield's own juvenilia), the Othering of indigenous non-Western peoples is almost entirely absent.

Via their inflections of modernist primitivism, the Woolf of *The Voyage Out* and the Lawrence of the narratives discussed here sublimate or displace the love stories and quests of the romance mode into their narrative departures from traditional realism. Yet their primitivist tropes are drawn from the same continuum of discursive resources that also charge the imperial erotic romances with anxiety and desire. In Mansfield's "Prelude" and "At the Bay," the libidinal energies of the imperial romance find their "exotic" correlatives only in the most abstract sense, in narratives that have to do, not with the love story or heterosexual eroticism, but with various representations of the mind's romanticization of reality. As such, Mansfield's stories offer a bridge into the subject matter of chapter 6, the modernist romance of interiority.

CHAPTER SIX

Modernism and the Romance of Interiority

In 1927, England's former minister of education, Eustace Percy, voiced a common perception of his era when he announced that "the greatest 'mind opiate' in the world is carrying the eye along a certain number of printed lines in succession. . . . The habit of reading is one of the most interesting psychological features of the present day."[1] Percy's view offers a good sample of the British establishment's reception of most of the romance novels discussed in the foregoing chapters. His narcotic or pharmacological metaphor is especially telling, as it reminds us that many among the cultural elite saw popular narrative as an enervating compensation for the psychic pain of the reality principle—a deleterious means for the "masses," who had attained near-universal literacy only as recently as the turn of the century, to medicate themselves against the afflictions of daily life.

In the view of Queenie Dorothy Leavis, her husband, Frank Raymond Leavis, and like-minded Arnoldians, the antidote to such mass-cultural doping was "serious" literature. In her widely influential *Fiction and the Reading Public* (1932), which has since become a touchstone to cultural studies, Q. D. Leavis tells us that this category features the works of those we now label the high modernists: Joyce and Woolf, Conrad and Lawrence. Quoting Ezra Pound, she laments that "when 'The pianola replaces / Sappho's barbitos' national life suffers; fantasy fiction is the typical reading of people whose normal impulses are starved of the means of expression" (209). She suggests that there has arisen a polarization, unique to the early twentieth century, of the fiction-reading public: on the one hand, "sophisticated" readers of realist and modernist literature; on the other, the less (or poorly) educated readers of "fantasy-fiction." Listing "highly popular novelists"—Florence Barclay, Hall Caine, Marie Corelli, and the American midwesterner Gene Stratton Porter (a woman romance writer)—Leavis says that they are "genuinely preoccupied with ethical problems, whatever side attractions there may be in the way of unconscious pornography and excuses for daydreaming" (64). Any concessions to these best-selling authors' forays into serious themes, however, are outweighed by negative aesthetic judgments. She avers that these four authors' most famous works—Barclay's *The Rosary,* Caines's *The Christian* (1897), Corelli's *The Sorrows of Satan,* and Stratton-Porter's *The Harvester* (1911)—"have aroused such torrents of enthusiasm because they excite in the ordinary person an emotional activity for which there is no scope in this life. These novels will all be found to make play with the key words of the emotional vocabulary which provoke the vague warm surges of feeling associated with religion substitutes—e.g., life, death, love, good, evil, sin, home, mother, noble, gallantry, purity, honour" (64). Nonetheless, she observes, there is "evidently a vast public that derives great pleasure from reacting this way" (65). The romances that Leavis lists, two of which are explored in previous chapters, did of course represent the tastes of common readers in Britain; records indicate that each of the four novels listed here was among the top two or three sellers within the twelve months following its publication—*The Sorrows of Satan* in 1895, *The Christian* in 1897, *The Rosary* in 1910, and *The Harvester* in 1912.[2] The heated terms of Leavis's description—"torrents of enthusiasm," "excite[d] . . . emotional activity," "warm surges of feeling," and "great pleasure"—connote simultaneously the effects of stimulants and of evangelical fervor. The literature of less-educated readers may be "genuinely preoccupied with ethical problems" but on the whole is judged to be precisely *non*-genuine—akin to artificial stimulation or bogus religiosity.

As the account of a divide between sets of readers, however, Leavis's famous *Fiction and the Reading Public* today suggests to us not a binary opposition but a complex symmetry between the experimentally modern and popular fiction of the early twentieth century—in particular, between best-selling romance and what we conventionally call modernism. Just as the modernist themes of self-abnegation and supreme sacrifice for art were borrowed from religious tropes to exalt the artist—think of Stephen Dedalus or Gustave von Aschenbach—so too may the consumption of popular romance be said, by Leavis's account, to offer the reader a pleasurable and parareligious exaltation of the emotions, through the appeal to the charged ideological notions represented by the "key words of the emotional vocabulary." Could not the relationship between the parareligious asceticism associated with some modernist texts and the quasi-religious enthusiasms here associated with increasingly secular romance texts be construed not as inversion but as a difference of kind or degree? What if "serious" modernist narratives might be seen to offer parallels, rather than inversions, of the compensatory psychic function of popular narrative?[3] However indirectly, Leavis's argument suggests a complementarity of affect, whereby the sublime quest of the modernist artist—and, frequently, of the modernist protagonist—finds a parallel phenomenon in the ecstatic transports of the romance protagonist and the "fantasy-fiction" reader.[4] It may be, as my earlier discussion of the popular sublime suggests, that the highbrow and the lowbrow species of exaltation, the differing means of parareligious transport, were not, when viewed from the angle of readers' reception, as neatly opposed as they might conventionally appear. We might read some high modernist narratives as consolatory or compensatory resources, in parallel with the "escapism" of the popular romance. In a discussion of Joyce's *Portrait of the Artist,* for example, one critic has recently suggested that "each of Stephen's romantic moments comes as a defense against some prior pain" and that the defense mechanism is also enjoyed by the reader.[5] I argue in this chapter that parallel interpretations of "romantic moments" may also be suggested by Katherine Mansfield's narratives, as well as those of other canonical modernist writers—in particular, West, Woolf, Lawrence, and the earlier Joyce (not only of *A Portrait* but also of *Dubliners*). Together, the examples raise the possibility that

Leavis's cathartic regimen of serious literary narrative might be no less powerful an anodyne than romantic and fantastic escapism.

These questions, triggered by the pharmacological and religious figures employed in Leavis's influential account of mass-marketed fiction,[6] may at first glance seem overgeneralizing, but they are meant to provoke, to push into the background the well-elaborated aesthetic and allegedly ethical differences between elite and popular literature in the period under scrutiny and instead to speculate on the anxieties and desires addressed by both "high" modernist and "low" modern narrative. My central contention in this final chapter is that such anxieties and desires overlapped—that modernist and romance narratives served parallel functions for their early twentieth-century readers and that, when it came to reader reception, more significant than the differences *between* these genres may have been their shared differences *from* late nineteenth- and early twentieth-century "high realism." In contrast to the social diagnoses of literary realism—intended to awaken, disturb, educate, and even galvanize readers into action—the metaphors and symbols of both modernist and popular-romance narratives may have acted therapeutically on the anxieties and longings that readers' quotidian social experience either actively engendered or at least did little to allay or satisfy. If, as Percy lamented in 1927, most of the popular "present-day reading discourage[d] thought," then, from a perspective that considers the reception and consumption of narrative in twentieth-century Western society, such reading may be more in a dialectical than a diametrically opposed relation with "serious" modern literature, and not least because the great works of Joyce, Lawrence, Woolf, and others centrally treat the problem of a social realm in which the mass-cultural compensations for and diversions from readers' social alienation should have to exist at all. Thereby, the modernist fiction-writers may be said to offer narrative compensations of their own, which, if considerably more self-reflexive in their complex symbolic systems, nonetheless succeed because of their psychic and emotional appeal, their psychoactive—no less than their overtly sociopolitical, philosophical, or "cerebral"—effects. In the case of these two fictional modes, what "elite" and "common" readers "got" from their literature may not have been so different, after all.

By way of speculating on this affinity, the following discussion takes as its main exhibit an early short story by Katherine Mansfield,

"The Tiredness of Rosabel." Mansfield's tale, written on the cusp of modernist experimentation in British fiction (circa 1908), offers a realist vignette of a day in the life of a young sales clerk in a London millinery shop. In anticipation of the modernist focus on the interior life, Mansfield's story chronicles the memories of the main character, Rosabel, of her day on the job and depicts a daydream fantasy triggered by two encounters—one with a best-selling romance novel, the other with clients at the hat shop. The story combines elements of three literary modes—realism, romance, and an emergent modernism—in a compact, dense representation of their interrelations. Mansfield's depiction of the reading of the popular romance provides a synecdoche of the lived context of lower- to middle-class women's (but not *only* women's) reading of the romance; its realist slice of life suggests reasons for the appeal of novels such as the one Mansfield chose to insert into her narrative, *Anna Lombard*. Moreover, both in content and in form, the story indexes the deep structural affinities shared by the popular romance and modernism, through their homologous cultural responses to the conditions of life under early twentieth-century modernity.

Ultimately, I argue, Mansfield's ambivalent but empathetic critique of the reading of popular romance may point toward an important strand of the modernist mode: what I have been calling the romance of interiority, a mode of representation that may be especially prevalent in writings not only by Mansfield but also by the early Joyce, Lawrence, West, and Woolf. The romance of interiority consists of dialectically altered elements of both the traditional romance mode of narrative and its offshoot, early nineteenth-century British Romanticism. As a concept, the romance of interiority is meant in part to counter the T. S. Eliot–inspired notion of modernist anti-Romanticism, which proposed that, within texts of literature, clues to objective reality could be found only in works that built upon classic monuments to civilization (Homer, Virgil, Dante, and so forth) and that otherwise the individual writer had little hope of gaining insight into an absolute Being from which that writer, as a denizen of twentieth-century modernity, was necessarily alienated.[7] The modernist version of the psychic inscape that I elucidate here builds instead upon an alternative literary tradition to the high classical—a tradition more democratic and readily available, often subsumed within the narrative at hand in a fashion that is intuitive or semiconscious, both for the reader and even, in some cases, for the writer. The romance of interiority denotes the linguistic quest for moments of access to the sublime or the absolute, in representations of psychic spaces through which such apertures, like a set of spiritual asymptotes,[8] are tantalizingly approached but never fully reached. What we witness here, I argue, is a strain of modernist narrative that both disenchants and re-enchants.

Katherine Mansfield's "Rosabel" and Compensatory Narratives

Katherine Mansfield wrote "The Tiredness of Rosabel" in 1908, at a watershed moment in British literary history. This, of course, was the year when Ezra Pound first arrived in London, and Ford Madox Hueffer started a journal, the *English Review*, that helped transform British literary conventions.[9] Though Henry James, Joseph Conrad, the New Woman novelists, and others had already been probing the boundaries of prose fiction—and though, to be strictly chronological, 1908 antedates Woolf's symbolic fulcrum of 1910—the year is generally recognized as a significant one for English-language modernism. It is fitting that a twenty-year-old Mansfield, just moved to London from the antipodes, should have at this moment written the story now generally regarded as the bridge between her juvenilia and mature work. "The Tiredness of Rosabel" has features of both dominant high realist and emergent modernist fictional modes; Mansfield here experiments for the first time in her career with free indirect discourse and internal monologue.[10] These are, of course, two characteristic modernist techniques, but "Tiredness" also features Mansfield's earliest experimentation with what Pamela Dunbar has called her "sophisticated techniques of indirection . . . including the use of fairytale and mythic parallels at odds with their chronicle-realist surfaces."[11] The fairytale and mythic parallels that Dunbar here identifies are significant; I would go a bit further and suggest that the story puts into play a sibling generic category—the romance narrative—at a literary historical moment when it was still this mode, and not any yet-to-be-named modernism, that was felt to be the aesthetic antithesis of realism.[12] In Raymond Williams's term, this older category of the romance might be labeled a residual cultural form[13]—though one that was destined not to fade away but rather to be reinvented.

Mansfield's story derives its content from the sterility and alienation of the protagonist's everyday life. In the opening sentences, she deploys the free indirect discourse later associated with Joyce's *Dubliners:* a measured, gently ironic, third-person voice that merges with Rosabel's thoughts:

> At the corner of Oxford Circus Rosabel bought a bunch of violets, and that was practically the reason why she had so little for tea—for a scone and a boiled egg and a cup of cocoa at Lyons are not ample sufficiency after a hard day's work in a millinery establishment. As she swung on to the step of the Atlas 'bus, grabbed her skirt with one hand and clung to the railing with the other, Rosabel thought she would have sacrificed her soul for a good dinner—roast duck and green peas, chestnut stuffing, pudding with brandy sauce—something hot and strong and filling.[14]

Rosabel is a modern type, a figure of common urban life: the lower-middle-class shopgirl on her evening commute home. At the outset, the mode of representation here is realist. Unlike, say, a Mrs. Dalloway or a Molly Bloom, Rosabel betrays no noteworthy tics of individual character through her represented flow of consciousness; nor does any linguistic experiment reflect the aleatory wanderings of the human mind. Her food cravings do not denote the singularities of a Leopold Bloom, with his unusual penchant for the inner organs of beasts and fowls; the point here is of a rather different kind, in that Rosabel has forgone heartier forms of sustenance by purchasing a bunch of violets with her tea money. Rosabel has sacrificed a good dinner for the more ethereal pleasures of the everyday aesthete; the purchase of the violets is "*practically* the reason why she had so little tea" on this evening, the adverb emphasizing our protagonist's dreamy impracticality, her romantic idealism.

We discover just how common this romantic impulse is when we meet Rosabel's alter ego, a romance-reading fellow-commuter on the bus beside her: "She sat down next to a girl very much her own age who was reading *Anna Lombard* in a cheap, paper-covered edition, and the rain had tear-spattered the pages" (3). As discussed in some detail in chapter 5, *Anna Lombard* was a best-selling romance of passion and intrigue set in India and Burma and excoriated in the respectable press for its alleged lewdness of sexual incident and description. Rosabel scorns this seemingly escapist and lowbrow reader, whose novel is damp with a figurative wash of emotion while she engages her lips, tongue, and fingers in a corporeal pleasure that mirrors the sensuality of the reading material: "[Rosabel] glanced at the book which the girl read so earnestly, mouthing the words in a way that Rosabel detested, licking her first finger and thumb each time that she turned the page. She could not see very clearly; it was something about a hot, voluptuous night, a band playing, and a girl with lovely, white shoulders" (3–4).[15] With characteristic descriptive economy, however, Mansfield has already established Rosabel's similar susceptibility to the romanticization of reality, as she has imagined that the drab city façades around her have transformed themselves into fairy palaces (3). Later, when she arrives at her flat and settles in for the evening, Rosabel forgoes her customary practice of reading in favor of daydreaming: "If she pulled the blind and put out the gas it was much more restful—Rosabel did not want to read" (4). But this choice to daydream rather than to read on this particular evening suggests that she experiences the same need that motivates her bus-riding alter ego's reading of a romance. Rosabel loses herself in a fantasy of love, whose buildup paraphrases the novel of her fellow-commuter: "Yes, it was a voluptuous night, a band playing, and *her* lovely white shoulders" (7). With a compassionate irony, Mansfield's narrator makes it clear that Rosabel's fantasy likewise takes the form of a romance narrative. Rosabel's self-distancing from the romance reader, as it turns out, has been a suspiciously energetic—and evidently unconscious—repression of her own self-recognition.

"The Tiredness of Rosabel" hints in its title at a causal link between the main character's—and, by extension, the reading bus-rider's, and many lower-middle-class shopgirls'—conditions of existence and fantasy life. Mansfield offers a fictional version of the later analysis offered by Leavis in *Fiction and the Reading Public.* Considering the link between reading and boredom, Leavis theorizes a change in the nature of work, a shift that accompanied the late nineteenth century's vast expansion of the reading public:

> It is generally recognised that the universal need to read something when not actively employed has been created

> by the conditions of modern life. The notes made by Mr. George Sturt (*Memoirs of a Surrey Labourer* [1907]), *Change in the Village* [1912], *The Wheelwright's Shop* [1923]) of the changes he himself has witnessed since 1884 in the lives of both town and country workers go a long way toward explaining this. He writes in detail of craftsmen for whose personal skills the introduction of modern methods has substituted machine-tending. He observes how the comeliness has been taken away from the peasant's life and his traditional way of living broken down, the ordinary worker everywhere losing the delight that a really interesting and varied round of duties gave. The old order made reading to prevent boredom unnecessary, whereas the narrowing down of labour that specialisation has produced has changed the working day from a sequence of interests to a repetition of mechanical movements of both body and mind. (48)

Without invoking Marx by name, Leavis offers a vivid, commonsensical version of the theory of the alienation of labor as a prime cause behind the popularity of escapist novel-reading.[16] The supplanting by machines of "craftsmen" and their "personal skill" may be interpreted here to signify that industrial means of production strip the workers of their potential for self-realization in their work. The ever more specialized division of labor causes a fragmentation of the processes of production, whereby the worker loses his/her sense of control and mastery and comes to feel like a powerless "cog in the machine." The lassitude and fatigue of modern readers are not the products of longer hours, then, but are instead *psychological* effects of the quality of the work, with its dull repetition, monochrome specialization, and general tendency to the worker's disempowerment. Leavis broadens her characterization of the reading material in this context to "something to read," momentarily dropping her focus on popular fiction and thus underscoring the psychic dimension of "reading to prevent boredom," irrespective of subject matter or content.

Considering Mansfield's story in light of Leavis's conception of worker alienation, we note that Rosabel, a lower-middle-class shop attendant, does not tend a factory machine. Yet her lack of satisfaction with her work implies the parallel repetitiveness of service work, with its stream of predictable clientele and its continual focus on one narrow aspect of daily living—in Rosabel's case, the sale of clothing accessories that she plays no part in creating or enjoying. As a common shopgirl, Rosabel experiences the alienation, if not exactly of Leavis's manual "craftsmen" then of the service-sector employee. She does not literally produce the hat with which she gratifies the unnamed customer and her male companion, Harry, but, as Mansfield's minutely observed description conveys, she does help produce the consumers' pleasures in the act of shopping:

> They had been very hard to please; Harry would demand the impossible, and Rosabel was almost in despair. Then she remembered the big, untouched box upstairs.
>
> "Oh, one moment, Madam," she had said. "I think perhaps I can show you something that will please you better." She had run up, breathlessly, cut the cords, scattered the tissue paper, and yes, there was the very hat—rather large, soft, with a great curled feather, and a black velvet rose, nothing else. They had been charmed. The girl had put it on and then handed it to Rosabel.
>
> "Let me see how it looks on you," she said, frowning a little, very serious indeed.
>
> Rosabel turned to the mirror and placed it on her brown hair, then faced them.
>
> "Oh, Harry, isn't it adorable," the girl cried. "I must have that!" She smiled again at Rosabel. "It suits you, beautifully."
>
> A sudden, ridiculous feeling of anger had seized Rosabel. She longed to throw the lovely, perishable thing in the girl's face, and bent over the hat, flushing.
>
> "It's exquisitely finished off inside, Madam," she said. (5–6)

Rosabel's instrumental role as a temporary menial to others is underscored by the well-to-do shopper's insistence that she herself try on the hat that the shopper will purchase and enjoy. The shopper's flattery only heightens Rosabel's sense of her lower social status. The encounter fills Rosabel with a carefully concealed anger, just as the presumptuous and condescending flirtation of the shopper's male escort irritates her with its "insolence" (6). At the same time, the encounter with the well-to-do and the flirtation of the attractive man will also provide the donnée of her later, solitary, nighttime romance narrative. (In a later section, I say more about this exemplary reworking of ordinary, everyday experience into an extraordinary romance narrative.)

Through her fictional depiction of this well-nigh-intimate scene of commerce, Mansfield conjures an early instance of the social interaction and psychic experience of what has recently been called the "immaterial labor" of our own, more fully developed consumer society. The function of "immaterial labor" has been theorized by Michael Hardt, who suggests that one of its important facets consists of

> the *affective labor* of human contact and interaction. . . . To one degree or another this affective labor plays a certain role throughout the service industries, from fast food servers to providers of financial services, embedded in the moments of human interaction and communication. This labor is immaterial, even if it is corporeal and affective, in the sense that all its products are intangible: a feeling of ease, well-being, satisfaction, excitement, passion—even a sense of connectedness or community. Categories such as in-person services or services of proximity are often used to identify this kind of labor, but what is essential to it, its "in-person" aspect, is really the creation and manipulation of affects.[17]

In her "in-person" role as a shopgirl, Rosabel, no differently than today's department store attendants, customer service reps, and "Walmart greeters," is shown to produce anticipation, excitement, and satisfaction—in other words, to "create" and "manipulate" affects among her customers. In and of itself, Hardt suggests, such affective labor can be a tremendous resource; it is best understood "by beginning from what feminist analyses of 'women's work' have called 'labor in the bodily mode'" ("Affective," 96).[18] When it has not been appropriated directly into the circuits of capital, in fact, "what affective labor produces are social networks, forms of community, biopower" (96). This is not a possibility for the lonely Rosabel, of course, as we see no evidence of her being plugged into any social networks or forms of community; her affective labor consists in part of repressing her actual emotional responses—she has to dissimulate her "anger" and her "flushing" face by bending over the hat and offering another useful piece of information about it. Working in the service of commodity exchange, Rosabel experiences an access of the particular species of alienation that may come of such "immaterial labor."

Nonetheless, the story also displays a libidinal exchange, "embedded in the moments of human interaction and communication," that complicates the depiction of Rosabel's social frustrations:

> The man leant over her as she made out the bill, then, as he counted the money into her hand—"Ever been painted?" he said.
>
> "No," said Rosabel shortly, realizing the swift change in his voice, the slight tinge of insolence, of familiarity.
>
> "Oh, well you ought to be," said Harry. "You've got such a damned pretty little figure."
>
> Rosabel did not pay the slightest attention. How handsome he had been! She had thought of no one else all day; his face fascinated her; she could see clearly his fine, straight eyebrows. (6)

The passage presents an interpretive knot, as it seems to belie the notion that we are witnessing a straightforward scene of service-worker exploitation. If readers may notice the double entendre of "ever been painted"—as a sitter for a portrait or as a painted lady of the night—Rosabel does not. This minutely observed moment offers a fine example of Mansfield's craft, her adept use of the modernist technique of free indirect discourse: what Rosabel tells herself about the encounter—that she did not pay Harry "the slightest attention"—is, of course, contradicted by what we are shown of her thoughts. Rosabel resents the well-to-do man's presumption, his masculine insolence and privileged overfamiliarity. Yet what Hardt calls the "intangible products" of the affective labor seem to be not all engendered on behalf of a consumer taking momentary advantage of a service worker; Hardt's catalogued feelings of "well-being, satisfaction, excitement, passion" register, however ambivalently, within Rosabel herself. Moreover, even as the daily indignities of Rosabel's work cause her to take refuge in compensatory fantasies, this encounter provides the raw material of that fantasy life, as her romantic daydream is catalyzed by her imagining herself in the place of Harry's shopping companion: "Suppose they changed places" (6). We might see her reverie as an example of what Michel de Certeau calls "making do," or the various tactics that the socially disempowered employ to rework the given circumstances of their lives in ways unanticipated by the empowered.[19] Nevertheless, this service worker/consumer interaction in the millinery stops well short of that "sense of connectedness or community" that a less alienated transaction of affective labor might betoken. Later in the story, Rosabel's impotent fantasy is conducted in a poignant condition of solitude that shows no sign of changing. Again, we witness Leavis's spur to the reading—or in this instance, the internalizing of the script—of "fantasy fiction": "To obtain vicarious satisfaction or compensation for life." Rosabel and the female commuter incarnate Leavis's "universal need to read something when not actively employed," a need that "has been created by the conditions of modern life."

Our close reading of Mansfield's story has not yet considered the significance of its final paragraph: "And the night passed. Presently the cold fingers of dawn closed over her uncovered hand; grey light flooded the dull room. Rosabel shivered, drew a little gasping breath, sat up. And because her heritage was that tragic optimism, which is all too often the only inheritance of youth, still half asleep, she smiled, with a little nervous tremor around her mouth" (8). The narrator's free indirect discourse has heretofore avoided any form of authorial intrusion, has been careful to *show* rather than to *tell* the reader about Rosabel's consciousness, without explicit judgment. But the story's final sentence provides a retroactive interpretation of the foregoing narrative. Here Mansfield might seem to underscore the distance between her narrator and her naive protagonist—and, implicitly, the difference between Rosabel's "low" fantasy and that fantasy's sobering inversion, the author's own "high" psychological realism. To today's reader, the final sentence feels like a tonal residue of previous literary eras, a sudden fall into univocal didacticism after the high-wire balance of irony and sympathy that has delicately conveyed Rosabel's consciousness. Alternatively, we might interpret this moment as an abrupt loss of artistic self-control on the part of a callow twenty-year-old writer—the sign of a fear that readers would not grasp her story's subtleties. Despite the formal inconsistency, however, the final note of moralizing omniscience does not undermine the writer's respect for her subject. In Mansfield's personal correspondence of the period, she uses very similar language to describe her own writing. In 1907, she wrote to her father's secretary, who was typing up Mansfield's earliest short stories at her father's New Zealand office, that her own fiction displayed "the tragic pessimism of youth."[20] In 1908, she told a friend about the prospect of returning to London after a brief sojourn home to New Zealand: "I cannot live with Father, and I must get back because I know I shall be successful—look at the splendid tragic optimism of Youth."[21] Whether optimistic or pessimistic, there is a self-ascribed "tragic" idealism here, a romanticism that might be seen to run at odds with her sometimes naturalistic realism, in both Mansfield's personal philosophy and her literary practice.

In fact, while Mansfield was never especially direct or systematic in articulating her literary goals and methods, we find a current of Romanticism, parallel to her character Rosabel's, in many of her statements of literary intention. She wrote to her would-be fiancé, Garnet Trowell, on 8 November 1908,

> Oh, Garnet, why is it we so love the strong emotions? I think it is because they give us such a keen sense of *Life*—a violent belief in our Existence.
>
> One thing I cannot bear and that is the mediocre—I like always to have a great grip of life—so that I intensify the so called small things—so that everything is truly significant.[22]

Here too we find an echo of a passage in "Rosabel"; early on in the character's fantasy, she imagines to herself, "The butler opened the door, Harry was waiting, they drove away together. . . . *That* was life, thought Rosabel!" (6). If the overcoming of mediocrity and the grasping of "life" require the intensifying of "the so called small things," then Mansfield and Rosabel perform the same mental activity upon different materials. Just as Rosabel invests her working day's mundane encounter with a heightening or intensifying fantasy narrative, so too does Mansfield make an emotionally significant narrative out of the most ordinary or mundane of experiences, a shopgirl's day-to-day worklife. In both cases, we witness presentation of the everyday or quotidian as enhanced by unaccustomed meanings. There is, of course, a major difference: while Rosabel fills her notion of "life" with a conventional script of romance, Mansfield, in her letter, leaves the content of "Life" suggestively blank; what counts for her is the "strong emotion"—"a keen sense," "a violent belief"—that would seem to fill the term *life* with significance. Yet both Mansfield's letter and Rosabel's daydream offer the re-enchantment of a disenchanted (workaday or "mediocre") reality. The shared term *life* is in both cases invested with extraordinary meaning, a noumenal shimmer.

The oft-capitalized term *Life* serves a quasi- or paramystical function elsewhere in Mansfield's writings. We might recall its centrality to one of her most anthologized stories, "The Garden-Party," which concludes with Laura's unfinished query of her brother Laurie: "'Isn't life,' she stammered, 'isn't life—' But what life was she couldn't explain. No matter. He quite understood. '*Isn't* it, darling?' said Laurie."[23] It also appears in Mansfield's declarations of literary intention. In a letter of 1919 to her husband, John Middleton Murry, she writes, apropos of the experience of the Great War,

> Now we know ourselves for what we are. In a way it's a tragic knowledge: it's as though, even while we live again, we face death. But *through Life:* that's the point. We see death in life as we see death in a flower that is freshly unfolded. Our hymn is to the flower's beauty: we would make that beauty immortal because we *know*. . . . But don't imagine I mean by this knowledge let-us-eat-and-drink-ism. No, I mean "deserts of vast eternity." But . . . I couldn't tell anybody *bang out* about those deserts: they are my secret. I might write about a boy eating strawberries or a woman combing her hair on a windy morning, and that is the only way I can ever mention them. But they *must* be there. Nothing less will do.[24]

Mansfield's phrasing "deserts of vast eternity" quotes Andrew Marvell's "To His Coy Mistress," but she disavows the directness of the poet's metaphor for mortality. Nonetheless, there is a Keatsian Romanticism to her talk of immortalizing the beauty of life through our knowledge of its fragility: the terms *death, life,* and *beauty* take on the aspect here of absolute essences. She admits that her only method of representing such absolutes in her writing is through indirection, is through the writing of precisely "the so called small things" (the eating boy, the grooming woman) that she imagines choosing as the subjects of her literary portraiture. Such small-scale, close-focus material would be her chosen means to access a tragic awareness "*through Life.*"

Mansfield's letter to Murry conflates two goals that late nineteenth-century criticism tended to see as belonging to the opposed genres of realism and romance: the mirrorlike, mimetic representation of "real life," and the symbolic representation of eternal absolutes. I suggest that in Mansfield's use of the term *life* we are witnessing an emerging modernist shibboleth—a keyword of what Northrop Frye, in a famous series of lectures,[25] would later call modernism's "secular scripture." In fact, in *The Secular Scripture,* Frye broadly characterizes the opposition between realism and the romance mode as follows: "In the fiction-writing of the last four or five centuries there has been a kind of reversible shuttle moving between imagination and reality, as [Wallace] Stevens uses those words. One direction is called 'romantic,' the other 'realistic.' The realist tendency moves in the direction of the representational and the displaced, the romantic tendency in the opposite direction, concentrating on the formulaic units of myth and metaphor" (37). If Mansfield's 1919 letter gestures toward both of these "tendencies," so too do "The Tiredness of Rosabel" and the letter to Garnet Trowell, with its literary program to "intensify the so called small things." Mansfield's deployment of the signifier *life,* both as a mysterious sign invoked by her fictional characters and as a goal of narrative representation expressed in her personal correspondence, tends to oscillate between these two seeming poles of generic expression. If "Rosabel" offers sharp verisimilitude regarding urban life of the Edwardian period, much as it was actually experienced by young, female city-dwellers of a certain class, so too does Rosabel's introspective Cinderella tale metaphorize an experience of intensity and emotional fulfillment that is supposed to be, as the cliché says, "what life is all about" ("*That* was life, thought Rosabel"). A point that bears repeating here is that no matter how pre-scripted Rosabel's fantasy, and no matter how commonplace, even banal, this character's interpretation of its meaning, Mansfield cues us to identify with the core desire expressed through such daydreaming.

Romance Subsumed in Joyce and Lawrence: The Representation of "Life"

If Mansfield delicately limns the social circumstances that sharpen the desire for the romance mode in the psychic life of a young woman, the young Joyce of "An Encounter," "Araby," and "The Dead" offers a complementary vision of the role of the romance narrative in the psychic interpellation of boy and man at the same historical moment of urban modernity captured in her tale. The unnamed narrator of "An Encounter" recounts the spell of the boy's adventure romance—tales of the Wild West to be found in such cheap magazines as the *Union Jack*, *Pluck*, and the *Halfpenny Marvel*—and how it induced him to play truant in a daylong quest, ultimately disappointed, for exciting adventures.[26] The young adolescent of "Araby" undertakes a displaced heroic quest, on behalf of his would-be beloved, under the influence of Walter Scott's *The Abbot* (1820), Pacificus Baker's *The Devout Communicant* (1813), and François Eugène Vidocq's *Memoirs of Vidocq* (1829). The first of these texts is a historical romance by the nineteenth century's famed originator of that subgenre; the latter two offer the contradictory combination of a traditional religious tract and a somewhat lurid memoir of Parisian crime and prostitution. This motley juxtaposition serves to mirror the contradictory experience of the protagonist, who would inhabit the romance narrative he desperately wants: "Her image accompanied me even in places the most hostile to romance" (31). Looking back, Joyce's adult narrator recounts the effects on his youthful idealism of the internalization of the love-and-quest romance under twentieth-century conditions. The bathos of the final scene of "Araby" parallels the pathetic conclusion of "Rosabel." The primary structural difference from Mansfield's tale is Joyce's inclusion of the protagonist's eventual disillusionment, as the boy feels the onrush of the reality principle in a way that Rosabel, still sleeping at the end of Mansfield's tale, has not. However, the commonalty remains: it is not the popular sublime that the two stories conjure but rather the *desire* for that sublimity amid somewhat sterile and desiccated modern landscapes. This desire is understood to be shared by readers, not only of the popular love-romance but also of the story at hand, perhaps in their spurred recollections of their own youth. That tacit sympathy is crucial here and illustrates again why the notion of a great divide between popular and modernist literature is too simplistic.

Joyce's tales of boys' romanticization of reality bear a significant relation to the mature male life depicted in *Dubliners*' final story. In the Gabriel Conroy of "The Dead," the depiction of interiority moves from the culs-de-sac of a demystifying realism to the sudden vistas of a re-enchanting modernism, through which are reintroduced the libidinal energies of Romanticism, in a dialectical subsumption. Famously, the last third of the narrative shifts focalization from the painstaking re-creation of the Dublin middle-class public sphere circa 1904 to the inner life of its conflicted protagonist, as recorded through his emotional oscillations. Here again, as in "Araby," we witness the disillusionment of the protagonist with the romantic narrative that he has been projecting upon his relation with his would-be beloved. A long-married man superimposes a romance story upon a late evening's passage in his relationship with his wife: "boy meets girl" in the glimpse of a defamiliarized Gretta on the stairs, listening to distant music; "boy suffers setbacks" (endless leave-takings, a snowy cab journey) in his pursuit of girl, while keeping spiritual faith with their unspoken bond; "boy gets girl," or is just about to do so, when the two are ready (as he believes) to consummate their love in the hotel room. The solipsism of this narrative becomes clear in Gabriel's emotional reversal, which reprises the final debacle of the boy in "Araby," here transformed into a middle-aged version of romantic defeat: "Gabriel felt humiliated. . . . While he had been full of memories of their secret life together, full of tenderness and joy and desire, she had been comparing him in her mind with another" (219). Under questioning, Gretta pieces together her own miniature romance narrative regarding Michael Furey—this time a tragic one, but no less self-dramatizing: "I think he died for me, she answered" (220). Gabriel accepts this explanation of the tubercular youth's demise—"So she had had that romance in her life: a man had died for her sake" (222)—because it augments, by displacement, the stature of his self-perceived romantic failure.

But in "The Dead," of course, we witness another phase, the movement beyond the callow anguish and anger of "Araby" and attendant on the recognition of romantic vanity. For at this point in "The Dead," the profound limits of the romance narrative as a psychic script—which limits, it has in part been Joyce's intention to reveal—paradoxically usher in a more abstract form of Romantic idealism. A dialectical turn—Gabriel's conceptual repositioning from subject to object of his thoughts—sparks the epiphany via which, his eyes filled with "generous tears," his identity dissolves in empathy for his wife. He now perceives Gretta both as a former young person, like any other, needing the romance script of her own life, and as a much older person, like any other, long since aware of the romance's supersession by reality but nonetheless unable to relinquish it. His discrete selfhood is further extinguished by the awe-inspiring magnitude of death, "general all over Ireland," even as that magnitude offers a form of secular consolation. Sublimity suffuses Gabriel's meditation on mortality, via which "his own identity was fading out into a grey impalpable world: the solid world itself which these dead had one time reared and lived in was dissolving and dwindling" (223). Through the invocation of the ancient Greek paradigm of "shades" of the underworld, Gabriel's felt communion with a form of the Absolute is here self-consciously portrayed as a human construction, as a structure erected of mythology, yet it gains its power by means of precisely that self-awareness. Having been deflated by the bracing incursion of the Real, with its reminder of the subject's inexorable isolation, desire reasserts itself through reascendant metaphors—tropes no longer of the consummation of romantic-erotic love but rather, on a more etherealized plane, of the prospect of unity between consciousness and Being.

This thumbnail interpretation of one of literary modernism's most celebrated tableaux has arrived somewhat hastily at its metaphysical culmination, but, relying on the general familiarity of the passage, I will here leave these suggestions as they stand and point to a parallel possibility regarding *A Portrait of the Artist as a Young Man.* This work has been the central illustration in discussions of Joyce's relation to the English Romantic poets and has been cited by the camp of those who see a powerful continuity between Wordsworthian Romanticism and Joycean modernism, one of whose members represents this view as follows: "[T]he concept of the epiphany itself is of course extremely Romantic, as is Joyce's presentation of it."[27] This approach sees in such passages as Stephen Dedalus's ecstatic vision of the "bird-girl" a modern culmination of the Wordsworthian "spot of time," that mystical moment in which the whole shape of the universe, and the unity of all created things, is suddenly available to the writer's cognition. Wordsworth unveils the term *spot of time* in *The Prelude*, but this notion is just as famously discernable within these lines from "Tintern Abbey": "A presence that disturbs me with the joy / Of elevated thoughts; a sense sublime / Of something far more deeply interfused' (lines 93–96). Critics have found evidence of the conscious influence of Wordsworth on Joyce's depiction of epiphanies—while writing *Dubliners* in 1905, he said in letters to his brother, "In my history of literature I have given the highest palms to Shakespeare, Wordsworth, and Shelley," and "I think Wordsworth of all English men of letters best deserves your word 'genius.'"[28] Deliberate (even ironic)[29] or not, these accesses to the Wordsworthian sublime in *A Portrait* are salient here in at least two respects.

First, Joyce illustrates the manner in which Stephen bends the discourse of courtly love to his own uses as a self-reflexive catalyst to his identity as an artist. In the epiphany of chapter 4, the anonymous girl is subjected to premodern romance lyricism—"her long fair hair was girlish; and girlish, and touched with the wonder of mortal beauty, her face"—while Stephen's regard for her is described in chivalric terms—"when she felt his presence and the worship of his eyes her eyes turned to him in quiet sufferance of his gaze" (176). This allusion to the medieval chivalric romance brings to mind the fantasy of the boy of "Araby," but here the fantasy's temporal duration is much shorter, nearly instantaneous; the psychic experience is of an entirely different order, as the profane usurps the sacred, and Stephen transits, before our eyes, from a Christian to a secular-aesthetic set of values: "—Heavenly God! cried Stephen's soul, in an outburst of profane joy. . . . To live, to err, to fall, to triumph, to recreate life out of life! A wild angel had appeared to him, the angel of mortal youth and beauty, an envoy from the fair courts of life, to throw open before him in an instant of ecstasy the gates of all the ways of error and glory. On and on and on and on!" (176–77). This transition is later underscored by a very different attitude toward the discourse of courtly love, in an anti-epiphanic moment recorded in Stephen's diary; on the verge of leaving Ireland to dedicate himself to the life of the artist-in-exile, he transcribes his last encounter with his university sweetheart: "Asked me, was I writing poems? About whom? I asked her. This confused her more and I felt sorry and mean. Turned off that valve at once and opened the spiritual-heroic refrigerating apparatus, invented and patented in all countries by Dante Alighieri" (253). With its modernized mockery of the love of the medieval poet for his Beatrice, this passage seems to invert the sublimity of the earlier epiphany, but Stephen's ecstasy suddenly surges again. Romantic love has been cast aside, yet the superseded discourse of the love-romance has been used as a catalyst toward another idealism, more abstract but no less elevated, as conveyed in the novel's final epiphany: "Welcome, O life! I go to encounter for the millionth time the reality of experience and to forge in the smithy of my soul the uncreated conscience of my race" (253). In his seaside epiphany, Stephen had exulted in his capacity "to live . . . to recreate life out of life"; here, he apostrophizes that entity as he is about to embark on his Daedelian quest. As in Katherine Mansfield's writing, so too in *A Portrait of the Artist,* the term *life* serves a quasi- or paramystical function, signifying an aperture into the secular absolute.

The heightened language of these epiphanies indicates a second aspect of Joyce's refashionings of Wordsworthian "spots of time," which is their semantic self-reflexivity—or, to put it another way, their portrayal of a sublime uninformed by traditionally conceived divinity. In the later passages from *A Portrait* that we have just observed, Joyce famously encodes the model of the artist supplanting the priest as the conduit to the absolute and in so doing draws attention to the aesthetic dimensions of the artist's language as the medium of illumination. As critics have long observed, this model may place Stephen in the role of individualist artist as the questing romantic hero, or as Luciferian antihero—and may also imply a critical distancing and a deflating irony on Joyce's part. Regarding these latter alternatives, it may be best to accept all as obtaining here, no matter how seemingly incommensurable, and to move on to a different point, which is that the epiphanies may convey certain effects upon readers. Jay Clayton has suggested that "many readers have found the content of Stephen's [epiphanic] visions silly. But their content is less important than their compensatory structure."[30]

He goes on to say that "they remain interesting as stages in the movement of the poetic mind away from something painful in the story and toward something exalting on the level of discourse," and he posits—through a combination of psychoanalytic and reader-response theories—that this psychic transaction may also occur in the reader (125). As proposed at the opening of this chapter, we can here recall our earlier explorations of the popular sublime; canonically modernist texts such as *A Portrait of the Artist* suggest that the high-cultural and the popular-romantic species of exaltation, these different conveyances of parareligious transport, were not, when viewed from the angle of readers' reception, so neatly opposed as they might conventionally appear. We might read certain modernist narratives as consolatory or compensatory resources, as etherealizations of the "low-modern" romance that could also convey, in certain of their passages, that vernacular mode's salving effects.

Before moving on to the literary theories of West and Woolf, which convey analogous conceptions of emergent modernism, I briefly return to D. H. Lawrence, another male modernist who may offer more evidence to support the speculations prompted by Mansfield's story. We have seen how the modernist primitivism of *Women in Love,* "The Woman Who Rode Away," and *The Plumed Serpent* shows certain affinities with the imperial erotic romance and conveys a Romanticism of the Other. Also pertinent in the present context are Lawrence's earliest canonized novels, *Sons and Lovers* (1913) and *The Rainbow* (1915), in which he begins the transformation of his fictional mode toward the modernist style that characterizes *Women in Love* and later works. If the narrative arc of *Sons and Lovers* can be summarized as the unfolding stages in protagonist Paul Morel's discovery of his libidinal selves, then the initial description of his first lover, the farmgirl Miriam Leivers, establishes some of the themes of that development:

> The girl was romantic in her soul. Everywhere was a Walter Scott heroine being loved by men with helmets or with plumes in their caps. She herself was something of a princess turned into a swine-girl in her own imagination. . . . So to Miriam, Christ and God made one great figure, which she loved tremblingly and passionately when a tremendous sunset burned out the

> western sky, and Ediths, and Lucys, and Rowenas, Brian de Bois Guilberts, Rob Roys, and Guy Mannerings, rustled in the sunny leaves in the morning, or sat in her bedroom aloft, alone, when it snowed. That was life to her. For the rest, she drudged in the house.[31]

This kind of dreamy innocence originally attracts Paul to Miriam, but of course the tone of this passage also anticipates his reaction against such internalization of romance narratives, together with the religious faith that accompanies it. Paul's development into an explicit agnosticism certainly represents one counterformation to his lover's Christian idealism, but there is another, less remarked-upon strand to his intellectual rebellion. Miriam's possessive approach to "Lad and Girl Love" (as one chapter title has it) troubles Paul with its alleged bloodlessness; soon he is petulantly crying, "I'm so damned spiritual with *you* always" and feeling that "[I]f he could have kissed her in abstract purity he would have done so. But he could not kiss her thus—and she seemed to leave no other way" (188). Lawrence establishes Miriam's ideals regarding love's exclusivity, into which she has been conditioned by her reading of romance literature, as a foil to the churning, conflicted representation of Paul's psychic and libidinal terrain, with its seismic fault lines—his powerful Oedipal fixation on his mother and his sexually fulfilling (but otherwise vexed) encounter with the married Clara Dawes.

That Lawrence was breaking risky new fictional ground in *Sons and Lovers* was of course attested by its scandalized reception, which is well documented. But this romantic-erotic *agon* between Miriam and Paul is not simply a matter of a renovated realist mode being precipitated as yet another reaction, so common since the late nineteenth century, against the romance mode. As John Beer concedes, critics have traditionally claimed that the early Lawrence embodies a sharp social realism and that in his "picture of English provincial society in *Sons and Lovers* and his deeper probing in *The Rainbow*," Lawrence's "frankness in sexual matters" issued "a welcome call for larger honesty in English cultural life," in the mode of the so-called sex-novel. But Beer also suggests that even these early works are a far cry from literary naturalism.[32]

The foregoing discussion of Joyce and Mansfield offers us one way to theorize how Lawrence here began to transmute literary realism. For all the narratological differences between Joyce and Lawrence (for example, Joyce's indirect discourse and internal monologues famously "show," while Lawrence's third-person omniscient often "tells"), we may be witnessing in *Sons and Lovers* and *The Rainbow* the emergence of a modernist discourse that, like Stephen Dedalus's, would renovate Romantic transcendence in part through the keyword *life*. Likewise, returning to the quotation above, we see that Miriam's view of Scott-style romance—"That was life to her"—recalls the perspective of Mansfield's Rosabel, who used the same phrase, "*That* was life" (*Stories*, 6), in her mental summary of the imagined romance with the rich shop client. Literally speaking, this echo of Mansfield's earlier but (as of 1913) unpublished story is pure coincidence; it comes as no surprise, however, that within the first month of Mansfield's friendship with Lawrence she read the manuscript of *Sons and Lovers* and was "deeply impressed."[33]

From the broad perspective that I am elaborating here, in fact, this identical formulation in similar narrative contexts (one difference, admittedly, being the urban versus agrarian settings of Rosabel and Miriam) is no coincidence; just as for Mansfield and for the Stephen Dedalus of *A Portrait*, so too for Lawrence's narrator and his character Paul Morel (one of the author's mouthpieces), the term *life* is richly overdetermined. This supercharged word serves not only as a pivot to narrative development in *Sons and Lovers* but also as a sign of Lawrence's intellectual bid for a new episteme. With Paul's guidance, Miriam will be challenged to resituate "life" elsewhere and to move beyond her internalized romance scripts. Upon asking why she is so drawn to Paul's sketches of local flora, she is told,

> "It's because—it's there is scarcely any shadow in it; it's more shimmery, as if I'd painted the shimmering protoplasm in the leaves and everywhere, and not only the stiffness of the shape. That seems dead to me. Only this shimmeriness is the real living. The shape is a dead crust. The shimmer is inside really."
>
> And she, with her little finger in her mouth, would ponder these sayings. They gave her a feeling of life again, and vivified things which had meant nothing to her. She managed to find some meaning in his struggling,

> abstract speeches. And they were the medium through which she came distinctly at her beloved objects. (152)

The problem of sexism in such passages—whereby intellectual intuition is, as so often in Lawrence's work, the province of "masculine" mastery—cannot be denied, but such perceptions of the noumena will also originate among the women of Mansfield's and West's and Woolf's fictions. In fairness to Lawrence, it should also be recorded that such neo-Romantic insights may on occasion originate with his female protagonists, as we see in *The Rainbow,* where precisely such a vision leads Ursula Brangwen to abandon the romance script (her favorite reading has been Tennyson's *Idylls of the King*) of love-as-consummation. At a climactic moment in the narrative, when betrothal to Anton Skrebensky is most likely, Ursula's botany professor asks, "I don't see why we should attribute some special mystery to life—do you?" (*Sons,* 440). Ursula will refute this view as, peering through her microscope at a single-cell organism, she has an epiphany: "She had passed away into an intensely-gleaming light of knowledge. She could not understand what it all was. She only knew that it was not limited mechanical energy, nor mere purpose of self-preservation and self-assertion. It was a consummation, a being infinite. Self was a oneness with the infinite. To be oneself was a supreme, gleaming triumph of infinity" (441). Following this glimpse of sublimity, this momentary dissolution of self in a vast web of biological life, Ursula rejects the prospect of marrying her lover, and the novel will end with her having found, for the time being, vocational and intellectual independence. But she has not, at the conclusion, achieved a contented stasis; a core desire will continually rearise. We are given to understand that it will not take exclusive or even primary form as the desire for romantic-erotic consummation.

Citing the above passage from *Sons and Lovers,* David Thorburn takes it to emblematize Lawrence's relationship to British Romanticism:

> Romanticism is also particularly preoccupied, according to Harold Bloom and others, with problems of consciousness and selfhood, with the mysteries within, with our passionate lives, and in that sense especially Lawrence is a direct descendant of the Romantic poets. . . . We might call Lawrence a Romantic vitalist, and link him

> especially to the apocalyptic Romanticism of poets like William Blake. Lawrence is constantly preoccupied by some energies or elements that are beneath the surface, that in some cases are inexpressible or challenge the possibilities of language, that are not even visible on the surface, but have a kind of authority for him.[34]

What we can add to this commonly accepted characterization is an emphasis on the centrality of that vitalism's etymological root, *vita,* as Lawrence's antonym, proposed through the experience of Paul Morel, to *religion:* "Paul and his mother now had long discussions about life. Religion was fading into the background. . . . Now life interested him more" (*Sons,* 256). It is certainly no accident that the theorizations worked out with Gertrude Morel, the object of Paul's fierce oedipalization, find their fleshly incarnation not in Paul's love for the spiritual Miriam but in his sexual experience, "ruthless in its primitiveness . . . like Adam and Eve" with the sensualist Clara Dawes:

> [T]hey lost their innocence and realised the magnificence of the power which drove them out of Paradise and across the great night and the great day of humanity. It was for each of them an initiation and a satisfaction. To know their own nothingness, to know the tremendous living flood which carried them always, gave them rest within themselves. If so great a magnificent power could overwhelm them, identify them altogether with itself, so that they knew they were only grains in the tremendous heave that lifted every grass blade to its little height, and every tree, and living thing, then why fret about themselves? They could let themselves be carried by life, and they felt a sort of peace each in the other. . . . Nothing could nullify it, nothing could take it away; it was almost their belief in life. (353–54)

Lawrence here transposes the site of the Romantic sublime from the encounter with grand natural phenomena to the subject's limitless interiorization, via which the self dissolves into mere "grains." As the reference to Adam and Eve connotes, this vision exemplifies

Lawrence's secular scripture; in such passages, the would-be transcendental signifier, *life,* denotes both self-negating libidinality and a vitalist sublime. The supersession of the romance mode entails a shifting in the quest-object, from the consummation of ideal love to an aperture into the biological absolute; in Paul's day-after reflection on this encounter, he concludes that the experience "had been impersonal, and not Clara" (354). For her part, Clara feels that "in the morning it was not the same. They had *known,* but she could not keep the moment" (354–55). In this refashioning of the quest into a series of psychic adventures, lasting plenitude eludes the lovers' grasp, and an ultimate stasis cannot be achieved.

Having briefly considered the early texts of both Lawrence and Joyce, we can now elaborate the speculations on realism, the romance, and modernism that were originally prompted by "The Tiredness of Rosabel." In the schema of Northrop Frye, Mansfield's characteristic story, together with her stated literary aims, could be seen as the index of a sea-change in the relative tides of realism and romance. Concerning that modal polarity, Frye asserts that "this 'romantic' and 'realistic' contrast is a nineteenth-century one. . . . [T]he prestige of 'realism' in the nineteenth century reflected the prevailing fashions of that culture, nearly all of which emphasized some form of correspondence, the paralleling of mental structures with something in the outer world. It was an age of representational painting and realistic fiction, and of . . . approaching works of literature as historical or psychological documents" (*Secular,* 45). As a characterization of the Victorian critical taste for realism and naturalism, Frye's generalization is perhaps as commonplace as it is unobjectionable; more striking is how he describes its fin-de-siècle supersession. Citing Wilde's aphorism "Life goes faster than Realism, but Romanticism is always in front of Life," Frye asserts, "Wilde was clearly the herald of a new age in literature, which would take another century or so to penetrate the awareness of critics. He is looking forward to a culture which would use mythical and romantic formulas in its literature with great explicitness, making once more the essential discovery about the human imagination, that it is always a form of 'lying,' that is, of turning away from the descriptive use of language and the correspondence form of truth" (46). Frye thus associates the popular romance with high modernism as together constituting the pendulum swing of "a new age in literature" away from high realism. The "explicit" use of "mythical and romantic formulas" refers to popular literature, exemplified for Frye by such writers as Marie Corelli, John Buchan, Elinor Glyn, and J.R.R. Tolkien (42–43). At the same time, Frye identifies the belated critical discovery of the imagination's healthy practice of "lying" with Wallace Stevens's doctrine, so prominent in the 1950s and '60s (Frye's critical era), of "supreme fictions." What modernism and the romance share, by this account, is a suspension of the Victorian precept that literary language must, if it is to be taken seriously, correspond to mind-independent, external reality. They do, of course, suspend that precept quite differently; whereas the romance partly ignores it, modernism generally interrogates it. "The romantic tendency is antirepresentational," writes Frye (38), and so too might we say, in extension of his claim that twentieth-century high literature has "shifted the center of interest back to the linguistic structure itself" (46), that the modernist tendency is *meta*representational, or represents the problems of representation. In both cases, again, we see a "turning away from the descriptive use of language and the correspondence form of truth."

Of course, this yoking of modernism and the popular romance has tended to run against our literary-historical thinking about the early twentieth-century contours of Anglo-American literature, ever since Andreas Huyssen, Peter Bürger, and others have demonstrated how, at least in part, high modernism can be said to be constituted by its very difference from mass culture.[35] Until quite recently, as I suggest in the introduction to this study, it has been unusual to see the formulaic production of mass-market paperbacks as one facet of the same phenomenon represented by modernism's self-conscious mythologizing (since, in part, postmodernism is usefully distinguished from modernism by its dissolution of a high-low distinction that the latter putatively kept in place). Yet this is what Frye's broad literary-historical lens would encourage us to do. This is a clarifying lens, as suggested above, and not least because the great divide between modernism and the romance may be as much a matter of cultural production, distribution, and reception—à la Bourdieu—as it is a matter of literary content qua content. The case of Mansfield's exemplary story illustrates the feature that "high" and "low" share, in contradistinction to a once-dominant, externalized realism: the depiction of interiority through what is ultimately more a *metaphorical* than a *referential* mode of discourse.

It then becomes possible to suggest, at the admitted risk of an idealizing reduction, that the difference between some high modernism and popular romance may be a matter more of degree than of kind: the one offers metaphors for life, while the other offers metaphors for life that thematize their own metaphoricity; the one is generally unself-conscious about its tropes, while the other is generally self-conscious about its own. The heuristic value of "The Tiredness of Rosabel" in this context is its service as a metafiction: it employs the realist mode to represent, via the synecdoche of its protagonist, the historical conditions that will bring about the double hegemony of "low" and "high" modern forms, that is, the mass-market romance and modernist interiorization. Mansfield demonstrates the power of the romance narrative over an ordinary shop attendant such as Rosabel at the same time that she asserts, through the everyday subject matter of the story, the inherent interest of the phenomenon of an individual's psychic compensations for an unsatisfying social reality.

To take this observation another step, we might say that Mansfield depicts the objective preconditions for high modernist literature: what Jameson labels "the increasing fragmentation both of the rationalized external world and of the colonized psyche."[36] As discussed earlier, in *The Political Unconscious,* Jameson offers a two-sided appraisal of modernism that can also be applied to the mass-market romance narrative; by this account, modernism is at once "an ideological expression" of capitalism's "reification of daily life" and "a Utopian compensation for everything that reification brings with it" (236). We can readily see how paperback fantasies of love and adventure meet the definition of "reification," as a turning of properly human interrelations into highly formulaic *things;* that the same books should be ennobled by this designation, as "Utopian compensation," may be less plain. But just as for Frye's literary-cyclical scheme of cultural history, so too for Jameson's historicism is the late nineteenth- to early twentieth-century period a moment of shifting to new incarnations of the romance. We may return to a passage from *The Political Unconscious* cited at the opening of chapter 2: "It is in the context of the gradual reification of realism in late capitalism that romance once again comes to be felt as the place of narrative heterogeneity and of freedom from that reality principle to which a now oppressive realist representation is the hostage. Romance now again seems to offer the possibility of sensing other historical rhythms, and of the demonic or Utopian transformations of a real now unshakably set in place" (104). In this ambitious account, the term *romance* might be replaced by the term *modernism;* if we take out the "once again" and the "again," we have two compelling sentences to explain the inexorable pull of modernism, from the early twentieth century to the present moment. The *magna opera* of anglophone modernism once were and have since been a kind of alternative to the sobering gravity of realist representation, and certainly they "seem to offer the possibility of sensing other historical rhythms"—the rhythms of the collective psychic experience of many, female and male, among the working and middle classes of early twentieth-century modernity.

Rebecca West and *The Strange Necessity*

The fiction-writing of Rebecca West's early years represents another thread in this inquiry, and one far less familiar to most readers than the works of Joyce and Lawrence. West's modernist phase is generally considered to run from her earliest publications in the 1910s through her novels of the 1920s. As a young woman, she was especially keen that her fiction-writing should lay claim to a high artistry evading the perceived traps of "sentiment." With her proclaimed aversion to what she saw as jejune writing by her popular female contemporaries, West criticized the best-selling romances of the authors we have considered here, both directly and savagely. In her 1928 essay "The Tosh-Horse," she decried Corelli, Barclay, and Dell as nonserious writers, declaring about their romances that "the best-sellers have, like the toad, a jewel in the head: the jewel of a demoniac vitality."[37] Alongside West's batrachian image of fellow novelists' works, her Flaubertian inversion of Mary Ward's achievement—the jibe that Mary Ward's career had been "one long specialization in the *mot injuste*" (*Strange,* 106)—conveys an undercurrent of anger at women romance writers.

Born in 1892, Rebecca West (pseudonym of Cicely Fairfield) had come of age in the era when Ward and Corelli earned enough on the proceeds of their fiction to enjoy near-universal celebrity.

By the time West published her attacks on Ward and Corelli, the twentieth century's bohemian avant-garde had reached its prime and, as suggested at the end of chapter 2, had begun to criticize the older cohort of British women romance writers for their mass appeal, their institutionalization as "respectable," and their formal and thematic conservatism. On behalf of the artistically ambitious writers of her generation, West implied that the female renegades of modernism were defining themselves as these romance writers' determinate negation or converse image on the literary field. The shared sex of the two camps did not generate a stance of solidarity, and in West's case, in particular, literary ambition and bohemian antagonism combined with a powerful feminism to rule out alliance with perceived cultural conservatives.

Of course, West's feel for the positions of women writers in the literary field would not seem to contravene later critical perceptions of a divide between "masculinist" modernism and a "feminized" mass culture. However, the discovery in 1996 of her novel *The Sentinel*—a 250-page manuscript left unfinished circa 1911—offers evidence that West may have protested too much in her deriding of the women's romance. Kathryn Laing, who discovered the manuscript in the University of Tulsa archives, characterizes *The Sentinel* as an example of women's suffrage fiction (protagonist Adela Furnival becomes a militant suffragette, in company with characters based on Emmeline and Christabel Pankhurst) in which "the tropes of popular fiction (romance and adventure) are blended with a realism reminiscent of journalistic texts."[38] We do not have space to go into the particulars of *The Sentinel* here—further interpretations of this relatively new discovery will be forthcoming—but Laing summarizes how West juxtaposes passages of "Zolaesque realism" with Gothic and melodramatic scenes, including moments of erotic longing that go "beyond the experience of the aesthetic to a near-religious vocation" (16–19). In fact, many passages of West's narrative instantiate the popular sublime that we have seen in best-selling romances. Moreover, as Laing asserts, "the language of Keatsian poetry is mingled with the militant rhetoric of the WSPU [Women's Political and Social Union]" (20). Intercalated with elements of the love-romance mode and Romantic lyricism, West's representations of psychic intensities anticipate modernist elaborations of deep interiority.[39] In sum, this is a work of juvenilia—West was seventeen to eighteen years old at its writing—whose callow idealism parallels that seen in Mansfield's early vignettes and whose underlying Romanticism, like Mansfield's, prefigures later pulses of would-be transcendence through modernist carapaces of ambiguity.

West's first published fiction, "Indissoluble Matrimony," appeared in Wyndham Lewis's *Blast* and is on the surface an antiromance narrative. But the jagged psychic abstractions of this satire on male egotism are tinged by the black-and-white moral grid of popular melodrama. Through West's sardonic indirect discourse, antihero George Silverton deliriously projects sexist and racist misreadings of his eminently sane and self-sufficient wife; Evadne wears the figurative white hat, and George the black, in this phantasmagoria of well-nigh cartoonish male paranoia. A few years later in West's career we find, embedded in the Jamesian psychodrama of post-traumatic stress disorder that is *The Return of the Soldier,* an idyllic love story, staged within the nostalgic fantasy of an island sanctuary and climaxing with the following tableau: "But tonight there was nothing anywhere but beauty. He lifted her in his arms and carried her within the columns and made her stand in a niche above the altar. . . . His love was changeless."[40] These lines would have been appropriate to a mass-market, Mills-and-Boon-style romance of the 1910s. But the passage does not represent the kind of parody that is seen in, say, Joyce's pastiche of the "sentimental" novel in *Ulysses'* "Nausicaa" episode. It represents the recounting by the female narrator of the male protagonist's own recounted memory of a love affair—a memory experienced as he returned to consciousness after being wounded in a battlefield of the Great War. West's layers of narrative mediation, employing a self-consciously Jamesian penumbra of representation, convey a quest for transcendence amid a gritty realist universe. If the language of the love reverie is idealized, it is nonetheless presented with dignity, without any narratorial snigger at putative sentimentality or at romance clichés. The conclusion to be drawn is not that West was hypocritical in lambasting the best sellers of the women romancists. It is instead that she was renovating, through the ambitious departures of *The Sentinel* and *The Return of the Soldier,* the same components of the romance mode that were being otherwise renovated in the secularizing, psychologizing texts sold to the masses: namely, the love story, the quest narrative, the representation of exalted states.

Unlike Mansfield, West lived long enough to publish literary-critical pieces that would shed explanatory light on such aspects of her fiction. Many readers have found the title essay of Rebecca West's *The Strange Necessity* (1928)—her lengthy meditation on the appeal of beauty in art and literature—to be dauntingly abstruse. As Carl Rollyson has pointed out in his biography of West, the title essay presents a sometimes meandering cultural commentary, the main current of which can seem to get lost in esoteric eddies.[41] West opens with sardonic criticism of the sentimentality of James Joyce's volume *Pomes Penyeach* (1927) and ends, 210 pages later, with speculations on the human physiological response to "great" art, especially great novels. In between, she moves from analyses of Benjamin Constant's *Adolphe* and Marcel Proust's fiction to reflections on shopping in Paris and gambling in Monte Carlo, with a long passage devoted to the discussion of Pavlov's experiments with dogs. The unhurried sinuosity of her argument is enough to make the contemporary reader marvel. But the essay patiently builds a theory of narrative that, despite its range of literary touchstones (from Shakespeare to Proust, from Austen to Mansfield), is recognizably modernist in all but name. West gradually assembles a unified literary-artistic theory that resembles, and is as subtle and suggestive as, Woolf's critical statements from the same period. Most significantly in our context, West's concluding passages articulate the crypto-Romanticism that runs as a powerful subcurrent through West's fiction of the 1910s and '20s.

West's occasion for the composition of *The Strange Necessity*, she tells us at the outset, was an autumn day spent walking the streets of Paris and pondering Joyce's poetry: "I shut the bookshop door behind me and walked slowly down the street that leads from the Odéon to the Boulevard Saint-Germaine in the best of all cities, reading the little volume [*Pomes Penyeach*] which had there been sold to me, not exactly pretentiously, indeed with a matter-of-fact briskness, yet with a sense of there being something on hand different from an ordinary commercial transaction" (1). We might compare this opening with Virginia Woolf's setup of *A Room of One's Own*, which was also originally written in 1928: "Here then I was . . . sitting on the banks of a river a week or two ago in fine October weather, lost in thought. That collar I have spoken of, women and fiction, the need of coming to some conclusion on a subject that raises all sorts of prejudices and passions, bowed my head to the ground."[42] This comparison between the occasions prompting West's and Woolf's essays may seem a superficial one—both tracts claim to recompose the thoughts of an autumn day spent in pleasant solitude—but "women and fiction" is also one of West's key subtexts in *The Strange Necessity.* For the real catalyst behind the essay is not Joyce's poetry; it is rather his *Ulysses,* whose controversial critical reception, as the latest candidate bidding to join the pantheon of masculine works of genius, provokes West's defense of her implicit claim, as a woman writer, to the status of a detached, clinical, unsentimental artist and critic.

At the heart of her argument is the quest for a common root to the "strange necessity," for the unitary human desire that binds the superficially disparate desires for love, art, and knowledge. Paradoxically, she avers that the appeal of great art is at once subjective and objective; that all human principles to organize the data of reality are projections of the mind, and yet that the "experiment" of a great work of fiction offers an ordering of experience that corresponds closely to structures of mind-independent, external reality. Anthony Trollope, a novelist she deems great, is said to offer readers a scientific achievement on par with the findings of Pavlov: "Anthony Trollope passed the whole of [his] material through his imagination . . . and having thus gained an accurate, non-sentimental view of it he told the truth about it so helped him God. At the end of it he has established just how certain kinds of people act in certain circumstances that uncover their attitudes to recurring and fundamental factors of life, just as Professor Pavlov has established how a certain kind of dog behaved when it was given meat powder under certain conditions" (87). So far from functioning as escapism, the "experiments" we call fictional narratives can, if composed with genius, teach us about the reality of life; that is, great works of fiction and literature generally (her other examples include works by Shakespeare, Madame de La Fayette, Benjamin Constant, Austen, Proust, Joyce, and Mansfield) constitute a form of empirical research. She would thereby defamiliarize literary art by analogizing it to empirical and positivistic scientific investigations, even as she says that great fiction also carries the supplement, the further dimension—absent from scientific empiricism—of ecstatic beauty, of the joy-bearing aesthetic.

West's analogy between the successful novel and empirical scientific research was motivated in part, as I have suggested, by her wish to be hard-nosed, nonmystifying, and rigorously critical, that is, to distance herself from too apparently mystical or intuitive a line of thought, given the continuity of those terms with contemporaneous feminized constructions of "the sentimental." West's ambition was to find a well-nigh-transcendent significance buried somewhere deep within the felt "necessity," as that "strange" force that subtends, or acts as common denominator to, what she categorized distinctly as love, art, and the desire for objective knowledge (this last she called the "What-is-it?" reflex [88]). In her essay's final passage, she offers a proposed synthesis:

> An analogy strikes me. Is it possible that the intense exaltation which comes to our knowledge of the greatest works of art and the milder pleasure that comes of our more everyday dealings with art, are phases of the same emotion, as passion and gentle affection are phases of love between a man and a woman? Is this exaltation the orgasm, as it were, of the artistic instinct, stimulated to its height by a work of art, which, through its analysis and synthesis of some experience enormously important to humanity (though not necessarily demonstrable as such by the use of the intellect), creates a proportionately powerful excitatory complex, which, in other words, halts in front of some experience which if left in a crude state would probably make one feel that *life* was too difficult, and transforms it into something that helps one to go on living? . . . But do I really love *life* so much that I derive this really glorious pleasure from something that merely helps me to go on living? That is incredible, considering that *life* has treated me as all the children of man like a dog from the day I was born. It is incredible, that is, if things are what they seem, if there is not a secret hidden somewhere. . . . And that I should feel this transcendent joy simply because I have been helped to go on living suggests that I know something I have not yet told my mind, that within me I hold some assurance regarding the value of *life,* which makes my fate different from what it appears, different, not lamentable, grandiose. (211–13; emphasis added)

The attempt at scientific objectivity being left behind, here a sudden Romanticism—previously hinted at, but repressed, in West's efforts to observe fine conceptual distinctions—comes rushing to the fore and exacts its revenge. The bridge to Mansfield, Joyce, Lawrence, and Woolf is to be found in the final use of the term *life,* which I have italicized in the quotation. In a deeply secular conception, West's concluding passage suggests that "life" is transformed in art, so that the representation of "life" in art captures and reaffirms "the value of life"—and in great art, actually catalyzes a "transcendent joy" within the reader or viewer. As do the other modernists, West deploys the term *life* after the fashion of Keatsian or Wordsworthian idealism, but again, this is a crypto-Romanticism, very much chastened, very much transformed by the cultural environs of the early twentieth century. If literary modernism is accurately characterized as realism raised to the next exponential power, then West seems to have gone through to the other side of both the strict materialism and the solipsistic psychologism of turn-of-the-century realism and to have arrived at a dialectically altered idealism.

West thus hazards a view of the power of literature and other art forms to capture the ineffable. The life-world captured in the most effective literary narratives and artistic works, she tells us, represents "our paradise from which we are exiled by some cosmic misadventure, and which we can re-enter at times by participating in the experience of those artists who are supposed by some mystical process to have gained the power to reproduce in this universe the conditions of that other" (211). Suggestive here is the fact that a writer with a modernist agenda would implicitly counterpose the representations of realism (here connoted by "this universe") with the representations of the romance (here connoted by "our paradise" and "that other" world, an otherworldly reality to which the writer or artist offers us access, or the ability to "re-enter," through her romances). As we have seen, one of the enduring, fundamental definitions of the English-language romance form is that it depicts a counter-real life-world, in which at least some of the laws of quotidian reality are suspended. Certainly, too, with her invocation of our "cosmic misadventure" and the artist/writer's "mystical process," here at the climax of a 210-page treatise on the sources of artistic and literary effectiveness, West lofts herself out of her earlier, hard-nosed analyses and into idealism, even at the risk of sounding "sentimental." West goes on to suggest that in the presence of authentic art or literature she feels "transcendent joy," which "suggests that I know something that I have not yet told my mind, that within me I hold some assurance regarding the value of life" (213). This juxtaposition of transcendence with the artistically conveyed "value of life" hints at the achievement by the successful fiction or artwork of the figuration of an exalted interior state, its representational quest having, however fleetingly, been achieved. That the theoretical criteria by which to judge all effective literary texts are, in West's most ambitious statement of her literary goals, conflated with the aspects of the romance mode is therefore telling.

A Modernist Quest

So runs West's theoretical subsumption of features of the romance mode within a modernist manifesto; I conclude this study with a consideration of parallel emphases in the canonical literary criticism of Virginia Woolf. If, as I argue here, Mansfield's 1908 story offers an encrypted prophecy of modernism's full-blown challenges to traditional realism, then by 1919, two years into her professional friendship with Mansfield, Woolf was posing the challenges explicitly. As she said in a review of a Dorothy Richardson novel, "We want to be rid of realism, to penetrate without its help into the regions beneath it."[43] In the same year, in the essay "Modern Fiction," Woolf famously suggested that if her immediate predecessors had produced a fiction too much focused on sociological exteriority, conveying character through class types and social milieux, then the emergent writers of modernism were variously seeking, through their new and strange literary forms, to capture psychological interiority. Woolf's criticism of the period thus yokes two psychoanalytic metaphors: the telos of literary practice should be to get "inside" human character and to penetrate that character's "depths." "For the moderns," she wrote, "the point of interest lies very likely in the dark places of psychology."[44] To define her project through an idealized conception of psychic interiority, she opposed a certain strain of turn-of-the-century realism. The notion of verisimilitude that Woolf proposed in "Modern Fiction" was indeed new. "Look within," she advised, "and life . . . is very far from being 'like this'"—like, that is, the depiction of life offered in the contemporary realist novel.

We return to one of the loci classici of Woolf studies: "The mind receives a myriad impressions—trivial, fantastic, evanescent. . . . [F]rom all sides they come, an incessant shower of innumerable atoms; and as they fall, the accent falls differently from of old . . . so that, if a writer were a free man . . . he could base his work upon his own feeling and not upon convention" ("Modern," 2308). In the present context, we may focus on Woolf's use of the term *feeling*—that is, the idea that the new novel should base itself on "feeling" rather than realist "convention." If, as a subject, the novelist should consult the inner domain of feeling as a resource in her project of literary mimesis, then, too, the object world has an inner essence belied by its outward and material appearances.

We may then recall another locus classicus, already cited at the end of the discussion of Corelli in chapter 3: "[L]ife is a luminous halo, a semi-transparent envelope surrounding us from the beginning of consciousness to the end. Is it not the task of the novelist to convey this varying, this unknown and uncircumscribed spirit, whatever aberration or complexity it may display, with as little mixture of the alien and external as possible?" ("Modern," 2308). While there is a "spirit" within the psyche of the individual—that desideratum lacking in the fiction of Bennett, Galsworthy, and Wells—there is furthermore a "spirit" that inheres in the object world of circumjacent life. Implicitly, Woolf seems to be offering a Kantian model of phenomena and noumena. If the phenomena of the external world are only appearances, then the novelist must try to penetrate through the envelope of the materially seen, to make it at least "semi-transparent," and get at the noumenal essences. Woolf's challenge in writing a manifesto that would applaud the exploratory foray into a new notion of verisimilitude is to arrive at the right words for these sought-after noumena, or extrasensual essences, of life. Much like Mansfield in her letters of literary intent, much like West in the concluding theorizations of *The Strange Necessity,* Woolf is self-conscious and speculative in "Modern Fiction" about this quest for the right words: "Whether we call it life or spirit, truth or reality, this, the essential thing, has moved off, or on, and refuses to be contained any longer in such ill-fitting vestments as we provide" (2308). Whatever it is called, this essential thing, Woolf suggests that one should seek to arrive at it through the consultation of one's inner feeling; there is presumably some correspondence between inner and outer noumena, some mode of intuitive access, some form of anterior passageway that opens between the two. Never does she directly settle upon a word or a phrase for this "thing," letting it nestle for a moment under this or that sign—but only, she is sure always to remind us, for a moment. Apparently, this transcendental category, this would-be touchstone of her criticism, eludes a permanent signifier. Woolf repeatedly admits her inability to plumb the real depths of her essay's central concept and arrive at a satisfyingly cognitive definition of the lacking "thing." Getting at the "thing" depends as much on feeling as on intellect—if not more. For this reason, her literary as well as literary-critical desideratum—to capture "life," or "spirit," or "the essential thing"—can be seen as a Romantic quest for transcendence and, as such, for a constantly receding horizon of meaning. If the modern fiction writers cannot achieve this goal through the various new modes of poeticized novelistic technique, she cannot quite achieve it, either, through the more discursive and rationalist discourse of her literary criticism.

I now offer a final bridge into some of the more recently developed terms of materialist and psychoanalytic criticism and to redescribe Woolf's (and Mansfield's and West's) problem through other language, in a speculative turn that I hope is licensed by Woolf's claim that "[f]or the moderns . . . the point of interest lies very likely in the dark places of psychology." In psycholinguistic discourse, we might rename Woolf's semantic efforts at pinning down "the essential thing"—"truth," "reality," "life," "spirit"—as a series of traditionally humanist metonymies, and her restless struggle with the elusiveness of the thing to be pinned down under the given term as the effect of a desire. Here again is the sentence that captures that double slipperiness, that greased-pig effect on both the realist novelists and Woolf as critic: "Whether we call it life or spirit, truth or reality, this, the essential thing, has moved off, or on, and refuses to be contained any longer in such ill-fitting vestments as we provide." This sentence may briefly enact what Jacques Lacan has called the "metonymy of desire," as the meaning of what Woolf is after jumps from one term to the next, like an electric charge along a row of lightning rods. To return to Woolf's metaphor, these meanings are now also unwilling or unable to stay put, both in their frayed and old-fashioned, realist "vestments" and in the critical writing that would pinpoint the novel's teleology.

The introduction of the temporal dimension here may indicate that the movement of Woolf's desired meanings out of their old clothes is sensed as a historical change. For "the novelist at present," she wrote, "the accent falls a little differently; the emphasis is upon something hitherto ignored; at once a different outline of form becomes necessary, difficult for us to grasp, incomprehensible to our predecessors" ("Modern," 2310). The idea here is that the desired meanings have not simply escaped the techniques of realist fiction but have not yet been recaptured in the experimental literature of the moment. As I have suggested, Woolf might be seen as anxious about the possibility that they never *will be* recapturable, in any totalizing and universalizing literary practice. If Woolf's text might be seen to enact this anxiety textually, along a Lacanian, metonymic axis of desire, and to do so in a self-conscious fashion, then she may also be suggesting the undermining of the once seemingly stable codes of meaning carried in realist literature. Here, we may take the notion of "codes," too, in a specifically materialist-psychoanalytic sense: Deleuze and Guattari have theorized that human desire has historically been contained and constrained by "codes" of meaning specific to various epochs of history. (As mentioned in chapter 5, *A Thousand Plateaus* presents "territorialization" and "codes" as overlapping phenomena, with the latter term emphasizing the phenomena's discursive constitution.) Deleuze and Guattari suggest that, in the past, both social and linguistic codes effectively riveted desire onto socially sanctioned objects, such as royal families, sacred priestesses, and the fetishes of ritual; further, they assert that such codes have increasingly been unraveled, or "decoded," through the intensifying stages of development of capitalist society, as the formerly intrinsic-seeming meanings of persons, objects, and institutions have become increasingly subject to exchange value. As Eugene Holland proposes, "capitalist decoding tends . . . to systematically strip the halo of meaning from all aspects of social life . . . and organizes society as a cash-nexus for the sake of surplus-accumulation alone rather than in any meaningful way."[45]

This theory is a vast and ambitious one, referring to social practices as much as linguistically mediated forms of meaning, but for our purposes, literary texts can be seen as both purveyors and dissolvers of such codes through history. The notion of codes is coextensive with Jameson's theorem that "the historically distinct and incompatible modes of realism and modernism" might be seen as "so many stages in a dialectic of reification, which seizes on the properties and subjectivities, the institutions and the forms of an older precapitalist lifeworld in order to strip them of their hierarchical or religious content."[46] By this reading, late nineteenth- and early twentieth-century realism—for example, the works of George Gissing and Theodore Dreiser—offer narratives that diagnose this problem of the stripping away of traditional social codes by the increasingly powerful operations of the cash nexus, of the mediation of once-direct human relationships by the abstract flows of exchange value. This kind of realism may also be seen in the Edwardian naturalists against whom Woolf would define the modern writers—certainly it describes John Galsworthy, whose best-known novel, *The Man of Property* (1906), is a chronicle of the voracious acquisitiveness of the late Victorian middle and upper-middle classes. Jameson further theorizes that modernism's turn from would-be social verisimilitude to language and symbolic systems offers a response to realism's sharp diagnoses of the draining of stable meaning-codes and that this response is simultaneously an escape from traditional codes of meaning and an escape into self-aware productions of meaning that are projected out upon the chaos of contemporary social life. In this sense, modernism exhibits a certain cynicism, insofar as its fictions of meaning recognize themselves as such; but they can also offer great pleasure and affirmation, in ways that are foreign to realism. For if high realism and naturalism had often come to damningly express the reification and rationalization of turn-of-the-century life, then modernism offered "substitute gratifications" in the face of the pessimistic sociopolitical awareness thereby raised; modernism, by Jameson's theory, "constitutes a Utopian compensation for everything lost in an increasingly quantified world, the place of the archaic and of feeling amid the desacralization of the market system."[47] What we may see in the case of Woolf's literary criticism, then, is an effort at an emancipatory decoding of old meanings that effectively recognizes itself as such. Woolf's project is motivated by an intuitively "felt" desire, and its metonymic or horizontal movement from term to term—"truth," "reality," "life," "spirit"—provisionally invests those terms with the function of sacralized keywords in a restabilized code of meaning. However, because the rhetorical deployment of the terms demonstrates that they cannot be ontologically grounded in the manner that social codes were once felt to be, Woolf ironizes her wish for the terms to be fixed as if along the vertical or metaphoric axis of discourse, in the manner, as Deleuze and Guattari theorize, of those "metaphoric associations of equivalence and meaning imposed on desire by social and/or linguistic codes operating in the name" of territorialized desire—of the earth, of a totem, of a sovereign entity, of God.[48] (For Deleuze and Guattari, decoding has positive effects under capitalism, and recoding has negative effects.)[49] In Woolf's case, this desire may be detected in the depth metaphor behind her claim, "We want to be rid of realism, to penetrate without its help into the regions beneath it." In lieu of the realist novel's demonstrations of how once-stable codes have given way to the brutal reification of social life—in response, as well, to realism's skating along the surfaces of a depthless and disenchanted social representation—Woolf may be seen as calling for a decoding of meaning, at the same moment that she enacts the impossibility of linguistically expressing that decoding.

But if that meaning cannot be captured adequately in a linguistic code, Woolf suggests (to repeat) that it can nevertheless be felt. If "he could base his work upon his own *feeling*," she says, the novelist might be able "to convey this varying, this unknown and uncircumscribed spirit." In light of her philosophically idealist formulation of life as a luminous, numinous halo and her appeal elsewhere to the Romantic poets, we might see her as a uniquely twentieth-century romanticist. As already suggested, Woolf's call to literary "interiorization" suggests that we might usefully place her brand of modernism in a triangulated relationship with the opposed modes of popular-romantic and "serious" realist fiction. By this account, in the wake of realism's social analyses, the fiction of Joyce and Lawrence, of Mansfield and Woolf, might be seen as seeking to re-enchant the literary representation of Woolf's and Mansfield's "Life" through a renewed emphasis on affect, both as an experience to be figured and as a component of the reader's experience. As the narrative instances have repeatedly shown, modernist fiction could be seen to parallel, at a "higher" or more etherealized level, the "subjective" emotionalism of the romance novel; the difference in this latest witnessing is the evidence of Woolf's (and West's) literary theory.

We have come full circle to the argument of the earlier chapters of this study. If much modernist fiction explicitly rejects the nostalgic, retrograde ideologies sometimes embodied in the popular romance, it nonetheless shares with that often-"feminine" genre a concern with what Rita Felski calls "the transcendence of quotidian reality and the material world" (*Gender,* 112). In fact, as historical phenomena, both the popular romance and the now-canonical fiction of "high" modernism can be seen thematically to share a hostility toward abstract calculation as the basis of social order—that is, the increasingly "workaday" world of rational, quantifiable, measured and managed time—as well as toward the "realistic" or "naturalistic" literary depiction of this workaday world. If the reifying logic of the market was, by the early twentieth century, tending to transform meaningful social qualities into calculable economic quantities—if, in Marxian terms, social value was tending toward abstract exchange value and human relations in the public sphere were increasingly drained of intrinsic meanings—then both the popular romance and some modernist experimentation can be seen as attempts to "decode" experience, in their different ways, with affectively oriented symbolic systems. In other words, the embryonic "women's romance" of the early twentieth century did indeed offer daydreams and fantasies, but those reveries might not be so far from the modernist project—foreshadowed by Mansfield's "Rosabel," embodied in certain texts by early Joyce and Lawrence, and theorized by West and Woolf—of what I am calling "the romance of interiority."

Literary quests for symbolic transcendence can take different forms, but unlike the social diagnoses of high realism, they do not offer the direct critique that can in turn inspire social change. Doubtless, Katherine Mansfield intended to portray her socially isolated Rosabel—kneeing before the window of her tiny flat, revising the scene from *Anna Lombard* into her own story—as a dreamy escapist. But Rosabel's libidinal transformation of a lonely and desiccated daily life may also represent a Utopian compensation, with powerful implications of its own. By prophesying the centrality of the women's romance to twentieth-century popular culture, by doing so through the generic means of a penetrating psychological realism, Mansfield might have chosen to come down aesthetically in favor of the latter, at the expense of the former. Yet her various declarations of literary intent, together with the powerful empathy of Rosabel's portrayal, look ahead to the sublimation of romance narrative into modernist quests after the representation of human interiority's truths or absolutes. Literary realism seemed to have abandoned the romance's yearning for the Absolute; the modernist story often reengaged that pursuit, not only on the level of content but also on the level of form itself. In their cerebral manner, in turn, the representational quest of some modernist narratives—the linguistic mission to access the sublime or the Absolute—may have been as quixotic as the ideals of love and adventure set out in countless romance novels. It has even been suggested, quite recently, that what used to be called the Absolute is the very name for the ultimate mirage of identity of form and content and that modernism comes into being as the quest for that Absolute. Be that as it may, my final point here is instead the possibility of an unlikely parallel between modernist texts and modern romances, which, so different in so many ways, may nonetheless have gained their ascendancy in tandem, by fulfilling psychic needs and desires in response to social circumstances that so often did not, and so often do not.

NOTES

Introduction

1. See Jane Eldridge Miller, *Rebel Women: Feminism, Modernism, and the Edwardian Novel* (London: Virago Press, 1994) for an example of recent scholarship that makes the case for a modernism of content. In connection with a host of novelists of the Edwardian period—Arnold Bennett, E. M. Forster, John Galsworthy, Ada Leverson, Amber Reeves, Olivia Shakespear, and Elizabeth von Arnim, among many others—Miller has proposed that "these works of fiction should be considered examples of the modernism of content, an antecedent stage to the more familiar, canonized modernism of form" (7).

2. David Trotter, *The English Novel in History, 1895–1920* (London: Routledge, 1993), vii.

3. Douglas Mao and Rebecca Walkowitz, eds., *Bad Modernisms* (Durham, NC: Duke University Press, 2006), 1.

4. See, in particular, Ann Ardis, "E. M. Hull, Mass Market Romance, and the New Woman Novel in the Early Twentieth Century," *Women's Writing* 3, no. 3 (1996): 287–96; Janet Galligani Casey, "Marie Corelli and Fin de Siècle Feminism," *English Literature in Transition* 32, no. 2 (1992): 163–78; the chapter on Elinor Glyn in Nicholas Daly, *Literature, Technology, and Modernity, 1860–2000* (Cambridge, UK: Cambridge University Press, 2004), 76–109; Annette Federico, *Idol of Suburbia: Marie Corelli and Late-Victorian Literary Culture* (Charlottesville: University of Virginia Press, 2000); Laura Frost, "The Romance of Cliché: E. M. Hull, D. H. Lawrence, and Interwar Erotic Fiction" in *Bad Modernisms,* ed. Douglas Mao and Rebecca L. Walkowitz (Durham, NC: Duke University Press, 2006), 94–118; Jill Galvan, "Christians, Infidels, and Women's Channeling in the Writings of Marie Corelli," *Victorian Literature and Culture* 31, no. 1 (March 2003): 83–97; Elizabeth Gargano, "'English Sheiks' and Arab Stereotypes: E. M. Hull, T. E. Lawrence, and the Imperial Masquerade," *Texas Studies in Literature and Language* 48, no. 2 (Summer 2006): 171–86; R. B. Kershner, "Modernism's Mirror: The Sorrows of Marie Corelli" in *Transforming Genres: New Approaches to the British Fiction of the 1890s,* ed. Nikki Lee Manos and Meri-Jane Rochelson (New York: St. Martin's Press,

1994), 67–86; Nickianne Moody, "Elinor Glyn and the Invention of 'It,'" *Critical Survey* 15, no. 3 (2003): 92–104; Carol Margaret Davison and Elaine M. Hartnell, eds., "Marie Corelli," special issue, *Women's Writing* 13, no. 2 (June 2006); Teresa Ransom, *The Mysterious Miss Marie Corelli: Queen of Victorian Bestsellers* (Gloucestershire, UK: Sutton Publishing, 1999).

5. The sole exception is Marie Corelli's late romance *Innocent: Her Fancy and His Fact* (New York: A. L. Burt Company, 1914). But this novel was described by her biographer Teresa Ransom as "one of her most popular books" (*Mysterious Miss Marie Corelli,* 192), and it was one of the nine of Corelli's thirty books that were adapted into a silent film (1921).

6. Desmond Flower, comp., *A Century of Bestsellers, 1830–1930* (London: National Book Council, 1934).

7. Philip Waller, *Writers, Readers, and Reputations: Literary Life in Britain, 1870–1918* (Oxford: Oxford University Press, 2006), 647; "Mrs. Humphry Ward's Profits" (unsigned), *Literary News,* April 1903, 116.

8. Richard L. Kowalczyk, "In Vanished Summertime: Marie Corelli and Popular Culture," *Journal of Popular Culture* 7 (Spring 1974): 862.

9. Rita Felski, *The Gender of Modernity* (Cambridge, MA: Harvard University Press, 1995), 8.

10. Pamela Regis, *A Natural History of the Romance Novel* (Philadelphia: University of Pennsylvania Press, 2003), 14.

11. Maria DiBattista and Lucy McDiarmid, eds., *High and Low Moderns: Literature and Culture, 1889–1939* (New York: Oxford University Press, 1996), 18.

12. Gillian Beer, *The Romance* (London: Methuen, 1970).

13. Clive Bloom, *Bestsellers: Popular Fiction since 1900* (Basingstoke, UK: Palgrave Macmillan, 2002), 86.

14. Fredric Jameson, *The Political Unconscious* (Ithaca, NY: Cornell University Press, 1981), 266.

Chapter One: Contexts of Popular Romance, 1885–1925

1. Suzanne Clark, *Sentimental Modernism: Women Writers and the Revolution of the Word* (Bloomington: Indiana University Press, 1991).

2. See Jonathan Rose, *The Intellectual Life of the British Working Classes* (New Haven, CT: Yale University Press, 2001) for accounts (derived from memoirs, autobiographies, library records, and readers' surveys) of male reading during this period. Corelli, Orczy, and Glyn are each mentioned several times.

3. Mary Hammond, *Reading, Publishing and the Formation of Literary Taste in England, 1880–1914* (Aldershot, UK: Ashgate, 2006), 6.

4. Q. D. Leavis, *Fiction and the Reading Public* (London: Chatto and Windus, 1932), 54.

5. On this point, Suzanne Clark cites Marlon Ross's argument that "women writers *could not be romantics:* romanticism was the shaping of desire by an ideology of masculinity" (Clark, *Sentimental Modernism,* 207–8; italics in original).

6. Beer, *Romance,* 21.

7. See Kate Flint, *The Woman Reader, 1837–1914* (Oxford, UK: Clarendon Press, 1993).

8. Regis, *Natural History,* 14.

9. See Melisa Brittain, "Erasing Race in the New Woman Review: Victoria Cross's *Anna Lombard,*" *Nineteenth-Century Feminisms* 4 (Spring/Summer 2001): 75–95. For citations of Moody's, Ardis's, and Frost's relevant works, see note 4 in the introduction.

10. Felski, *Gender of Modernity,* 120.

11. Peter Brooks, *The Melodramatic Imagination* (New Haven, CT: Yale University Press, 1976), 16.

12. D. H. Lawrence, *Kangaroo* (New York: Viking Press, 1923), 220.

13. "Elinor Glyn," in *Comic Poems* (New York: Everyman Publishers, 2001), 91. Scholars have been unable to locate the original published source of this anonymous verse (if one exists).

14. Anthony Glyn, *Elinor Glyn: A Biography* (New York: Doubleday, 1955), 132.

15. Stenographer's record from the shorthand notes of Messrs. Barnett and Barrett. The Royal Courts of Justice, London, 21 December 1915 (British Library archives, London).

16. Ibid.

17. Elinor Glyn, *Romantic Adventure: Being the Autobiography of Elinor Glyn* (New York: E. P. Dutton, 1937), 98.

18. John Feather, *A History of British Publishing* (London: Routledge, 1988), 175.

19. See the Correspondence of the Society of Authors, British Library archives, London.

20. Letter from Bryne and Cutcheon Law Office, New York, to Herbert Thring, Society of Authors, undated [presumably 1912] (British Library archives, London).

21. Letter from Bryne and Cutcheon Law Office, New York, to Herbert Thring, Society of Authors, 22 May 1912 (British Library archives, London).

22. Fredric Jameson, "Reification and Utopia in Mass Culture," *Social Text* 1, no. 1 (1979): 137.

23. Ian Buchanan, *Fredric Jameson: Live Theory* (London: Continuum International Publishing Group, 2006), 74.

24. John Sutherland has shown that the twentieth-century commercialization of the fiction book trade in Britain lagged significantly behind that of North America. By way of evidence, reliable best-seller lists did not appear in Britain until the 1970s, and the Net Book Agreement, the 1900

price-fixing arrangement between publishers and booksellers, was annulled in 1995. John Sutherland, "The True Birth of the Bestseller," lecture at Fales Library, New York University, 30 March 2007. A good account of the relatively late rationalization of the popular fiction industry in Britain is offered by Clive Bloom in the chapter "Genre: History and Form" in *Bestsellers,* 85–106. Joseph McAleer, in his *Popular Reading and Publishing in Britain, 1914–1950* (Oxford, UK: Clarendon Press, 1992), dates the shift considerably earlier, claiming that "[a]fter 1914 . . . the commercialization of popular fiction promoted the genre and even the imprint over the particular author" (38).

25. Algernon Methuen, *Sir Algernon Methuen, Baronet: A Memoir* (London: Methuen, 1925), 8. This admission was offered exactly thirty years after Methuen published Corelli's *The Sorrows of Satan* (1895), a novel whose initial sales exceeded that of any previous work of fiction at that point in British history. By 1919, Methuen had sold 202,000 copies of *The Sorrows of Satan* (McAleer, *Popular Reading,* 26).

26. Peter Keating, *The Haunted Study: A Social History of the English Novel, 1875–1914* (London: Secker and Warburg, 1989), 208.

27. David Trotter differs from Peter Keating in his categorization of the "sex novel"; labeling it as synonymous with the "problem novel," he dates the era of the "sex novel" in Britain as 1895 to 1914 and effectively treats the category as overlapping with the New Woman novel. David Trotter, "Edwardian Sex Novels," *Critical Quarterly* 31, no. 1 (1989): 95. Such taxonomies cannot be scientifically determined, of course, and so I view these two literary historians' categorizations, which are equally well documented, as equally valid.

28. I here accept without qualification Virginia Woolf's well-known categorization from the 1924 essay "Mr. Bennett and Mrs. Brown."

29. Trotter, "Edwardian Sex Novels," 104.

Chapter Two: Mary Ward's Romances and the Literary Field

1. For example, the *Pall Mall Gazette* titled its review of *Robert Elsmere* "A Romance of the New Religion" (5 April 1888, 2–3), and William Gladstone, in his article "'Robert Elsmere' and the Battle of Belief," referred to the text as a "propagandist romance" (*Nineteenth Century* 23 [May 1888], 767).

2. Keating, *Haunted Study,* 175.

3. I am speaking here of canonical literature by women in this period. Since the time when Williams published his accounts of nineteenth- and early twentieth-century fiction—the most well known of which is probably *The English Novel from Dickens to Lawrence* (New York: Oxford University Press, 1970)—there have, of course, been many fine studies of the heterogeneous fiction by women in the period; these studies include Elaine Showalter, *A Literature of Their Own: British Women Novelists from Brontë to Lessing* (Princeton:

Princeton University Press, 1977); Ann Ardis, *New Women, New Novels: Feminism and Early Modernism* (New Brunswick, NJ: Rutgers University Press, 1990); Miller, *Rebel Women;* and Valerie Sanders, *Eve's Renegades* (New York: St. Martin's Press, 1996).

4. Showalter, *Literature of Their Own,* 61.

5. See Miller, *Rebel Women.*

6. W. H. Meyers, "George Sand," *Nineteenth Century* 1 (April 1877): 229.

7. Guizot is quoted in Hugh Walker, *The Literature of the Victorian Era* (Cambridge: Cambridge University Press, 1910), 707.

8. See Ellen Miller Casey, "Edging Women Out? Reviews of Women Novelists in *The Athenaeum,* 1860–1900," *Victorian Studies* 39, no. 2 (Winter 1996): 158. Casey offers this list of the women novelists to whom the descriptives *artist, genius,* or *great* were applied: Jane Austen, Elizabeth Gaskell, George Sand (recognized as a woman), Frances Ternan Trollope, George Eliot (recognized as a woman), Charlotte and Emily Brontë, Olive Schreiner, Margaret L. Woods, John Oliver Hobbes (recognized as a woman), Margaret Oliphant, Lily Dougall, and Mary Wilkins Freeman. The three not identified by the *Athenaeum* as women were the author of *St. Olave's* (Eliza Tabor Stephen), E. O. Somerville (Edith Somerville), and Martin Ross (Violet Ross). Casey, "Edging Women Out?" 158n25.

9. "Silly Novels by Lady Novelists" is the title of an article by Eliot in the *Westminster Review,* October 1856.

10. Edith Simcox, "George Eliot," *Nineteenth Century* 9 (May 1881): 782.

11. Each of the fields on this list, according to Bourdieu, is a subset of the broadest field of all, that of class relations. Nonetheless, each of these subfields is semiautonomous and functions by its own rules. See "The Field of Cultural Production, or: The Economic World Reversed," the first chapter of Pierre Bourdieu, *The Field of Cultural Production,* ed. Randal Johnson (New York: Columbia University Press, 1993), esp. 37–40. Thus does Bourdieu avoid certain kinds of reductionism, such as the notions that either economics or too broadly defined "power" must wholly determine the relations of the agents—individual or collective—on a given field. What the fields *do* share is a homologous functioning, whereby agents take positions on the field and engage in competition for control of the interests and resources that are specific to the field in question. Here I borrow from the gloss provided by Randal Johnson in his superb introduction to the English translation of *The Field of Cultural Production* (6).

12. Bourdieu, *Field of Cultural Production,* 163–64.

13. In Bourdieu's lexicon, "strategy" is a crucial notion, indicating the mode of individual agency on the field. It conveys the effectiveness of conscious intention, while allowing as well that the actant's tactics often half succeed, fail entirely, or produce unintended consequences.

14. The three forms of (noneconomic) capital most important to literary historians are probably the cultural, social, and symbolic. *Cultural capital*

refers to cultural knowledge as a resource of power; it consists in "the incorporation of symbolic, cognitive, and aesthetic competences via implicit learning processes mainly within the family socialization" (Christian Joppke, "The Cultural Dimensions of Class Formation and Class Struggle: On the Social Theory of Pierre Bourdieu," *Berkeley Journal of Sociology* 31 [1986]: 57). Cultural capital can take objective form in cultural goods, artifacts, books, and so on; beyond the family, it is accrued through social associations and formal and informal schooling. *Social capital* refers generally to the power that comes from social associations, such as memberships in various kinds of groups, both formal and informal; the strategic use and accumulation of such capital can bring the profit of improved position, as through "social climbing." *Symbolic capital* is perhaps the trickiest (and most important) form of noneconomic capital in Bourdieu's theory. It effectively embraces all the other species of capital and is the most abstract form, constituted as it is within the recognition *(reconnaissance)* of others. Neither one's literary allusions nor one's objets d'art nor one's social connections can function as valuable unless they are recognized as valuable by those individuals and groups who form one's social context. As Joppke asserts, "Because symbolic capital is dependent on its activation and affirmation by actual communicative practices, and in this respect cannot be objectified, institutionalized, or incorporated, it is merely a subjective reflection, acknowledgement and legitimation of a given distribution of economic, cultural, and social capital" ("Cultural Dimensions," 60). Symbolic capital might thus be said to have a dialectical relationship with the other forms of capital; as a concept it underscores the fact that none of the positive properties that circulate on the literary field ever *permanently* or *objectively* inheres in any of the individuals, groups, works, or literary forms that are held to partake of those properties. The structure of the literary field is always contingent and evolving as a matrix of subjective perceptions, power relations, and objectified embodiments of symbolic capital.

15. Toril Moi, "Appropriating Bourdieu: Feminist Theory and Pierre Bourdieu's Sociology of Culture," *New Literary History* 22, no. 4 (Autumn 1991): 1038.

16. *Heteronomous* is Bourdieu's antonym to *autonomous.* It indicates how success for the mass-market novelist is determined by a form of capital—economic—that strictly speaking does not find its value within the field of cultural (or literary) production but in effect "impinges from outside," from the broader field of economic power in society at large. See Bourdieu, *Field of Cultural Production,* 38.

17. Gaye Tuchman and Nina Fortin, *Edging Women Out: Victorian Novelists, Publishers, and Social Change* (New Haven, CT: Yale University Press, 1989), 1.

18. Ibid., 93.

19. In "Edging Women Out?" Ellen Miller Casey offers interesting evidence, counter to the evidence of Tuchman and Fortin, that women

novelists were not "edged out" between the years 1860 and 1900. She demonstrates that the percentage of novels published per year by women, as compared to the percentage published by men, declined only slightly, and not in a unilinear way. Her data are extremely useful but exclusively limited to a survey of reviews from one prestigious journal of the era, the *Athenaeum.* Moreover, she does not successfully refute Tuchman and Fortin's main argument, which is not that women were barred from the literary field altogether but that the collective symbolic capital of contemporary women novelists declined as male writers took the novel more seriously over the decades.

20. On this list of writers, see especially chapter 1 in Vineta Colby, *The Singular Anomaly: Women Novelists of the Nineteenth Century* (New York: New York University Press, 1970).

21. John Sutherland, *Mrs. Humphry Ward: Eminent Victorian, Pre-eminent Edwardian* (Oxford: Oxford University Press, 1991), 97.

22. Quoted in William S. Peterson, *Victorian Heretic: Mrs. Humphry Ward's* Robert Elsmere (Leicester: Leicester University Press, 1976), 102.

23. Sutherland, *Mrs. Humphry Ward,* 100, 103.

24. Quoted in ibid., 100.

25. Letter from G. L. Craik to Ward, 27 February 1885 (quoted in ibid., 107).

26. Mary Augusta Ward, *A Writer's Recollections* (London: W. Collins and Sons, 1918), 233.

27. Clyde de L. Ryals, "Editor's introduction" to *Robert Elsmere,* by Mary Augusta Ward (Lincoln: University of Nebraska Press, 1967), xxxiii–xxxiv.

28. Patricia Meyer Spacks, *Boredom* (Chicago: University of Chicago Press, 1995), 153–54.

29. Judith Wilt, *Behind Her Times: Transition England in the Novels of Mary Arnold Ward* (Charlottesville: University of Virginia Press, 2005), 48.

30. Laura Fasick, "The Ambivalence of Influence: The Case of Mary Ward and Charlotte Yonge," *English Literature in Transition* 37, no. 2 (1994): 150.

31. Judith Wilt also notes this generic cross-pollination, not only in *Robert Elsmere* but also in Ward's novels of the 1890s and the Edwardian decade; she designates Ward as "generically conservative in her attempt to consolidate across the decades the moral force that wedded romance fiction to Victorian realism" (*Behind Her Times,* 1).

32. Although Olive Schreiner's *The Story of an African Farm* (1883) is today categorized as an early New Woman novel, I follow Jane Eldridge Miller and other scholars in taking the first half of the 1890s to be the moment when the New Woman novels fully emerged (Miller, *Rebel Women,* 14).

33. Letter from Ward to George Smith, 27 January 1888 (Mrs. Humphry Ward Collection, Claremont Colleges).

34. Ibid.

35. Letter from Ward to George Smith, 22 February 1888 (Mrs. Humphry Ward Collection, Claremont Colleges).

36. "New Novels," *Scotsman,* 5 March 1888, 3.

37. Letter from Ward to George Smith, 6 March 1888 (Mrs. Humphry Ward Collection, Claremont Colleges).

38. Letter from Ward to George Smith, 14 March 1888 (Mrs. Humphry Ward Collection, Claremont Colleges). Joseph Shorthouse had published *John Inglesant: A Romance* in 1881, after Mary Ward had convinced her then publisher Macmillan to take the book.

39. Ward, *Writer's Recollections,* 236–37.

40. Ward was resummoned the next day after breakfast, and so their debate took place over the course of two days, 8 and 9 April 1888. For an account of their discussion, see Peterson, *Victorian Heretic,* 166–67.

41. Ward, *Writer's Recollections,* 245–46.

42. William Sharp, "New Novels," *Academy* 33, no. 828 (17 March 1888): 184.

43. "A Romance of the New Religion," *Pall Mall Gazette,* 5 April 1888, 2–3.

44. Letter from Ward to George Smith, 2 May 1888 (Mrs. Humphry Ward Collection, Claremont Colleges).

45. Letter from George Smith to Ward, 3 May 1888 (Mrs. Humphry Ward Collection, Claremont Colleges).

46. Letters from Ward to George Smith, 8 and 11 May 1888 (Mrs. Humphry Ward Collection, Claremont Colleges).

47. Introductory Notes, Honnold Collection, Claremont Colleges.

48. Letter from George Smith to Ward, 30 August 1888 (Mrs. Humphry Ward Collection, Claremont Colleges).

49. See Sanders, *Eve's Renegades,* 114–25; and Ardis, *New Women, New Novels,* 156–59.

50. Beth Sutton-Ramspeck, "Shot Out of the Canon: Mary Ward and the Claims of Conflicting Feminisms," in *Victorian Women Writers and the Woman Question,* ed. Nicola Diane Thompson (Cambridge: Cambridge University Press, 1999), 210.

51. All of these letters are to be found in the unpublished correspondence of Mary Augusta Ward at the Harry Ransom Humanities Center, University of Texas at Austin.

52. As Gisela Argyle illustrates, literary historians today tend to see *The Marriage of William Ashe* (1905) as the last of Ward's "serious" novels. See Argyle, "Mrs. Humphry Ward's Fictional Experiments in the Woman Question," *Studies in English Literature, 1500–1900* 43, no. 3 (Autumn 2003): 941.

53. Mary Augusta Ward, *Lady Rose's Daughter* (New York: Harper and Brothers, 1903), 1.

54. The time of the narrative is never specifically dated, but there are numerous clues. One of the heroine's would-be paramours, Captain Warkworth, is described as "the man who distinguished himself in the Mahsud

expedition" (11). Because he is just starting his military career, the action cannot take place long after the date of the actual Mahsud-Waziri Expedition into Waziristan (in present-day Pakistan), which was 1881.

55. "Lady Rose's Daughter" (unsigned review), reprint from *Times Saturday Review* in *Literary News: A Monthly Journal of Current Literature* (New York) 24 (April 1903): 100.

56. Ibid., 100.

57. Ibid., 101.

58. John Cawelti, *Adventure, Mystery, and Romance: Formula Stories as Art and Popular Culture* (Chicago: University of Chicago Press, 1976), 41–42.

59. "Thomas Arnold Dead," Saturday Review of Books and Art, *New York Times,* 17 November 1900, BR11.

60. See Janet P. Trevelyan, *The Life of Mrs. Humphry Ward* (London: Constable 1923), 176. Quoted in Sutherland, *Mrs. Humphrey Ward,* 197.

61. As Ward records in her 1918 memoir, she had later in her life come to believe in the possibility of such visual hallucinations. Apropos the present context, she recorded the late-night apparition of an aged William Wordsworth before her daughter Dorothy, when Dorothy was sleeping in Dorothy Wordsworth's former bedroom, at Rydal Mount in the Lake District, in the early hours of 14 September 1911 (Ward, *Writer's Recollections,* 110–12).

62. The American Harriet Beecher Stowe was a transatlantic exception—an earlier woman novelist who had sold copies of *Uncle Tom's Cabin* in the hundreds of thousands.

63. Feather, *History of British Publishing,* 155.

64. Letter from Ward to George Smith, 4 June 1894 (Mrs. Humphry Ward Collection, Claremont Colleges).

65. Ibid.

66. Feather, *History of British Publishing,* 155.

67. Ibid.

68. Letter from Ward to George Smith, 12 July 1894 (Mrs. Humphry Ward Collection, Claremont Colleges).

69. Virginia Woolf, *The Diary of Virginia Woolf,* vol. 1, *1915–1919,* ed. Anne Olivier Bell (New York: Harcourt Brace Jovanovich, 1977), 300.

70. Virginia Woolf, *The Letters of Virginia Woolf,* vol. 2, *1912–1922,* ed. Nigel Nicolson and Joanne Trautmann (New York: Harcourt Brace Jovanovich, 1976), 68.

71. Rebecca West, *The Strange Necessity* (New York: Doubleday, 1928), 106.

72. Woolf, *Letters,* 2:62.

73. *Harvest* was the second-to-last novel that Ward wrote (in 1918) but was often treated as Ward's last novel because it was published after her last-written novel, *Cousin Philip* (1919).

74. Katherine Mansfield, "Mrs. Humphry Ward's Last Novel," *Athenaeum* 4697 (7 May 1920): 606.

Chapter Three: Marie Corelli and the Discourse of Romance

1. To be fair to Coetzee, of course, I should note that the quoted passage can be read as evidencing the self-importance of his eponymous protagonist, the novelist and intellectual Elizabeth Costello.

2. This is true despite the fact that Corelli's efforts to procure symbolic and social capital were no less assiduous than Ward's. Corelli, having heard about the visits (described in the previous chapter) that Gladstone had paid to Mary Augusta Ward in April 1888, sent at least four letters to Gladstone from May to July 1889, begging him to review her romance *Ardath.* As he had done with Ward, Gladstone called upon Corelli (on 4 June 1889), but she had a decidedly less successful colloquy with him about the themes of her romances (they included, at that early date in her career, *A Romance of Two Worlds, Vendetta,* and *Ardath*). In a follow-up letter, she again requested that Gladstone review her romances or at least mention them in his "masterly thoughts on these psychological questions" (Corelli, letter of 5 June 1889; quoted in Brian Masters, *Now Barabbas Was a Rotter: The Extraordinary Life of Marie Corelli* [London: Hamish Hamilton, 1978], 89). He never did.

3. These nine included *Boy* (1900), *Jane* (1900), *Delicia* (1900), *The Master Christian* (1900), *Temporal Power* (1902), *God's Good Man* (1904), *The Treasure of Heaven* (1906), *Holy Orders* (1908), and *The Devil's Motor: A Fantasy* (1910). Over this period, she published articles, pamphlets, and nonfiction books as well.

4. For hard evidence to support this claim, see Masters, *Now Barabbas,* 6.

5. See Kowalczyk, "In Vanished Summertime"; Masters, *Now Barabbas;* Janet Galligani Casey, "Marie Corelli and Fin de Siècle Feminism," *English Literature in Transition* 32, no. 2 (1992): 163–78; Kershner, "Modernism's Mirror"; Felski, *Gender of Modernity,* 115–44; Peter Keating, introduction to *The Sorrows of Satan,* by Marie Corelli (Oxford: Oxford University Press, 1996), ix–xx; Ransom, *Mysterious Miss Marie Corelli;* Federico, *Idol of Suburbia;* Galvan, "Christians, Infidels"; Julia Kuehn, *Glorious Vulgarity: Marie Corelli's Feminine Sublime in a Popular Context* (Berlin: Logos, 2004); and Carol Margaret Davison and Elaine M. Hartnell, eds., "Marie Corelli," special issue, *Women's Writing* 13, no. 2 (June 2006).

6. Felski, *Gender of Modernity;* Kershner, "Modernism's Mirror"; Federico, *Idol of Suburbia.* In their introduction to a recent (June 2006) issue of the journal *Women's Writing* devoted to Corelli's romances, Carol Margaret Davison and Elaine M. Hartnell urge that "the ideological and aesthetic complexities repeatedly identified in Corelli's works justify their reappraisal" (183).

7. In making this observation about Corelli's relationship to genre, I again follow the lead of Davison and Hartnell, who write, "The fin de

siècle witnessed a proliferation of new novel types—among them the boy's adventure novel, the spiritual romance, and science fiction—and the experimental Corelli was certainly of her age with her unique blend of sensationalism, mysticism, romance, and the Gothic (to name but a few styles she employed)" (183).

8. Nickianne Moody, "Moral Uncertainty and the Afterlife: Explaining the Popularity of Marie Corelli's Early Novels," *Women's Writing* 13, no. 2 (June 2006): 202.

9. Kershner, "Modernism's Mirror," 76.

10. Claude Lévi-Strauss, *Structural Anthropology*, trans. Claire Jacobson and Brooke Schoepf (New York: Basic Books, 1963), 229.

11. I have chosen to emphasize these issues in this order because they seem to me to predominate in this sequence, but of course they are often closely related and are not confined respectively to the three romances in question.

12. See Pierre Macherey, *A Theory of Literary Production*, trans. G. Wall (London: Routledge, 1978).

13. See Masters, *Now Barabbas*, 143; Ransom, *Mysterious Miss Marie Corelli*, 81; Moody, "Moral Uncertainty," 191.

14. As Julia Kuehn records in her study of Corelli, "according to two advertisements in the *Pall Mall Gazette* of 18 and 23 October 1895, the first two editions of the *Sorrows*—the first with 15,000 and the second with 5,000 copies—were exhausted before publication, so that a third edition of another 5,000 copies was already in the press when the novel was released" (*Glorious Vulgarity*, 216).

15. W. T. Stead, "*The Sorrows of Satan*—and of Marie Corelli," *Review of Reviews* 12 (July–December 1895): 453. Stead says that the novel's sales reached this figure by the end of 1895. The novel was published on 21 October of that year, hence my calculation of ten weeks.

16. Kuehn, *Glorious Vulgarity*, 12.

17. Marie Corelli, *The Sorrows of Satan, or the Strange Experience of One Geoffrey Tempest, Millionaire: A Romance*, ed. Peter Keating (Oxford: Oxford University Press, 1996), xi. All citations from Corelli's novel are from this edition.

18. See note 5, above.

19. In this characterization of the melodramatic mode, I draw in particular on Juliet John, *Dickens's Villains: Melodrama, Character, Popular Culture* (Oxford: Oxford University Press, 2001).

20. For more on Buddhism and Hinduism in Corelli, see J. Jeffrey Franklin, "The Counter-Invasion of Britain by Buddhism in Marie Corelli's *A Romance of Two Worlds* and H. Rider Haggard's *Ayesha: The Return of She*," *Victorian Literature and Culture* 31, no. 1 (March 2003): 19–42.

21. Reasserting the thesis of Jane Tompkins and Nina Baym regarding American literary culture at the turn of the century, Felski argues in her discussion of Corelli that "sentiment, melodrama, and sensationalism" are "key aspects of women's popular culture of the time" (*Gender of Modernity*, 142).

While I certainly do not intend to refute that generalization, I am suggesting that *The Sorrows of Satan* was a melodramatic romance that was neither experienced as exclusively "women's popular culture" in the 1890s nor read by women alone. The evidence suggests that many men read and enjoyed this novel.

22. See Frank Rahill, *The World of Melodrama* (University Park: Pennsylvania State University Press, 1967): "[I]t was the English romance that determined the last phase in the evolution of the pantomime into melodrama. . . . The gothic tales of Mrs. Radcliffe and 'Monk' Lewis took Paris by storm. . . . [M]elodrama, when it made its way onto the British stage at the dawn of the nineteenth century, did so not as an interloping alien but rather as a returning native son, whose unfamiliar aspect was nothing more than a superficial polish acquired on the Grand Tour" (110).

23. Ibid., xiv.

24. See, for instance, Erin Marie Smith, "Trembling on the Boundary: Melodrama and the Victorian Novel, 1846–1876," *Dissertation Abstracts International* 60, no. 11 (May 2000): 4023; Lauren D. McKinney, "From New Money to New Woman: Social Change and Melodrama in Three British Novels of the 1890s," *Dissertation Abstracts International* 56, no. 9 (March 1996): 3595A; Annette Doblix Klemp, "Dickens and Melodrama: Character Presentation and Plot Motifs in Six Novels," *Dissertation Abstracts International* 45, no. 12 (June 1985): 3646A.

25. It was dramatized for the London stage by Herbert Woodgate and Paul M. Berton in 1897 (Waller, *Writers, Readers, and Reputations,* 787).

26. Danish director Carl Theodor Dreyer's loose adaptation of Corelli's novel, *Blade af Satans Bog (Leaves from Satan's Book),* in 1919 also has a significant place in film history. This silent film "follows Satan's banishment from Heaven, with the conditions for his return based upon the charge to tempt and try mankind. Influenced by the episodic structure of D. W. Griffith's 'Intolerance,' the film takes place in four chapters from different time periods as Satan appears as various characters, including a Pharisee persecuting Jesus of Nazareth, a monk during the Spanish Inquisition, a servant during the French Revolution, and Russian monk in Finland in 1918." University of Nevada–Reno, "The Feature Films of Carl Theodor Dreyer," http://www.scs.unr.edu/~schmidta/ featurefilms.html.

27. Thomas F. G. Coates and R. S. Warren Bell, *Marie Corelli: The Writer and the Woman* (Philadelphia: George W. Jacobs and Company, 1903).

28. In April 1900, Corelli wrote the following explanation of her denomination of Anglicanism to the vicar of Stratford-on-Avon, the Reverend George Arbuthnot:

> Dear Mr. Arbuthnot,—It is very sweet and kind of you to write me such a nice letter, and though I do not belong to your form of the Christian faith, nor to the Roman Catholic form either now,

> I have the greatest respect and reverence for both. I am one of a very numerous "fraternity" (we are perhaps between 50,000 and 100,000 altogether)—who are bound to try our best to follow the teachings of Christ as enunciated by himself—and we are not, by the rules of our Order, allowed to attend public worship, "That we may be seen of men." Our rules are somewhat difficult and arbitrary, and render us liable to a good deal of misconception—hence we have chosen as our motto, "In the world ye shall have tribulation, but be of good cheer—I have overcome the world." If you would like to form an idea of what we try to do, I will copy the "Daily Paradise" from my little private Manual (each member of our Order has one), as I think it will rather interest you. We are all at one in our Faith in the Divinity of Jesus Christ and his Message, as being the only way to truth and life: of final salvation, so far as this earth and its inhabitants are concerned, and any doubter of this first grand principle would be requested to resign his or her membership. But we do not accept any of the Church forms. We simply, as far as it is humanly possible to do, obey the words of Christ as spoken by himself—even at all risk of inconvenience to ourselves and misjudgement by our friends. (Quoted in Ransom, *Mysterious Miss Marie Corelli,* 102)

Corelli's "Order" is entirely imaginary, and precisely where she discovered those statistics regarding possible adherents remains a mystery. Kuehn observes, "The Order, like the Manual, seems to be Corelli's own invention, but there are several allusions to something of the kind in Corelli's work, as in *The Life,* where the heroine attends the mysterious Order of the Cross and Star, which has its own book of faith. Corelli thus teases the reverend with the suggestion of a hidden order working to undermine the authority of the clergy and the established religions. She mentions the large number of believers and, implicitly, asserts her own authority through her popularity. This she designates the hidden order as a valid form of Christianity, not just occult" (*Glorious Vulgarity,* 237).

29. This religious openness may in part explain the attraction of Queen Victoria to Corelli's romances. As one of her biographers states, Victoria exhibited "her own idiosyncratic brand of Christianity, which was an eclectic and contradictory amalgam of both High and Low Church ritual, with an emphasis on the devotional element rather than the traditional fear of God's punishment, coupled with a strong belief in the afterlife—a belief that fuelled a considerable interest in the paranormal." Helen Rappaport, *Queen Victoria: A Biographical Companion* (New York: ABC-CLIO, 2003), 312.

30. Quoted in Ransom, Mysterious Miss Marie Corelli, 85.

31. This quotation was recorded by the anonymous journalist who published "Priest Denounces Realistic Novels: Fiction Stronger than the

Pulpit, Father McMahon Asserts" in the *New York Times* on 27 January 1903. By 1903, Corelli's persistent anti-Catholicism had been made explicit in her novel *The Master Christian* (1900), and Father McMahon's attack may in part have been motivated by this fact.

32. For an analysis of these elements of Corelli's religious ontology in *The Sorrows of Satan,* see especially Elaine M. Hartnell, "Morals and Metaphysics: Marie Corelli, Religion, and the Gothic," in Davison and Hartnell, "Marie Corelli," 284–303.

33. Franklin, "Counter-Invasion of Britain," 30.

34. Hartnell, "Morals and Metaphysics," 284.

35. Robyn Hallim, "Marie Corelli: Science, Society, and the Best Seller," dissertation, University of Sydney, May 2002, 85.

36. National Library of New Zealand, "The Corelli Collection," http://www.natlib.govt.nz.

37. Corelli's philosophy in *The Sorrows of Satan* is also conveyed in part by the forms of the gothic, another subgenre of the romance, as Elaine M. Hartnell and Benjamin F. Fisher demonstrate. See Hartnell, "Morals and Metaphysics"; Benjamin F. Fisher, "Marie Corelli's *Barabbas, The Sorrows of Satan,* and Generic Transition," in Davison and Hartnell, "Marie Corelli," 304–20.

38. Brooks, *Melodramatic Imagination,* 16.

39. Coates and Bell, *Marie Corelli,* 165.

40. In their preface, Coates and Bell say, "[We] beg to offer Miss Corelli our grateful thanks for permitting us to have access to letters, papers, and other documents necessary to authenticate our facts" (4). I have found no evidence that Corelli, who was sensitive to slights and misinterpretations and was highly aware of what was published about her, ever objected to any aspect of Coates and Bell's 352-page treatment of her life and literary themes.

41. Eric Hobsbawm, *The Age of Empire, 1875–1914* (New York: Vintage, 1987), 10.

42. Ibid., 40. Hobsbawm describes the situation as no less than an ideological crisis, such that the liberal bourgeoisie "had triumphed by shattering the social cohesion of ancient hierarchies and communities, by choosing the market against human relations, Gesellschaft against Gemeinschaft" (104). This condition, in part brought about by the triumph of Victorian liberalism, was by the 1890s a social reality in severe tension with the laissez-faire conviction that the market would ultimately be fair and just in rewarding individual effort.

43. The phrase *deterritorialized capital accumulations* is taken from the theory of Gilles Deleuze and Félix Guattari, in particular *Anti-Oedipus: Capitalism and Schizophrenia* [1972], trans. Robert Hurley, Mark Seem, and Helen R. Lane (Minneapolis: University of Minnesota Press, 1983) and *A Thousand Plateaus: Capitalism and Schizophrenia* [1980], trans. Brian Massumi

(Minneapolis: University of Minnesota Press, 1987). A good gloss on what the phrase signifies in the present context is to be found in Eugene Holland, *Deleuze and Guattari's Anti-Oedipus: Introduction to Schizoanalysis* (London: Routledge, 1999), 19–20.

44. See "antinomy," in *Webster's New Collegiate Dictionary* (Springfield, MA: G. and C. Merriam Company, 1981).

45. It should be stated, of course, that the phrase *must also come into play* needs two qualifications: the necessity is emphasized because the terms of a binary opposition must implicitly entail one another to be structurally intelligible; second, this effect is achieved more intuitively than intellectually among readers.

46. Unsigned review of *The Sorrows of Satan,* by Marie Corelli, *Shafts* 8, no. 3 (November 1895): 111.

47. Quoted in Masters, *Now Barabbas,* 135.

48. James Stanley Little, "New Novels," *Academy* 48, no. 1219 (14 September 1895): 202.

49. Jameson, *Political Unconscious,* 255–56.

50. This point is also a methodological one: both Rita Felski and Julia Kuehn are correct to see in such Corelli romances as *The Sorrows* the instantiation of the popular sublime, and we can complement those readings via a historicizing (as I attempt here) that helps explain how the collective necessity of the popular sublime was ideologically generated.

51. Coates and Bell, *Marie Corelli,* 341–42.

52. Ibid., 57.

53. Ibid.

54. Quoted in Rose, *Intellectual Life,* 129.

55. Ibid., 139, 253.

56. Quoted in Federico, *Idol of Suburbia,* 65.

57. Jameson, *Political Unconscious,* 104.

58. Raymond Williams, *The English Novel from Dickens to Lawrence,* 16.

59. Ibid.

60. Recent critics have elucidated how Corelli's opposition to turn-of-the-century feminist activism and thought is countered in some ways by her frequent depictions of strong, independent female characters. Janet Galligani Casey, for example, has demonstrated that for all her allegiance to Victorian strictures regarding "feminine" virtues, Corelli's female characters serve to promote women's equality, through their author's "general fervor and sincerity in asserting dignity and respect for women" ("Marie Corelli," 176).

61. Marie Corelli, *The Treasure of Heaven* (New York: Dodd, Mead and Company, 1906), 1–2. All citations from Corelli's novel are from this edition.

62. Quoted in Ransom, *Mysterious Miss Marie Corelli,* 150.

63. Jean Radford, ed., "Introduction," *The Progress of Romance: The Politics of Popular Fiction* (London: Routledge and Kegan Paul, 1986), 10.

64. "To those who suggested her reading was desultory, she retorted that Byron and Keats also read everything they could lay their hands on, and it did them no harm." Masters, *Now Barabbas,* 27.

65. Quoted in George Bainton, ed., *The Art of Authorship* (London: James Clarke and Company, 1890), 7.

66. Ibid.

67. I am referring to Corelli's set of literary allusions as her small-r, rather than capital-R, "romantic canon," because the specific movement of early nineteenth-century English Romanticism should be seen as a late development in (and subset of) the centuries-old tradition of romance literature. I draw this view from the work of Harold Bloom; see in particular his collection *Romanticism and Consciousness: Essays in Criticism* (New York: W. W. Norton and Company, 1970).

68. George Sturt, *Change in the Village* [1912] (London: Caliban Books, 1984), 194.

69. Northrop Frye, *Anatomy of Criticism* (Princeton: Princeton University Press, 1957), 151.

70. Ibid., 157.

71. Corelli's writing career spanned thirty-eight years, from the publication of her first novel, *A Romance of Two Worlds,* in 1886, to her death in 1924.

72. As Corelli's biographer Brian Masters shows, the last of Corelli's "big successes"—novels that sold over 100,000 copies—was *The Life Everlasting,* published in 1911 (*Now Barabbas,* 244). However, Corelli received a larger advance for the 1914 manuscript of *Innocent* (£5,000) than she did for *The Treasure of Heaven* (£4,500), which was by far the more successful of the two books (ibid., 168).

73. R. A. Scott-James, *Modernism and Romance* (London: John Lane, 1908), 109.

74. Marie Corelli, *Innocent: Her Fancy and His Fact* (New York: A. L. Burt Company, 1914), 65. All citations from Corelli's novel are from this edition.

75. As if to underscore her effectively preindustrial upbringing, when Innocent departs to make a name for herself as a writer in London, she feels "sick and giddy" on her first train ride: "[S]he imagined herself as being torn away from the peaceful past and hurled into a stormy future" (213–14). Like motor cars in *The Treasure of Heaven,* machines such as the train (which had existed in England since the 1820s) are in *Innocent* depicted as negative synecdoches for the onrush of modernity. This Luddite vision may be seen as a Corellian example of the romantic anticapitalism that characterizes any number of late-Victorian and Edwardian writers, from William Morris to E. M. Forster.

76. Corelli scholar Julia Kuehn chronicles Corelli's relationship with Severn as follows: "Corelli's acquaintance with Arthur. . . culminated in Corelli and Severn's cooperation on *The Devil's Motor* in 1910. The writer

and the painter planned another joint work, a factual book on Shakespeare's Stratford-on-Avon, written by Corelli and illustrated by Severn. It was assigned for 1912, then postponed and finally abandoned in 1915, as the relationship between the author and the painter had become more and more strained over the years and finally ended in 1917." Julia Kuehn, "Marie Corelli's Love Letters to Arthur Severn," in *The Victorian Web: Literature, History, and Culture in the Age of Victoria,* ed. George P. Landow, http://www.victorianweb.org/authors/corelli/corelliov.html.

77. Federico, *Idol of Suburbia,* 141.

78. Severn's letters to Corelli have been lost, presumably destroyed by their recipient before her death in 1924.

79. Letter from Corelli to Arthur and Joan Severn, 28 January 1907 (Marie Corelli Collection, University of Detroit Mercy).

80. Letters from Corelli to Arthur Severn, 29 and 31 May 1912 (Marie Corelli Collection, University of Detroit Mercy).

81. Letters from Corelli to Arthur Severn, 17 and 26 November 1912 (Marie Corelli Collection, University of Detroit Mercy).

82. Letter from Corelli to Arthur Severn, 30 March 1907 (Marie Corelli Collection, University of Detroit Mercy).

83. Letter from Corelli to Arthur Severn, 29 May 1912 (Marie Corelli Collection, University of Detroit Mercy).

84. Letter from Corelli to Arthur Severn, 26 August 1912 (Marie Corelli Collection, University of Detroit Mercy).

85. Letters from Corelli to Arthur Severn, 12 August and 14 November 1912 (Marie Corelli Collection, University of Detroit Mercy).

86. Letter from Corelli to Arthur Severn, 23 April 1913 (Marie Corelli Collection, University of Detroit Mercy).

87. Letter from Corelli to Arthur Severn, 27 December 1914 (Marie Corelli Collection, University of Detroit Mercy).

88. The figurative style of Jocelyn's paintings is described when Innocent views one of his works, *Wild Weather* (see text): "So faithfully . . . rendered that it was like nature itself" (267). Far from the avant-garde modernist styles of the prewar period, this description brings to mind early nineteenth-century Romantic painting.

89. Percy Wyndham Lewis, ed., *Blast* (1914; facsimile repr., Santa Rose, CA: Black Sparrow Press, 1989), 20–21.

90. The three categories of novel Corelli mentions here were on the historical cusp between popular and (in the properly twentieth-century term) mass-market fiction in 1914. Each subgenre had its famous British innovators in the late Victorian and Edwardian periods—H. G. Wells with his science fiction, Arthur Conan Doyle with his detective fiction, and Elinor Glyn (author of the scandalous *Three Weeks*) with her "sex-novel." Each subgenre would go on, after the Edwardian period, to become a booming mass-cultural category, with many profitable imitators of the earlier masters and developing

niche markets of readers. (Though the term *sex-novel* soon went out of favor, its practice lived on in best-selling erotic romances through the rest of the twentieth century.)

91. Fredric Jameson, *A Singular Modernity* (London: Verso, 2002), 141.

92. I am thinking here of Katherine Mansfield's later stories, such as "Prelude" and "At the Bay," in which a new multiperspectivism begins to interrogate the realist convention of the single third- or first-person narrator. These stories, published in the years before her death in 1923, clearly influenced the development of her friend Virginia Woolf's modernist techniques. I discuss them in chapter 5.

93. Jameson, *Singular Modernity*, 164.

94. Felski, *Gender of Modernity*, 143.

95. Virginia Woolf, "Modern Fiction," in *The Norton Anthology of English Literature*, 6th ed. (New York: Norton, 1996), 2308.

Chapter Four: The Women's Romance and the Ideology of Form

1. Corelli sided with morally uplifting popular fiction as a bulwark against the depravity of "modern" literature; West, whose fiction appeared in the romance-deriding *Blast* (ed. Wyndham Lewis, 1914), later published an essay in *The Strange Necessity* (1927) mocking the "tosh horse" fiction of such popular romanciers as Corelli, whom she singles out by name.

2. On this phenomenon of the romance-within-modernist text, see especially Nicholas Daly, *Modernism, Romance, and the Fin de Siècle* (Cambridge: Cambridge University Press, 1999).

3. Pierre Bourdieu, "Passport to Duke," in *Pierre Bourdieu: Fieldwork in Culture*, ed. Nicholas Brown and Imre Szeman (Lanham, MD: Rowman and Littlefield, 2000), 245.

4. At the time of this writing, foremost among these websites is one entitled, after the Scarlet Pimpernel's alter ego, "Sir Percy's Place" (http://sirpercy.org/info/orczy_bio.htm [accessed 4 January 2008]).

5. Emma Orczy, *Links in the Chain of Life* (London: Hutchinson and Company, 1947), 101–5.

6. These figures regarding publication history are in the front matter of Baroness Orczy, *The Scarlet Pimpernel: A Romance*, "Popular Edition" (London: Greening and Co., 1909), iv.

7. Cecily Close, "Arthur Greening, Publisher of *The Scarlet Pimpernel*," *La Trobe Journal* 78 (Spring 2006): 45.

8. Waller, *Writers, Readers, and Reputations*, 641.

9. For an exploration of the revival of such masculine romance, see especially Daly, *Modernism, Romance.*

10. Georg Lukács, *The Historical Novel*, trans. Hannah and Stanley Mitchell (Lincoln: University of Nebraska Press, 1983), 31.

11. Emma Orczy, *The Scarlet Pimpernel* [1905] (New York: Signet Classic, 1974), 9. All citations from Orczy's novel are from this edition.

12. Lukács, *Historical Novel,* 34.

13. Here one might object that *The Scarlet Pimpernel*'s readers could not be aware, until the publication of Orczy's autobiography decades later, of this displacement of the author's personal experiences of class conflict, and thus the novel could not function for anyone but its author as so specific an allegory. But perhaps one of the meanings of Frye's notion of the romance's psychological archetypes is that such a narrative, when successful with readers, "radiates a glow of subjective intensity" (*Anatomy of Criticism,* 304) that conduces to the reader's libidinal cathexis. Thus, when Frye tells us that "a suggestion of allegory is creeping in around" the "fringes" of the romance narrative (304), what he means is that readers are freer with the romance than with realism to bring their own unconscious or semiconscious material into play and to organize that material allegorically through the romance characters and plot. Both Chauvelin, as a source of trauma, and the Pimpernel, as a savior, may be successful characters insofar as they allow individual readers to allegorize them, however semi- or unconsciously, via their own psychic agendas.

14. Frye, *Anatomy of Criticism,* 151.

15. In keeping with this idealization of romantic love, Percy, for his part, "was but a man madly, blindly, passionately in love, and as soon as her light footsteps had died away within the house, he knelt down . . . and in the very madness of his love he kissed one by one the places where her small foot had trodden" (128). His irrepressible love for Marguerite cannot be squelched even by the fact that she has been aiding and abetting the Jacobin enemy.

16. There may be exceptions, nineteenth-century romances that likewise exhibit this representation of amoral and secular transcendence through erotic love, such as *Wuthering Heights* and some gothic novels. But the point here is the suddenly increasing tendency toward such a phenomenon represented by popular works such as Orczy's.

17. See Felski, *Gender of Modernity,* 130.

18. By way of historically proximate contrast with the secularism of Orczy's romance, we might consider Corelli's early romances, such as *A Romance of Two Worlds* (1886) and *The Soul of Lilith* (1892), in which, as Jill Galvan points out, the protagonists serve as "a channel of spiritual knowledge between worlds" ("Christians, Infidels," 86).

19. This sentence from *The Anatomy of Criticism* is also important to Jameson's reading of Frye on the romance. See Jameson, *Political Unconscious,* 110–50.

20. Radford, "Introduction," 11.

21. See in particular Joan Hardwick, *Addicted to Romance: The Life and Adventures of Elinor Glyn* (London: Andre Deutsch, 1994); Penelope Dell, *Nettie and Sissie: The Biography of Ethel M. Dell and Her Sister Ella* (London: Hamish

Hamilton, 1977); and Anonymous, *The Life of Florence L. Barclay: A Study in Personality, by One of Her Daughters* (London: Putnam, 1921), for which the author/daughter does not offer her name in the text.

22. G. P. Putnam's Sons advertisement, *Publishers' Weekly* 78, no. 2018 (1 October 1910): 1322.

23. *Newsbasket,* March 1912, 67; quoted in McAleer, *Popular Reading,* 34. The *Newsbasket* article refers to Barclay's "books" because by 1912 she had published three more romances: *The Mistress of Shenstone* (1910), *The Following of the Star* (1911), and *Through the Postern Gate* (1911).

24. Waller, *Writers, Readers, and Reputations,* 702.

25. This passage from the 10 November 1909 issue of the *Nation* is quoted from the online publication of archival research on Barclay's *The Rosary* by Bethany Sulc, a student in Professor John Unsworth's course "20th-Century American Bestsellers," taught at the University of Virginia at Charlottesville, circa 2000. See http://www3.isrl.illinois.edu/~unsworth/courses/bestsellers (accessed 15 November 2009).

26. Ibid., *Bookman* (date unknown).

27. Waller, *Writers, Readers, and Reputations,* 725.

28. MacAleer, *Popular Reading,* 38–39; see also Hammond, *Reading, Publishing,* 161.

29. Waller, *Writers, Readers, and Reputations,* 717.

30. Barclay's novel both takes its title from and quotes the popular American song entitled "The Rosary," which was first published in 1898. Its lyrics were written by Robert Cameron Rogers; its music, by Ethelbert Nevin. At the peak of its popularity, around the time of Barclay's novel, its religious connotation was primarily Catholic. See Theodore Raph, *The American Song Treasury* (Mineola, NY: Dover, 1986), 343.

31. Florence Barclay, *The Rosary* (New York: G. P. Putnam's Sons, 1909), 67. All citations from Barclay's novel are from this edition.

32. Jameson, *Political Unconscious,* 142.

33. Anonymous, *Life of Barclay,* 240.

34. Frye, *Anatomy of Criticism,* 151.

35. Jameson, *Political Unconscious,* 142.

36. See Trotter, "Edwardian Sex Novels."

37. Ibid., 100.

38. Keating, *Haunted Study,* 208.

39. Ibid., 210.

40. For a recent discussions of Glyn's later career in Hollywood, and her contribution to the creation of the first "It girl" of the cinema, Clara Barton, see especially Nickianne Moody, "Elinor Glyn and the Invention of 'It,'" *Critical Survey* 15, no. 3 (2003): 92–104; and chapter 4 of Nicholas Daly, *Literature, Technology and Modernity, 1860–2000* (Cambridge: Cambridge University Press, 2004), titled "'It': The Last Machine and the Invention of Sex Appeal," 76–109.

41. Waller, *Writers, Readers, and Reputations,* 641.

42. Hardwick, *Addicted to Romance,* 121.

43. Elinor Glyn, *Three Weeks* (London: Duckworth, 1907), 80. All citations from Glyn's novel are from this edition.

44. See Elinor Glyn, *The Reason Why,* condensed by Barbara Cartland, Barbara Cartland's Library of Love (London: Duckworth, 1979).

45. Glyn, *Romantic Adventure,* 99.

46. Joan Hardwick offers more evidence of the influence of medieval romance on the young Glyn: "Like her American contemporary Edith Wharton, the young Elinor revelled in the poems about lovelorn maidens and knights in shining armour doing gallant deeds for love and honour. . . . She claimed later in life that it was at this time that she learnt great quantities of poetry by heart including 'Guinevere' and 'Elaine.' The influence of this poetry encountered so young can be seen clearly in her writing as an adult. For not only are the *Idylls* frequently mentioned in her novels and essays, they provide that romantic sense of the relationships between men and women which she never really discarded" (*Addicted to Romance,* 14).

47. Anonymous, "Elinor Glyn Talks about Her American Critics," *New York Times,* 6 October 1907, 12.

48. See, for instance, Annette Kuhn, "The Trouble with Elinor Glyn: Hollywood, *Three Weeks* and the British Board of Film Censors," *Historical Journal of Film Radio and Television* 28, no. 1 (2008): 23–35; Vincent L. Barnett, "The Novelist as Hollywood Star: Author Royalties and Studio Income in the 1920s," *Film History: An International Journal* 20, no. 3 (2008): 281–93; Vincent L. Barnett, "Picturization Partners: Elinor Glyn and the Thalberg Contract Affair," *Film History: An International Journal* 19, no. 3 (2007): 319–29; and Daly, "It," in Daly, *Literature, Technology,* 76–109.

49. Anonymous review of *Three Weeks* in *Saturday Review of Politics, Literature, Science and Art* 2694, no. 103 (15 June 1907): 754.

50. Brooks, *Melodramatic Imagination,* 16.

51. David R. Shumway, *Modern Love: Romance, Intimacy, and the Marriage Crisis* (New York: New York University Press, 2003), 76.

52. *Three Weeks*'s diatribes against conventional marriage reflect the same concerns thematized in the Edwardian marriage problem novel, that most progressive realist subgenre of the century's first decade in Britain. As exemplified by the works of E. M. Forster, Ada Leverson, John Galsworthy, Arnold Bennett, Amber Reeves, Elizabeth von Arnim, Mrs. Dudeney, and M. P. Willcocks, the marriage problem novel interrogated the institution of marriage to introduce more radical questions about the contours of male-female relations in British society. In this respect, suggests Jane Eldridge Miller, "the marriage problem novel, with its distinctive moods of dissatisfaction and alienation, is indicative of a new, modern sensibility which was radically suspicious of tradition and received ideas" (*Rebel Women,* 83). Miller argues that *Three Weeks,* when set against the backdrop of

the sober marriage problem novel, appears to have "far more to do with the Edwardian vogue for 'smartness' and 'naughtiness' than with the Woman Question" (71). If Glyn's heroine is meant to express dissatisfaction and alienation with the heterosexual status quo, then by comparison with the feminist realism of the time, her alternative model for male-female relations may indeed appear to be, in Miller's term, "pure escapism." In suggesting that Glyn's romance offers "the familiar comfort of a conventional and morally correct ending," however, Miller may dismiss too readily the novel's subversiveness, as its conclusion celebrates the royal elevation of a child born of a glorified adulterous union and vindicates the lady's scandalous claim to Paul, "I feel myself ennobled, exalted, because you are my lover, and our child, when it comes to us, will have a noble mind" (Glyn, *Three Weeks,* 195). The lady's socially iconoclastic pronouncements seem to take their provenance in libidinal fantasies of life under ancient or medieval social orders and are too idiosyncratic to be reduced to mere reinforcements of any Edwardian status quo.

53. Tennyson's poetry did, however, influence Glyn's thematic aims (see note 47 above).

54. When Paul asks Mme. Zalenska whether the classical Greeks were perhaps wise about love, she responds, "they were wise, they did not educate the wives and daughters, they realised that to perform well domestic duties a woman's mind should not be over-trained in learning. Learning and charm and grace of mind were for others, the *hetaerae* of whom they asked no tiresome ties" (*Three Weeks,* 193–94). *The Oxford Companion to Classical Literature* characterizes the *hetaerae:* "As the law forbade the marriage of Athenian citizens [all males] except with the daughters of other Athenian citizens, a sort of irregular union with foreign women was frequent in the 5th and 4th cc. These women, known as hetaerae (*hetairai,* literally 'companions,' and including concubines and courtesans), were often Ionians, whose charm was increased by a high degree of intelligence and education, making them more agreeable companions than the cloistered Athenian women. The most famous of these hetaerae was Aspasia." Sir Paul Harvey, *The Oxford Companion to Classical Literature* (Oxford: Oxford University Press, 1980), 450.

Chapter Five: The Imperial Erotic Romance

1. See Edward Said, *Culture and Imperialism* (New York: Alfred A. Knopf, 1993); and Anne McClintock, *Imperial Leather: Race, Gender, and Sexuality in the Colonial Conquest* (New York: Routledge, 1995).

2. Corrine Saunders, *A Companion to Romance, from Classical to Contemporary* (Malden, MA: Blackwell, 2004), 406.

3. See Susan Jones, "Into the Twentieth Century: Imperial Romance from Haggard to Buchan," in Saunders, *A Companion to Romance,* 406–23; and

Laura Chrisman, *Rereading the Imperial Romance: British Imperialism and South African Resistance in Haggard, Schreiner, and Plaatje* (New York: Oxford University Press, 2000).

4. Two other examples of the imperial romance from the period—instances that fit under the general rubric I am applying to Cross, Dell, and Hull—would be Robert Hichens's *The Garden of Allah* (1904) and Elinor Glyn's *His Hour* (1909).

5. Jenny Sharpe, *Allegories of Empire: The Figure of Woman in the Colonial Text* (Minneapolis: University of Minnesota Press, 1993).

6. "Theodora: A Fragment" opens Elaine Showalter's anthology *Daughters of Decadence: Women Writers of the Fin de Siècle* (New Brunswick, NJ: Rutgers University Press, 1993), which was published in response to a renewed interest in the feminism of late nineteenth-century writers in Britain.

7. Shoshana Milgram Knapp, "Revolutionary Androgyny in the Fiction of 'Victoria Cross,'" in *Seeing Double: Revisioning Edwardian and Modernist Literature,* ed. Carola M. Kaplan and Anne B. Simpson (New York: St. Martin's Press, 1996), 10.

8. Said, *Culture and Imperialism,* 134–35.

9. Knapp, "Revolutionary Androgyny," 83.

10. Speculating on Cory's attitudes toward the recently annexed India in which she grew up, we may consider those of a female Anglo-Indian writer who was twenty years Cory's senior, Flora Annie Steel (1847–1929), the author of the fictional works *Tales of the Punjab* (1894) and *On the Face of the Waters* (1896), in addition to the autobiographical *The Garden of Fidelity* (London: Macmillan, 1929). In the autobiography, Steel writes, "The Indian Mutiny was then the Epic of the Race. It held all possible emotion, all possible triumph" (226). If we assume that Steel voices the prevalent Anglo-Indian view of the mutiny in the decades that followed it, then the ideological transgressions of Cory's/Cross's *Anna Lombard* stand out in stark relief. Consider this summary of Steel's attempts at racial rapprochement in *On the Face of the Waters* (published five years before *Anna Lombard*): "[S]he could not escape the conventions of the colonialist genre in which Indians (or any non-Europeans) are seen as the other and the Western self is tested against this other, who is essentially passive but capable of unbelievable violence when aroused. . . . Steel's intention, as she states in the preface, was to bring the two races closer to forgiving and forgetting what went on during the mutiny. But her attempt ends up a revenge novel that flatters the British ruling class." Rebecca Saunders, "Gender, Colonialism, and Exile: Flora Annie Steele and Sara Jeanette Duncan in India," in *Women's Writing in Exile,* ed. Mary Lynn Broe and Angela Ingram (Chapel Hill: University of North Carolina Press, 1989), 308.

11. If the lyrics penned by Vivian Cory's older sister evince colonialist discourse regarding the culture of India, it is a form of discourse, parallel to that of Vivian's fictions, that would elevate the Eastern culture as superior in passion to that of the English. The last lines of "Kashmiri Song" address the

hands of the poet's lost lover, which she remembers loving in the gardens of Shalimar, in a sublime wish for self-destruction: "I would rather have felt you round my throat, / Crushing out life, than waving me farewell." Two months after the death of her husband in 1904, Adela Cory Nicolson committed suicide in an explicit effort to join him.

12. Robert J. C. Young, *Colonial Desire: Hybridity in Theory, Culture, and Race* (New York: Routledge, 1995), 9.

13. The word *miscegenation* was first coined in 1864, in an anonymous pamphlet published in London and New York (Young, *Colonial Desire,* 9).

14. See Brittain, "Erasing Race." As Brittain points out, the major exception to this panning of the novel was the positive appraisal of influential reviewer W. T. Stead, who saw in the role-reversing depiction of female "promiscuity" a warning to male readers about the pain that their own philandering would cause their spouses.

15. Knapp, "Revolutionary Androgyny," 83.

16. Victoria Cross [Vivian Cory], *Anna Lombard* (New York: Kensington Press, 1901), 1. All quotations from Cross's romance come from this edition.

17. The Lombards were a Germanic tribe mentioned in Tacitus's *Germania* (98 A.D.) as the "Langobardi."

18. Quoted in Ania Loomba, *Colonialism/Postcolonialism* (New York: Routledge, 1998), 115.

19. Although there is no evidence that Cross had read Conrad's *An Outcast of the Islands* (1896), it is useful to contrast the hero in this section of the narrative to Conrad's antihero Willem, whose antiromantic decline is portrayed as resulting from miscegenation and other "uncivilized" temptations.

20. In point of fact, imperial policy regarding interracial marriage in Burma was, by the 1890s (the time at which the novel is set), on the cusp of a shift away from such tolerance as is depicted here: "Few English women or missionaries lived in 1860s Burma, which was administered from India, resulting in a higher frequency of both intermarriage and liaisons than in India, with its larger European population and more elaborate colonial administrative structure. Even so, by the 1890s the government threatened to transfer officers for marrying Burmese women, and ultimately the administration made it clear that having such wives would damage their official prospects." Margaret Strobel, *European Women and the Second British Empire* (Bloomington: Indiana University Press, 1991), 3.

21. Again, as Melisa Brittain suggests, Cross writes under the progressive influence of the New Woman novelists and implicitly defends "a representation of active white female sexuality" ("Erasing Race," 91). The term *implicitly* is especially important here, as we have already seen Cross's stated apologia for the novel, which tries to divert our readerly attention from the novel's violated taboo of a sexual relationship between a white woman and a "black" man. Nonetheless, I think Brittain (along with other scholars such as Shoshana Milgram Knapp) correctly identifies this

feminist discourse as constitutive of *Anna Lombard* as a whole—no matter how we interpret the novel's last chapter, wherein, as Brittain has it, the text "rechannel[s] . . . Anna's transgressive sexuality into white heterosexual marriage" with Gerald (91).

22. Kumari Jayawardena, *The White Woman's Other Burden: Western Women and South Asia during British Colonial Rule* (New York: Routledge, 1995), 4.

23. jay dixon [*sic*], *The Romance Fiction of Mills and Boon, 1909–1990s* (London: UCL Press, 1999), xi.

24. Regis, *Natural History,* 29.

25. "Barclay's books were . . . harbingers of the new fiction, not only because we see in *The Rosary* a thousand Mills and Boon romances (Barclay overwhelmingly appealed to women) but because her work was inherently modern in its approach to writing fiction (and especially women's domestic fiction). . . . This was a legacy that was soon to be developed by writers such as Ethel M. Dell and Barbara Cartland." Bloom, *Bestsellers,* 89–90.

26. Regis, *Natural History,* 108.

27. Dell, *Nettie and Sissie,* xiv.

28. dixon, *Romance Fiction,* 43–46.

29. dixon further explains that "[a]round the period of the First World War the aristocratic heroes of Mills and Boon books cease[d] to be as explicitly passionate, perhaps mirroring the historical reality of upheavals in the social structure. As Naomi Mitchison states that it was not unusual for a man in his twenties to be a virgin in the First World War, the displacement of sexuality onto men of other nationalities may have had its basis in reality" (*Romance Fiction,* 51).

30. Sharpe, *Allegories of Empire,* 3.

31. Nancy L. Paxton, *Writing under the Raj: Gender, Race, and Rape in the British Colonial Imagination, 1830–1947* (New Brunswick, NJ: Rutgers University Press, 1999), 6.

32. Loomba, *Colonialism/Postcolonialism,* 107.

33. Ethel Dell, *The Way of an Eagle* (London: Virago, 1996), 13. All quotations from Dell's romance come from this edition.

34. Paxton, *Writing under the Raj,* 5.

35. P. Dell, *Nettie and Sissie,* 21.

36. These four authors' actual experiences and novelistic representations together offer a cross section of colonial life as lived by married Anglo-Indian women. Steel's husband worked in the Indian Civil Service; Diver was married to an army officer; Perrin, to an officer in the Indian Public Works Program; and Penny, to a Christian missionary active in Madras (Paxton, *Writing under the Raj,* 31).

37. Peter Morey, *Fictions of India: Narrative and Power* (Edinburgh: Edinburgh University Press, 2000), 2–3.

38. Sharpe, *Allegories of Empire,* 6–7.

39. Ibid., 6.

40. Sarah Wintle, "*The Sheik:* What Can Be Made of a Daydream," *Women: A Cultural Review* 7, no. 3 (Winter 1996): 292.

41. Rachel Anderson, "Hull, E(dith) M(aude)," in *Twentieth-Century Romance and Historical Writers,* ed. Aruna Vasudevan (London: St. James Press, 1994), 333.

42. Quoted in Wintle, "*The Sheik,*" 292.

43. These include *The Desert Healer* (1923), *The Sons of the Sheik* (1926), *Camping in the Sahara* (nonfiction; 1926), *The Lion-Tamer* (1928), and *The Captive of Sahara* (1931).

44. Scholars may rightly quibble with this claim, pointing to Robert Hichens's *The Garden of Allah* (1904) and Elinor Glyn's *His Hour* (1910), among other possible candidates for the ur-text of the desert romance. Nonetheless, in the popular imagination and in the romance industry, Hull is generally held to be the founder of this subgenre.

45. These are titles published in New York City alone, by such houses as Harlequin, Dell, Silhouette, Bantam, Avon, and St. Martin's.

46. As I mention in the introduction to this study, Hull's romance has occasioned a good deal of critical scrutiny in the past few years. Readings tend to focus, as does my own, on racial representations (see especially Gargano, "English Sheiks"); on the figure of the New Woman, as embodied in the novel's heroine (see especially Ardis, "E. M. Hull"); or on the status of the text as women's pornography (see especially Frost, "Romance of Cliché"). All of these interpretations are compelling and vindicate the claim that this romance was culturally pivotal in the history of British popular fiction. I would complement such discussions of Hull's *representativeness* with a defense of this text's *singularity* at the time of its appearance. While Hull's novel represents an instance of the kind of women's romance novel that would come to dominate the paperback markets of future decades, we should remember that *The Sheik* was, in its moment, unique—and not only because of its sexual explicitness. As is true of all of the popular narratives discussed in this study, the popular romance of the late nineteenth and early twentieth centuries was shaped by commercial exigencies but only in loose and open-ended fashion; the genre was just on the cusp of rationalized codification for mass production. In other words, there were limits proscribing what the romance could represent, but there were no blueprints or recipes for what had to go into the romance to guarantee sales. Although I have sought to delineate a taxonomy of the popular romance of the period and have in this chapter "abstracted out" certain shared characteristics of imperial erotic romances, each of the texts exhibits a certain haecceity, which I would in this context define as a particular assemblage of textualized desires that is constituted by the collective energies of its sociohistorical contexts.

47. E. M. Hull, *The Sheik* [1919] (Philadelphia: Pine Street Press, 2001), 59. All quotations from Hull's romance come from this edition.

48. Susan Blake, "What 'Race' Is the Sheik? Rereading a Desert Romance," in *Doubled Plots: Romance and History*, ed. Susan Strehle and Mary Paniccia Carden (Jackson: University Press of Mississippi, 2003), 78. Blake discerns contradictions, parallel to those seen in this passage, in the racial logic of Raoul's account of the sheik's true origins: "The contradictions in Raoul's explanation betray the necessity to make the romantic hero safely English while distancing marital impropriety through the victimized and deserting wife's Spanish nationality and the cruel husband's Scottish title [the earl of Glencaryll]" ("What 'Race,'" 76). In other words, Raoul would elevate Ahmed by labeling him biologically English, even as he symbolically spares English identity from the besmirching associations of spousal desertion and marital cruelty by emphasizing, at the ugly parts of the story, the Spanish and Scottish lineages of Ahmed's mother and father.

49. Blake explains the broader implications of this undecideability: "If Raoul's version of events overwrites Diana's, the Sheik is English, Diana is rescued (from racial heresy as well as miscegenation), and the novel, like a skillful argument, questions racial boundaries only to prove their validity in the end. If Diana's perspective prevails, the Sheik is symbolically Arab; what is rescued by the revelation of his English parentage is not Diana but the story of an Englishwoman falling in love with an Arab; and we can read the story as an expression of either the desire to cross racial boundaries or the fetishization, the other side of demonization, of nonwhite sexuality" ("What 'Race,'" 83). As Blake suggests here, Diana's desire to stay with the culturally Other sheik represents the concurrent demonization and fetishization of nonwhite male sexuality.

50. I offer the following excursus on the historical specificity of *The Sheik* as a post–Great War novel. Hull populates the opening pages with French, British, American, and other Western nationals enjoying themselves at a ball in the Biskra Hotel, in a North African outpost of the French empire comparable to Tunis or Algiers. This social event is described by Lady Conway, a British matron worried about what the other foreign nationals will think of Diana Mayo's excursion into the desert: "I thoroughly disapprove of the expedition of which this dance is the inauguration. I consider that even by contemplating such a tour alone in the desert with no chaperon or attendant of her own sex, with only native camel drivers and servants, Diana Mayo is behaving with a recklessness and impropriety that is calculated to cast a slur not only on her own reputation, but also on the prestige of her country. I blush to think of it. We English cannot be too careful of our behavior abroad. No opportunity is slight enough for our continental neighbors to cast stones, and this opportunity is very far from being slight. It is the maddest piece of unprincipled folly I have ever heard of" (1). The first chapter hereby telegraphs the novel's discreet and distanced relationship to geopolitical reality. The 1922 *Bookman* blurb records that Hull wrote *The Sheik* "as a means of personal distraction during the war"; it is thus noteworthy that her narrative

opens with a character who is highly aware of the actions of the English abroad as reflecting on their national character and is concerned that "continental neighbors" may use any occasion, however slight, "to cast stones" at the English as a nation. When we recall that the novel was published in the year after the war ended, we cannot help but read this opening social scene, with its "chattering men and women of all [Western] nationalities" (6), as allegorically nationalistic, in light of the global colonial rivalries that helped to precipitate the Great War. Hull's narrator emphasizes the cosmopolitan composition of a European cohort in a non-Western setting, hovering on the eve, the periphery, or the aftermath (the moment is not specified) of a war that, strikingly, the text never alludes to. It is instructive, moreover, to note what a contrast *The Sheik* sets to John Buchan's *Greenmantle* (1916), a contemporaneous adventure romance, which also features a multinational Western cohort in an "Eastern" environment. The second half of *Greenmantle* is set in the Ottoman Empire, where the text thematizes a gulf between Islamic and Western culture—in this case, the rise of a Jihadist prophet-leader against the European *entente* powers. Improbable as it may sound, Buchan configures the Great War as an imaginative stage for swashbuckling derring-do and old-fashioned codes of masculine honor, as though it were being fought in the Crimea of the 1850s. But the European slaughter had by war's end become unlikely material for the representations of romance, and so Hull, publishing her novel only three years after Buchan's, gestures toward this social context only through the allegorical form of its characters' counterposed nationalities.

51. As Ann Ardis suggests in "E. M. Hull," a more notably foregrounded historical aspect of *The Sheik* is its reflection, both positive and negative, of popular British views of the New Woman. At the novel's opening, Diana Mayo offers a frank self-appraisal of her unfeminine ways: "When God made me He omitted to give me a heart. I have never loved anyone in my life. My brother and I have tolerated each other, but there has never been any affection between us. . . . I have never obeyed anyone in my life; I do not wish to try the experiment" (11). Ardis identifies the last sentence here as a direct quotation of female protagonists from more than one New Woman novel of the 1890s; by this form of renunciation, female characters from Sarah Grand's *The Heavenly Twins* (1893) and Iota's *The Yellow Aster* (1894) "reject compulsory heterosexuality, marriage as a vocation for women, and confinement in the domestic sphere" ("E. M. Hull," 291). Ardis's contention here is that *The Sheik*, so far from endorsing conservative verities of sexual and racial Otherness, is self-consciously intended by its author to honor and extend the socially interrogative, frequently resistive tendencies of the New Woman novel. There is good evidence to support this interpretation, but I think it is also important to register the deep ambivalence of *The Sheik*'s third-person narrative voice in its initial representation of Diana's indomitability. Diana's original independence is shadowed by the calamity to come: "The idea of marriage—even in its highest form, based on mutual consideration

and mutual forbearance—was repugnant to her. She thought of it with a shiver of absolute repulsion. To Aubrey [her brother] it was distasteful, but to her cold, reserved temperament it was a thing of horror and disgust. That women could submit to the degrading intimacy and fettered existence of married life filled her with scornful wonder" (35). Later, at the camp of the sheik, Diana will be subjected to a de facto marriage of no "mutual consideration" or "mutual forbearance" and will be literally forced to obey her de facto husband. She will thereafter fall in love with the conjugal tyrant. Yet, as Ardis implies, reading this narrative as one of antifeminist *ressentiment,* as exacting a nasty comeuppance for the haughty pride of the New Woman character, would be too simple. Hull's narrator repeatedly insists that Diana's unusual upbringing—no parents, an older brother acting as surrogate father—has made her what she is, and this fictive circumstance may have offered female readers the vehicle for an enabling "orphan fantasy," a venue for alternative self-imagining through identification with the heroine. A marker of *The Sheik*'s singularity is the contrast with the Electra-like heroines of *Anna Lombard* and *The Way of an Eagle,* with their initial protection by ideal father figures, by means of which the narratives enact the bumpy transference to new love-objects (Gerald Etheridge, Nick Ratcliffe) before the readers' eyes. It may be a liberatory aspect of *The Sheik* that, unlike the earlier romances, Hull's novel portrays no filial piety in its independent heroine.

52. Here I borrow again from Fredric Jameson's comments on the romance mode: "A first specification of romance would then be achieved if we could account for that way in which, in contrast to realism, its inner-worldly objects such as landscape or village, forest or mansion—mere temporary stopping places on the lumbering coach or express-train itinerary of realist representation—are somehow transformed into folds in space, into discontinuous pockets of homogeneous time and of heightened symbolic closure, such that they become tangible analoga or perceptual vehicles for *world* in its larger phenomenological sense" (*Political Unconscious,* 112).

53. Phillip Wegner, *Imagined Communities: Utopia, the Nation, and the Spatial Histories of Modernity* (Berkeley: University of California Press, 2002), 13.

54. Jones, "Into the Twentieth Century," 408.

55. Derek Brewer, "The Popular English Metrical Romances," in *A Companion to Romance,* ed. Corrine Saunders (Malden, MA: Blackwell, 2004), 45.

56. Ernst Bloch, *The Principle of Hope,* trans. Neville Plaice (Cambridge, MA: MIT Press, 1986), 371.

57. See Deleuze and Guattari, *Thousand Plateaus.*

58. Two more canonical fiction-writers, traditionally associated with modernism, who might have been examined here are Conrad and Forster. But the Conrad of *Heart of Darkness* (1899) and *Lord Jim* (1901) has been the subject of exhaustive critical discussion vis-à-vis primitivism, and the Forster of *A Passage to India* is not generally considered a formal modernist.

59. Ronald Bogue, *Deleuze and Guattari* (New York: Routledge, 1989), 88.

60. On this line of interpretation, see especially Rachel Blau DuPlessis's chapter "'Amor Vin—': Modifications of Romance in Woolf," in DuPlessis, *Writing beyond the Ending* (Bloomington: Indiana University Press, 1985), 47–65.

61. Virginia Woolf, *The Voyage Out* [1915] (New York: Barnes and Noble Classics, 2004), 27. All quotations from Woolf's novel come from this edition.

62. Woolf offers a self-conscious symbolization of a "prehistory," synchronically latent in all humanity, in *The Waves* (1931) and *Between the Acts* (1941). "Virginia Woolf's first and last novels, *The Voyage Out* and *Between the Acts,* are the two works which engage most directly with ideas of the primeval. In *The Voyage Out* it is necessary to travel to remote countries to discover it. The primitive is still figured as outside self. But in *The Waves,* and even more in *Between the Acts,* the prehistoric is seen not simply as part of a remote past, but as contiguous, continuous, a part of ordinary present-day life." Gillian Beer, "Virginia Woolf and Pre-History," in *Virginia Woolf: A Centenary Perspective,* ed. Eric Warner (New York: St. Martin's Press, 1984), 102.

63. Roger Fry's first and second postimpressionist exhibits in London (1910–11, 1912) and the founding of the Omega Workshops (1913) both occurred within the nine-year span (1906–15) of Woolf's composition of *The Voyage Out.* On Woolf's fascination with "the primitive," as mediated through such modernist venues, see Lois J. Gilmore, "Virginia Woolf, Bloomsbury, and the Primitive," in *Virginia Woolf and Communities: Selected Papers from the Eighth Annual Conference on Virginia Woolf,* ed. Jeanette McVicker and Laura Davis (New York: Pace University Press, 1999), 127–35.

64. Francesca Herrick, lecture at exhibit titled "Beyond Bloomsbury: Designs of the Omega Workshops" at the Courtauld Institute in London, 13 September 2009.

65. This passage from *Melymbrosia,* the earliest extant complete draft of *The Voyage Out,* has been interpreted as depicting "the ambience of a lesbian utopia in an Edenic setting." Patricia Juliana Smith, "'The Things People Don't Say': Lesbian Panic in *The Voyage Out,*" in *Lesbian Readings of Virginia Woolf,* ed. Eileen Barrett and Patricia Cramer (New York: New York University Press, 1997), 137.

66. Ibid., 138.

67. Marianna Torgovnick, *Gone Primitive: Savage Intellects, Modern Lives* (Chicago: University of Chicago Press, 1990).

68. See in particular Brett Neilson, "D. H. Lawrence's 'Dark Page': Narrative Primitivism in *Women in Love* and *The Plumed Serpent,*" *Twentieth-Century Literature* 43, no. 3 (Fall 1997): 310–25; Jad Smith, "Völkisch Organicism and the Use of Primitivism in Lawrence's *The Plumed Serpent,*" *D. H. Lawrence Review* 30, no. 3 (2002): 7–24; and Laura Frost, "The Romance of Cliché: E. M. Hull, D. H. Lawrence, and Interwar Erotic Fiction," in *Bad*

Modernisms, ed. Douglas Mao and Rebecca L. Walkowitz (Durham, NC: Duke University Press, 2006), 94–118.

69. D. H. Lawrence, *Women in Love* (London: Penguin Books, 1995), 78. All quotations from Lawrence's novel come from this edition.

70. Neilson, "D. H. Lawrence's 'Dark Page,'" 313.

71. Paul DeMan, "The Rhetoric of Temporality," in DeMan, *Blindness and Insight: Essays in the Rhetoric of Contemporary Criticism* (Minneapolis: University of Minnesota Press, 1983), 187–228.

72. For her reading of "The Woman Who Rode Away," see Frost, "Romance of Cliché," 107–8.

73. D. H. Lawrence, "Surgery for the Novel—Or a Bomb," in *Selected Literary Criticism*, ed. Anthony Beal (London: Heinemann, 1967), 11–18.

74. D. H. Lawrence, "The Woman Who Rode Away," in *The Cambridge Edition of the Works of D. H. Lawrence: The Woman Who Rode Away and Other Stories*, ed. Dieter Mehl and Christa Jansohn (Cambridge: Cambridge University Press, 2002), 40. All quotations from Lawrence's short story come from this edition.

75. As Jane Stafford and Mark Williams explain, "Maoriland is a name for New Zealand still occasionally encountered, although it is no longer in everyday use. It is an archaic word with colonial associations, politically suspect in a postcolonial age. 'Maoriland' suggests the smug paternalism of a period now regarded with embarrassment, a world in which Maori warriors in heroic attitudes and Maori maidens in seductive ones adorned romantic portraits and tourist postcards." Stafford and Williams, *Maoriland: New Zealand Literature, 1872–1914* (Wellington: Victoria University Press, 2006), 10.

76. Nicholas Thomas quoted in ibid., 165.

77. Katherine Mansfield, *The Katherine Mansfield Notebooks*, ed. Margaret Scott (Minneapolis: University of Minneapolis Press, 1997), 140–41, 148–49.

78. Stafford and Williams, *Maoriland*, 166.

79. Katherine Mansfield, "Summer Idylle," in *Katherine Mansfield Notebooks*, 75. All quotations from Mansfield's story are from this source.

80. Sydney Janet Kaplan, *Katherine Mansfield and the Origins of Modernist Fiction* (Ithaca, NY: Cornell University Press, 1991), 46. This is also the view of the most recent transcriber and editor of Mansfield's barely legible journal handwriting, Margaret Scott; see Scott, *Katherine Mansfield Notebooks*, 75. Scott's text is the source manuscript of my reading here.

81. My interpretation of "Summer Idylle" owes much to that of Sydney Janet Kaplan, who writes that "the short piece is as dense and compact as poetry. As in the symbolist poetry that Mansfield had been reading, each object radiates a multiplicity of meanings" (*Katherine Mansfield*, 49). My reading emphasizes the Romantic, organicist cast of Mansfield's numinous symbolism.

82. Antony Alpers points out this connection between "Kezia" and the cassia plant in his biography of Mansfield. He also clarifies that "Kezia" is both a variation on "Cass," Mansfield's childhood nickname, and (as Mansfield penciled into the endpaper of her Bible) a reference to the second daughter of Job. Antony Alpers, *The Life of Katherine Mansfield* (New York: Viking Press, 1980), 190.

83. Katherine Mansfield, "Prelude," in *Stories by Katherine Mansfield,* ed. Jeffrey Meyers (New York: Vintage Classics, 1991), 72. Subsequent quotations from Mansfield's short stories come from this edition.

84. Patricia Moran, "Unholy Meanings: Maternity, Creativity, and Orality in Katherine Mansfield," *Feminist Studies* 17, no. 1 (Spring 1991): 118.

85. Katherine Mansfield, "At the Bay," in *Stories by Katherine Mansfield,* 131.

86. Quoted in Alpers, *Life of Katherine Mansfield,* 189.

Chapter Six: Modernism and the Romance of Interiority

1. Quoted in Q. D. Leavis, *Fiction and the Reading Public* (London: Chatto and Windus, 1932), 56.

2. Waller, *Writers, Readers, and Reputations,* 647.

3. All of these questions might be best answered by an ethnographic study of a group of readers from the early part of the twentieth century, after the mode of Janice Radway's study of 1970s–80s U.S. readers in *Reading the Romance: Women, Patriarchy, and Popular Literature* (Chapel Hill: University of North Carolina Press, 1991). But such an ethnography would, for obvious reasons of temporal distance, here be impossible, and thus this argument will let Leavis's *Fiction and the Reading Public* stand in as its ethnographic data on the reading habits of the early twentieth-century readers in the United Kingdom.

4. A text that combines these phenomena might be the "Nausicaa" episode of James Joyce's *Ulysses,* with its gentle satire on the romantic daydreams of Gerty McDowell.

5. Jay Clayton, "A Portrait of the Romantic Poet as a Young Artist: Literary History as Textual Unconscious," in *Joyce: The Return of the Repressed,* ed. Susan Stanford Friedman (Ithaca, NY: Cornell University Press, 1993), 125.

6. In contrast, contemporary metaphors for the reading of mass-market romance often tend to be oriented around consumption. For example, the *New York Times* reported that "in 1997 . . . 38 percent of all adult popular fiction books sold were romance novels. . . . Some readers consume as many as 14 books a month. . . . That kind of voracity demands constant feeding." Bruce Weber, "For Romance Novelists, Profits without Honor," *New York Times,* 3 August 1999, B1–2.

7. John Beer, *Post-Romantic Consciousness: Dickens to Plath* (Basingstoke, UK: Palgrave Macmillan, 2003), 114–15.

8. I take the mathematical term *asymptote* to mean a straight line that is the limiting value of a curve or, in this metaphorical instance, of a trajectory of language; that limit becomes a tangent to the trajectory at infinity.

9. The journal was launched, in Hueffer's terms, "with the definite design of giving imaginative literature a chance in England." Arthur Mizener, *The Saddest Story: A Biography of Ford Madox Ford* (New York: World Publishing, 1971), 154.

10. Critic Sydney Janet Kaplan, for instance, cites the story as Mansfield's first move toward literary experiment: "By 1908 in 'The Tiredness of Rosabel,' Mansfield was working with states of consciousness as a way of giving shape and depth to a short story" (*Katherine Mansfield,* 11).

11. Pamela Dunbar, *Radical Mansfield: Double Discourse in Katherine Mansfield's Short Stories* (New York: St. Martin's Press, 1997), xv.

12. For the historical background of the realism-romance debate in British literary criticism of the 1880s through 1910s, see in particular Keating, *Haunted Study.*

13. See the chapter of Raymond Williams's *Marxism and Literature* titled "Dominant, Residual, and Emergent" (New York: Oxford University Press, 1977), 121–27.

14. Katherine Mansfield, "The Tiredness of Rosabel," in *Stories by Katherine Mansfield,* 3.

15. As Antony Alpers suggests, the source for this description appears to come from page 17 of the (1908?) paperback edition of *Anna Lombard* (at the British Library in London): "I took her out on the terrace, found her a chair and then dutifully brought her the ice and sat beside her. . . . [T]he purple sky above was throbbing, beating, palpitating with the light of stars and planets, and a low, large, yellow moon was sinking towards the horizon, reddening as it sank. What a night for the registration or consummation of vows! One of those true voluptuous tropic nights when the soft, hot air itself seems to breathe of the passions. It was a night on which, as the Frenchman said, all women wished to be loved. . . . She sat sipping her ice cheerfully and diligently, for ice, like virtue, does not last long in the tropics." Quoted in Alpers, *Life of Katherine Mansfield,* 80–81.

16. "What constitutes the alienation of labour? Firstly, the fact that labour is *external* to the worker, i.e., does not belong to his essential being; that he therefore does not confirm himself in his work, but denies himself, feels miserable and not happy. . . . Hence the worker feels himself only when he is not working; when he is working he does not feel himself. He is at home when he is not working, and not at home when he is working. . . . [His labour] is therefore not the satisfaction of a need but a mere *means* to satisfy needs outside himself. . . . Just as in religion the spontaneous activity of the human imagination, the human brain and the human heart detaches itself and reappears as the alien activity of a god or of a devil, so the activity of the worker is not his own spontaneous activity. It belongs to another, it is a

loss of his self." Karl Marx, *Capital,* vol. 3 (Harmondsworth, UK: Penguin, 1981), 322–24.

17. Michael Hardt, "Affective Labor," *Boundary* 2 26, no. 2 (Summer 1999): 95–96.

18. See also Dorothy Smith, *The Everyday World as Problematic: A Feminist Sociology* (Boston: Northeastern University Press, 1987), 78–88.

19. Michel de Certeau, "'Making Do': Uses and Tactics," in *The Consumer Society Reader,* ed. Martyn J. Lee (Oxford: Blackwell Publishing, 2000), 162–74.

20. Quoted in Alpers, *Life of Katherine Mansfield,* 51.

21. Ibid., 60.

22. Ibid., 259.

23. Katherine Mansfield, "The Garden-Party," in *Stories by Katherine Mansfield,* 297.

24. Quoted in Alpers, *Life of Katherine Mansfield,* 76.

25. Northrop Frye, *The Secular Scripture: A Study of the Structure of Romance* (Cambridge, MA: Harvard University Press, 1976).

26. James Joyce, "An Encounter," in *Dubliners* (New York: Penguin Books, 1996), 19. Subsequent quotations from Joyce's *Dubliners* stories come from this edition.

27. Morris Beja, *Epiphany in the Modern Novel* (London: Peter Owen, 1971), 79.

28. Richard Ellmann, ed., *James Joyce: Letters II* (New York: Viking Press, 1966), 90, 91.

29. Hugh Kenner argues that, contrary to the Wordsworthian spirit, Joyce ironizes Stephen's pretensions and self-importance in the epiphany sequences of *Portrait of the Artist.* Kenner, *Dublin's Joyce* (Boston: Beacon Press, 1956), 109–33.

30. Clayton, "Portrait," 125.

31. D. H. Lawrence, *Sons and Lovers* (Harmondsworth, UK: Penguin Books, 1978), 142. All quotations from Lawrence's novel come from this edition.

32. Beer, *Post-Romantic Consciousness,* 122.

33. Roger Norburn, *A Katherine Mansfield Chronology* (Basingstoke, UK: Palgrave Macmillan, 2008), 27.

34. David Thorburn, "Horse Dealer's Daughter: The Shimmer Within," lecture 12, course no. 2539, "Masterworks of Early 20th-Century Literature" (Chantilly, VA: Teaching Company, 2007).

35. Andreas Huyssen, *After the Great Divide: Modernism, Mass Culture, Postmodernism* (Bloomington: Indiana University Press, 1986); Peter Bürger, *Theory of the Avant-Garde* (Minneapolis: University of Minnesota Press, 1984).

36. Jameson, *Political Unconscious,* 236.

37. Rebecca West, *The Strange Necessity* (New York: Doubleday, 1928), 356. Subsequent quotations of West's essays come from this edition.

38. Kathryn Laing, "'The Sentinel': Rebecca West's Buried Novel," *Tulsa Studies in Women's Literature* 19, no. 1 (Spring 2000): 14.

39. By way of illustration of some of these stylistic features of West's first novel, the following passage, in which the primary male character sees the protagonist Adela asleep at her desk, nicely conveys West's superheated language, which veers between the passion of a romance novel and the psychic turbidity of D. H. Lawrence:

> Quite suddenly he realized that he wanted this woman. The knowledge appalled him. He was swaying, biting his lips, closing his eyes till that fiery tide of blood should leave his throat. She was necessary to him. He wanted her irrationally, with an uncertainty of purpose, with a desire that was mysteriously mental and physical. At the same second that his soul shivered in awe at the thought of intimacy with her spirit, he fiercely desired to crush her warm, heaving bosom against his body, lay a greedy mouth on her throbbing throat, and drink in the clean scent of her flesh, kiss her, hurt her, assault her. That rather shocked him. He sat down again heavily and tried to get control of himself. There was a stupid feeling of ill-usage in his amazement. It seemed as if some emanation from him had met an emanation from her sleeping body; their casual union had brought to birth this whipping passion. The chance thing was hurting him horribly. Work he was used to, tumult and war, discouragement and contumely, the exertion of courage; but not to desire. He had been too busy for these exclusively personal emotions. Under the brutal onslaught of this passion he felt slightly degraded, surprisingly animalized. In every way this thing shocked him. (Rebecca West, *The Sentinel* [Oxford: Legenda, 2002], 104–5)

40. Rebecca West, *The Return of the Soldier* (New York: Penguin, 1998), 41.

41. Carl Rollyson, *Rebecca West* (New York: Scribner, 1996), 122–27.

42. Virginia Woolf, *A Room of One's Own* (San Diego: Harcourt Brace Jovanovich, 1957), 5.

43. Virginia Woolf, "Review of *The Tunnel* by Dorothy Richardson," in *Contemporary Writers*, ed. Jean Guiguet (New York: HBJ, 1965), 122.

44. Woolf, "Modern Fiction," 2310.

45. Eugene Holland, "From Schizophrenia to Social Control," in *Deleuze and Guattari: New Mappings in Politics, Philosophy, and Culture*, ed. Eleanor Kaufman and Kevin Jon Heller (Minneapolis: University of Minnesota Press, 1998), 67.

46. Fredric Jameson, *The Cultural Turn* (London: Verso, 1998), 148.

47. Jameson, *Political Unconscious*, 236–37.

48. Holland, "From Schizophrenia," 65.

49. For Deleuze and Guattari, desire is alienated into representation, because desire is naturally *productive* in material ways. In their view, representation has usurped the place of a directly material, bodily process of the "desiring-machine." Marx, analogously, theorizes an alienation of originally organic labor power. Thus, Deleuze and Guattari are closer to Marx than to Freud and Lacan, who theorize a psychic *lack*. This understanding of representation may parallel that of Virginia Woolf's text in "Modern Fiction."

BIBLIOGRAPHY

Alpers, Antony. *The Life of Katherine Mansfield.* New York: Viking Press, 1980.

Altick, Richard D. *The English Common Reader: A Social History of the Mass Reading Public, 1800–1900.* Chicago: University of Chicago Press, 1957.

Anderson, Rachel. "Hull, E(dith) M(aude)." In *Twentieth-Century Romance and Historical Writers,* edited by Aruna Vasudevan, 333. London: St. James Press, 1994.

Anonymous. *The Life of Florence L. Barclay: A Study in Personality, by One of Her Daughters.* London: Putnam, 1921.

Ardis, Ann. "E. M. Hull, Mass Market Romance, and the New Woman Novel in the Early Twentieth Century." *Women's Writing* 3, no. 3 (1996): 287–96.

———. *New Women, New Novels: Feminism and Early Modernism.* New Brunswick, NJ: Rutgers University Press, 1990.

Argyle, Gisela. "Mrs. Humphry Ward's Fictional Experiments in the Woman Question." *Studies in English Literature, 1500–1900* 43, no. 3 (Autumn 2003): 939–57.

Bainton, George, ed. *The Art of Authorship.* London: James Clarke and Co., 1890.

Bakhtin, Mikail M. *The Dialogic Imagination: Four Essays by M. M. Bakhtin.* Translated by Caryl Emerson and Michael Holquist. Austin: University of Texas Press, 1981.

Baldick, Chris. *Oxford English Literary History,* vol. 10, *1910–1940: The Modern Movement.* Oxford: Oxford University Press, 2004.

Barclay, Florence. *The Rosary.* New York: G. P. Putnam's Sons, 1909.

Barnett, Vincent L. "The Novelist as Hollywood Star: Author Royalties and Studio Income in the 1920s." *Film History: An International Journal* 20, no. 3 (2008): 281–93.

———. "Picturization Partners: Elinor Glyn and the Thalberg Contract Affair." *Film History: An International Journal* 19, no. 3 (2007): 319–29.

Beer, Gillian. *The Romance.* London: Methuen, 1970.

———. "Virginia Woolf and Pre-History." In *Virginia Woolf: A Centenary Perspective,* edited by Eric Warner, 99–123. New York: St. Martin's Press, 1984.

Beer, John. *Post-Romantic Consciousness: Dickens to Plath.* Basingstoke, UK: Palgrave Macmillan, 2003.

Beja, Morris. *Epiphany in the Modern Novel.* London: Peter Owen, 1971.

Bennett, Arnold. *Sacred and Profane Love.* London: Chatto and Windus, 1905.

Blake, Susan. "What 'Race' Is the Sheik? Rereading a Desert Romance." In *Doubled Plots: Romance and History,* edited by Susan Strehle and Mary Paniccia Carden, 67–85. Jackson: University Press of Mississippi, 2003.

Bloch, Ernst. *The Principle of Hope.* Translated by Neville Plaice. Cambridge, MA: MIT Press, 1986.

Bloom, Clive. *Bestsellers: Popular Fiction since 1900.* Basingstoke, UK: Palgrave Macmillan, 2002.

Bloom, Harold. *Romanticism and Consciousness: Essays in Criticism.* New York: W. W. Norton and Company, 1970.

Bogue, Ronald. *Deleuze and Guattari.* New York: Routledge, 1989.

Bourdieu, Pierre. *The Field of Cultural Production.* Edited by Randal Johnson. New York: Columbia University Press, 1993.

———. "Passport to Duke." In *Pierre Bourdieu: Fieldwork in Culture,* edited by Nicholas Brown and Imre Szeman, 241–46. Lanham, MD: Rowman and Littlefield, 2000.

Brewer, Derek. "The Popular English Metrical Romances." In *A Companion to Romance,* edited by Corrine Saunders, 45–64. Malden, MA: Blackwell, 2004.

Brittain, Melisa. "Erasing Race in the New Woman Review: Victoria Cross's *Anna Lombard.*" *Nineteenth-Century Feminisms* 4 (Spring/Summer 2001): 75–95.

Brooks, Peter. *The Melodramatic Imagination: Balzac, Henry James, Melodrama, and the Mode of Excess.* New Haven, CT: Yale University Press, 1976.

Brown, Nicholas, and Imre Szeman, eds. *Pierre Bourdieu: Fieldwork in Culture.* Lanham, MD: Rowman and Littlefield, 2000.

Buchanan, Ian. *Fredric Jameson: Live Theory.* London: Continuum International Publishing Group, 2006.

Bürger, Peter. *Theory of the Avant-Garde.* Minneapolis: University of Minnesota Press, 1984.

Caine, Hall. *The Christian: A Story.* London: Heinemann, 1897.

Casey, Ellen Miller. "Edging Women Out? Reviews of Women Novelists in *The Athenaeum,* 1860–1900." Victorian Studies 39, no. 2 (Winter 1996): 151–71.

Casey, Janet Galligani. "Marie Corelli and Fin de Siècle Feminism." *English Literature in Transition* 32, no. 2 (1992): 163–78.

Cawelti, John. *Adventure, Mystery, and Romance: Formula Stories as Art and Popular Culture.* Chicago: University of Chicago Press, 1976.

Chrisman, Laura. *Rereading the Imperial Romance: British Imperialism and South African Resistance in Haggard, Schreiner, and Plaatje.* New York: Oxford University Press, 2000.

Clark, Suzanne. *Sentimental Modernism: Women Writers and the Revolution of the Word.* Bloomington: Indiana University Press, 1991.

Clayton, Jay. "A Portrait of the Romantic Poet as a Young Artist: Literary History as Textual Unconscious." In *Joyce: The Return of the Repressed,* edited by Susan Stanford Freidman, 114–27. Ithaca, NY: Cornell University Press, 1993.

Close, Cecily. "Arthur Greening, Publisher of *The Scarlet Pimpernel.*" *La Trobe Journal* 78 (Spring 2006): 39–55.

Coates, Thomas F. G., and R. S. Warren Bell. *Marie Corelli: The Writer and the Woman.* Philadelphia: George W. Jacobs and Company, 1903.

Coetzee, J. M. *Elizabeth Costello.* New York: Viking, 2003.

Colby, Vineta. *The Singular Anomaly: Women Novelists of the Nineteenth Century.* New York: New York University Press, 1970.

Conrad, Joseph. *An Outcast of the Islands.* New York: D. Appleton and Company, 1896.

Corelli, Marie. *Free Opinions, Freely Expressed on Certain Phases of Modern Social Life and Conduct.* London: Archibald Constant and Company, 1905.

———. *Innocent: Her Fancy and His Fact.* New York: A. L. Burt Company, 1914.

———. *The Life Everlasting: A Reality of Romance.* London: Hodder and Stoughton, 1911.

———. *The Sorrows of Satan, or the Strange Experience of One Geoffrey Tempest, Millionaire: A Romance* [1895]. Edited by Peter Keating. Oxford: Oxford University Press, 1996.

———. *The Treasure of Heaven: A Romance of Riches.* New York: Dodd, Mead and Company, 1906.

Cross, Victoria [Vivian Cory]. *Anna Lombard.* New York: Kensington Press, 1901.

———. "Theodora: A Fragment." In *A New Woman Reader: Fiction, Articles and Drama of the 1890s,* edited by Carolyn Christensen Nelson, 70–90. Hertfordshire, UK: Broadview Press, 2000.

———. *The Woman Who Didn't* [1895]. Victorian Women Writers Project, edited by Perry Willett. http://www.indiana.edu/letrs.vwwp/cross/womanwho.html. 1999.

Daly, Nicholas. *Literature, Technology and Modernity, 1860–2000.* Cambridge: Cambridge University Press, 2004.

———. *Modernism, Romance, and the Fin de Siècle.* Cambridge: Cambridge University Press, 1999.

Davison, Carol Margaret, and Elaine M. Hartnell, eds. Introduction to "Marie Corelli." Special issue, *Women's Writing* 13, no. 2 (June 2006): 181–87.

de Certeau, Michel. "'Making Do': Uses and Tactics." In *The Consumer Society Reader,* edited by Martyn J. Lee, 162–74. Oxford: Blackwell Publishing, 2000.

Deleuze, Gilles, and Félix Guattari. *Anti-Oedipus: Capitalism and Schizophrenia* [1972]. Translated by Robert Hurley, Mark Seem, and Helen R. Lane. Minneapolis: University of Minnesota Press, 1983.

———. *A Thousand Plateaus: Capitalism and Schizophrenia* [1980]. Translated by Brian Massumi. Minneapolis: University of Minnesota Press, 1987.

Dell, Ethel. *The Way of an Eagle* [1912]. London: Virago, 1996.

Dell, Penelope. *Nettie and Sissie: The Biography of Ethel M. Dell and Her Sister Ella.* London: Hamish Hamilton, 1977.

DeMan, Paul. "The Rhetoric of Temporality." In *Blindness and Insight: Essays in the Rhetoric of Contemporary Criticism,* by DeMan, 187–228. Minneapolis: University of Minnesota Press, 1983.

DiBattista, Maria, and Lucy McDiarmid, eds. *High and Low Moderns: Literature and Culture, 1889–1939.* New York: Oxford University Press, 1996.

dixon, jay [*sic*]. *The Romance Fiction of Mills and Boon, 1909–1990s.* London: UCL Press, 1999.

Doyle, Sir Arthur Conan. *The Adventures of Sherlock Holmes.* New York: Grosset and Dunlap, 1892.

———. *The Lost World.* New York: Berkley Medallion, 1965.

Dunbar, Pamela. *Radical Mansfield: Double Discourse in Katherine Mansfield's Short Stories.* New York: St. Martin's Press, 1997.

Duncan, Ian. *Modern Romance and Transformations of the Novel.* Cambridge: Cambridge University Press, 1992.

DuPlessis, Rachel Blau. "'Amor Vin—': Modifications of Romance in Woolf." In *Writing beyond the Ending,* by DuPlessis, 47–65. Bloomington: Indiana University Press, 1985.

Eliot, George. "Silly Novels by Lady Novelists." *The Westminster Review* 66 (October 1856): 442–61.

Ellmann, Richard. *James Joyce.* Rev. ed. Oxford: Oxford University Press, 1982.

———, ed. *James Joyce: Letters II.* New York: Viking Press, 1966.

Fanon, Frantz. *The Wretched of the Earth* [1961]. Translated by Constance Farringdon. Harmondsworth: Penguin, 1967.

Fasick, Laura. "The Ambivalence of Influence: The Case of Mary Ward and Charlotte Yonge." *English Literature in Transition* 37, no. 2 (1994): 141–54.

Feather, John. *A History of British Publishing.* London: Routledge, 1988.

Federico, Annette. *Idol of Suburbia: Marie Corelli and Late-Victorian Literary Culture.* Charlottesville: University of Virginia Press, 2000.

Felski, Rita. *The Gender of Modernity.* Cambridge, MA: Harvard University Press, 1995.

Fisher, Benjamin F. "Marie Corelli's *Barabbas, The Sorrows of Satan,* and Generic Transition." In Davison and Hartnell, "Marie Corelli," 304–20.

Flint, Kate. *The Woman Reader, 1837–1914.* Oxford, UK: Clarendon Press, 1993.

Flower, Desmond, comp. *A Century of Bestsellers, 1830–1930.* Introduction by Desmond Flower. London: National Book Council, 1934.

Forster, E. M. *Howard's End.* Boston: Bedford, 1997.

Franklin, J. Jeffrey. "The Counter-Invasion of Britain by Buddhism in Marie Corelli's *A Romance of Two Worlds* and H. Rider Haggard's *Ayesha: The Return of She.*" *Victorian Literature and Culture* 31, no. 1 (March 2003): 19–42.

Friedman, Susan Stanford, ed. *Joyce: The Return of the Repressed.* Ithaca, NY: Cornell University Press, 1993.

Frost, Laura. "The Romance of Cliché: E. M. Hull, D. H. Lawrence, and Interwar Erotic Fiction." In *Bad Modernisms,* edited by Douglas Mao and Rebecca L. Walkowitz, 94–118. Durham, NC: Duke University Press, 2006.

Frye, Northrop. *Anatomy of Criticism.* Princeton: Princeton University Press, 1957.

———. *The Secular Scripture: A Study of the Structure of Romance.* Cambridge, MA: Harvard University Press, 1976.

Galsworthy, John. *The Man of Property.* New York: Signet, 1967.

Galvan, Jill. "Christians, Infidels, and Women's Channeling in the Writings of Marie Corelli." *Victorian Literature and Culture* 31, no. 1 (March 2003): 83–97.

Gargano, Elizabeth. "'English Sheiks' and Arab Stereotypes: E. M. Hull, T. E. Lawrence, and the Imperial Masquerade." *Texas Studies in Literature and Language* 48, no. 2 (Summer 2006): 171–86.

Gilmore, Lois J. "Virginia Woolf, Bloomsbury, and the Primitive." In *Virginia Woolf and Communities: Selected Papers from the Eighth Annual Conference on Virginia Woolf,* edited by Jeanette McVicker and Laura Davis, 127–35. New York: Pace University Press, 1999.

Gladstone, W. E. "'Robert Elsmere' and the Battle of Belief." *Nineteenth Century* 23 (May 1888): 766–88.

Glyn, Anthony. *Elinor Glyn: A Biography.* Garden City, NY: Doubleday, 1955.

Glyn, Elinor. *The Reason Why.* Condensed by Barbara Cartland. Barbara Cartland's Library of Love. London: Duckworth, 1979.

———. *Romantic Adventure: Being the Autobiography of Elinor Glyn.* New York: E. P. Dutton, 1937.

———. *Three Weeks.* London: Duckworth, 1907.

Hallim, Robyn. "Marie Corelli: Science, Society, and the Bestseller." Dissertation, University of Sydney, May 2002.

Hammond, Mary. *Reading, Publishing and the Formation of Literary Taste in England, 1880–1914.* Aldershot, UK: Ashgate, 2006.

Hardt, Michael. "Affective Labor." *Boundary 2* 26, no. 2 (Summer 1999): 89–100.

Hardt, Michael, and Kathi Weeks, eds. *The Jameson Reader.* Oxford, UK: Blackwell, 2000.

Hardwick, Joan. *Addicted to Romance: The Life and Adventures of Elinor Glyn.* London: Andre Deutsch, 1994.

Hartnell, Elaine M. "Morals and Metaphysics: Marie Corelli, Religion, and the Gothic." In Davison and Hartnell, "Marie Corelli," 284–303.

Harvey, Paul. *The Oxford Companion to Classical Literature.* Oxford: Oxford University Press, 1980.

Hobsbawm, Eric. *The Age of Empire, 1875–1914.* New York: Vintage, 1987.

Holland, Eugene. *Deleuze and Guattari's Anti-Oedipus: Introduction to Schizoanalysis.* London: Routledge, 1999.

———. "From Schizophrenia to Social Control." In *Deleuze and Guattari: New Mappings in Politics, Philosophy, and Culture,* edited by Eleanor Kaufman and Kevin Jon Heller, 65–73. Minneapolis: University of Minnesota Press, 1998.

Hull, E. M. *The Sheik* [1919]. Philadelphia: Pine Street Press, 2001.

Huyssen, Andreas. *After the Great Divide: Modernism, Mass Culture, Postmodernism.* Bloomington: Indiana University Press, 1986.

Jameson, Fredric. *The Cultural Turn.* London: Verso, 1998.

———. *The Political Unconscious.* Ithaca, NY: Cornell University Press, 1981.

———. *Postmodernism; or, the Cultural Logic of Late Capitalism.* Durham, NC: Duke University Press, 1991.

———. "Reification and Utopia in Mass Culture." *Social Text* 1, no. 1 (1979): 130–48.

———. *A Singular Modernity.* London: Verso, 2002.

Jayawardena, Kumari. *The White Woman's Other Burden: Western Women and South Asia during British Colonial Rule.* New York: Routledge, 1995.

John, Juliet. *Dickens's Villains: Melodrama, Character, Popular Culture.* Oxford: Oxford University Press, 2001.

Johnson, Randal. Introduction to *The Field of Cultural Production,* by Pierre Bourdieu, 1–25. New York: Columbia University Press, 1993.

Jones, Enid Huws. *Mrs. Humphry Ward.* London: Heinemann, 1973.

Jones, Susan. "Into the Twentieth Century: Imperial Romance from Haggard to Buchan." In *A Companion to Romance,* edited by Corrine Saunders, 406–23. Malden, MA: Blackwell, 2004.

Joppke, Christian. "The Cultural Dimensions of Class Formation and Class Struggle: On the Social Theory of Pierre Bourdieu." *Berkeley Journal of Sociology* 31 (1986): 51–78.

Joyce, James. *Dubliners.* Edited by Robert Scholes and A. Walter Litz. New York: Viking Penguin, 1996.

———. *A Portrait of the Artist as a Young Man.* New York: Signet, 1991.

———. *Ulysses.* New York: Vintage International, 1990.

Kaplan, Sydney Janet. *Katherine Mansfield and the Origins of Modernist Fiction.* Ithaca, NY: Cornell University Press, 1991.

Keating, Peter. *The Haunted Study: A Social History of the English Novel, 1875–1914.* London: Secker and Warburg, 1989.

———. Introduction to *The Sorrows of Satan,* by Marie Corelli, ix–xx. Oxford: Oxford University Press, 1996.

Kenner, Hugh. *Dublin's Joyce.* Boston: Beacon Press, 1956.

Kershner, R. B. "Modernism's Mirror: The Sorrows of Marie Corelli." In *Transforming Genres: New Approaches to the British Fiction of the 1890s,* edited by Nikki Lee Manos and Meri-Jane Rochelson, 67–86. New York: St. Martin's Press, 1994.

Klemp, Annette Doblix. "Dickens and Melodrama: Character Presentation and Plot Motifs in Six Novels." *Dissertation Abstracts International* 45, no. 12 (June 1985): 3646A.

Knapp, Shoshana Milgram. "Revolutionary Androgyny in the Fiction of 'Victoria Cross.'" In *Seeing Double: Revisioning Edwardian and Modernist Literature,* edited by Carola M. Kaplan and Anne B. Simpson, 3–20. New York: St. Martin's Press, 1996.

Kowalczyk, Richard L. "In Vanished Summertime: Marie Corelli and Popular Culture." *Journal of Popular Culture* 7 (Spring 1974): 850–63.

Kuehn, Julia. *Glorious Vulgarity: Marie Corelli's Feminine Sublime in a Popular Context.* Berlin: Logos, 2004.

———. "Marie Corelli's Love Letters to Arthur Severn." In *The Victorian Web: Literature, History, and Culture in the Age of Victoria,* edited by George P. Landow. http://www.victorianweb.org/authors/corelli/corelliov.html.

Kuhn, Annette. "The Trouble with Elinor Glyn: Hollywood, *Three Weeks* and the British Board of Film Censors." *Historical Journal of Film, Radio, and Television* 28, no. 1 (March 2008): 23–35.

Lacan, Jacques. "The Agency of the Letter in the Unconscious, or Reason since Freud." In *Ecrits: A Selection.* Translated by Alan Sheridan, 146–78. New York: W. W. Norton and Company, 1977.

Laing, Kathryn. "'The Sentinel': Rebecca West's Buried Novel." *Tulsa Studies in Women's Literature* 19, no. 1 (Spring 2000): 9–26.

Lawrence, D. H. *Kangaroo.* New York: Viking Press, 1923.

———. *The Plumed Serpent* [1926]. New York: Vintage, 1959.

———. *Sons and Lovers.* Harmondsworth, UK: Penguin Books, 1978.

———. "Surgery for the Novel—Or a Bomb." In *Selected Literary Criticism,* edited by Anthony Beal, 11–18. London: Heinemann, 1967.

———. "The Woman Who Rode Away" [1924]. In *The Cambridge Edition of the Works of D. H. Lawrence: The Woman Who Rode Away and Other Stories,* edited by Dieter Mehl and Christa Jansohn, 39–71. Cambridge: Cambridge University Press, 2002.

———. *Women in Love* [1920]. London: Penguin Books, 1995.

Leavis, F. R. *The Great Tradition.* London: Chatto and Windus, 1948.

Leavis, Q. D. *Fiction and the Reading Public.* London: Chatto and Windus, 1932.

Lévi-Strauss, Claude. *Structural Anthropology.* Translated by Claire Jacobson and Brooke Schoepf. New York: Basic Books, 1963.

Lewis, Percy Wyndham, ed. *Blast.* 1914. A facsimile reprint of the original edition. Santa Rosa, CA: Black Sparrow Press, 1989.

———. *Blast 2: War Number.* 1914. A facsimile reprint of the original edition. Santa Rosa, CA: Black Sparrow Press, 1989.

Literary News. "Mrs. Humphry Ward's Profits." 24, no. 4 (April 1903): 116.

Little, James Stanley. "New Novels." *Academy* 48, no. 1219 (14 September 1895): 202.

Loomba, Ania. *Colonialism/Postcolonialism.* New York: Routledge, 1998.

Lukács, Georg. *The Historical Novel.* Translated by Hannah and Stanley Mitchell. Lincoln: University of Nebraska Press, 1983.

Macherey, Pierre. *A Theory of Literary Production.* Translated by G. Wall. London: Routledge, 1978.

Mansfield, Katherine. *The Katherine Mansfield Notebooks.* Edited by Margaret Scott. Minneapolis: University of Minneapolis Press, 1997.

———. "Mrs. Humphry Ward's Last Novel." *Athenaeum* 4697 (7 May 1920): 606.

———. *Stories by Katherine Mansfield.* Edited by Jeffrey Meyers. New York: Vintage Classics, 1991.

———. "Summer Idylle." In *The Katherine Mansfield Notebooks,* edited by Margaret Scott, 75–76. Minneapolis: University of Minneapolis Press, 1997.

Mao, Douglas, and Rebecca L. Walkowitz, eds. *Bad Modernisms.* Durham, NC: Duke University Press, 2006.

Marx, Karl. *Capital,* vol. 3. Harmondsworth, UK: Penguin, 1981.

Masters, Brian. *Now Barabbas Was a Rotter: The Extraordinary Life of Marie Corelli.* London: Hamish Hamilton, 1978.

Maugham, W. Somerset. *Of Human Bondage.* New York: Bantam Books, 1991.

McAleer, Joseph. *Popular Reading and Publishing in Britain, 1914–1950.* Oxford, UK: Clarendon Press, 1992.

McClintock, Anne. *Imperial Leather: Race, Gender, and Sexuality in the Colonial Conquest.* New York: Routledge, 1995.

McKinney, Lauren D. "From New Money to New Woman: Social Change and Melodrama in Three British Novels of the 1890s." *Dissertation Abstracts International* 56, no. 9 (March 1996): 3595A.

Methuen, Algernon. *Sir Algernon Methuen, Baronet: A Memoir.* London: Methuen, 1925.

Meyers, W. H. "George Sand." *Nineteenth Century* 1 (April 1877): 221–41.

Miller, Jane Eldridge. *Rebel Women: Feminism, Modernism, and the Edwardian Novel.* London: Virago Press, 1994.

Mizener, Arthur. *The Saddest Story: A Biography of Ford Madox Ford.* New York: World Publishing, 1971.

Modleski, Tania. *Loving with a Vengeance: Mass-Produced Fantasies for Women.* Hamden, CT: Archon, 1982.

Moi, Toril. "Appropriating Bourdieu: Feminist Theory and Pierre Bourdieu's Sociology of Culture." *New Literary History* 22, no. 4 (Autumn 1991): 1017–49.

Moody, Nickianne. "Elinor Glyn and the Invention of 'It.'" *Critical Survey* 15, no. 3 (2003): 92–104.

———. "Moral Uncertainty and the Afterlife: Explaining the Popularity of Marie Corelli's Early Novels." In Davison and Hartnell, "Marie Corelli," 188–205.

Moran, Patricia. "Unholy Meanings: Maternity, Creativity, and Orality in Katherine Mansfield." *Feminist Studies* 17, no. 1 (Spring 1991): 105–25.

Morey, Peter. *Fictions of India: Narrative and Power.* Edinburgh: Edinburgh University Press, 2000.

Neilson, Brett. "D. H. Lawrence's 'Dark Page': Narrative Primitivism in *Women in Love* and *The Plumed Serpent.*" *Twentieth-Century Literature* 43, no. 3 (Fall 1997): 310–25.

Norburn, Roger. *A Katherine Mansfield Chronology.* Basingstoke, UK: Palgrave Macmillan, 2008.

Orczy, Baroness [Emmuska]. *The Scarlet Pimpernel: A Romance.* "Popular Edition." London: Greening and Co., 1909.

Orczy, Emmuska. *Links in the Chain of Life.* London: Hutchinson and Company, 1947.

———. *The Scarlet Pimpernel* [1905]. New York: Signet Classic, 1974.

Paniccia Carden, Mary, and Susan Strehle. "Introduction: Reading Romance, Reading History." In *Doubled Plots: Romance and History,* edited by Mary Paniccia Carden and Susan Strehle, xi–xxxiii. Jackson: University Press of Mississippi, 2003.

Paxton, Nancy L. *Writing under the Raj: Gender, Race, and Rape in the British Colonial Imagination, 1830–1947.* New Brunswick, NJ: Rutgers University Press, 1999.

Peterson, William S. *Victorian Heretic: Mrs. Humphry Ward's* Robert Elsmere. Leicester: Leicester University Press, 1976.

Porter, Gene Stratton. *The Harvester.* Project Gutenberg Etext, 1995. http://sailor.gutenberg.org/etext95/tharv10.txt.

Radford, Jean. "Introduction." In *The Progress of Romance: The Politics of Popular Fiction.* Edited by Jean Radford, 1–20. London: Routledge and Kegan Paul, 1986.

Radway, Janice A. *Reading the Romance: Women, Patriarchy, and Popular Literature.* Chapel Hill: University of North Carolina Press, 1991.

Rahill, Frank. *The World of Melodrama.* University Park: Pennsylvania State University Press, 1967.

Ransom, Teresa. *The Mysterious Miss Marie Corelli: Queen of Victorian Bestsellers.* Gloucestershire, UK: Sutton Publishing, 1999.

Raph, Theodore. *The American Song Treasury.* Mineola, NY: Dover, 1986.

Rappaport, Helen. *Queen Victoria: A Biographical Companion.* New York: ABC-CLIO, 2003.

Regis, Pamela. *A Natural History of the Romance Novel.* Philadelphia: University of Pennsylvania Press, 2003.

Robins, Elizabeth. *A Dark Lantern.* London: Macmillan and Company, 1905.

Rollyson, Carl. *Rebecca West.* New York: Scribner, 1996.

Rose, Jonathan. *The Intellectual Life of the British Working Classes.* New Haven, CT: Yale University Press, 2001.

Ryals, Clyde de L. Editor's introduction to *Robert Elsmere,* by Mary Augusta Ward, vii–xxxix. Lincoln: University of Nebraska Press, 1967.

Said, Edward. *Culture and Imperialism.* New York: Alfred A. Knopf, 1993.

Sanders, Valerie. *Eve's Renegades: Victorian Anti-Feminist Women Novelists.* New York: St. Martin's Press, 1996.

Saunders, Corrine. *A Companion to Romance, from Classical to Contemporary.* Malden, MA: Blackwell, 2004.

Saunders, Rebecca. "Gender, Colonialism, and Exile: Flora Annie Steel and Sara Jeannette Duncan in India." In *Women's Writing in Exile,* edited by Mary Lynn Broe and Angela Ingram, 304–24. Chapel Hill: University of North Carolina Press, 1989.

Scott, Margaret, ed. *The Katherine Mansfield Notebooks.* Minneapolis: University of Minneapolis Press, 1997.

Scott-James, R. A. *Modernism and Romance.* London: John Lane, 1908.

Sharp, William. "New Novels." *Academy* 33, no. 828 (17 March 1888): 183–84.

Sharpe, Jenny. *Allegories of Empire: The Figure of Woman in the Colonial Text.* Minneapolis: University of Minnesota Press, 1993.

Showalter, Elaine, ed. *Daughters of Decadence: Women Writers of the Fin de Siècle.* New Brunswick, NJ: Rutgers University Press, 1993.

———. *A Literature of Their Own: British Women Novelists from Brontë to Lessing.* Princeton: Princeton University Press, 1977.

Shumway, David R. *Modern Love: Romance, Intimacy, and the Marriage Crisis.* New York: New York University Press, 2003.

Simcox, Edith. "George Eliot." *Nineteenth Century* 9 (May 1881): 778–801.

Smith, Dorothy. *The Everyday World as Problematic: A Feminist Sociology.* Boston: Northeastern University Press, 1987.

Smith, Erin Marie. "Trembling on the Boundary: Melodrama and the Victorian Novel, 1846–1876." *Dissertation Abstracts International* 60, no. 11 (May 2000): 4023.

Smith, Esther Marian Greenwell. *Mrs. Humphry Ward.* Boston: Twayne, 1980.

Smith, Jad. "Völkisch Organicism and the Use of Primitivism in Lawrence's *The Plumed Serpent.*" *D. H. Lawrence Review* 30, no. 3 (2002): 7–24.

Smith, Patricia Juliana. "'The Things People Don't Say': Lesbian Panic in *The Voyage Out.*" In *Lesbian Readings of Virginia Woolf,* edited by Eileen

Barrett and Patricia Cramer, 128–45. New York: New York University Press, 1997.

Spacks, Patricia Meyer. *Boredom.* Chicago: University of Chicago Press, 1995.

Stacpoole, Horace de Vere. *The Blue Lagoon, A Romance.* Philadelphia: J. B. Lippincott, 1908.

Stafford, Jane, and Mark Williams. *Maoriland: New Zealand Literature, 1872–1914.* Wellington: Victoria University Press, 2006.

Stansky, Peter. *On or About 1910: Early Bloomsbury and Its Intimate World.* Cambridge, MA: Harvard University Press, 1997.

Stead, W. T. "*The Sorrows of Satan*—and of Marie Corelli." *Review of Reviews* 12 (July–December 1895): 453–64.

Steel, Flora Annie. *The Garden of Fidelity.* London: Macmillan, 1929.

Strobel, Margaret. *European Women and the Second British Empire.* Bloomington: Indiana University Press, 1991.

Sturt, George. *Change in the Village* [1912]. London: Caliban Books, 1984.

Sutherland, John A. *Fiction and the Fiction Industry.* London: Athlone Press, 1978.

———. *Mrs. Humphry Ward: Eminent Victorian, Pre-eminent Edwardian.* Oxford: Oxford University Press, 1991.

Sutton-Ramspeck, Beth. *Raising the Dust: The Literary Housekeeping of Mary Ward, Sarah Grand, and Charlotte Perkins Gilman.* Athens: Ohio University Press, 2004.

———. "Shot Out of the Canon: Mary Ward and the Claims of Conflicting Feminisms." In *Victorian Women Writers and the Woman Question,* edited by Nicola Diane Thompson. 204–22. Cambridge: Cambridge University Press, 1999.

Thomas, Nicholas. *Possessions: Indigenous Art/Colonial Culture.* London: Thames and Hudson, 1999.

Thorburn, David. "Horse Dealer's Daughter: The Shimmer Within." Lecture 12, course no. 2539, "Masterworks of Early 20th-Century Literature." Chantilly, VA: Teaching Company, 2007.

Torgovnick, Marianna. *Gone Primitive: Savage Intellects, Modern Lives.* Chicago: University of Chicago Press, 1990.

Trevelyan, Janet P. *The Life of Mrs. Humphry Ward.* London: Constable, 1923.

Trotter, David. "Edwardian Sex Novels." *Critical Quarterly* 31, no. 1 (1989): 92–106.

———. *The English Novel in History, 1895–1920.* London: Routledge, 1993.

Tuchman, Gaye, and Nina Fortin. *Edging Women Out: Victorian Novelists, Publishers, and Social Change.* New Haven, CT: Yale University Press, 1989.

Walker, Hugh. *The Literature of the Victorian Era.* Cambridge: Cambridge University Press, 1910.

Waller, Phillip. *Writers, Readers, and Reputations: Literary Life in Britain, 1870–1918.* Oxford: Oxford University Press, 2006.

Ward, Mary Augusta. *Lady Rose's Daughter.* New York: Harper and Brothers, 1903.

———. *The Marriage of William Ashe.* London: Harper and Brothers, 1905.

———. *Robert Elsmere* [1888]. Edited by Clyde de L. Ryals. Lincoln: University of Nebraska Press, 1967.

———. *A Writer's Recollections.* London: W. Collins and Sons, 1918.

Weber, Bruce. "For Romance Novelists, Profits without Honor." *New York Times,* 3 August 1999, B1–2.

Wegner, Phillip. *Imagined Communities: Utopia, the Nation, and the Spatial Histories of Modernity.* Berkeley: University of California Press, 2002.

Wells, H. G. *The First Men in the Moon.* London: G. Newnes, 1901.

———. *Kipps, the Story of a Simple Soul.* New York: Scribner, 1905.

West, Rebecca. *The Return of the Soldier.* New York: Penguin, 1998.

———. Review of *A Writer's Recollections,* by Mary Augusta Ward. *Bookman* 45 (December 1918): 106–7.

———. *The Sentinel.* Oxford: Legenda, 2002.

———. *The Strange Necessity.* New York: Doubleday, 1928.

Williams, Raymond. *The English Novel from Dickens to Lawrence.* New York: Oxford University Press, 1970.

———. *Marxism and Literature.* New York: Oxford University Press, 1977.

Wilt, Judith. *Behind Her Times: Transition England in the Novels of Mary Arnold Ward.* Charlottesville: University of Virginia Press, 2005.

———. "Transition Time: The Political Romances of Mrs. Humphry Ward's *Marcella* (1894) and *Sir George Tressday* (1896)." In *The New Nineteenth Century: Feminist Readings of Underread Victorian Fiction,* edited by Barbara Leah Harman and Susan Meyer, 225–46. New York: Garland, 1996.

Wintle, Sarah. "*The Sheik:* What Can Be Made of a Daydream." *Women: A Cultural Review* 7, no. 3 (Winter 1996): 291–302.

Woolf, Virginia. *The Diary of Virginia Woolf,* vol. 1, *1915–1919.* Edited by Anne Olivier Bell. New York: Harcourt Brace Jovanovich, 1977.

———. *The Letters of Virginia Woolf,* vol. 2, *1912–1922.* Edited by Nigel Nicolson and Joanne Trautmann. New York: Harcourt Brace Jovanovich, 1976.

———. "Modern Fiction." In *The Norton Anthology of English Literature,* 2306–11. 6th ed. New York: Norton, 1996.

———. *Moments of Being: Unpublished Autobiographical Writings.* Edited by Jeanne Schulkind. New York: Harvest/HBJ, 1976.

———. "Review of *The Tunnel* by Dorothy Richardson." In *Contemporary Writers,* edited by Jean Guiguet, 122. New York: HBJ, 1965.

———. *A Room of One's Own.* San Diego: Harcourt Brace Jovanovich, 1957.

———. *The Voyage Out* [1915]. New York: Barnes and Noble Classics, 2004.

Young, Robert J. C. *Colonial Desire: Hybridity in Theory, Culture, and Race.* New York: Routledge, 1995.

INDEX

www.ingramcontent.com/pod-product-compliance
Lightning Source LLC
Chambersburg PA
CBHW020946310726
48980CB00001B/72

* 9 7 8 0 8 2 1 4 1 9 7 0 0 *